The Longman Companion to

European Nationalism 1789–1920

The Longman Companion to

European Nationalism 1789–1920

Raymond Pearson

Longman

London and New York

Longman Group UK Limited,
Longman House, Burnt Mill,
Harlow, Essex CM20 2JE, England
and Associated Companies throughout the world.

*Published in the United States of America
by Longman Publishing, New York*

First published 1994

ISBN 0582 07229 8 CSD
ISBN 0582 07228 X PPR

British Library Cataloguing-in-Publication Data
A catalogue record for this book is
available from the British Library

Library of Congress Cataloging in Publications Data
Pearson, Raymond.
   The Longman companion to European nationalism, 1789–1920 / Raymond
Pearson.
      p. cm. – (Longman companions to history)
   Includes bibliographical references and index.
   ISBN 0–582–07229–8. – ISBN 0–582–07228–X (pbk.)
      1. Europe–Politics and government–1789–1900. 2. Europe–
–Politics and government–1871–1918. 3. Nationalism–Europe–
–History–19th century. 4. Nationalism–Europe–History–20th
century. I. Longman (Firm) II. Title. III. Series.
D359.7.P43   1993
940–dc20
                                                    92–46026
                                                       CIP

Set by 7LL in 9½/11 pt New Baskerville
Produced by Longman Singapore Publishers (Pte) Ltd.
Printed in Singapore

Contents

List of Maps

Preface

The scope of the *Companion to European Nationalism, 1789–1920* is ambitious. Geographical coverage extends throughout Europe, from Russia to Portugal and from Turkey to Iceland. Thematic range includes social and cultural as well as ideological, military and political dimensions. Chronological treatment stretches from 1789, when the outbreak of the French Revolution first generated the modern concept of the 'nation', to 1919–1920, when the Paris Peace Settlement appeared to endorse nationalism as the legitimacy of the new European establishment.

To effect an historically sound coverage of the whole of Europe over the 'long nineteenth century', the material on offer in this *Companion* is divided into eight sections of variable text length but, it is hoped, comparable reference value.

Section I comprises an **International chronicle**, setting the indispensable background context for nineteenth-century nationalism, divided thematically into 'Military' and 'Diplomatic' calendars of events.

The career of nationalism is inexplicable without an appreciation of the degree to which history and geography overlapped in the nineteenth century. The geopolitical dimension is therefore introduced early, not (as is so often the practice) relegated to a token appendix. Section II is accordingly an **Historical atlas** of 12 maps illustrating the impact of nationalism upon the political cartography of nineteenth-century Europe.

Reinforcing this geopolitical emphasis, Section III departs from the conventions of most reference volumes in providing a **Geopolitical gazetteer**. Concentrating on territorial jurisdiction, this section is subdivided into four categories according to politico-constitutional status. 'Old States' are defined as those established or resident political entities which maintained a sovereign independence throughout the nineteenth century. 'New States' are those novel entities which emerged with permanent independent and sovereign status in the course of the period 1789–1914. 'Ex-States' are those sovereign or autonomous political entities which were liquidated, incorporated or superseded over the nineteenth century. Finally, 'Sub-States' are those identifiable territories which engaged the allegiance of their inhabitants but failed to achieve recognition as sovereign states over the period 1789–1914 (although some accomplished the political break-through in 1919–1920).

Section IV comprises **National chronologies** of the major political, military, social, intellectual and cultural events of the nineteenth-century careers of all the principal nations and nationalities of Europe (presented in alphabetical order from the Albanians to the Welsh). While conventionally (and quite properly) conceding pride of place and coverage to such leading nations as the Germans and Italians, a determined effort to safeguard equitable treatment of the smaller nations of Europe has been undertaken.

Section V provides **Statistical tables** of economic, social but especially demographic material useful to an understanding of the societal infrastructure affecting the development of nationalism.

Biography has always been among the most accessible approaches to an historical period and now often performs the necessary corrective role of re-humanising a history in danger of becoming de-humanised by statistics-based disciplines. Section VI furnishes **Nationalist biographies** of leading personalities of nineteenth-century nationalism, presented in alphabetical order (from Ali Pasha Tepalene to Ypsilanti). Where appropriate, entries for individual 'life-histories' include details of original writings and recommended biographies.

Section VII is a **Political glossary** of terms and concepts, presented in alphabetical order (from 'Absolutism' to 'Zollverein'). Terms contemporary to the nineteenth century as well as those currently employed by academic specialists in the increasingly sophisticated social-science discipline of the study of nationalism are both included.

Predictably and necessarily, the final Section VIII is a **Select bibliography** of the massive volume of material published in English on the phenomenon of European nationalism, subdivided into three parts. 'Analytical' introduces the principal theoretical, philosophical and synoptic works published on the global phenomenon of nationalism. 'General' provides coverage of publications on the broad career of nationalism within the specific confines of nineteenth-century Europe. 'National' furnishes individual bibliographies for each of the principal nations and nationalities of nineteenth-century Europe (presented in alphabetical order from 'Albania' to 'Wales').

At least as handy as a handbook, *European Nationalism 1789–1920* is intended to be user-friendly, even companionable, for specialist and general reader alike.

Acknowledgements

I must express my gratitude to the various individuals — and groups of individuals — who have influenced my (no doubt idiosyncratic) choice of historical material presented in this *Companion* volume. Firstly, my sincere thanks to my academic colleagues Sean Connolly, Peter Pyne and Ken Ward for their stimulating opinions on the general phenomenon of nationalism, together with their specialist expertise on (respectively) its Irish, Spanish and German manifestations. Secondly, a retrospective salute to the students enlisted over the last ten years on the final-year history courses on 'Nationalism' and 'Nationality Problems in Modern Europe' at the University of Ulster, whose extravagantly varied responses to the topic identified areas where a reference volume would be most helpful. Thirdly, I have been strongly influenced in my compilation of material by a three-year stint as A-level History Examiner, which provided unique insights into what sixth formers need to know to tackle effectively the complex phenomenon of nineteenth and twentieth-century nationalism. Finally, I must thank John Stevenson, one of the General Editors of the *Companion* series, and Longman Higher Education, for their genuinely constructive comments on the original text.

Raymond Pearson
University of Ulster
October 1992

SECTION I

International chronicle

1. Military

The Russian-Ottoman War of 1768–1774 The Ottoman Empire declares war in October 1768 after Russian troops burn the Ottoman town of Balta. In July 1770, the Russian fleet defeats the Ottomans off Chesme. By 1771, the Russians have occupied Crimea, Moldavia and Wallachia. This geopolitically critical territorial advance by Russia is undermined by the Pugachev Rebellion, which compels Empress Catherine the Great to end the war with the Ottomans prematurely by the Treaty of Kutchuk Kainardji in July 1774.

The war that, by establishing the weakness of the Ottoman Empire vis-à-vis the expansionist Russian Empire, effectively poses the long-running 'Eastern Question'.

The Russian-Austrian-Ottoman War of 1787–1792 The Ottoman Empire declares war on Russia in August 1787. Joining Russia in February 1788, Habsburg Austria overruns Moldavia while Russia defeats the Ottomans at sea. By 1789, the scale of the Austro-Russian advance is signalling the collapse of Ottoman power in Europe. However, Russia becomes diverted by war with Sweden while Austria is increasingly restrained by Prussia and Britain. Austria agrees to the Treaty of Sistova with the Ottomans in August 1791 and Russia makes peace at Jassy in January 1792.

A war which confirms the international repercussions of the decline of the Ottoman Empire and identifies the Russian and Austrian empires as the principal long-term rivals for self-interested exploitation of the Ottoman Empire's territorial shrinkage in the Balkans.

The Russian-Swedish-Danish War of 1788–1790 In June 1788, Gustavus III of Sweden attempts to exploit Russia's current campaign against the Ottoman Empire by declaring war on Russia. The combination of mutiny in the Swedish army and invasion of Sweden by Denmark frustrates his ambitions for 1788. Gustavus defeats the Danes in 1789 and routs the Russian fleet at Svenskund in 1790; but, by the Treaty of Varela, settles for peace on the basis of the pre-war geopolitical status quo.

The Austrian-Belgian War of 1789–1790 Revolt against Habsburg authority starts in the Austrian Netherlands in October 1789. A declaration of independence under the name of 'Belgium' is issued in December 1789. The 'Belgians' are crushed by the Austrian military, who re-enter Brussels in December 1790.

A short-lived revolt important for placing 'Belgium' on the geopolitical map and political agenda of Europe (preparatory to its independence after 1830).

The French Revolutionary War of 1792 The first alliance against revolutionary France is agreed by Habsburg Austria and Prussia in February 1792. Hostilities start in April 1792, with the Prussians checked at Valmy in September 1792 and the Austrians defeated at Jemappes in November 1792.

A war of intended restoration transformed by the surprisingly effective military performance of revolutionary France, making necessary a broader anti-French coalition of anti-revolutionary states.

The War of the First Coalition, 1793–1795 The French advance into the Low Countries, 'Germany' and 'Italy', together with the execution of King Louis XVI, prompts the formation of the First Coalition of Habsburg Austria, Prussia, Britain, Spain, Naples and Holland in 1793. The Allies experience some early successes, notably the Austrian victory at Neerwinden in March 1793 and the British seizure of Toulon in August 1793. With Carnot reorganising its army, France rallies, defeating the Austrians at Wattignies in October 1793, overrunning the Austrian Netherlands/Belgium in June 1794 and the Netherlands in December 1794, and invading Spain and Piedmont. The First Coalition splinters, with Prussia, Spain and the Netherlands making peace with France by the Treaties of Basle over April–July 1795.

The war that demonstrates the formidable challenge to the *ancien régime* represented by revolutionary France and the necessity of concerted action by *ancien régime* Powers to prevent a French geopolitical takeover of central and western Europe.

The French Campaign in Italy, 1796–1797 A series of military victories is scored by Napoleon Bonaparte over the Austrians in northern Italy: at Lodi in May 1796, at Arcola in November 1796 and especially at Rivoli in January 1797. Habsburg Austria is forced into a geopolitical accommodation with France at Campo Formio in October 1797.

The war which features the debut (and first triumph) of Napoleon Bonaparte.

The French Expedition to Egypt, 1798–1801 With only Britain – supreme at sea – remaining to challenge France by late 1797, Napoleon leads an expedition to Egypt to threaten British possessions in the East in May 1798. Napoleon defeats the Mameluke rulers of Egypt in the Battle of the Pyramids in July 1798 but the French fleet is destroyed by the British at the Battle of the Nile in Aboukir Bay in August 1798. The French forces move north to seize Syria but are halted at Acre in May 1799. After defeating the Turks at Aboukir in July 1799, Napoleon returns to France. The French expeditionary force under Kléber defeats the Turks and Mamelukes at Heliopolis in March 1800 but then suffers defeat by the British at Alexandria, leading to surrender in August 1801.

A disastrous Napoleonic venture on the periphery of Europe, poorly exploited by the anti-French Powers.

The War of the Second Coalition, 1798–1802 By December 1798, Britain (led by Pitt) has organised the Second Coalition against France, comprising Habsburg Austria, Russia, Portugal, Naples, the Ottoman Empire and Britain itself. The campaign by a Russian army (led by Suvorov) in northern Italy achieves some success during mid-1799 but disputes between Russia and Austria lead to Russia quitting the Second Coalition in October 1799. The Ottoman Empire also makes peace with France in January 1800. In June 1800, Napoleon (now First Consul of France) wins a decisive victory over the Austrians at Marengo, forcing Austria to sign the Treaty of Lunéville in February 1801. Portugal makes peace with France's ally Spain in September 1801 and even Britain (briefly) comes to terms with France by the Treaty of Amiens in March 1802.

The combination of chronic disunity among the anti-French Powers and the stunning Napoleonic victory at Marengo shatters the Second Coalition.

The War of the Third Coalition, 1804–1807 In May 1803, war breaks out again between France and Britain. A new, Third Coalition comprising Britain, Austria, Russia and Sweden is formed over 1804–1805. While the British triumph at sea, defeating the combined navies of France and Spain at Trafalgar in October 1805, on land the combined armies of Austria and Russia are destroyed at Austerlitz in December 1805, perhaps Napoleon's most brilliant victory. Austria is forced to make peace at Pressburg in December 1805. When Prussia joins the Coalition in summer 1806, she is promptly defeated at the battles of Jena and Auerstadt in October 1806. Napoleon fights the inconclusive but damaging battle of Eylau against Russia and Prussia in February 1807, then the more decisive battle of Friedland against Russia in June 1807. As a consequence, France and Russia make peace at Tilsit in July 1807.

Triumphant at sea but defeated on land, the Third Coalition proves more united and formidable than its predecessor, making Napoleon attempt to split the alliance of his enemies by offering a long-term geopolitical division of Europe between France and Russia.

The Russian-Ottoman War of 1806–1812 The Ottoman Empire declares war over Russian territorial claims in the Balkans in December 1806. Russia gradually forces back the Ottoman armies, capturing Belgrade (and much of the Ottoman army) in February 1811. Fearing an imminent war with France, Russia settles with the Ottomans by the Treaty of Bucharest in May 1812, occupying Bessarabia.

Another military episode in the continuing 'Eastern Question', running alongside the larger conflict being played out in central Europe.

The Russian-Swedish War of 1808–1809   With Napoleon's support, as agreed at Tilsit in July 1807, Alexander I of Russia attacks Sweden. By the Treaty of Fredericksham in September 1809, Russia acquires Finland from Sweden.

The Peninsular War of 1808–1814   Having conquered Portugal in 1807, Napoleon attempts to make his brother Joseph King of Spain in 1808. Encouraged by Britain, Spain rebels against French domination, forcing a French surrender at Baylen in July 1808. A British army lands at Lisbon in August 1808, expelling the French from Portugal after the battle of Vimeiro. The British expeditionary force under Moore is defeated at Corunna in January 1809. Under Wellesley (later Wellington), British forces advance steadily eastward, defeating the French at Talavera (July 1809), defending Torres Vedras (1809–1811) and then inflicting defeats at Salamanca (July 1812) and Vittoria (June 1813) before invading southern France and winning the battle of Toulouse in April 1814.

The relative credit due to British military intervention and Spanish guerrilla action in the slow defeat of the French is still a matter of controversy, as is the larger question of the degree to which the 'Spanish Ulcer' really debilitated the military resources of Napoleonic Europe.

The Austrian-French War of 1809   Austria is encouraged by French defeats in the Peninsular War to declare war on France in February 1809. The Austrians have a (rare) victory over the French at Aspern in May 1809 but are badly defeated at Wagram in July 1809. With Vienna occupied, Austria is compelled to sue for peace in October 1809.

An opportunist attack by Austria, ill-advised both in terms of lack of allies and premature timing. Austria is confirmed as both the second most-persistent opponent of France (after Britain) and the *ancien régime* Power most frequently and most seriously defeated by Napoleon.

The French Invasion of Russia, 1812   In May 1812, the détente between France and Russia established at Tilsit (1807) finally breaks down and Napoleon, encouraged by alliance with Prussia in February 1812, invades Russia. The French capture Smolensk (August 1812), have the military edge in the bloody battle of Borodino (September 1812) and occupy the Russian capital of Moscow. When the Russians refuse to negotiate, Napoleon decides to abandon Moscow (October 1812) and withdraw westwards. Harassed by the Russians, the frost-bitten French army finally evacuates Russian territory only in December 1812.

Another ill-judged Napoleonic foray to the European periphery, resulting in an unmitigated military disaster for Napoleon and the loss of most of his *Grande Armée* of 500,000 troops.

The War of the Fourth Coalition, 1813–1814 An alliance prompted by the French disaster in Russia. In February 1813, Prussia switches sides from France to Russia (soon followed by Sweden). In May 1813, Napoleon defeats the combined Russians and Prussians at Lützen and Bautzen. Brokered by Britain, the Coalition is formally founded in June 1813. Austria joins the Coalition in August 1813 but is promptly defeated at Dresden. Napoleon is decisively defeated by the combined armies of Russia, Prussia and Austria at Leipzig, the 'Battle of the Nations', in October 1813. The Allies cross the Rhine into France, capturing Paris in March 1814.

The decisive – but still close-run – campaign against Napoleon, sometimes described (usually by Germans) as the 'War of Liberation'.

The 'Hundred Days', 1815 In March 1815, Napoleon returns from exile on Elba to raise France. He confronts the British, Prussian and Dutch armies in 'Belgium', defeats the Prussians at Ligny but is beaten by Wellington's combined British and Dutch forces at Waterloo (June 1815), aided by the Prussians. Napoleon abdicates again and the Allies reoccupy Paris in July 1815.

The Spanish Uprising of 1820–1823 In early 1820, Spanish troops mutiny to secure a liberal constitution, forcing King Ferdinand VII to submit. A virtual civil war ensues, ending in 1823 when a French army (backed by Austria and Russia at the Congress of Verona) invades Spain and restores Ferdinand VII to full power.

A civil war 'resolved' by Great Power interventionist invasion favouring the monarchical status quo.

The Greek War of Liberation, 1821–1829 In April 1821, Greek nationalists raise the standard of independent Greece, defying Ottoman authority. Though bloodily beaten by Ottoman forces, the Greeks successfully engage first Western sympathy and then Great Power intercession. In July 1827, Britain, France and Russia agree to support the cause of independent Greece. Britain destroys the Ottoman fleet at Navarino in October 1827. Russia declares war on the Ottoman Empire in April 1828, advancing through Moldavia and Wallachia. The Ottoman Empire is forced to concede an independent Greece by the Treaty of Adrianople (September 1829).

A nationalist uprising against imperial authority 'resolved' by Great Power diplomatic and military intervention favouring a new nation-state.

The Belgian War of Liberation, 1830–1833 The 'Belgians' rebel against Dutch rule in August 1830, encouraged by the successful Greek example of national uprising and sparked by the 'July Revolution' in

France. Britain, France and Prussia are sympathetic to the Belgian cause, favouring the dissolution of the Dutch-Belgian union of 1815. The Dutch resist and have to be coerced by the Powers (notably by French seizure of Antwerp in December 1832) into accepting the independence of Belgium, formally guaranteed by the Treaty of London only in April 1839.

A western-European equivalent of the Greek War of Liberation: another nationalist uprising against 'imperial' authority is resolved by Great Power diplomatic and military intervention favouring a new nation-state.

The (First) Polish Uprising, 1830–1831 Excited by the successful Greek War of Liberation and the current Belgian uprising, Polish nationalists rebel against Russian authority and expel the Russian garrison from Warsaw in November 1830. The Russians refuse to negotiate, reoccupying Warsaw in September 1831. Most Polish nationalists are either exiled to Siberia or flee into exile in France.

Poland fails to become the eastern-European equivalent of Belgium because of the military power available to Russia and its inability to engage Western Great Power diplomatic or military commitment.

The (First) Egyptian-Ottoman War, 1832–1833 Mehemet Ali of Egypt, disappointed that his only reward for aiding the Greek cause against the Ottomans is the Governorship of Crete, invades Ottoman territory in 1832. He captures Acre and defeats the Ottoman army at Koniah. As his price of peace, Ali secures the formal independence of Egypt from the Ottoman Empire, plus the acquisition of Syria and Adana.

Another indication of the accelerating enfeeblement of the Ottoman Empire: not only external Great Powers but internal 'vassals' are exploiting Ottoman weakness to their own territorial advantage.

The (First) Carlist War, 1834–1839 Civil war breaks out in Spain in 1834 when a coalition of regional (especially Basque), aristocratic and Catholic interests supports the claim of the conservative Don Carlos against his niece Queen Isabella. Supported by the army, the liberals and the Powers of Britain and France, Isabella gradually defeats the Carlist forces over 1837–1839.

A protracted and damaging civil war, without major Great Power intervention, which fails to resolve any principal Spanish issue.

The Second Egyptian-Ottoman War, 1839–1841 In April 1839, the Ottomans attack Mehemet Ali of Egypt but are defeated at Nezib. France is sympathetic to Ali but Britain, Russia, Austria and Prussia intervene diplomatically in July 1840 to protect the Ottoman Empire. The British bombard Beirut and capture Acre (September–November 1840), forcing Ali to withdraw from Syria. Peace is made in July 1841 and the 'Straits Convention' is negotiated to stabilise the Ottoman Empire.

Having kept out of the First Egyptian-Ottoman War, the Powers are persuaded by the frailty of the Ottoman Empire to intervene diplomatically and then militarily on its behalf in the Second Egyptian-Ottoman War.

The Hungarian Uprising of 1848–1849 Encouraged by revolution in France, the Hungarians claim autonomy within the Habsburg Empire, which is recognised by Emperor Ferdinand I in March 1848. However, with the covert backing of the Emperor, the Croats under Jelačić invade Hungary in September 1848, prompting vigorous Hungarian resistance. After December 1848, under the new Emperor Franz Josef, the Empire strikes back hard against the Hungarians, capturing the Hungarian capital of Budapest in January 1849. Dogged fighting by the Hungarian militia, which recaptures Budapest in May 1849, persuades Franz Josef to invite military aid from Russia. Tsar Nicholas I despatches Russian forces into Hungary, defeating the Hungarians at Temesvár and forcing their surrender at Világos in August 1849.

Though defeated, the Hungarians demonstrate their national strength by forcing the Austrian Empire to summon external aid from the Russian 'Gendarme of Europe' to counter the Hungarian challenge. A war indicating the vulnerability of the Austrian Empire, the strength of the Russian Empire and the improving prospects for Hungarian nationalism.

The Austrian-Piedmontese War of 1848–1849 Encouraged by revolt in Milan (in Austrian Lombardy-Venetia) in March 1848, Piedmont-Sardinia declares war on the Austrian Empire but is defeated at Custozza in July 1848. An armistice signed at Vigevano is breached after six months by Piedmont, which is again defeated at Novara in March 1849. Piedmont has to sue for peace by the Treaty of Milan in August 1849.

A brave, lone attempt by Piedmont to raise the flag of 'Italy' founders, even when directed against an Austrian Empire politically embarrassed and militarily stretched by the 'Year of Revolutions'.

The (First) Danish-Prussian War, 1848–1850 In March 1848, the predominantly German provinces of Schleswig and Holstein rebel against Danish rule. Prussia supports Schleswig-Holstein from April 1848, forcing Denmark to accept the truce of Malmö in August 1848. War returns briefly in April 1849. Peace is established by the Treaty of Berlin in July 1850, with the Great Powers (including Prussia) guaranteeing Denmark's territorial integrity by the Treaty of London in May 1852.

Prussia's first attempt to expand territorially at the expense of Denmark proves militarily feasible but diplomatically unsuccessful.

Ottoman-Montenegrin Wars of 1852–1853 and 1858 On both occasions, the Ottomans declare war after Montenegro seizes adjacent territory, the Austrian Empire intervenes to protect Montenegro and peace treaties expand and legitimise Montenegrin jurisdiction.

An indication of how even a tiny nation can defy the declining Ottoman Empire if sponsored or protected by a Great Power.

The Crimean War of 1853–1856 Russia claims protectorship of Christians within the Ottoman Empire in April 1853, refuted by the Ottoman Empire in May 1853. In July 1853 Russia invades the Danubian Principalities until Austria secures the withdrawal of both Russian and Ottoman forces. Following the Russian destruction of the Ottoman fleet at Sinope in November 1853, Britain and France decide to ally with the Ottomans in March 1854. Britain and France invade Crimea to besiege the strategically crucial base of the Russian Black Sea fleet at Sebastopol in September 1854 (joined by Piedmont after January 1855). Battles are fought against the Russians at Alma (September 1854), Balaclava (the occasion of the glorious – if unnecessary – Charge of the Light Brigade immortalised by Tennyson) in October 1854, and Inkerman (November 1854) before Sebastopol is finally captured in September 1855. Peace terms restoring the status quo are initialled in February 1856, under threat of Austria joining the war on the Allied side. The war is formally ended by the Treaty of Paris in March 1856.

War losses: Russia 100,000; France 93,600; Ottoman Empire 35,000; Britain 22,200; Piedmont 2,200; Total 253,000. The only war involving four Great Powers (Britain, France, Russia and the Ottoman Empire) for the century between 1815 and 1914, with profound effects upon Russia both internationally and especially domestically.

The Franco-Piedmontese-Austrian War of 1859 In July 1858, Emperor Napoleon III of France agrees at Plombières to help Piedmont-Sardinia unite northern Italy. War is declared by Austria, then Piedmont in April 1859, and by France in May 1859. The combined French and Piedmontese forces prove victorious at the bloody battles of Magenta and Solferino (both June 1859). Napoleon III outrages Piedmont by making peace with Austria at Villafranca in July 1859, without consulting Cavour. By the Treaty of Zurich in November 1859, Piedmont acquires Lombardy and Parma from Austria.

War losses: Austria 40,000; France 19,000; Piedmont 7,600; Total 66,600. After the disappointment of 1848–1849, Piedmont makes solid progress towards the territorial 'Unification of Italy' by attracting the Great Power military backing of France, to the detriment of the increasingly defensive multi-national Austrian Empire.

The Second Polish Uprising, 1863–1864 Encouraged by France's sponsorship of 'Italy' in 1859, the Poles hope for Western support for 'Poland' and rebel against Russian rule in January 1863. In February 1863, Prussia self-interestedly allies with Russia jointly to suppress the

Uprising. By August 1864, the Uprising has been neutralised by a combination of harsh military suppression and expedient politico-social concession.

Unable – as in 1830–1831 – to engage the military backing of any sympathetic Great Power (even France), Poland cannot defeat the combined repressive power of Russia and Prussia. 'Poland' remains the largest 'nation without a state' in Europe, the most frustrated inmate of the tsarist 'Prison of Nations'.

The Danish-Prussian-Austrian War of 1864 In February 1864, Prussia and Austria declare war on Denmark in support of the predominantly-German Danish provinces of Schleswig and Holstein. Most of Schleswig-Holstein (and the Danish army) is captured by July 1864. By the Treaty of Vienna in October 1864, Denmark is forced to cede Schleswig and Holstein to Prussia and Austria.

War losses: Denmark 11,000; Prussia 2,400; Austria 1,100; Total 14,500. A sequel to the War of 1848–1850 with a different outcome: Prussia proves successful in claiming 'German' territory possessed by a non-German state, thereby posing as the 'Champion of German Unification'.

The Austrian-Prussian-Italian (Seven Weeks) War of 1866 In June 1866, Prussia and its ally Italy declare war on Austria, ostensibly over the sharing of Schleswig-Holstein. On the northern (Austrian-Prussian) front, Prussia defeats the Austrians decisively at the battle of Sadowa (or Königgrätz) in July 1866. On the southern (Austrian-Italian) front, the Austrians defeat the Italians at the (second) battle of Custozza in June 1866. The northern-front war is ended by the Treaty of Prague (August 1866) excluding Austria from 'Germany'. The southern-front war is ended by the Treaty of Vienna (October 1866) forcing Austria to relinquish Venetia to Italy.

War losses: Austria 112,400; Prussia 22,300; Italy 11,200; Total 145,900. A mixed result militarily for the Prussian-Italian alliance but a diplomatic triumph: Prussia assumes the leadership of 'Germany'; Italy switches Great Power sponsor from France (in 1859) to Prussia (in 1866) to achieve the expulsion of Austria from all northern Italy and the near-completion of 'Italian Unification'.

The Franco-Prussian War of 1870–1871 In July 1870, Napoleon III declares war on Prussia over a disagreement on the Spanish succession and French resentment at alleged insults in the 'Ems Telegram'. The Prussian army outmanoeuvres the French, defeating then capturing most of the French army at Sedan (September 1870) and Metz (October 1870). Napoleon III is captured at Sedan and Paris falls to the Prussian army after a siege from September 1870 to January 1871. National resistance in the provinces is attempted but France accepts defeat by March 1871, formalised by the Treaty of Frankfurt in May 1871.

War losses: France 580,000; Prussia 130,000; Total 710,000. Amassing the highest casualties since the Napoleonic Wars, the Franco-Prussian War delivers a stunning blow to French pride, symbolising the replacement of France as the dominant continental Great Power by the new 'Germany'.

The Second Carlist War, 1872–1876   After King Amadeo is chosen as successor to Queen Isabella of Spain in November 1870, conservative forces rebel in support of (the second) Don Carlos against the republican government established in Madrid. Though strongly backed in the Basque provinces, Don Carlos is defeated, signing the Convention of Amovebeita in May 1872. Amadeo abdicates in February 1873 prompting another Carlist campaign. With the restoration of the monarchy by the proclamation of King Alfonso in September 1874, the Carlist forces lose support everywhere except the Basque provinces. Don Carlos is forced into exile from Spain in February 1876.

Like the First Carlist War (1834–1839), the sequel Second Carlist War proves a divisive and damaging political and military conflict conducted without Great Power intervention, emphasising the irremediable decline of a decolonising empire on the periphery of Europe.

The Russian-Ottoman War of 1877–1878   Over 1875–1876, nationalist revolts against Ottoman rule in Bosnia Herzegovina and 'Bulgaria' are ruthlessly and bloodily suppressed. Serbia and Montenegro declare war on the Ottomans in July 1876. Further reprisals culminate in the 'Bulgarian Atrocities' (condemned by Western public opinion led by William Gladstone in September 1876). Russia declares war on behalf of its Slav compatriots in the Balkans in April 1877. Capturing the strategically crucial Ottoman fortress of Plevna in December 1877, Russia advances over the Shipka Pass to take Adrianople and threaten Constantinople in January 1878. The Ottoman Empire is forced to agree to the Russian-imposed geopolitical settlement of San Stefano in March 1878.

Once again, spreading Balkan nationalism (and its ferocious harassment by the Ottoman Empire) is exploited by Russia as a Pan-Slavist pretext for military intervention and territorial aggrandisement which threaten to overturn the increasingly precarious power-balance in what now remains of Ottoman Europe.

The Serbian-Bulgarian War of 1885–1886   In September 1885, the new state of Bulgaria provocatively defies neighbours and Great Powers alike by unilaterally annexing Eastern Rumelia, denied to 'Big Bulgaria' under the Congress of Berlin (1878). Serbia declares war on Bulgaria in pursuit of territorial compensation but is immediately and ignominiously routed by the 'Prussians of the Balkans' at Slivnitsa in November 1885 (a battle which provides the setting for George

Bernard Shaw's play *Arms and the Man*). An Austrian ultimatum to Bulgaria saves Serbia and secures a peace settlement at Bucharest in March 1886, which confirms the territorial status quo.

The first major quarrel between new Balkan states, demonstrating that the past solidarity of alliance between emergent national states against the retreating Ottoman Empire is being replaced by internecine competition for the territorial legacy of the moribund Ottoman Europe.

The Greek-Ottoman War of 1896–1898 After their unsuccessful revolt of 1866–1869, the Cretans rise again against Ottoman rule in February 1896. Concessions over autonomy granted by the Ottomans in July 1896 fail to undermine the Cretan campaign for union with Greece. Greece declares war in support of Crete in April 1897 and is promptly defeated, inducing the Great Powers to intervene to impose an armistice in May 1897. Peace between Greece and the Ottoman Empire is signed by the Treaty of Constantinople in December 1897 but the last Turkish troops do not evacuate autonomous Crete until December 1898.

A further episode in the continuing diplomatic and (where necessary) military campaign to realise 'Greater Greece', necessarily at the territorial expense of the collapsing Ottoman Empire.

The Russo-Japanese War of 1904–1905 Russian-Japanese imperial rivalry in Manchuria and Korea, seeking since the 1890s to exploit the weakness of China (the 'Sick Man of Asia'), becomes war in February 1904. A catalogue of disasters for Russia: the Russian Pacific fleet is badly damaged at Port Arthur by Japanese surprise attack (February 1904); Port Arthur surrenders (January 1905); the Russian army is forced to retreat at Mukden (March 1905); the Russian Black Sea fleet mutinies, led by the battleship *Potemkin* (April 1905); and the Russian Baltic fleet provokes the Dogger Bank Incident with Britain (October 1904) on the way round the world to be sunk at Tsushima (May 1905). Hostilities are concluded by the Treaty of Portsmouth, New Hampshire in September 1905.

A war of colonial expansionism which soon assumes broader implications: the humiliating defeat for Russia contributes to radical domestic unrest in the 'Revolution of 1905'; the Japanese victory announces the advent of a new military Great Power, breaking the nineteenth-century European monopoly of the 'Great Power Club'.

The Italian-Ottoman War of 1911–1912 In September 1911, Italy declares war on an Ottoman Empire weakened by the Young Turk Revolution in the hope of acquiring territory in Africa. In November 1911 Italy defeats the Ottomans in north Africa, and occupies Rhodes and the Dodecanese in the Aegean in May 1912. The Ottoman Empire cedes the islands of Rhodes and the Dodecanese, and the mainland African territories of Cyrenaica and Tripoli (now Libya) to Italy by the Treaty of Ouchy in October 1912.

An opportunistic land-grab by Italy designed to compete with Greece for acquisition of the islands of the eastern Mediterranean and to create an Italian African Empire. As has increasingly been the case over the nineteenth century, the 'Sick Man of Europe' (the Ottoman Empire) is in no condition to resist a determined attack.

The First Balkan War, 1912–1913 Encouraged by Italy's land-grabbing over 1911–1912, the Balkan states of Serbia, Bulgaria, Montenegro and Greece declare war on the Ottoman Empire in October 1912, soon overrunning most of remaining Turkey-in-Europe. Redistribution of the ex-Ottoman territories among the Balkan combatants is agreed by the ambassadorial Treaty of London in May 1913.

A throw-back to the anti-Ottoman Balkan solidarity of the earlier nineteenth century, now almost (but not quite) achieving the Ottomans' complete territorial expulsion from Europe.

The Second Balkan War, 1913 War breaks out in June 1913 when Bulgaria, which incurred two-thirds of the casualties in the First Balkan War, demands an increased share of ex-Ottoman territory at the expense of ex-allies Serbia and Greece. Bulgaria is soon defeated by an alliance of Serbia, Greece, Rumania and even the Ottoman Empire. A fresh redistribution of territory to the disadvantage of Bulgaria and advantage of Serbia, Greece, Rumania and the Ottoman Empire is effected by the Treaty of Bucharest (August 1913) and Ottoman treaties with Bulgaria (September 1913) and Greece (November 1913).

A continuation of the later nineteenth-century competitive land-grab mentality of the new Balkan states first demonstrated by the Serbian-Bulgarian War of 1885–1886.

Losses in both Balkan Wars: Ottomans 70,000; Bulgaria 50,000; Serbia and Montenegro 33,500; Greece 7,500; Rumania 1,500; Total 162,500.

The First World War, 1914–1918 The long-expected Great Power conflict is triggered by Austria-Hungary's declaration of war on Serbia (following the assassination of Archduke Franz Ferdinand in Sarajevo) on 28 July 1914. Russia mobilises to support Serbia, prompting German support for Austria-Hungary. France and then Britain intervene to complete the diplomatic and military confrontation of the 'Entente Allies' against the 'Central Powers' by mid-August 1914.

1914 The expected short war fails to materialise. On the western front, the German Schlieffen Plan (originally drafted in 1905) fails to achieve the projected capture of Paris, partly due to French and British counter-attack at the First Battle of the Marne (September 1914), partly because of the unexpected speed of Russian mobilisation to the East. The war on the eastern front opens earlier than Germany expects, leading to early Russian advances but then disasters at Tannenberg (August 1914) and the Masurian Lakes (September 1914). On the southern front, the Austro-Hungarians are stubbornly held by the Serbs.

1915 Both sides attempt to respond to the 'longer war'. The Central Powers advance relentlessly on the eastern front against Russia (the most conspicuous victim of the 'short war mentality'), occupying Russian Poland and taking Warsaw in August 1915. The Allies attempt 'weak point strategy' both to relieve pressure on Russia and break the deadlock on the western front by attracting Italy to their side (from May 1915), by despatching outflanking expeditionary forces to Salonika in Greece (from October 1915) and Gallipoli in Turkey (from April 1915), they hope to force the Straits and establish better communication between the Allies. On the western front, a stalemate of trench warfare is established. On the southern front, Serbia is finally defeated and overrun by the Austro-Hungarians.

1916 The military stalemate of a 'long war' continues on both fronts. On the western front, offensives are launched by both sides (the Germans against Verdun from February 1916 and the Allies on the Somme from July 1916), but despite horrendous casualties no decisive advantage is gained. At sea, the battle of Jutland (May–June 1916) is the principal naval engagement of the war, an inconclusive confrontation in which the British fleet loses more ships but the German fleet returns permanently to port. On the eastern front, the Russian army rallies, going onto the offensive against the Ottoman Empire in the Caucasus (from January 1916) and against the Austro-Hungarians (from March 1916). Russia inflicts a defeat on the Austro-Hungarians by the Brusilov Offensive of June–July 1916 but is embarrassed by the collapse of Rumania under combined German, Austro-Hungarian and Bulgarian attack in December 1916.

1917 Both sides are offered hope for the resolution of the 'long war'. In early 1917, the Allies make modest advances on the western front and welcome to their camp the U.S.A. (which declares war on Germany in April 1917 and on Austria-Hungary in December 1917). On the defensive on the western front, the Central Powers have victories elsewhere later in 1917: on the southern front, Austria-Hungary routs the Italians at Caporetto in October–November 1917; and on the eastern front, the February Revolution ends the tsarist empire and undermines the Russian war effort (from April 1917) while the October Revolution brings the Bolsheviks to power, leading first to an armistice in November 1917 and subsequently to the separate Peace of Brest-Litovsk which takes Bolshevik Russia out of the war in March 1918.

1918 The decisive last struggle. Cheered by the Central Powers' victory on, then dissolution of, the eastern front, Germany finds herself fighting on one front for the first time. Concentrating previously divided forces, Germany launches three great offensives on the western front in March, May and July 1918. American aid becomes vital to the

Allied defeat of the final German offensive at the Second Battle of the Marne (July–August 1918) and the Fourth Battle of Ypres (September 1918). With Austria-Hungary, Bulgaria and the Ottoman Empire defeated by October 1918, Germany agrees to an armistice with the Allies on 11 November 1918.

War fatalities

	Military	Civilian	Total
Austria-Hungary	1,200,000	300,000	1,500,000
Belgium	14,000	30,000	44,000
British Empire	908,000	30,000	938,000
Bulgaria	87,000	275,000	362,000
French Empire	1,363,000	40,000	1,403,000
Germany	1,774,000	760,000	2,534,000
Greece	5,000	132,000	137,000
Italy	460,000	–	460,000 +
Montenegro	3,000	–	3,000 +
Ottoman Empire	325,000	2,150,000	2,475,000
Portugal	7,000	–	7,000 +
Rumania	336,000	275,000	611,000
Russian Empire	1,700,000	2,000,000	3,700,000
Serbia	125,000	650,000	775,000
Total Fatalities	*8,307,000*	*6,642,000*	*14,949,000*

The First World War inflicts unprecedented material and human damage (15 million dead) on Europe and the wider world. With an impact on all aspects of European society almost impossible to exaggerate, the 'Great War' (as it is known to contemporaries) necessarily constitutes both the death agony of nineteenth-century Europe and the traumatic birth of twentieth-century Europe.

The Russian Civil War of 1918–1920 Following the Bolshevik assumption of power in Russia in October 1917, armed conflict develops in three distinct (though related) forms:

Civil war The confrontation between the Bolshevik-led 'Reds' and the anti-Bolshevik 'Whites' shifts from a political quarrel (in 1917) to a civil war of internecine ferocity and atrocity fought over most parts of Russia until finally resolved by the Red Army defeating and expelling the last 'White' army from Russia in December 1920.

War of foreign intervention The Allies intervene militarily (although not in great strength) from early 1918, initially in an attempt to maintain an eastern front in the First World War, subsequently to reinforce 'White' efforts to dislodge the Bolshevik government. British, French, American and Japanese expeditionary forces only serve to discredit the 'Whites' and are withdrawn from European Russia by 1920 (and Asiatic Russia by 1922).

War of national emancipation The civil war between Russians is exploited by nationalists eager to effect a mass escape from the ex-tsarist 'Prison of Nations'. The Finns, Estonians, Latvians, Lithuanians, Belorussians, Ukrainians, Armenians, Georgians and Azeris all claim sovereignty and independence from Russia, with varying degrees of success.

War losses The combined deaths from military action, economic dislocation, social collapse and resultant disease and famine have been estimated to total as many as 14 million.

A war on a scale still unappreciated in the West, dwarfing the First World War in its demographic impact upon Russia (deaths 1914–1918: 3.7 million; deaths 1918–1921: up to 14 million). Deaths in the Russian Civil War match the combined deaths incurred by all combatant states in the First World War.

The Polish-Russian War of 1919–1920 Reconstituted by the Allies at the Paris Peace Settlement, Poland attempts to exploit Bolshevik difficulties in the Russian Civil War, invading Russia to acquire more eastern territory in April 1919. By Spring 1920, the Red Army is successfully counter-attacking but is then held by the Polish army in the 'Miracle on the Vistula', the battle of Warsaw in August 1920. The war is effectively halted by mutual exhaustion in October 1920, with a settlement of the Russian-Polish border finally agreed by the Treaty of Riga in March 1921.

Essentially the most important episode in the Russian Civil War's 'national emancipation' dimension, resulting in Poland becoming the largest state in eastern Europe (outside Russia).

The Hungarian-Rumanian War of 1919 Resentful of the October 1918 armistice terms and anticipating territorial losses imposed by the Allies, Hungary sanctions a Communist government headed by Bela Kun in March 1919 and invades Slovakia. Rumania attacks Hungary to gain Transylvania, capturing Budapest and toppling the Kun government in August 1919. Under Allied pressure, the Rumanians withdraw from Hungary in November 1919. The territorial losses feared by the Hungarians (including the surrender of Transylvania to Rumania) are confirmed by the Treaty of Trianon in June 1920.

A war licensed by the Allies to effect the territorial reduction of Hungary (on the losing Central Powers' side in the First World War) and reward Rumania (on the winning Allied side) by permitting her to become the second-largest state in eastern Europe (after Poland).

The Greek-Turkish War of 1920–1923 Refusing to condone their territorial losses to Greece as accepted by the Ottoman Empire at the Treaty of Sèvres (August 1920), the Turks under Mustapha Kemal resist the Greek takeover. Over 1921 Kemal organises Turkish resistance into an effective national fighting force. In September 1922 Kemal drives the Greeks from their last mainland stronghold of Smyrna and confronts the British expeditionary force in the Dardanelles at Chanak. Turkish control over the Straits and Constantinople area is conceded by the Convention of Mudania in October 1922, a prelude to the Treaty of Lausanne in July 1923, which adapts 'Sèvres' to the territorial exclusion of the Greeks and the territorial integrity of Turkey.

The war which challenges (successfully) the imposed Allied settlement at the end of the First World War and establishes a tolerable territorial 'answer' to the 150-year-old 'Eastern Question'.

2. Diplomatic

1772 August: *First Partition of Poland.* Russia takes territories east of the rivers Duna and Dnieper; Prussia takes west Prussia (except Danzig) and Ermland; Habsburg Austria takes eastern Galicia and Iodomenia. Territorial jurisdiction of state of Poland reduced by one third.

1774 July: *Treaty of Kutchuk-Kainardji.* Ends war between Russian and Ottoman Empires: Russia acquires Crimea and the Black Sea littoral as far as the mouth of the river Dnieper plus the right of navigation in Ottoman waters. Conventionally regarded as the start of the 'Eastern Question'.

1783 September: *Treaty of Versailles.* Independence of U.S.A. conceded by Britain, witnessed by France and Spain.

1784 January: *Convention of Constantinople.* Ottoman Empire formally recognises Russian acquisition of Crimea and northern littoral of Black Sea.

1788 November: *Treaty of Uddevalla.* Denmark agrees to withdraw from Sweden.

1790 January: *Convention of Berlin.* Britain, Prussia and Netherlands agree over Austrian Netherlands (Belgium).
 July: *Convention of Reichenbach.* Prussia and Austria agree policy over Netherlands and Ottoman Empire.
 August: *Treaty of Varela.* Ends war between Russia and Sweden.

1791 August: *Treaty of Sistova.* Ends war between Habsburg and Ottoman Empires (with Austria acquiring Orsova).
 August: *Declaration of Pillnitz.* Austria and Prussia threaten military intervention against revolutionary France (if supported by other Powers).

1792 January: *Treaty of Jassy.* Russian and Ottoman Empires establish river Dnieper as their common border.
 February: *Treaty of Berlin.* Austria and Prussia promise mutual support in war against France.

1793 February: *First Coalition.* Britain, Austria, Prussia, Netherlands, Spain and Piedmont-Sardinia against France.
 May: *Second Partition of Poland.* Russia and Prussia (without Austria) seize more territory, leaving rump Polish state.

1794 April: *Treaty of the Hague.* Between Netherlands, Britain and Prussia.

September: *St Petersburg Alliance.* Between Russia, Britain and Austria.

1795 April–July: *Treaties of Basle.* Between France and Prussia, Netherlands and Spain effectively bring First Coalition to an end.

October: *Third Partition of Poland.* Russia, Austria and Prussia dismember the remainder of Poland. The state of Poland disappears from the geopolitical map of Europe until the First World War.

1796 May: *Armistice of Cherasco.* Piedmont-Sardinia quits war against France, surrendering Nice and Savoy to France.

1797 October: *Treaty of Campo Formio.* French-Austrian territorial settlement. Austria recognises French conquests (Austrian Netherlands/Belgium and Ionian Islands). Northern 'Italy' partitioned between France (Cisalpine Republic) and Austria (Venetia, Istria and Dalmatia). Promise of a future congress at Rastatt to partition 'Germany': France to get most of left-bank (west) Rhineland; Austria to get Salzburg and part of Bavaria.

1798–1799: *Second Coalition.* Britain, Russia, Austria, Portugal and Naples against France.

1800 December: *Armed Neutrality of the North.* Combination of Russia, Sweden and Denmark revived by France as anti-British shipping alliance.

1801 February: *Treaty of Lunéville.* Establishes peace between France and Austria (with France securing the left bank of the River Rhine).

1802 March: *Treaty of Amiens.* Establishes peace between France and Britain, Spain and Netherlands. Provides only a 14-month breathing-space in the war between Britain and France.

1803 February: *Diet of Ratisbon.* Reconstitutes 'Germany', abolishing most ecclesiastical princedoms and imperial cities.

1804: *Third Coalition.* Britain, Russia, Austria and Sweden against France.

1805 December: *Treaty of Schönbrunn.* Between France and Prussia: Prussia loses Cleves, Neuchâtel and Ansbach, gaining Hanover in compensation.

December: *Treaty of Pressburg.* Between Austria and France. Austria loses territory to French client states and pays war indemnity of 40,000 francs.

1806 July: *Treaty of Paris.* Establishes the *Confederation of the Rhine.* 16 territories of western 'Germany' united geopolitically as a Napoleonic client-state.

November: *Berlin Decree.* Institutes the 'Continental System' to blockade Britain into submission through the closure of continental ports (extended to Russia in 1807, Spain and Portugal in 1808).

1807 April: *Treaty of Bartenstein.* Russia and Prussia agree to continue war against France.

July: TREATY OF TILSIT. Establishes geopolitical détente between France and Russia. Public provisions: France recognises Russian hegemony in eastern Europe; Russia recognises French hegemony in central and western Europe, particularly with regard to the halving of the territory of Prussia and the creation of the Kingdom of Westphalia and Grand Duchy of Warsaw. Secret provisions: Russia to support France by joining the 'Continental System' against recalcitrant Britain; France to support Russia by facilitating her territorial designs on Sweden and Ottoman Europe.

October: *Treaty of Fontainebleau.* France and Spain agree to partition Portugal.

1808 August: *Convention of Cintra.* France permitted to evacuate Portugal without British harassment.

October: *Erfurt Conference.* Reaffirms cooperation between France and Russia, in presence of German princes. A public relations exercise by Napoleon designed to stabilise Napoleonic Europe.

1809 September: *Treaty of Frederiksham.* Sweden cedes Finland to Russia.

October: *Treaty of Vienna.* As the price of peace, Austria cedes territory to France (Illyria and Trieste) and her client states (Galicia to Grand Duchy of Warsaw, Salzburg to Bavaria).

1812 April: *Treaty of Åbo.* Secret alliance between Russia and Sweden. Sweden accepts the transfer of Finland to Russia in exchange for Russian support for Sweden acquiring Norway from Denmark.

May: *Treaty of Bucharest.* Ends war between Russian and Ottoman Empires: Russian annexation of Bessarabia.

July: *Alliance of Örebro.* Between Britain, Russia and Sweden against France.

1813 February: *Treaty of Kalisch.* Forges alliance between Prussia and Russia against France.

June: *Treaty of Reichenbach.* Russia, Prussia and Austria agree on the abolition of the Grand Duchy of Warsaw and Confederation of the Rhine.

September: *Treaty of Teplitz.* Establishes agreement between Russia, Prussia and Austria on war aims against France.

1814 January: *Treaty of Kiel:* Geopolitical land deal in Scandinavia. Since Sweden has already lost Finland to Russia (1809), Denmark cedes Norway to Sweden, receiving Pomerania in compensation.

March: *Treaty of Chaumont.* Britain, Russia, Prussia and Austria promise not to make separate peace with Napoleonic France.

April: *Treaty of Fontainebleau.* Following abdication, Napoleon is granted princedom of Elba for exile.

May: *(First) Treaty of Paris.* France reduced to her 1792 borders, preparatory to comprehensive peace settlement at Vienna.

1815 April: Britain, Russia, Prussia and Austria form new alliance to defeat Napoleon during his last 'One Hundred Days'.

June: THE CONGRESS OF VIENNA SETTLEMENT. International assembly of Great Powers meeting from September 1814 to June 1815 to determine the geopolitical structure of Europe after the (double) defeat of Napoleon.

Delegates: Metternich (Austria), Castlereagh (Britain), Alexander I and Capodistrias (Russia), Hardenberg (Prussia) and Talleyrand (France). Gentz as Secretary General of Congress. The principal provisions as follows.

Three new geopolitical creations: the 'United Kingdom of the Netherlands'; a 'German Confederation' of 39 states under Austrian presidency; the free city of Cracow.

Two subject kingdoms created: 'Lombardy-Venetia', ruled by the Emperor of Austria; 'Poland', ruled by the Tsar of Russia.

Restoration of legitimate dynasties in Spain, Naples, Piedmont, Tuscany and Modena.

Re-establishment of the Swiss Confederation.

Austria acquires Lombardy-Venetia, Dalmatia, Carniola, Salzburg and Galicia.

Prussia acquires Posen, Danzig, most of Saxony and Westphalia (and Pomerania from Sweden).

Russia acquires most of Poland (and 1808 acquisition of Finland from Sweden and 1812 acquisition of Bessarabia from Ottoman Empire confirmed).

Additional general principles: free navigation of the rivers Rhine and Meuse; condemnation of the slave trade; promotion of Jewish rights (especially in 'Germany'); updating and consolidation of diplomatic protocol.

The Vienna Settlement restores the dynastic principle with few concessions to nationalism in a broad geopolitical matrix which lasts without major revision for almost 50 years.

September: *Holy Alliance.* On the initiative of Tsar Alexander I, the monarchs of Russia, Austria and Prussia declare their faith in Christian brotherhood. Famously condemned by Castlereagh as 'a piece of sublime mysticism and nonsense'.

November: *Second Treaty of Paris.* Reduces France to her 1789 frontiers, exacts indemnity and authorises five-year Allied military occupation of France. Under Article VI, the Powers of Britain, Russia, Austria and Prussia agree to hold regular meetings to discuss problems and decide joint action 'most salutary for the repose and prosperity of the nations and for maintaining the peace of Europe' (subsequently termed the 'Congress System').

1818: *Congress of Aix-La-Chapelle.* First of the 'Congress System' meetings. Britain, Russia, Austria and Prussia extend their alliance to include France, settle the question of war indemnity and end their occupation of France after only three years. France readmitted to the 'Great Power Club'. Early signs of dissent about the purpose of the Congress System: Britain rejects a Russian proposal for an alliance guaranteeing all prevailing systems of government in Europe.

November: *Quadruple Alliance* of Britain, Russia, Austria and Prussia secretly renewed as safeguard against possible French revanche.

1820 October–December: *Congress of Troppau.* Second of Congress System meetings. Called by Tsar Alexander I, alarmed at revolts in Spain, Portugal, Piedmont and Naples. Metternich produces *Troppau Protocol*, authorising united intervention if international order and stability are threatened. Agreed by Russia and Prussia but publicly opposed by Britain, causing the Congress to break down.

1821 January–May: *Congress of Laibach.* Seen as the third of the Congress System meetings, though really only a resumption of the adjourned Troppau Congress. Austria and Russia are prepared to intervene in 'Italy' and 'Greece' but Britain objects and withdraws.

1822 October–December: *Congress of Verona.* Fourth of the Congress System meetings, last to be attended by Britain. On discovering that Austria and Russia are supporting French intervention in Spain, Britain protests and withdraws permanently.

1824 June–1825 April: *Congress of St Petersburg.* Fifth of the Congress System meetings, though Britain pointedly absent. Rows between Russia and Austria ensure that no more meetings are called. The end of the ten-year career of the 'Congress System'.

1826 April: *Protocol of St Petersburg.* Britain and France agree that Greece should become an autonomous state.

1827 July: *Treaty of London.* Britain, Russia and France threaten force if Ottoman Empire does not observe the Protocol of St Petersburg.

1828 February: *Peace of Turkmenchai.* Russia acquires parts of Armenia from Ottoman Empire and Azerbaidzhan from Persia.

1829 September: *Treaty of Adrianople.* Between Russian and Ottoman Empires. Provisions: independence of Greece granted; Russia occupies Danubian Principalities of Moldavia and Wallachia; Russian access to the Straits and acquisition of Georgia and Armenia recognised.

1830 December: *London Conference.* Britain, France and Prussia agree to the dissolution of the United Kingdom of the Netherlands (1815) and authorise the creation of an independent Belgium.

1833 July: *Treaty of Unkiar-Skelessi.* Between Russian and Ottoman Empires. Public provision: a defensive accord between the Russian and Ottoman Empires valid for eight years. Secret provision: Ottomans agree to close Dardanelles to foreign warships at Russian request while allowing Russian ships free access from the Black Sea. The ideal arrangement for Russia: she can get out of the Black Sea at will but no-one else can get in without her express permission.

September: *Agreement of Münchengrätz.* Metternich and Tsar Nicholas I agree on joint maintenance of the Ottoman Empire and the partition of Poland (assisting each other where necessary).

October: *Agreement of Berlin.* Austria, Russia and Prussia reaffirm the interventionist Troppau Protocol (1820).

1834 April: *Quadruple Alliance.* Formed between Britain, France, Spain and Portugal to establish stability in the Iberian peninsula through the promotion of liberal constitutions.

1839 April: *Treaty of London.* Great Powers guarantee the 'independent and perpetually neutral state' of Belgium. This is the 'scrap of paper' over which Britain enters the First World War in August 1914.

1840 July: *Quadruple Alliance.* Britain, Russia, Austria and Prussia support the Ottoman Empire against overthrow or partition.

1841 July: *Straits Convention.* Britain, Russia, Austria, Prussia, France and the Ottoman Empire agree to close the Dardanelles to all but Ottoman warships. Supersedes the Treaty of Unkiar-Skelessi (1833), bottling up the Russians in the Black Sea.

1849 May: *Convention of Balta Liman.* Russian and Ottoman Empires agree on joint seven-year occupation of Danubian Principalities.

August: *Treaty of Milan.* Establishes peace between Austria and Piedmont-Sardinia after war of 1848–1849.

1850 July: *Treaty of Berlin.* Establishes peace between Prussia and Denmark after war over Schleswig-Holstein.

November: *Convention of Olmütz.* Prussia concedes to Austria over Schleswig-Holstein and Hesse-Cassel.

1852 May: *Treaty of London.* Britain, France, Russia, Austria, Prussia and Sweden guarantee the territorial integrity of Denmark.

1854 March: Alliance between Britain, France and Ottoman Empire signed in Constantinople (opening the Crimean War).

April: *Vienna Agreement.* Britain, France, Austria and Prussia agree to maintain the territorial integrity of Ottoman Empire.

June: *Treaty of Boyadjii-Keuy.* Ottoman Empire permits Austria to occupy the Danubian Principalities (to deny them to Russia).

December: Treaty of alliance between Britain, France and Austria signed at Vienna, securing Austria's neutrality in Crimean War.

1855 January: *Turin Military Convention.* Britain, France and Piedmont-Sardinia ally against Russia.

November: *Stockholm Agreement.* Made between Britain, France and Sweden for the maintenance of the Kingdom of Sweden and Norway.

1856 March: PEACE OF PARIS. Britain, France, Piedmont, Russia, Austria, Prussia and Ottoman Empire conclude the Crimean War with a settlement to the political and military disadvantage of Russia.

Principal provisions: Russia cedes mouth of Danube and part of Bessarabia to the Danubian Principalities (which are guaranteed by the Powers); Russia surrenders Kars in the Caucasus back to the Ottoman Empire; Russia relinquishes all claims to religious protectorship over Christians within the Ottoman Empire; Black Sea neutralised militarily; international commission to regulate traffic on Danube established.

Napoleon III of France's attempts to introduce a more general geopolitical revision of European frontiers (favouring Italy) are blocked by Britain and Austria.

April: Britain, France and Austria guarantee the territorial integrity and independence of the Ottoman Empire.

1858 July: *Pact of Plombières.* Secret agreement between Napoleon III of France and Cavour of Piedmont-Sardinia. Piedmont to attack Austria, supported by France, and effect the transformation of Habsburg Italy (Lombardy-Venetia) into a Piedmont-headed 'Kingdom of Upper Italy'.

August: *Paris Agreement.* France, Britain, Russia, Prussia, Piedmont and Ottoman Empire agree to join Moldavia and Wallachia into the 'United Danubian Principalities' (soon renamed 'Rumania').

1859 June: *Peace of Villafranca.* Ends war between Austria and France/Piedmont. Piedmont to be ceded Lombardy.

November: *Treaty of Zurich.* Austria, France and Piedmont confirm provisions of Peace of Villafranca: Piedmont gains Lombardy.

1860 March: *Treaty of Turin.* Between France and Piedmont. Piedmont cedes Nice and Savoy to France (for services rendered to Piedmont in the war of 1859, as agreed by the Pact of Plombières).

1864 August: *Geneva Convention.* Created for the 'Protection of the Wounded in War'.

October: *Treaty of Vienna.* Ends war between Denmark and Austria/Prussia. Denmark renounces claims to Schleswig and Holstein.

1865 August: *Convention of Gastein.* Between Austria and Prussia: Austria to gain Holstein, Prussia to gain Schleswig.

1866 July: Preliminary peace between Prussia and Austria at Nikolsburg.

August: *Treaty of Prague.* Ends Austrian-Prussian 'Seven Weeks' War.

Prussia gains both Schleswig and Holstein, and becomes head of the 'North German Confederation'.

October: *Treaty of Vienna.* Ends Austrian-Italian War. Austria cedes Venetia to Italy at Prussian insistence.

1870 August: *London Agreements.* Britain, France and Prussia confirm independence and neutrality of Belgium.

1871 March: *London Agreement.* Britain, France, Russia, Germany, Italy, Austria-Hungary and Ottoman Empire end neutralisation of the Black Sea operative since 1856 (or, more accurately, acquiesce to Russian remilitarisation of the Black Sea).

May: *Treaty of Frankfurt.* Ends Franco-Prussian War of 1870–1871. France cedes Alsace and most of Lorraine to Germany and must suffer German military occupation until a war indemnity of 5 million francs is paid.

1872 September: *League of the Three Emperors* (or *Dreikaiserbund*). Formed by the emperors of Germany, Russia and Austria-Hungary meeting in Berlin, as an act of monarchical solidarity against subversion.

1873 May–June: *Schönbrünn Agreement.* Austria-Hungary and Russia to cooperate against subversion.

1877 January: *Convention of Budapest.* Austria-Hungary promises Russia neutrality in the event of war between Russia and Ottoman Empire.

February: Peace Treaty between Serbia and Ottoman Empire.

March: *London Protocol.* Great Powers demand Ottoman reforms.

1878 March: TREATY OF SAN STEFANO. Ends Russian-Ottoman War of 1877–1878. Provisions: establishes 'Big Bulgaria', a new Slav state stretching from the Black Sea to the Aegean; Russia gains territory in the Caucasus at Ottoman expense; Serbia and Montenegro enlarged territorially; independence of Serbia, Montenegro and Rumania confirmed.

Ambitious geopolitical settlement by Russia, designed to transfer crucial Ottoman territories in Europe to Russia and her Slav allies, thereby converting the Balkans into a permanent Russian sphere of dominance.

July: CONGRESS OF BERLIN. A concerted effort by the Great Powers to counter the Russian geopolitical takeover of the Balkans posed by the Treaty of San Stefano. Attended by delegates from Britain, France, Austria-Hungary, Italy and the Russian and Ottoman Empires, hosted by Bismarck in the role of 'Honest Broker'.

Provisions: the cancellation of 'Big Bulgaria' and its replacement by a smaller autonomous principality of Bulgaria and 'Eastern Rumelia' (a province nominally under Ottoman jurisdiction but provided with a Christian governor) to the south of Bulgaria; independence of Serbia and Rumania acknowledged; independence of enlarged Montenegro acknowledged; Rumania granted southern Dobrudja in return for ceding Bessarabia to Russia; Austria-Hungary granted right to occupy Bosnia-Herzegovina and the Sanjak of Novi Bazar; Britain acquires Cyprus from Ottomans.

Successful, self-interested intercession by the Great Powers to stabilise the Balkans after the Russian-Ottoman War of 1877–1878 and prevent the Russian takeover proposed by the Treaty of San Stefano. The geopolitical matrix established by the 'Berlin Settlement' lasts some 30 years, until the Balkan Wars on the eve of the First World War.

August: *Treaty of Therapia.* Between Britain and Ottoman Empire regarding British occupation of Cyprus.

1879 October: *Dual Alliance.* Germany and Austria-Hungary sign secretly in Vienna. It provides for mutual aid in the event of war with Russia, and neutrality in the event of war with any other Power.

1881 June: *Alliance of the League of the Three Emperors.* Germany, Russia and Austria-Hungary commit themselves to consultation over developments in Balkans. Renewed in 1884, lapses in 1887.

1882 May: *Triple Alliance.* Between Germany, Austria-Hungary and Italy. Anti-France provisions: if Italy is attacked by France, Germany and Austria-Hungary will support Italy; if Germany is attacked by France, Italy will support Germany; if any signatory is attacked by more than one Great Power, the other two signatories will support her. Renewed in 1887, 1891, 1902 and 1912.

1883 March: Dual Alliance of Germany and Austria-Hungary (1879) extended for a further five years.

October: Alliance between Austria-Hungary and Rumania, later extended to Germany and Italy. Renewed in 1892, 1896, 1902 and 1913.

1884 March: Alliance of the League of the Three Emperors (1881) renewed.

1885 February: *Act of Conference of Berlin.* Conference convened by Bismarck from November 1884 to produce international settlement of European Powers' imperial claims to central Africa. Delegates from 15 imperial states, including Austria-Hungary, Belgium, Britain, Denmark, France, Germany, Italy, Netherlands, Ottoman Empire, Portugal, Russia, Spain and Sweden. Broadly successful international initiative to prevent the European 'Scramble for Africa' precipitating general war through a public exercise in negotiated imperial partition.

1886 March: *Treaty of Bucharest.* Ends war between Serbia and Bulgaria.

1887 February, March and December: *Mediterranean Agreements.* Britain, Italy and Austria-Hungary agree to preserve stability in the Balkans and Mediterranean. A series of secret agreements implicitly directed against both France and Russia, allowed to lapse in 1896.

June: *Reinsurance Treaty.* Between Germany and Russia, following the lapse of the Alliance of the League of the Three Emperors. Provisions: each signatory to be neutral in any war involving the other, unless Germany attacks France or Russia attacks Austria-Hungary. Germany also promises to support Russian ambitions regarding Bulgaria and the Straits. Lapses in 1890.

1888 October: *Suez Canal Convention.* Signed at Constantinople. All Great Powers agree on internationalisation and neutralisation of the Suez Canal.

1890 July: *Berlin Agreement.* Between Britain and Germany. Britain cedes Heligoland to Germany in exchange for Zanzibar. Perceived by contemporaries as an indicator of Anglo-German rapprochement.

1891 August: *Paris Agreement.* France and Russia agree on joint action if either is attacked (by Germany).

1892 August: Preliminary French-Russian military convention.

1893 December: *French-Russian Military Convention.* Signed in St Petersburg. France and Russia promise reciprocal military aid in the event of war with Germany. Ratified in 1894, reaffirmed in 1899 and reinforced by a naval convention in 1912. Effectively precipitates the *Dual Entente* of France and Russia.

1896: First Modern Olympic Games, organised by Coubertin in Athens, provides new arena for nationalistic competition between states.

1897 May: *Vienna Agreement.* Austria-Hungary and Russia agree not to press competing interests in the Balkans but to maintain the status quo.
  December: *Treaty of Constantinople.* Establishes peace between Greece and Ottoman Empire (over Crete).

1898–1899: *Fashoda Incident.* Clash of British and French imperialist expansionism over Egypt staged at Fashoda in Sudan, July to November 1898. France eventually backs down, renouncing claims to the Nile valley in March 1899. Incident sours French-British relations.

1899 May–July: *(First) Hague Peace Conference.* International conference called by Tsar Nicholas II of Russia to limit armaments. Russian initiative interpreted by many of the delegates from 26 states as admission that Russia cannot keep up with the arms race. Decision to institute a permanent Court of Arbitration at The Hague (established in 1901).

1900 December: *Rome Agreement.* Between Italy and Austria-Hungary over Albania.

1902 November: Treaty between France and Italy, publicly over spheres of influence in north Africa, secretly agreeing that Italy will be neutral in any war involving France.

1904 March: *Treaty of Sofia.* Establishes alliance between Serbia and Bulgaria.

April: *Entente Cordiale.* Britain and France settle various colonial disputes, France allowing Britain a free hand in Egypt in exchange for Britain allowing France a free hand in Morocco. Dispels much of the Anglo-French antagonism generated by the Fashoda Incident (1898–1899), introducing a new era of Anglo-French rapprochement.

October: France and Spain agree over future partition of Morocco.

1905 March: Tangier Incident prompts *(First) Moroccan Crisis.* Kaiser William II provocatively declares support for Moroccan independence to frustrate French and Spanish designs and disrupt the newly-established Entente Cordiale.

July: *Treaty of Björkö.* Kaiser William II bamboozles Tsar Nicholas II into agreeing that Germany and Russia form a defensive alliance against attack by any other Power. An attempt by William II to disrupt the Russian-French Dual Entente instantly disavowed by both the Russian and German foreign offices.

August: *Anglo-Japanese Alliance.*

September: *Treaty of Portsmouth, New Hampshire.* Ends 1904–1905 war between Russia and Japan. Territorial losses for Russia (including Port Arthur); territorial gains for Japan (including Korea).

The Japanese victory in war demonstrates that military Great Power status is no longer a European monopoly. The American venue of the peace treaty, facilitated by President Theodore Roosevelt of U.S.A., serves notice that political and diplomatic Great Power status is also no longer a European monopoly. Within five years of the dawning of the twentieth century, the military, diplomatic and political monopoly of the European Great Powers has been breached.

1906 January–April: *Algeçiras Conference.* Convened at German insistence to settle the (First) Moroccan Crisis. Thirteen participant states agree on a compromise formula of joint French and Spanish policing of Morocco under a Swiss Inspector-General respecting the authority of the Sultan of Morocco. The mischief-making attempt by William II and Bülow to disrupt the Entente Cordiale backfires, instead strengthening Anglo-French rapprochement.

1907 June–October: *Second Hague Peace Conference.* Produces a series of conventions designed to civilise the conduct of warfare.

August: *Anglo-Russian Entente.* Effected by agreement in St Petersburg on relative spheres of British and Russian influence in Persia and attitudes to Afghanistan and Tibet.

Completes the 'third leg' of the *Triple Entente* between France, Russia and now Britain (though the 'Triple Entente' was never formalised and did not constitute a military alliance until after the outbreak of the First World War).

1908–1909: *Bosnian Crisis.* Austria-Hungary formally annexes Bosnia-Herzegovina (occupied since 1878) in October 1908, returning Sanjak of Novi Bazar as a concession to the Ottomans. Russia acquiesces in belief that Austria-Hungary will pay pre-agreed 'compensation' in the form of support for Russian acquisition of the Straits. Aehrenthal (Austria-Hungary) outmanoeuvres Izvolsky (Russia), embittering empty-handed Russia towards Austria-Hungary (and establishing the political climate and venue for the detonation of the First World War).

1911 July: *Agadir Crisis* (or *Second Moroccan Crisis*). German gunboat *Panther* provocatively sent to Moroccan port of Agadir 'to protect German interests'. Britain fears the establishment of a German naval base threatening Gibraltar, France is alarmed at new threat to her plans for Morocco. Further solidifies Anglo-French Entente Cordiale against Germany.

November: *Berlin Convention.* Between France and Germany. France is conceded predominance in Morocco in return for German territorial gains at the expense of the French Congo. A face-saving but ill-tempered conclusion to the Second Moroccan Crisis.

1912 February–June: *Balkan League.* Bulgaria and Serbia, then Greece and Montenegro, line up against the Ottoman Empire by a series of agreements brokered by Russia.

July: French-Russian naval convention.

September: Anglo-French naval convention.

October: *Treaty of Ouchy.* Brings Italian-Ottoman War to an end. Italy ceded Tripoli, Cyrenaica and Dodecanese by Ottoman Empire.

1913 May: *Treaty of London.* Ends First Balkan War of 1912–1913 between Ottoman Empire and Balkan League states. Provisions: Turkey-in-Europe reduced to area around Constantinople; combatant Balkan states of Bulgaria, Serbia, Greece and Montenegro all gain territory; new independent state of Albania established (blocking Serbian access to the Adriatic and frustrating Montenegrin expansion along the Adriatic littoral).

August: *Treaty of Bucharest.* Ends Second Balkan War of 1913, establishing peace between Bulgaria, Greece, Serbia, Montenegro, Rumania and the Ottoman Empire. Provisions: territory in Thrace and Macedonia claimed by Bulgaria in First Balkan War now redistributed between Serbia and Greece; Bulgaria forced to cede southern Dobrudja to Rumania.

Another anti-Bulgarian geopolitical settlement (like the Congress of Berlin in 1878), fuelling Bulgarian frustration.

November: Naval convention of Triple Alliance.

1914 June: *London Agreement.* Britain and Germany agree over the Baghdad Railway.

September: *London Declaration.* Allied Powers of Britain, France and Russia undertake not to make separate peace with the Central Powers.

1915 March–April: *Constantinople Agreements.* Secret promise from Britain and France that Russia will receive Constantinople and the Straits at the end of the war. Effectively, an Allied bribe to keep Russia in the war as her war effort gets into difficulties.

Represents the expedient abandonment of the nineteenth-century Western strategy of propping up the moribund Ottoman Empire against the territorial expansionism of Russia.

April: *Treaty of London.* Secret agreement between Britain, France and Italy. Italy is promised territorial gains on the Adriatic littoral at the expense of Austria-Hungary at the end of the war in return for joining the Allied camp in May 1915. Italy allows herself to be bribed onto the Allied side by the promise of the post-war acquisition of 'Italia Irredenta'.

1916 May: *Sykes-Picot Note.* Secret agreement between Sir Mark Sykes (for Britain) and Georges Picot (for France) to partition the Ottoman Empire at the end of the war. Britain to get Transjordan, Iraq and northern Palestine; France to get Syria and Lebanon; some provision for an 'Arab state'.

1917 April: *Treaty of St Jean de Maurienne.* Secret agreement between Britain, France, Russia and Italy authorising an Italian share in the post-war partition of the Ottoman Empire. Italy to receive the Aegean littoral in western Anatolia around Smyrna. Another component in the planned (but never realised) European partition of the Ottoman Empire by the Allied Powers.

November: *Balfour Declaration.* Policy statement by British Foreign Secretary Arthur Balfour declaring British support for the establishment of a Jewish homeland in Palestine.

1918 January: *Fourteen Points.* Speech by President Woodrow Wilson of U.S.A. establishes an Allied blueprint for the post-war geopolitical settlement of Europe.

March: TREATY OF BREST-LITOVSK. Between Bolshevik Russia and the Central Powers, taking Russia out of the war by a separate peace.

Negotiations between the Central Powers and the Bolshevik delegation headed by Leon Trotsky continue from December 1917 until February 1918, when the Austro-German military advance into Russia forces the Bolshevik Government into acceptance of crippling terms. Vladimir Lenin, the Bolshevik leader, ignores the London Declaration (September 1914) and Constantinople Agreements (April 1915), arguing that the Bolshevik Government is not morally or politically bound by tsarist undertakings.

Provisions: as the near-exorbitant price of a separate peace, Russia surrenders its western and southern borderlands, almost halving its

European jurisdiction. Ukraine, Finland, Poland and the Baltic States of Estonia, Latvia and Lithuania become nominally independent states within the Central Powers' sphere of influence. Newly conquered territory in the Caucasus is returned to the Ottoman Empire.

The Brest-Litovsk Treaty simultaneously: (1) demotes Russia from a Great Power to (at best) a second-rate power by confiscating much of her most valuable European possessions (and reversing the last 300 years of tsarist expansionism); and (2) establishes a multinational eastern empire of the German and Austrian Central Powers on a grandiose scale unprecedented since the Napoleonic Empire.

The (short-lived) Brest-Litovsk settlement represents a geopolitical transformation of eastern Europe unmatched for a century.

May: *Treaty of Bucharest.* Between Rumania and the Central Powers; takes Rumania out of the war by a separate peace.

1919 January: *Paris Peace Conference* opens, dominated by the 'Big Four': Woodrow Wilson (U.S.A.), David Lloyd George (Britain), Georges Clemenceau (France) and Vittorio Orlando (Italy).

June: TREATY OF VERSAILLES. Between Germany and the Allies.

Territorial provisions: Germany cedes all her overseas colonies to the Allies; Germany returns Alsace-Lorraine to France and northern Schleswig to Denmark; Germany cedes Eupen-Malmédy to Belgium and parts of Prussian Poland, East Prussia and upper Silesia to revived state of Poland; Germany cedes Danzig (to be administered by new League of Nations) and Memel; Rhineland and Saar to be demilitarised and occupied by the Allies for 15 years; territorial union (or *Anschluss*) between Germany and Austria expressly forbidden.

Non-territorial provisions: Germany must sign Clause 231, the 'war guilt clause', which justifies the imposition of liability for war reparations and a restriction of the German army to 100,000 men; the Covenant of the new League of Nations is agreed and signed.

The Treaty of Versailles formally supersedes the Treaty of Brest-Litovsk, replacing the short-lived German eastern European empire with a German state stripped of its overseas colonies and territorially reduced within Europe. 'Versailles', which comes into operation in January 1920, is viewed within Germany as a humiliating diktat effecting an intolerable rebuff to the rising power and legitimate ambitions of Germany.

September: TREATY OF ST GERMAIN. Between Austria and the Allies.

Provisions: Austria cedes South Tyrol and Julian March to Italy; Slovenia, Bosnia-Herzegovina and Dalmatia to new Kingdom of the Serbs, Croats and Slovenes; Bohemia and Moravia to new state of Czecho-Slovakia; Galicia to revived state of Poland; and Bukovina to Rumania. Hungary recognised as an independent state; *Anschluss* between Austria and Germany forbidden. As a loser in First World War, Austria is held liable for war reparations, and its armed forces limited to 30,000.

'St Germain' effects the formal dissolution of Austria-Hungary, with Austria losing all non-German territories of the former Habsburg Empire (as well as one-third of the Empire's German-speaking population). Coming into force in July 1920, 'St Germain' sanctions the geopolitical transformation of east-central Europe, replacing a single multi-national empire with a collection of novel political entities claiming to be nation-states.

November: TREATY OF NEUILLY. Between Bulgaria and the Allies.

Provisions: as a loser in First World War, Bulgaria must cede territory to Serbia and Greece (Western Thrace), becomes liable for war reparations and has its armed forces limited to 20,000.

The Neuilly Settlement comes into force in August 1920: Bulgaria is treated more generously – or less vindictively – than the other Central Powers defeated in the First World War but 'Neuilly' is still viewed within Bulgaria as the latest in a sequence of Western anti-Bulgarian treaties (which included Berlin in 1878 and Bucharest in 1913).

1920 February: *(First) Treaty of Tartu.* Bolshevik Russia recognises the independence of Estonia.

June: TREATY OF TRIANON. Between Hungary and the Allies.

Provisions: Hungary (granted independence by Treaty of St Germain) cedes Transylvania and half of Banat to Rumania; Croatia and Voivodina to new Kingdom of Serbs, Croats and Slovenes; part of northern Slovakia to revived state of Poland; most of Slovakia and Ruthenia to new state of Czecho-Slovakia; Fiume to Italy; and Burgenland to Austria. On the losing side in the First World War, Hungary becomes liable for war reparations and has its armed forces limited to 35,000.

Together with 'St Germain', 'Trianon' constitutes the most territorially-revolutionary of the treaties of the Paris Peace Settlement. Hungary is reduced by two-thirds territorially (ceding to Rumania alone more territory than remains to 'rump Hungary') and suffers a drop in state population from 21 million (1914) to 8 million (1920). Represents an externally-imposed geopolitical disaster to which 'Trianon Hungary' and the Hungarians could never be reconciled.

July: *Treaty of Moscow.* Bolshevik Russia recognises the independence of Lithuania.

August: *Treaty of Riga.* Bolshevik Russia recognises the independence of Latvia.

August: TREATY OF SÈVRES. Between Ottoman Empire and the Allies.

Provisions: Ottoman Empire renounces all claims to territory inhabited by non-Turks, ceding Thrace and western Anatolia to Greece; Rhodes and Dodecanese to Italy; Syria, Mesopotamia and Palestine become League of Nations' mandates; Arabia and Armenia become independent; the Straits are demilitarised and administered by the League of Nations.

'Sèvres' is the last of the constituent treaties of the Paris Peace Settlement (and the shortest-lived). Though not partitioning the Ottoman Empire as drastically as earlier envisaged by the Allies (in 1916–1917), the Sèvres Settlement still reduces the Turkish state territorially to a size intolerable to Turkish national sentiment.

October: *(Second) Treaty of Tartu.* Bolshevik Russia recognises the independence of Finland (again).

November: *Treaty of Rapallo.* Between Italy and Kingdom of the Serbs, Croats and Slovenes: temporary accommodation of Adriatic territorial disputes (Italy gets Zara, 'Yugoslavia' gets Split and Sebenico, and Fiume becomes independent) and joint pledge to observe peace treaties to prevent Habsburg restoration.

1921 March: *Treaty of Riga.* Formal end to Polish-Russian War and definition of the border between independent Poland and Bolshevik Russia.

1922 October: *Convention of Mudania.* Demilitarised Straits and Constantinople area (administered by the League of Nations under the Treaty of Sèvres) are restored to Turkish jurisdiction.

1923 July: Treaty of Lausanne. Between Turkey and the Allies. The Ottoman Empire is replaced by Turkey (headed by Mustapha Kemal), which refuses to recognise 'Sèvres' and forces a renegotiated settlement through the Turkish-Greek War of 1920–1923.

Provisions: Turkey disavows all Ottoman imperial claims to non-Turkish populated territory; foreign Powers retain islands in eastern Mediterranean (Britain keeps Cyprus, Italy keeps Dodecanese) but are excluded from mainland of Anatolia/Asia Minor; the Straits remain demilitarised.

The Treaty of Sèvres (an Allied diktat signed by the moribund Ottoman Empire) proves the only treaty of the Paris Peace Settlement of 1919–1920 to be successfully challenged before the Second World War. 'Sèvres' is replaced by 'Lausanne', which provides an internationally acceptable and stable territorial settlement for the new nation-state of Turkey.

Historical atlas

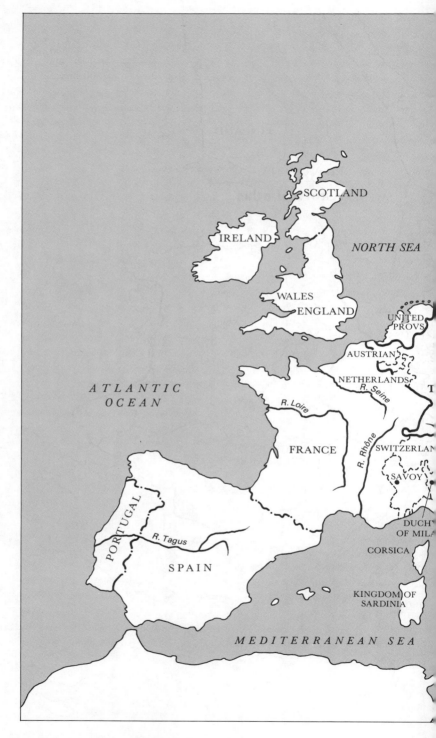

1. *Europe in the late eighteenth century*

39

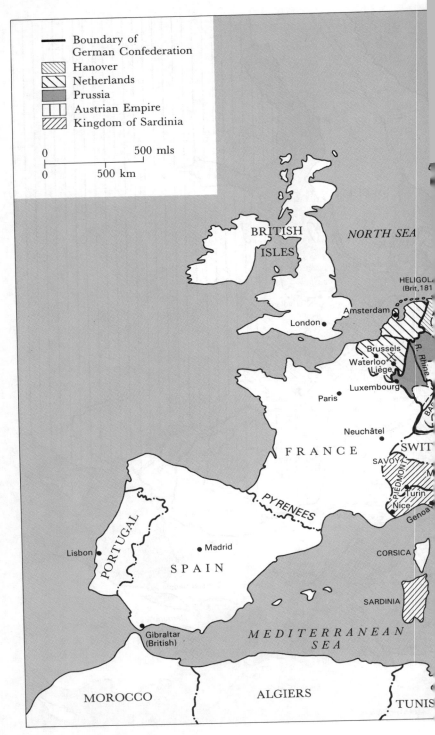

3. *Europe in 1815*

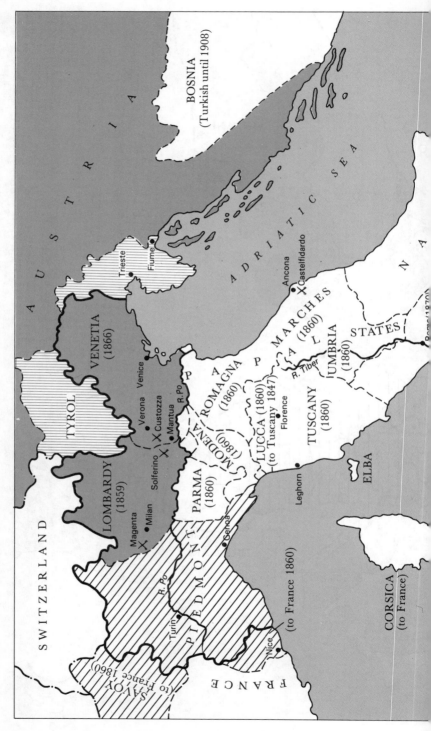

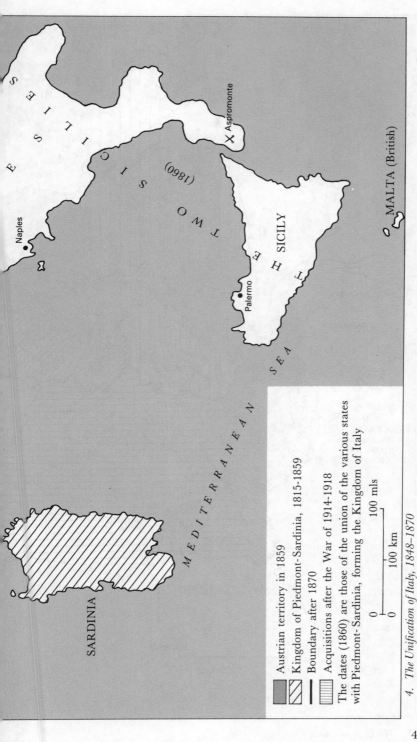

4. *The Unification of Italy, 1848–1870*

Legend:
- Austrian territory in 1859
- Kingdom of Piedmont-Sardinia, 1815-1859
- Boundary after 1870
- Acquisitions after the War of 1914-1918

The dates (1860) are those of the union of the various states with Piedmont-Sardinia, forming the Kingdom of Italy

0   100 mls
0   100 km

SARDINIA

MEDITERRANEAN SEA

Naples

THE TWO SICILIES

THE (1860)

Aspromonte ✕

SICILY

Palermo

MALTA (British)

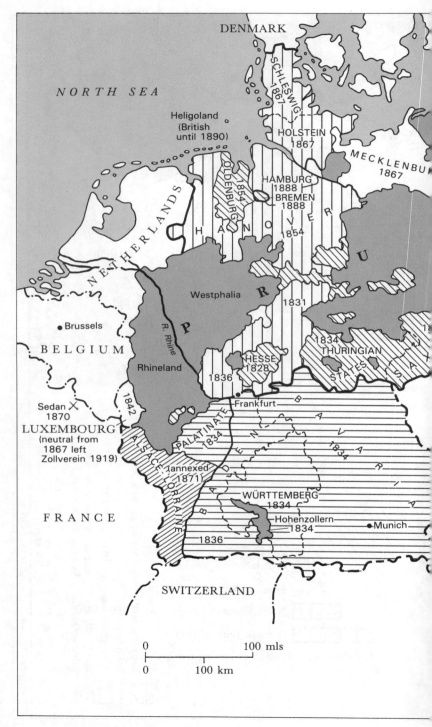

5. *The Unification of Germany, 1818–1871*

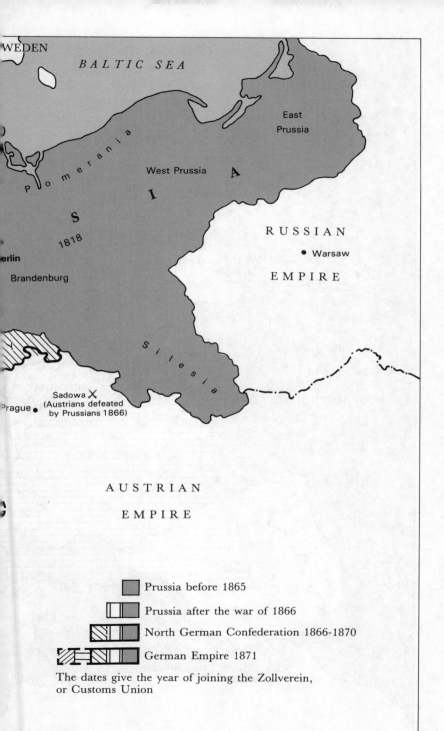

SWEDEN

BALTIC SEA

East
Prussia

West Prussia

P o m e r a n i a

A

S I

1818

erlin

Brandenburg

RUSSIAN

• Warsaw

EMPIRE

S i l e s i a

Sadowa ✕
(Austrians defeated
by Prussians 1866)

Prague •

AUSTRIAN

EMPIRE

Prussia before 1865

Prussia after the war of 1866

North German Confederation 1866-1870

German Empire 1871

The dates give the year of joining the Zollverein,
or Customs Union

6. *Europe in 1871*

7. *The Habsburg Empire, 1867–1918 (political)*

POLAND

Cracow

Lemberg
(Lvov)

G A L I C I A

RUTHENIA

R U S S I A

SLOVAKIA

N G A R Y

Czernowitz

BUKOVINA

Budapest

I N G D O M   O F
H U N G A R Y

TRANSYLVANIA

Kronstadt

BANAT

AVONIA

Belgrade

R. Danube

RUMANIA
Independent from Ottoman Empire 1878

• Bucharest

jevo

SERBIA
Independent from
Ottoman Empire 1878

R. Danube

SANJAK
OF NOVIBAZAR
Occupied by Austria
1878-1912

MONTENEGRO

BULGARIA
Independent from Ottoman Empire 1878

ALBANIA
Established 1913

0	100 mls
0	100 km

49

8. *The Habsburg Empire, 1867–1918 (ethnic)*

RUSSIA

POLAND

Cracow

P O L E S

Isolated
POLES

Lemberg ★

R U T H E N I A N S

UKRAINE

SLOVAKS

Czernowitz •

M A G Y A R S

Budapest ★

RUMANIANS

Hermannstadt

Kronstadt •

R. Danube
Belgrade

RUMANIA

SERBS

SERBIA

R. Danube

SANJAK OF
NOVIBAZAR

MONTENEGRO

ALBANIA

The Peoples of the Empire (1910)

⦀ Germans 12 million (24%)	▨ Rumanians 3·5 million (6%)	
▤ Magyars 10 million (20%)	▨ Italians 0·75 million (1·5%)	
▦ Slavs 23 million (46%)		

★ Cities with large Jewish populations
2 million Jews in all (4%)

51

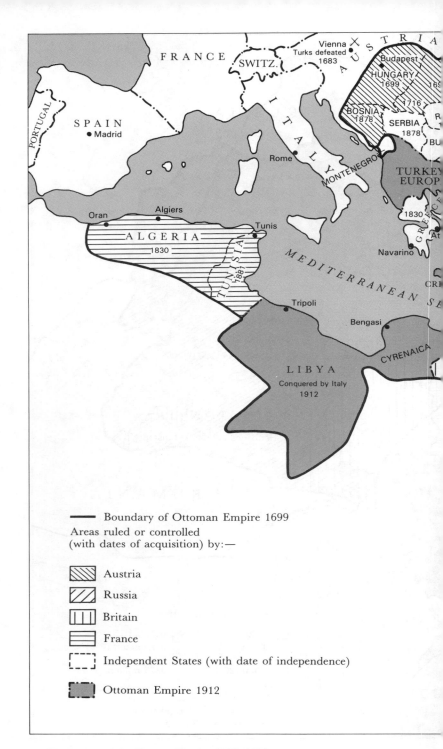

9. *The Decline of the Ottoman Empire, 1815–1912*

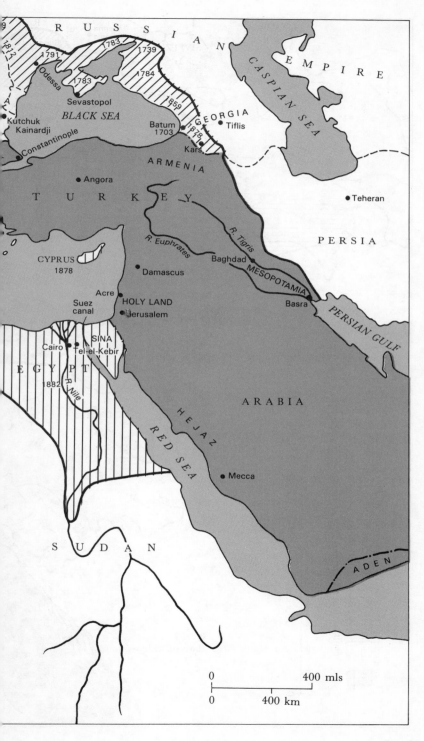

RUSSIAN EMPIRE

1821
1791
1783
1739
1784
1783
1759
Odessa
Sevastopol
BLACK SEA
Kutchuk Kainardji
Batum
1703
1878
GEORGIA
Tiflis
CASPIAN SEA
Constantinople
Kars
ARMENIA
Angora
Teheran
T U R K E Y
PERSIA
R. Euphrates
R. Tigris
CYPRUS
1878
Damascus
Baghdad
MESOPOTAMIA
Acre
Suez canal
HOLY LAND
Jerusalem
Basra
PERSIAN GULF
Cairo
SINAI
Tel-el-Kebir
E G Y P T
1882
R. Nile
ARABIA
H E J A Z
RED SEA
Mecca
S U D A N
ADEN

0   400 mls
0   400 km

53

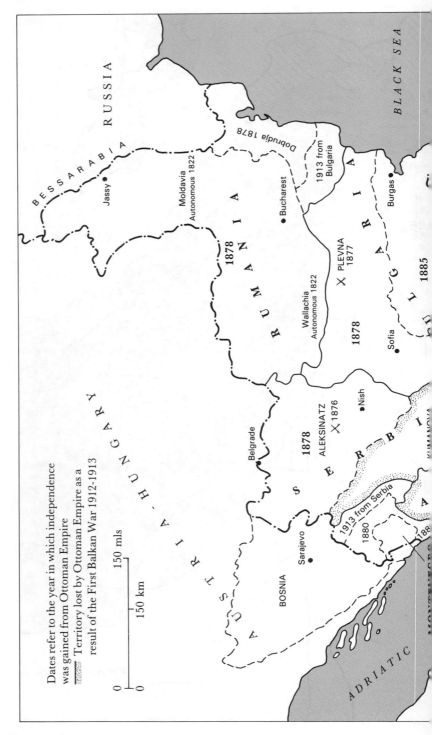

Dates refer to the year in which independence
was gained from Ottoman Empire

▨▨▨ Territory lost by Ottoman Empire as a
result of the First Balkan War 1912-1913

150 mls

150 km

BLACK SEA

RUSSIA

BESSARABIA

Jassy

Moldavia
Autonomous 1822

Dobrudja 1878

1913 from
Bulgaria

RUMANIA

1878

Bucharest

Wallachia
Autonomous 1822

Burgas

BULGARIA

PLEVNA
× 1877

1878

Sofia

1885

AUSTRIA-HUNGARY

Belgrade

SERBIA

1878

ALEKSINATZ
× 1876

Nish

KUMANOVA

Sarajevo

BOSNIA

1913 from Serbia

1880

ADRIATIC

MONTENEGRO

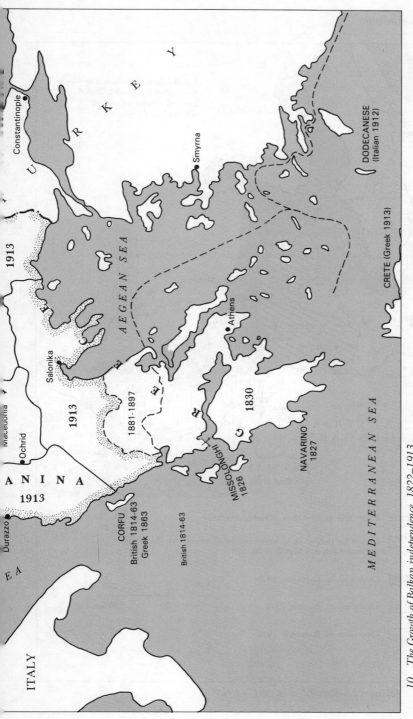

10. *The Growth of Balkan independence, 1822–1913*

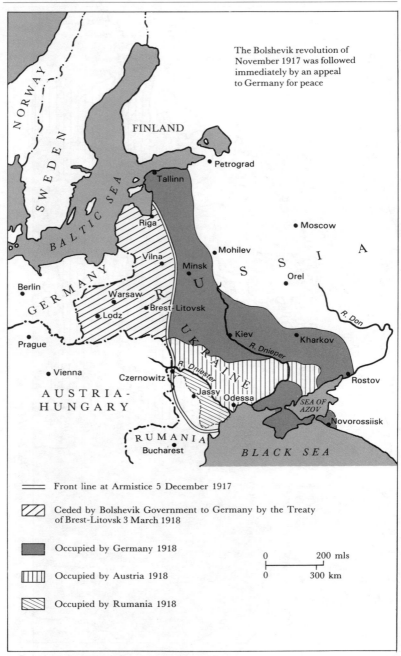

The Bolshevik revolution of
November 1917 was followed
immediately by an appeal
to Germany for peace

Front line at Armistice 5 December 1917

Ceded by Bolshevik Government to Germany by the Treaty
of Brest-Litovsk 3 March 1918

Occupied by Germany 1918

Occupied by Austria 1918

Occupied by Rumania 1918

0   200 mls
0   300 km

11. Russian Territorial Losses, 1917–1918

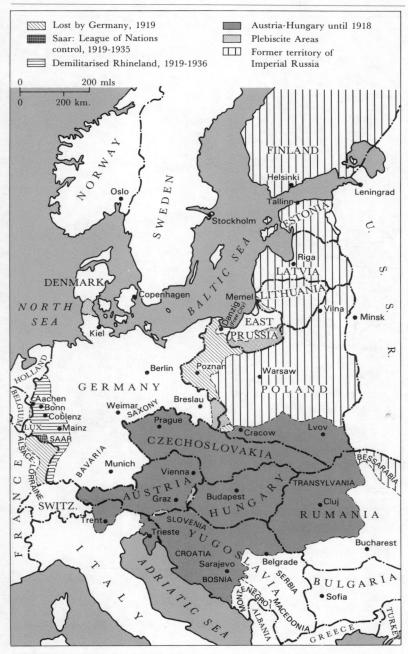

Legend

- Lost by Germany, 1919
- Saar: League of Nations control, 1919-1935
- Demilitarised Rhineland, 1919-1936
- Austria-Hungary until 1918
- Plebiscite Areas
- Former territory of Imperial Russia

0   200 mls
0   200 km.

NORWAY
Oslo
SWEDEN
Stockholm
FINLAND
Helsinki
Tallinn
Leningrad
ESTONIA
Riga
LATVIA
LITHUANIA
U. S. S. R.
DENMARK
Copenhagen
Memel
Vilna
Minsk
NORTH SEA
Kiel
Danzig (Free City)
EAST PRUSSIA
Berlin
Poznan
Warsaw
POLAND
HOLLAND
BELGIUM
GERMANY
Aachen
Bonn
Coblenz
Weimar
SAXONY
Breslau
LUX.
Mainz
SAAR
Prague
Cracow
Lvov
ALSACE-LORRAINE
BAVARIA
Munich
CZECHOSLOVAKIA
BESSARABIA
FRANCE
SWITZ.
Trent
Vienna
Graz
AUSTRIA
Budapest
HUNGARY
TRANSYLVANIA
Cluj
RUMANIA
ITALY
SLOVENIA
Trieste
YUGOSLAVIA
CROATIA
Sarajevo
BOSNIA
MONTENEGRO
ALBANIA
Belgrade
SERBIA
MACEDONIA
BULGARIA
Sofia
Bucharest
GREECE
TURKEY
ADRIATIC SEA
BALTIC SEA

12. *Europe's Frontiers, 1919–1937*

Geopolitical gazetteer

1. Old States

'Old States' may be defined as those (13) established or resident political entities which maintained a sovereign independence throughout the nineteenth century.

Denmark   An independent sovereign state which suffers substantial territorial shrinkage throughout the nineteenth century, recovering slightly in the early twentieth century. In the French camp over the Napoleonic period, Denmark is punished by having to cede Norway to Sweden and Heligoland to Britain by the Treaty of Kiel (1814), and Pomerania and Rugen to Prussia by the Vienna Settlement (1815), receiving only the Duchy of Lauenburg in compensation. Denmark incorporates the semi-independent duchies of Schleswig/Slesvig and Holstein in 1846, prompting inconclusive war with Prussia in 1848. After defeat in war in 1864, Denmark cedes Schleswig, Holstein and Lauenberg to Prussia and Austria by the Treaty of Vienna (October 1864). Retains Iceland (granted limited home rule in 1874). Denmark remains neutral in the First World War but, following a plebiscite, recovers Danish-speaking north Slesvig from Germany in July 1920. Overall, a victim of the Vienna Settlement and German unification but a minor beneficiary of the Versailles Settlement.

France   An independent sovereign Great Power which experiences major fluctuation in jurisdiction occasioned by the vicissitudes of territorial loss and gain throughout the nineteenth century. Over the Revolutionary and Napoleonic periods, France expands, both seizing neighbouring territory to effect a 'Greater France' and establishing a *cordon sanitaire* of dependent client-states (see **Ex-States**). On the defeat of Napoleon, France is reduced to her 1792 borders by the First Treaty of Paris (1814), then to her 1789 borders by the Second Treaty of Paris (1815). France acquires Savoy and Nice from Piedmont in 1860 (as payment for joining Piedmont against Austria in the War of 1859). France loses Alsace and Lorraine (except for Belfort and Meurthe-et-Moselle) to Germany after losing the Franco-Prussian War of 1870–1871. During the First World War, France loses substantial territory to the German advance in Flanders but all occupied territories (plus Alsace-Lorraine) are restored to France by the Versailles Settlement (1919).

Habsburg Empire   A sovereign independent Great Power throughout the nineteenth century. Two changes in nomenclature and one adjustment of constitution occur: in 1804/1806 the Habsburg monarch abandons the title of Holy Roman Emperor in favour of Austrian Emperor; and in 1867 the so-called *Ausgleich* converts the unitary Austrian Empire into the Dual Monarchy of Austria-Hungary. The Habsburg Empire ceases to exist at the end of the First World War by the terms of the Treaty of St Germain (1919).

The multinational Habsburg Empire experiences massive changes in territorial jurisdiction through the war. Over the last quarter of the eighteenth century, the Empire acquires Galicia through the First and Third Partitions of Poland (1772 and 1795). In the Napoleonic period, the Empire loses influence and territory to France and her client states, notably by the treaties of Campo Formio (1797), Lunéville (1801), Pressburg (1805) and Vienna (1809), prompting a reduction of Habsburg power in 'Germany', 'Italy', 'Belgium' and 'Poland'. At the Vienna Settlement (1815), the Empire's losses in 'Germany', 'Belgium' and 'Poland' are tacitly confirmed but compensation is provided by the acquisition of Lombardy-Venetia in northern Italy.

The Empire absorbs independent Cracow in 1846 but is expelled from Lombardy in 1859 by France and Piedmont, and from Venetia in 1866 by Prussia and Piedmont. The principal casualty of both Italian and German unification, Austria-Hungary increasingly looks east for territorial compensation at the expense of the Ottoman Empire, occupying Bosnia-Herzegovina in 1876 (formally annexed in 1908).

During the First World War, Austria-Hungary makes enormous territorial gains to the south (at the expense of Serbia and Montenegro), to the west (at the expense of Italy) but especially to the east (at the expense of Russia and Rumania). By the Treaty of Brest-Litovsk (1918), Austria-Hungary almost doubles her peacetime territorial jurisdiction. However, not only are all wartime gains forfeit at the end of the war but the defeated Habsburg Empire is politically dissolved and territorially partitioned by the Treaty of St Germain (1919).

Monaco An independent principality on the French Riviera, ruled since 1297 by the Genoese dynasty of Grimaldi. Annexed by France in 1793, Monaco is reinstated under the protection of Piedmont by the Vienna Settlement of 1815. In 1848, Monaco loses Menton and Roquebrunne to France but is compensated by France's formal recognition of its independence in 1861. Effectively 'Greater Monte Carlo', Monaco maintains a dependent and occasionally troubled relationship with France. Though excused French taxes, the Manegasques fear that a customs union signed in 1865 will be followed by French takeover and territorial absorption.

Netherlands A state undergoing bewildering changes of political status, nomenclature and jurisdiction before political and territorial stabilisation from the mid-nineteenth century.

The independent United Provinces are occupied by France in 1795, with the southern provinces being annexed directly to 'Greater France' and the northern provinces licensed as a French client-state, the Batavian Republic. The Kingdom of Holland is constituted by Napoleon 1806–1810, then annexed into 'Greater France' (1810–1813). After this brief disappearance of Holland/Netherlands from the geopolitical map of Europe, the independent Netherlands are confirmed by the Vienna Settlement (1815).

The Netherlands are divided into three independent territories over the nineteenth century: Belgium (the ex-Austrian Netherlands/ southern provinces of the United Provinces) rebels against Dutch authority in 1830, achieving general recognition of its independence by the Treaty of London (1839); Luxembourg becomes an independent Grand Duchy in 1890; and the 'rump' Netherlands retain their independence and territorial integrity unchanged after 1890.

Ottoman Empire A declining Muslim Great Power grappling often lethargically and always unsuccessfully with the twin issues of internal political reform and territorial decolonisation throughout the nineteenth century.

In 1800, the Ottoman Empire is a three-continent phenomenon, occupying extensive territories in western Asia, north Africa and south-eastern Europe. The nineteenth century is a period of accelerating territorial retreat and shrinkage towards the Turkish heartland of Anatolia, to the advantage of rival empires and a succession of emergent European, African and eventually Asian nation-states. Ottoman withdrawal from south-eastern Europe results in the competitive advance of the Russian and Habsburg Empires and the recognition of Greece (1830), Serbia (1878), Rumania (1856/1878), Bulgaria (1878) and Albania (1912) as independent states. In the First Balkan War (1912–1913), Ottoman jurisdiction in Europe is reduced to a tiny Turkey-in-Europe around the capital of Constantinople.

Although the Ottoman military performance in the First World War surprises the Allies, Ottoman exclusion from Europe is confirmed and European territorial designs on Anatolia are licensed by the Treaty of Sèvres (1920). By setting its signature to the European Powers' partition of Anatolia, the Ottoman Empire is totally discredited and is replaced by the Turkish Republic (1923) which negotiates an improved territorial settlement by the Treaty of Lausanne (1923). Patently the weakest of the dynastic empires of Europe, the Ottoman Empire provides nationalism with most (if not the most famous) of its victories over the nineteenth century.

Portugal An independent sovereign state taxed by the responsibilities of overseas empire and an increasing challenge to traditional monarchism (resident since 1128) from republicanism (which results in the proclamation of a republic in 1910). Portugal's overseas territorial jurisdiction shrinks substantially over the course of the nineteenth century (notably with the loss of Brazil in 1822) but its

African empire remains intact and *within* Europe its long-established borders are unchanged and its jurisdiction geopolitically stable.

Russian Empire Occupying substantial proportions of both Europe and Asia, the tsarist empire is the largest and most multinational state in the world. The Tsar enjoys unlimited autocratic power until the granting of a semi-constitutional system headed by the *Duma* (Parliament) in 1905. Overstrained by the First World War, tsarism collapses in February 1917, succeeded briefly by the liberal Provisional Government and then, in October 1917, by the Bolshevik Government (Soviet Union after 1922).

The Russian Empire experiences phenomenal gains in territory throughout the nineteenth century, succeeded by almost equally phenomenal losses of territory after the First World War. Nineteenth-century gains in Europe include: most of eastern Poland by the Partitions of 1772, 1793 and 1795; Crimea and the Black Sea littoral 1774 and 1791; Georgia 1801; Finland (as separate Grand Duchy) 1808/1809; Bessarabia 1812; Azerbaidzhan 1813; Mingrelia 1857; and Abkhazia 1864. Nineteenth-century gains in Asia include: Tashkent 1865; Samarkand and Bukhara 1868; Khiva 1873; Askhabad 1881; and Merv 1885. Gains in Manchuria and Korea over the 1890s are ceded to Japan after the Russo-Japanese War of 1904–1905.

In the First World War, the Russian Empire loses 'Poland' to the advancing Central Powers. The weak Provisional Government and hard-pressed Bolshevik Government are besieged by separatist claims to independence from Finland, Estonia, Latvia, Lithuania, Belorussia, Ukraine, Armenia, Georgia and Azerbaidzhan over the period 1917–1918. The Treaty of Brest-Litovsk (March 1918) excludes Bolshevik Russia from the western borderlands of the ex-Russian Empire, which fragment into nation-states. All but Finland, Estonia, Latvia and Lithuania are reclaimed by Bolshevik Russia by 1921.

Russia experiences the greatest territorial gains within Europe over the nineteenth century and the greatest territorial losses over the early twentieth century of any European state.

San Marino An independent 'Most Serene Republic' which successfully resists first Papal and then Italian claims to its territory. Respected by Napoleon, who even offers to expand the republic into a 'Greater San Marino' in 1797. Formally recognised as independent by the Vienna Settlement (1815). Offers asylum to Italian freedom-fighters, notably Garibaldi, during the wars of the *Risorgimento*. A series of treaties with Italy after 1862 effects a customs union but confirms its independence.

Spain A sovereign state throughout the nineteenth century (except for four years as a client-state of the Napoleonic Empire, 1808–1812). Like its neighbour Portugal, Spain is tried by the twin issues of constitutional struggle (prompting the divisive and damaging Carlist civil wars) and the increasingly precarious maintenance of overseas empire. Attempting to centralise into a unitary state over the nineteenth century, Spain resists the developing nationalist movements of the Basques and Catalans. Whilst losing its South American mainland- empire in the 1820s and its North American island-empire in the 1890s, Spain retains its traditional borders and territorial jurisdiction *within* Europe unchanged over the nineteenth century (and stays neutral in the First World War).

Sweden An independent monarchical state profoundly affected by the Napoleonic Wars, which alter Sweden's geopolitical disposition, puncture its traditional Great Power pretensions in the Baltic and set its face against involvement in any war thereafter. Sweden is shifted geopolitically westward and northward by the Napoleonic Wars, losing Finland to Russia by the Treaty of Fredericksham (1809) and Pomerania to Prussia by the Vienna Settlement (1815); but acquiring Norway from Denmark by the Treaty of Kiel (1814). Sweden admits concessions towards the autonomy of the Norwegians over the nineteenth century and finally (and amicably) recognises the independence of Norway in 1905.

Switzerland Existing as a union of cantons since the fifteenth century, Switzerland is reduced to the client 'Helvetic Republic' under Napoleon (1798–1803) but is re-established as the 'Swiss Confederation' at the Congress of Vienna (1815), with its 'perpetual neutrality' guaranteed by the Great Powers.

The constitution of modern Switzerland emerges from the political crisis of 1847–1848. After the defeat of the secessionist *Sonderbund* of Roman Catholic cantons, a new democratic constitution, combining effective central government with cantonal autonomy, is adopted in 1848. The territorial jurisdiction of Switzerland increases with the addition of Neuchâtel (previously a fief of Prussia) in 1857. Though an 'old' state, Switzerland stabilises itself constitutionally and territorially only in the mid-nineteenth century.

United Kingdom A sovereign Great Power created by the incremental territorial union of the Kingdom of England with the Principality of Wales (1536), the Kingdom of Scotland (1707) and Ireland (1800). Although Wales, Scotland and Ireland can all advance historical claims to be 'ex-states' rather than 'sub-states', their distinctive cultural identities are not constitutionally recognised by the British government over the nineteenth century. While the overseas British Empire expands phenomenally over the nineteenth century, there are only minor changes in British jurisdiction within Europe (usually involving strategic islands, like Heligoland, Malta and Cyprus) and no territorial changes to or within the United Kingdom itself.

2. New States

'New States' may be defined as those novel political entities emerging with permanent independent and sovereign status in the course of the period 1789–1914. In chronological order of formal independence, the (12) New States of nineteenth-century Europe were:

1806 Liechtenstein
1829 Greece
1839 Belgium
1858 Montenegro
1861 Italy
1871 Germany
1878 Serbia
1878 Rumania
1878 Bulgaria
1890 Luxembourg
1905 Norway
1913 Albania

Albania Part of the Ottoman Empire from the late fifteenth century, 'Albania' experiences an early episode of effective autonomy under Ali Pasha of Janina in the early nineteenth century but has to wait until granted independence after the Balkan Wars by the London Ambassadorial Conference of May 1913 and the Treaty of Bucharest of August 1913.

On independence, Albania becomes a Muslim principality with the German Prince William of Wied as (imported) head of state. Albania remains in a condition of anarchy throughout the First World War, divided by internal claimants to power and invaded by expansionist adjoining states. Real independence is only established after a long territorial wrangle between the neighbouring states of Greece, Italy and the Kingdom of the Serbs, Croats and Slovenes in November 1921. As the smallest and most recent of the new Balkan states, Albania is necessarily the most unstable and vulnerable.

Belgium Prior to independence, 'Belgium' is initially the Austrian Netherlands (until surrender by the Habsburgs by the Treaty of Campo Formio in 1797), then a province of Napoleonic 'Greater France' (1797–1813) and finally the southern province of the United Netherlands (1814–1830). Exasperated by the rapidly switching but uniformly distasteful experiences of Austrian, French and Dutch rule, the Belgians demand their own state. Independence is proclaimed in 1830 but only achieved against Dutch resistance by Great Power backing, officially by international guarantee of the neutrality of Belgium by the Treaty of London (1839).

The neutrality of Belgium guaranteed in 1839 is reaffirmed during the Franco-Prussian War of 1870–1871 but breached by German invasion in 1914, occasioning British entry into the First World War. All but the extreme north-west of Belgium is occupied by Germany throughout 1914–1918, under the governor-generalship of Von der Goltz. All occupied territory is restored to Belgium by the Versailles Treaty (1919), with the bonus of the acquisition of Eupen-Malmédy from Germany in September 1920.

Belgium is an historical anomaly: conspicuously not a nation-state, it is still precipitated by the rising tide of nationalism. With its population one half Flemish (living in the Dutch-orientated north-western region of Flanders) and one-half Walloon (living in the French-orientated south-eastern region of Wallonia), Belgium never possesses any credibility as a nation-state, but is self-interestedly maintained in an age of nationalism by the Great Powers.

Bulgaria An ancient Slav state of the eastern Balkans bordering the Black Sea, Bulgaria languishes within the Ottoman Empire from 1393 until independence in 1878, granted first by the Treaty of San Stefano, then by the Congress of Berlin. Bulgaria is officially an autonomous principality from 1878 to 1911, promoted to an independent kingdom in 1911.

From independence, Bulgaria is obsessed with territorial expansion, necessarily at the expense of its Balkan neighbours. Inspiration comes from the 'Big Bulgaria' (with access to both the Black and Aegean Seas) projected by the Russian-sponsored Treaty of San Stefano in March 1878 but replaced by a 'Small Bulgaria' (without access to the Aegean) at the Congress of Berlin in July 1878. From 1878 onwards, Bulgaria is intent on restoring 'Big Bulgaria'. Bulgaria defies both the Great Powers and its Balkan neighbours by seizing eastern Rumelia in 1885. Acquiring considerable ex-Ottoman territory in Thrace and Macedonia during the First Balkan War (1912–1913), Bulgaria loses most of its gains to Rumania (southern Dobrudja) and Serbia and Greece in the Second Balkan War (1913).

Fighting in the First World War on the side of the Central Powers, Bulgaria regains lost territory from Serbia in 1915 and southern Dobrudja from Rumania in late 1916. All wartime territorial gains made at the expense of Serbia, Rumania and Greece (all on the Allied side) are forfeit at the end of the war by the punitive Treaty of Neuilly (November 1919).

Germany Prior to the proclamation of the 'German Empire' in 1871,

'Germany' first comprises a multitude of states and principalities within the 'Holy Roman Empire' (before 1806); is then divided between Austria, Prussia and the Napoleonic 'Confederation of the Rhine' (from 1806 to 1815); next comprises a 'German Confederation' of 39 states headed by Austria but increasingly dominated by Prussia (between 1815 and 1866); and is briefly divided between the Prussian-dominated 'North German Confederation' and various southern German states between 1866 and 1870 (see **Ex-States**).

The German Empire is less multinational than any other European empire, with Polish, French and Danish minorities together constituting only 6 per cent of the population of what approximates to a German nation-state. As the political creator of the German Empire, Prussia plays so dominant a role in post-1871 Germany (both within and outside the bounds of the constitution) that many non-Prussian Germans view the so-called 'new' German Empire as only a geopolitical stratagem to effect a 'Greater Prussia' or 'Prussian Empire'. At very least, the process of geopolitical 'Unification' in the 1860s represents only an early phase in the protracted political, social and cultural evolution of modern Germany.

Germany achieves substantial territorial expansion by the Franco-Prussian War of 1870–1871, taking most of Alsace-Lorraine from France by the Peace of Frankfurt (1871). In the First World War, Germany achieves massive territorial expansion to the west (at the expense of Belgium and France) but especially to the east (at the expense of Russia), as formally established by the Treaty of Brest-Litovsk in March 1918.

All wartime territorial gains are forfeit by the Treaty of Versailles in June 1919, which, to the mortification of Germany, also authorises the surrender of peripheral peacetime territories: Alsace-Lorraine 'returns' to France; northern Schleswig/Slesvig 'returns' to Denmark; the Wartheland is ceded to the revived state of Poland (the 'Polish Corridor'); and the demilitarised Rhineland is to be occupied by the Allies for 15 years. After territorial expansion born of military success in 1870–1871 and 1914–1918, Germany pays the price of defeat in 1918–1919, being geopolitically reduced by the Allies to a jurisdiction substantially smaller than that of the German Empire at its creation in 1871.

Greece A captive territory of the Ottoman Empire from the mid-fifteenth century until a combination of local nationalist defiance and Great Power diplomatic and then military support secures its independence by the Treaty of Adrianople in 1829.

From independence in 1829, territorial expansion to achieve a 'Greater Greece' is the overriding concern. At independence, Greece comprises the Morea, Euboea, the Cyclades and the mainland south of Anta and Thessaly. Acquisitions include: the Ionian Islands from

Britain (a protectorate since 1815) in 1863–1864; Thessaly and Anta (part of Epirus) from the Ottoman Empire in 1881; Crete in 1897–1898; Macedonia, western Thrace (including the city and port of Salonica) and almost all the Aegean islands except the Dodecanese (Italian) at the end of the Second Balkan War in 1913.

During the First World War, as the Allies open a southern front at Salonica (from 1915), much of the northern territory of Greece is invaded (notably by Bulgaria) or under threat. By the Treaties of Neuilly in 1919 and Sèvres in 1920, all Greece's peacetime territories are confirmed, with the addition of western Thrace (ceded by Bulgaria) and eastern Thrace (ceded by the Ottoman Empire). Greece attempts territorial expansion to the Anatolian mainland at the expense of the collapsing Ottoman Empire but is expelled by nationalist Turkish forces (most dramatically from Smyrna in 1922), an exclusion from Asia confirmed by the Treaty of Lausanne in 1923. The dream of a 'Greater Greece' or 'Aegean Empire' reminiscent of classical times is imperfectly realised (though never entirely dispelled).

Italy Famously dismissed by Metternich as 'a geographical expression', 'Italy' is an agglomeration of squabbling mini-states in the late eighteenth century. Under Napoleon, northern 'Italy' is reconstituted as a dependent collection of French client-republics. After the unconvincing partial restoration of the pre-Napoleonic *ancien régime* in Italy by the Congress of Vienna in 1815, a 'Unification of Italy' is effected by the Kingdom of Piedmont-Sardinia (playing a role similar to that of Prussia in German Unification) over the 1850s and 1860s. The Kingdom of United Italy is proclaimed, a little prematurely, in March 1861. Piedmont-Sardinia acquires Lombardy from Austria in 1859 (at the price of ceding Nice and Savoy to France for French services rendered in the war of 1859). Naples and Sicily unite with Piedmont-Sardinia over 1860–1861 to effect the Kingdom of Italy. Italy acquires Venetia from Austria for services to Prussia in the Austro-Prussian War of 1866. The incorporation of Rome in 1870 completes the basic 'Unification of Italy'.

After 1870, two geopolitical issues remain. The first is the question of converting what critics condemn as a 'Piedmontese Empire' or 'Greater Piedmont' into a genuinely united Italy (though never really comparable to the role of Prussia within Germany). The second issue is Italian territorial expansion, either in pursuit of an overseas Italian empire (for example, by the seizure of the Dodecanese from the Ottoman Empire in 1912) or to realise *Italia Irredenta* (the unification of remaining peripheral lands claimed by Italy to effect a nation-state of 'Greater Italy').

In the First World War, Italy joins the Allies by the Treaty of London in April 1915 on the secret promise of *Italia Irredenta* and hopes for overseas empire. A share in the Allied partition of the Ottoman Empire is promised by the secret Treaty of St Jean de Maurienne in April 1917. Italy is, however, disappointed territorially at the end of the First World War. Wartime losses to Austria (notably after Caporetto in October 1917) are restored by the Treaty of St Germain in 1919; but only some of the *Irredenta* territory promised in 1915 and very little of the Ottoman territory promised in 1917 is secured by Italy. The seizure of Fiume in September 1919 demonstrates that, to extreme nationalists, the persistence of *Italia Irredenta* means that the unification of Italy remains incomplete.

Liechtenstein Becomes an independent mini-state situated between Austria and Switzerland on the abolition of the Holy Roman Empire in 1806. Enters into a customs union with Switzerland but successfully resists moves to be absorbed into a 'Greater Switzerland' over the nineteenth century.

Luxembourg An independent Grand Duchy from 1890, situated between Germany, France and Belgium. Part of the Holy Roman Empire until its abolition in 1806, Luxembourg is annexed into 'Greater France' under Napoleon. By the Congress of Vienna in 1815, the King of the Netherlands also becomes Grand Duke of Luxembourg (to compensate for the loss of Nassau to Prussia). With the emergence of Belgium, the Treaty of London of 1839 assigns the western part of Luxembourg to Belgium, with the eastern part remaining a Grand Duchy attached to the Dutch crown. Under pressure from France, Luxembourg has its neutrality guaranteed by the London Conference of 1867. In 1890, Luxembourg becomes independent (because the new Dutch Queen Wilhelmina, as a woman, is disqualified by the current Luxembourg constitution from being Grand Duchess of Luxembourg). There are no subsequent territorial changes: although invaded and occupied by Germany throughout the First World War, Luxembourg has its independent status and territory restored by the Treaty of Versailles in 1919.

Montenegro Nominally under Ottoman rule since the fifteenth century, the ideal guerrilla warfare terrain of the 'Black Mountain' ensures practical autonomy long before formal independence is granted in 1858. Before and after independence, Montenegro is ruled by the Petrović dynasty, first as a principality (1858–1910), then as a Kingdom (1910–1918). Always allied to its larger Slav neighbour Serbia, Montenegro expands spectacularly at Ottoman expense over the later nineteenth century: Montenegro's territorial jurisdiction is doubled by the Congress of Berlin in 1878; and doubled again after the Balkan Wars when, by the Treaty of Bucharest (1913), Montenegro and Serbia partition the Sanjak of Novi Bazar.

Allied to Serbia (as usual) in the First World War, Montenegro suffers a similar fate, being overrun by the Austrians in 1915 and wiped out as an independent entity. In 1918, a Serb-dominated assembly at Podgorica abolishes the Montenegrin monarchy and votes for the union of Montenegro with Serbia. Thereafter, Montenegro becomes a component of the Kingdom of the Serbs, Croats and Slovenes (later Yugoslavia).

Norway Before independence in 1905, Norway enjoys considerable autonomy under both its nineteenth-century imperial masters. Part of Denmark from the fourteenth century until 1814, Norway is conceded a national assembly from 1807. Attached to the Kingdom of Sweden and Norway from 1814, Norway receives various constitutional concessions from Sweden but insists on independence in 1905. Prince Carl of Denmark becomes King Haakon VII of Norway, 1905–1957. Norway remains territorially unchanged throughout the nineteenth and early twentieth centuries and (like Sweden) opts for neutrality in the First World War.

Rumania Officially part of the Ottoman Empire until granted independence by the Congress of Berlin in 1878. Prior to independence, 'Rumania' comprises the territories of Moldavia and Wallachia, which are united as the Danubian Principalities in 1858 and recognised by the Ottoman Empire as united autonomous principalities in 1861. Recognised as an independent principality from 1878, Rumania becomes a kingdom in 1881. Rumania experiences mixed fortunes territorially over the late nineteenth and early twentieth centuries. At the Congress of Berlin in 1878, Rumania gains northern Dobrudja from the Ottoman Empire but must cede southern Bessarabia to Russia. By the Treaty of Bucharest (ending the Balkan Wars in 1913), Rumania acquires southern Dobrudja from Bulgaria.

In the First World War, Rumania at first remains neutral, then joins the Allies (in the hope of territorial gain) in late 1916. Overrun by the Central Powers in 1917, Rumania makes a separate peace at Bucharest in May 1918 involving the return of southern Dobrudja to Bulgaria. Rumania opportunistically re-declares war on the Central Powers in November 1918.

By joining the Allied side (twice), Rumania may lose the war but wins the peace. By the Treaties of St Germain, Neuilly and Trianon (1919–1920), a 'Greater Rumania' is constructed: to the original principalities of Moldavia and Wallachia (or Regat) are added southern Bessarabia (from Russia), southern Dobrudja again (from Bulgaria), Bukovina (from pre-1919 'Austria') and Transylvania (from pre-1919 'Hungary'). Doubling its pre-1919 territorial jurisdiction, Rumania becomes the greatest territorial beneficiary of the Paris Peace Settlement among existing states.

Serbia Over the early nineteenth century, 'Serbia' passes through various phases of recognition before being granted full independence at the Congress of Berlin in 1878: previously merely a province of the Ottoman Empire, Serbia becomes a tributary principality under Ottoman suzerainty in 1817, then an autonomous principality in 1830. Promoted from a principality to a kingdom in 1882, Serbia witnesses a vicious and long-standing rivalry between the Obrenović and Karageorgević dynasties for the Serbian crown. Serbia experiences sweeping fluctuations in its jurisdiction over the late nineteenth and early twentieth centuries. Together with independence, Serbia receives the southern territory around Nish by the Congress of Berlin in 1878. Successful in the Balkan Wars, Serbia doubles its territory through partitioning the Sanjak of Novi Bazar (with its ally Montenegro) and acquiring areas of Macedonia from the Ottoman Empire by the Treaty of Bucharest (1913).

In the First World War, Serbia is effectively obliterated from the geopolitical map of Europe by the Austro-Hungarian army over late 1915, leaving what remains of 'Serbia' – its battered but unbowed army – to decamp to Corfu for the rest of the war. A conspicuous victim of the First World War, Serbia becomes a leading beneficiary of the Paris Peace Settlement, promoted by the Allies as the heartland of the new Kingdom of the Serbs, Croats and Slovenes (later Yugoslavia) established in late 1918. Serbia is perceived as having the same latter-day role in the 'Unification of Yugoslavia' as Prussia in the unification of Germany and Piedmont in the unification of Italy, inevitably inviting accusations that the 'new' Yugoslavia is really only a 'Greater Serbia' or 'Serbian Empire'.

3. Ex-States

'Ex-States' may be defined as those sovereign or autonomous political entities that were liquidated, incorporated or superseded over the period 1789–1914. In chronological order of discontinuation, the (30) Ex-States of nineteenth-century Europe were:

1795 Poland
1797 Cispadane Republic
       Lombardic Republic
1799 Parthenopean Republic
       Roman Republic
1801 Georgia
       Cisalpine Republic
1802 Helvetic Republic
1803 Lemanic Republic
1805 Ligurian Republic
       Republic of Italy
1806 Batavian Republic
       Holy Roman Empire
1813 Illyrian Republic
       Confederation of the Rhine
1814 Grand Duchy of Warsaw
1815 Kingdom of Italy
1830 United Kingdom of the Netherlands
1832 Congress Poland
1846 City of Cracow
1849 Venetian Republic
       Grand Duchy of Posen
1860 Kingdom of the Two Sicilies
1861 Kingdom of Piedmont-Sardinia
1862 Danubian Principalities
1866 German Confederation
1870 Papal States
1871 Kingdom of Bavaria
       North German Confederation
       Kingdom of Prussia

Batavian Republic (1795–1806) Following the French defeat of the Dutch in late 1794 and occupation of Amsterdam in January 1795, the

Treaty of Basle is signed between France and the United Provinces in May 1795: the Dutch agree to abolish the Stadtholdership and establish a 'Batavian Republic' dominated by France. In September 1801, a new constitution converts the Batavian client-republic into a French puppet-state. The Batavian Republic ends with its (short-term) conversion into a Kingdom of Holland under Napoleon's brother Louis Bonaparte in June 1806.

Bavaria (1805–1871) The most powerful state of southern 'Germany', Bavaria is recognised by the Austrian Empire as a kingdom by the Peace of Pressburg in December 1805. A leading state within the new Confederation of the Rhine established by Napoleon in July 1806, Bavaria retrieves its independence in 1815. Bavaria's Roman Catholic population and geopolitical situation favour Austria against Prussia in the mid-nineteenth century unification of Germany. Although the monarchy (under the notoriously unstable Wittelsbach dynasty) weathers rising nationalist and liberal protest, Bavaria loses its sovereignty but retains its title of Kingdom on the creation of the German Empire in 1871.

Cisalpine Republic (1797–1801) A nominally-independent client-republic in northern Italy ('on this–southern–side of the Alps') concocted by Napoleon in June 1797 from his conquests of 1796–1797. Confirmed by the Treaty of Campo Formio in October 1797, the Cisalpine Republic comprises Lombardy, old Venetian territories west of the river Adige and south as far as Modena, Emilia, Ferrara and Bologna. Re-established in June 1800, the Cisalpine Republic is reconstituted as the Italian Republic in 1801, with Napoleon as its president from January 1802. The Republic is subsumed into the Kingdom of Italy in 1805. With the defeat of Napoleon in 1814–1815, the ex-Republic's territories are allocated to the Austrian Empire as part of 'Lombardy-Venetia' by the Vienna Settlement of 1815.

Cispadane Republic (1796–1797) An early ephemeral client-republic in northern Italy ('on this–southern–side of the River Po') concocted by Napoleon in October 1796 from his recent conquests. Comprising the provinces of Emilia, Bologna and Modena, the Cispadane Republic is subsumed by the larger Cisalpine Republic to the north in July 1797.

Confederation of the Rhine (1806–1813) A Napoleonic geopolitical concoction comprising Bavaria, Württemberg, Hesse-Darmstadt, Baden, Saxony and 12 other states designed to consolidate the French hold on western 'Germany'. In return for the subordination of the smaller member-states to the larger member-states (notably Bavaria and Württemberg) and the introduction of the French legal code and constitution, the Confederation provides an army of 63,000 for its 'Protector' Napoleon. Formed in July 1806 implicitly as a *cordon sanitaire* against Austria and Prussia, the Confederation collapses after Napoleon's defeat at the Battle of Leipzig in October 1813 but its seven-year existence is influential in promoting the concept of German (originally both anti-Prussian and anti-Austrian) unification.

Congress Poland (1815–1832) The majority of 'Poland' as constituted by the Napoleonic Grand Duchy of Warsaw is granted to Russian jurisdiction as an autonomous Kingdom of Poland by the Vienna Congress of 1815. Perceived as a concession both to the Polish nation and to nationalism in general, Congress Poland falls victim to increasingly reactionary tsarism after only 16 years. Formally granted a constitution by Tsar Alexander I in November 1815, Congress Poland is never permitted a Polish king and has its constitution revoked by Tsar Nicholas I in February 1832 as punishment for the Polish Uprising of 1830–1831.

Cracow (1815–1846) The capital of medieval Poland, Cracow is claimed by Habsburg Austria by the Third Partition (1795) and subsequently ceded by Austria to the Napoleonic Grand Duchy of Warsaw in 1809. Claimed by both Russia and Austria in 1815, Cracow is established as an independent city-republic under the joint protection of Russia, Austria and Prussia as a compromise solution by the Congress of Vienna. After 1832, the disappearance of Congress Poland leaves Cracow as the only survivor and symbol of Poland. As the centre of Polish nationalism, Cracow is annexed by Austria 'in self-defence' in November 1846, wiping all geopolitical vestiges of Poland from the map of Europe. The 'Grand Duchy of Cracow' remains Austrian from 1846 until the collapse of Austria-Hungary and reconstitution of Poland in 1918–1919.

Danubian Principalities (1856–1862) Quarrelled over by the rival Ottoman, Russian and Habsburg Empires up to and during the Crimean War, the principalities of Moldavia and Wallachia are recognised and guaranteed by the Great Powers at the Treaty of Paris in 1856. In August 1858, the Powers sanction the creation of separate but identical administrations in Moldavia (at Jassy) and Wallachia (at Bucharest). In December 1861, the principalities unite, receiving recognition of their union into the autonomous principality of 'Rumania' in 1862 and their formal independence from the Ottoman Empire at the Congress of Berlin in 1878. The transitional geopolitical precursor of Rumania.

Georgia (until 1801) A traditional independent kingdom in the Trans-Caucasus which accepts Russian suzerainty in 1783 before being annexed into the Russian Empire in 1801. Although little Russification is attempted by tsarist authority, no political autonomy or national recognition is permitted Georgia over the nineteenth century. Georgia proclaims its independence after the fall of the tsarist empire in May 1918 but is forcibly reclaimed by the Bolshevik government in April 1921.

German Confederation (1815–1866) An entity of 39 loosely-linked German states, with no central administration or executive but with a Diet under the presidency of Austria, established by the Congress of Vienna in June 1815 (and supplemented in June 1820). Compared to the political membership of over 300 states in the pre-1806 Holy Roman Empire, the German Confederation is a significant shift towards geopolitical unification. Each member-state is independent in internal affairs, war between member-states is forbidden and war against a foreign state is only acceptable with the permission of the Diet of the Confederation. As headed by Austria, the German Confederation is seen as an apparatus favouring Austrian authority in 'Germany', or at very least resisting Prussian ambitions for 'Germany'. After defeating Austria in 1866, Prussia replaces the German Confederation with its 'own' North German Confederation.

Helvetic Republic (1798–1802) A Swiss client-state of France created by Napoleon following his victories over Austria in 1796–1797. Though permitted a degree of autonomy, the Helvetic Republic established in April 1798 is another component in the Napoleonic restructuring of the entire north Italian/Swiss/north Adriatic region. In 1802–1803, Napoleon abandons the idea of the Republic and permits the return of the Swiss Confederation.

Holy Roman Empire (to 1806) Originally a Germanic and Italian political entity created by Otto I, crowned first Holy Roman Emperor by the Pope in 962. From 1273 the Empire is dominated by the Habsburgs, who acquire eastern territories outside the boundaries of the original Empire. By the eighteenth century, the Empire comprises an agglomeration of over 300 German mini-states dominated by Austria. As part of his geopolitical restructuring of central Europe, especially the creation of the Confederation of the Rhine, Napoleon insists on the formal abolition of the Holy Roman Empire in August 1806. Anticipating the change, the Habsburg Franz I changes his title from Holy Roman Emperor to Emperor of Austria from August 1804. The Holy Roman Empire has an heir after 1815 in the Austrian-led German Confederation.

Illyrian Republic (1805–1813) A client-republic created by Napoleon (in what becomes northern Yugoslavia a century later) from territories confiscated from Austria. Ruled by Marshal Marmont, 1805–1810 (created Duke of Ragusa in 1808), the Republic enjoys little autonomy but still benefits from exposure to Western influences and reforms. The Republic collapses with the defeat of Napoleon and its territory is returned to Austria at the Congress of Vienna in 1815, but the fleeting first experience of 'statehood' serves as an inspiration for the Illyrian movement for the unification of the South Slavs over the nineteenth century. A precursor of Yugoslavia.

Italy, Republic of (1801–1805), Kingdom of (1805–1815) After the Treaty of Lunéville (February 1801), Napoleon converts his earlier creation, the Cisalpine Republic, into the Italian Republic (with himself as President). The Republic in turn is converted in 1805 into the Kingdom of Italy (including Venice from 1806) with Napoleon crowned as King of Italy.

Lemanic Republic (1798–1803) A Napoleonic client-republic centred on Geneva, created in January 1798 after Napoleon's victories over the Austrians in 1796–1797. Like the Helvetic Republic, the Lemanic Republic is part of Napoleon's restructuring of the territory of the Swiss Confederation, abandoned after 1803.

Ligurian Republic (1797–1805) A Napoleonic client-republic centred on Genoa, created in June 1797 after Napoleon's victories over the Austrians in 1796–1797 as a component in his geopolitical restructuring of northern 'Italy'. Following the annexation of Piedmont into 'Greater France' in September 1802, the Republic is abolished by Napoleon in June 1805 and annexed as a *département* of 'Greater France'. At the Congress of Vienna in 1815, Genoa is awarded to Piedmont-Sardinia.

Lombardic Republic (1796–1797) A Napoleonic client-republic centred on Milan, created in May 1796 after Napoleon's victories over the Austrians in northern Italy. In 1797, the Lombardic and Cispadane Republics are amalgamated into the larger Cisalpine Republic in a new phase of Napoleon's geopolitical restructuring of northern 'Italy'.

Netherlands, United Kingdom of (1814–1830) After the Napoleonic subordination and then incorporation of the United Provinces of the Netherlands into 'Greater France', an independent United Kingdom of the Netherlands comprising Holland, 'Belgium' (the ex-Austrian Netherlands) and Luxembourg is created in 1814 under the hereditary Stadtholder William of Orange-Nassau. Confirmed by the Congress of Vienna in 1815, the United Kingdom is effectively dissolved by the Belgian revolt of 1830–1831, leading to formal (if reluctant) Dutch acceptance of the independence of Belgium in 1839.

North German Confederation (1866–1871) A union of 21 German states north of the river Main created by Bismarck after the Prussian defeat of Austria in 1866. The Confederation is intended both to subordinate northern 'Germany' to Prussia and to allay the fears of the southern German states about Prussian territorial expansionism. The constitution of the Confederation, as formally adopted in April 1867, does allow certain autonomy to individual member-states but foreign policy and military affairs are the sole prerogative of the Prussian-dominated 'confederal' government. The Confederation is conventionally perceived as a Machiavellian ploy by Bismarck in his Grand Design for the unification of all Germany; but some historians believe that

Bismarck would have preferred German unification to stop at this point. Not really a 'confederation' at all, the North German Confederation is (by the forced adherence of the southern German states of Bavaria, Württemberg and Baden) superseded by the German Empire; but its supposedly 'confederal' constitution is adopted with few substantive changes as the imperial constitution in April 1871.

Papal States (until 1870) Substantial territories of central 'Italy' under the secular jurisdiction of the Papacy until their incorporation into united Italy in 1870. Briefly annexed to France by Napoleon in 1809, the Papal States become a byword for reactionary misrule and resist territorial annexation by Italy over the 1860s only through the protection of French troops. The withdrawal from Rome of the French military presence in 1870, occasioned by the Franco-Prussian War, leaves the Papacy defenceless. The addition of the Papal States completes the territorial unification of Italy (*Italia Irredenta* aside). Technically, the Papal States are reduced to the Vatican City, the tiny area of temporal jurisdiction now left to a Papacy which (especially under Pius IX) considers itself the 'Prisoner in the Vatican'.

Parthenopean Republic (January to July 1799) A short-lived client-republic of France centred on Naples; another component in Napoleon's geopolitical restructuring of 'Italy', on this occasion at the expense of the Kingdom of the Two Sicilies (Naples and Sicily).

Piedmont-Sardinia (1748–1861) State of north-western 'Italy' organising the unification of Italy in the 1850s and 1860s. United as a kingdom under the Savoy dynasty in 1748, Piedmont-Sardinia is overthrown by Napoleon in 1798 and annexed into 'Greater France' in September 1802 but re-established in 1814 (with the addition of Genoa in 1815). Under King Charles Albert, Piedmont attempts to expel the Austrians from Lombardy in 1848–1849 under the slogan *Italia fara da se* but is defeated. Under King Victor Emmanuel II, Prime Minister Cavour engages French support for the expulsion of Austria from Lombardy in 1859 (surrendering Savoy and Nice to France in payment). Piedmont-Sardinia is subsumed into the united Kingdom of Italy proclaimed in March 1861. The Piedmontese capital of Turin remains capital of Italy until 1865, symbolising the continuing authority of Piedmont-Sardinia within the new Italy. Like Prussia within Germany after 1871, Piedmont within Italy after 1861 is seen as retaining a dominant position within the new state.

Poland (until 1795) The sprawling Polish Commonwealth is cynically divided between the neighbouring powers of Russia, Austria and Prussia by the Polish Partitions of 1772, 1793 and 1795. Disappearing from the geopolitical map of Europe in 1795, 'Poland' remains *par excellence* the 'nation without a state' throughout the nineteenth century, the single most blatant defiance of the principle of nationalism.

Gestures towards Polish nationalism are permitted over the early nineteenth century. Napoleon concedes a Grand Duchy of Warsaw (1807–1813) which collapses on his defeat. After adjusting the Great Power division of 'Poland' in Russia's favour (in effect a Fourth Partition), the Congress of Vienna in 1815 authorises an autonomous Kingdom of Poland, which is revoked by Russia in 1832. The Congress of Vienna also permits the city-republic of Cracow, which is annexed by Austria in 1846. The Grand Duchy of Posen becomes the last territorial vestige of Poland but suffers final incorporation into Prussia in 1849. From the mid-nineteenth century, no independent or autonomous manifestation of 'Poland' is allowed by Russia and Prussia/Germany (though some concessions are granted by Austria-Hungary).

Politically advantaged by the First World War and the collapse or defeat of the partitioning powers, Poland is reconstituted as a sovereign state by the Paris Peace Settlement of 1919–1920. Polish opinion remains (dare one say) polarised between the concept of a compact Polish nation-state (as demanded by Dmowski) and a larger, federal Polish commonwealth (as promoted by Pilsudski).

Posen, Grand Duchy of (1815–1849) Assigned to Prussia by the Second Partition of Poland in 1793, the Polish Grand Duchy is confirmed as Prussian territory by the Congress of Vienna in 1815. The Grand Duchy of Posen (or Poznan) contrives a measure of autonomy until 1831, like Congress Poland within the Russian Empire. With Russian revocation of the constitution of Congress Poland following the Polish Uprising of 1830–1831, Prussia follows suit by pruning the vestigial autonomy of the Grand Duchy. After the Austrian annexation of Cracow in 1846, Prussia decides to convert Posen from a grand duchy to a province in 1849.

With Poles constituting the largest national minority within the German Empire, Posen presents some problems of assimilation, especially in the 1870s and 1900s. By the Treaty of Versailles in 1919, Posen becomes (as Poznan) part of the reconstituted state of Poland.

Prussia (until 1871) A traditional kingdom under the Hohenzollern dynasty expanding in territory, military power and political authority over the early nineteenth century to effect the unification of Germany over the 1860s and dominate the new German Empire from 1871. After early humiliation by Napoleon, Brandenburg-Prussia plays a crucial role in the military defeat of Napoleon (1813–1815). Prussia acquires the Rhineland, Pomerania, Posen and half of Saxony at the Congress of Vienna in 1815. In 1848–1849, Prussia falters as prospective champion of German unification. Under Bismarck, Prussia defeats the traditional claim of Austria to authority over 'Germany' in 1866, first sponsoring the North German Confederation and then expanding its territorial jurisdiction to create the German Empire in 1871. After 1871, the Kingdom of Prussia is officially subsumed within the new sovereign

German Empire. However, even more than Piedmont-Sardinia within Italy, Prussia plays a dominant role within the new Germany, prompting non-Prussian critics to condemn the new state as merely a 'Greater Prussia' or 'Prussian Empire'.

Roman Republic (1798–1799) A client-republic centred on Rome, established by Napoleon in February 1798 as a component in his geopolitical restructuring of 'Italy'.

(**1849**) Following the flight of Pope Pius IX in November 1848, Mazzini proclaims a Roman Republic (to replace the Papal States) in February 1849. French troops enter the Papal States in April, overthrowing the Roman Republic in July 1849.

Two Sicilies, Kingdom of the (until 1860) Independent kingdom of southern Italy and Sicily, centred on Naples and Palermo. Briefly converted by Napoleon into the Parthenopean Republic from January to July 1799. Re-established at the Congress of Vienna in 1815, the Kingdom continues under precarious and reactionary Bourbon government until overthrown in 1860. Sicily unsuccessfully attempts independence from Naples (1848–1849). As self-appointed champion of Italian unification, Garibaldi captures Sicily in May 1860 and Naples in September 1860. After a plebiscite in October, the Kingdom of the Two Sicilies is formally united with Piedmont/Italy in December 1860. The territories of the Kingdom of the Two Sicilies are divided into separate provinces of the new united Kingdom of Italy.

Venetian Republic (1848–1849) Proclaimed by Daniele Manin in defiance of Habsburg authority in Venetia in March 1848, the Venetian Republic falls to the Austrians in August 1849. Reverting to Austrian jurisdiction after 1849, Venice (as part of Venetia) is ceded by Austria to Italy in July 1866, confirmed by plebiscite in October 1866.

Warsaw, Grand Duchy of (1807–1813) A client-state created by Napoleon to attract Polish support to Napoleonic Europe and weaken the *ancien régime* powers of Russia, Austria and especially Prussia (all of which had partitioned Poland between 1772 and 1795). The Grand Duchy is created in July 1807 by the Treaty of Tilsit between France and Prussia, whereby Prussia cedes all lands taken from Poland since 1772 to make the France-sponsored Grand Duchy. The Grand Duchy cannot survive the defeat of Napoleon at Leipzig in October 1813 and is redivided in a 'Fourth Partition' between Russia, Austria and Prussia at the Congress of Vienna in 1815.

4. Sub-States

'Sub-States' may be defined as those identifiable territories engaging the allegiance of their inhabitants but which fail to achieve recognition as sovereign states over the period 1789–1914.

Alsace-Lorraine Territories comprising, at different times, the most easterly provinces of France and the most westerly provinces of Germany. Alsace becomes part of France in 1648, Lorraine only in 1766. After the Franco-Prussian War of 1870–1871, Alsace (except Belfort) and Lorraine (including Metz and Strasbourg) are ceded to the new German Empire by the Peace of Frankfurt (May 1871) and declared German 'imperial territory' in June 1871. Alsace-Lorraine is treated severely under Bismarck, declared a *Reichsland* under a governor-general in August 1879. Treatment becomes more lenient after 1890, culminating in the granting of a degree of autonomy in May 1911. The loss of Alsace-Lorraine represents a humiliation to France which irretrievably sours Franco-German relations between 1871 and 1914. After the First World War, Alsace-Lorraine is restored to France by the Treaty of Versailles in June 1919. The classic instance of territorial revanchism in late nineteenth-century Europe.

Andorra A tiny republic with a majority-Spanish population in the eastern Pyrenees, officially a co-principality under the joint suzerainty of France and Spain (in the person of the Bishop of Urgell) since 1278 but enjoying considerable autonomy in the nineteenth century.

Armenia A territory claimed by the Armenians in north-east Anatolia and southern Trans-Caucasia, most of which is annexed by the Russian Empire from the Ottoman Empire over the nineteenth century. Despite growing nationalist movements within both 'Russian Armenia' and 'Ottoman Armenia' during the late nineteenth century, neither empire acknowledges 'Armenia' politically. After the fall of the tsarist empire, nationalists proclaim the independence of Armenia in May 1918 and an Armenian delegation to the Paris Peace Conference in 1919 claims a 'Greater Armenia' reaching to the Mediterranean, but the new state is forcibly re-absorbed by the Bolshevik government of Russia by December 1920. By a new 'Armenian Partition', almost half 'Russian Armenia' is ceded to the Ottoman Empire/Turkey under the Treaty of Kars in March 1921.

Austria/Cisleithania Under the Dual Monarchy of Austria-Hungary

(1867–1918), the northern and western 'half' of Habsburg jurisdiction is officially termed 'Cisleithania' (the territory 'on this side of the river Leitha', the physical frontier-marker between 'Austria' and 'Hungary'). Comprising some 40 per cent of the area and 60 per cent of the population of Austria-Hungary, 'Cisleithania' is a de-politicised geographical term for 'Austria' (with 'Transleithania' serving the same purpose for 'Hungary'). Under the *Ausgleich* constitution (1867–1918), neither 'Austria' nor (still less) 'Hungary' is a sovereign independent state.

Azerbaidzhan   A Muslim territory of the Trans-Caucasus, part of which is acquired by Russia from Persia in the early nineteenth century (notably by the Treaty of Turkmenchai in 1828). Effectively partitioned between Russia and Persia over the nineteenth century, Azerbaidzhan is occupied by the Turks after the fall of tsarism in 1917 and reunited under Ottoman rule. 'Russian Azerbaidzhan' declares its independence in May 1918 but is forcibly reincorporated into Bolshevik Russia by the Red Army in May 1920.

Belorussia/Belarus   An ill-defined territory of north-western European Russia centred on Minsk and inhabited by the Belorussians, a Slav group closely related to the Russians but with their own distinctive language. With native nationalism slow to develop, the tsarist empire makes no concessions to political autonomy over the nineteenth century, even adopting cultural and linguistic Russification to assimilate the Belorussians. After the fall of tsarism, an independent Belorussia is proclaimed in 1917 but suffers a three-way 'Belorussian Partition' between Bolshevik Russia, Poland and Lithuania over 1919–1920.

Bessarabia   A classic disputed territory of the Balkans, centred on Kishinev/Chisinău and located between the rivers Pruth and Dniestr, Bessarabia passes backwards and forwards between the Russian Empire and Rumania. Bessarabia is acquired by Russia from the Ottoman Empire by the Treaty of Bucharest in May 1812, confirmed by the Congress of Vienna in 1815. Following defeat in the Crimean War, Russia is forced to cede part of Bessarabia back to the Ottoman Empire and part to the new Danubian Principalities by the Peace of Paris in March 1856. Russia is returned Bessarabia by Rumania (the reconstituted Principalities), by the Congress of Berlin in July 1878. In the First World War, the Central Powers occupy Bessarabia, which falls under Austro-Hungarian jurisdiction by the Treaty of Brest-Litovsk in March 1918. In November 1918, Rumania claims and occupies Bessarabia again, a territorial acquisition tacitly confirmed by the Treaty of Trianon in June 1920 which authorises 'Greater Rumania'.

Bohemia   The most north-westerly province of the Habsburg Empire, centred on Prague and inhabited mostly by Czechs. Originally an administrative division of the Empire, the 'Kingdom of Bohemia' develops economic muscle and cultural self-assurance over the nineteenth century, becoming the heartland of Czech nationalism. Although concessions to autonomy are granted by 'Austria' in the late nineteenth century, Bohemia never achieves her ambition of equal status with 'Austria' or at least 'Hungary' in a tri-partite power-sharing constitution. After the First World War, Bohemia becomes the single most important territorial component in the new state of Czecho-Slovakia, as confirmed by the Treaty of St Germain in September 1919.

Bosnia-Herzegovina A multi-ethnic, geographically ill-defined territory in the mid-Balkans which becomes the principal prize in the rival expansionism of Serbia and Austria-Hungary. Under Ottoman rule since the fifteenth century, Bosnia-Herzegovina rebels in 1875. By the terms of the Congress of Berlin in July 1878, Bosnia-Herzegovina remains under Ottoman suzerainty but is occupied by Austria-Hungary. Bosnia-Herzegovina is developed by the Habsburgs into a valuable property after 1878. In October 1908, Austria-Hungary is alarmed by the Young Turk Revolution into formally annexing Bosnia-Herzegovina (the most Muslim territory in the Balkans). Land-locked Serbia is outraged, seeing Bosnia-Herzegovina as the territorial bridge to her ally Montenegro and providing access to the Adriatic. Anti-Austrian nationalist activity within Bosnia-Herzegovina is encouraged by Serbia, culminating in the assassination of the Archduke Franz Ferdinand, the heir to the Habsburg throne, in the Bosnian capital of Sarajevo in June 1914. In the First World War that follows, Bosnia-Herzegovina is overrun and occupied by the Austrians from late 1915. By the Treaty of St Germain in September 1919, Bosnia-Herzegovina becomes a component in the new Kingdom of the Serbs, Croats and Slovenes (subsequently Yugoslavia).

Brittany/Breiz The most north-westerly region of France, an independent entity until incorporated by France in 1532. Retains strong cultural and linguistic links with its 'Celtic cousins' in Cornwall and Wales. After 1790, the centralising French Revolution divides the historic province into five deliberately artificial departments. From the mid-nineteenth century, the solidly Roman Catholic protagonists of 'Breiz' claim that the 1532 incorporation was accompanied by guarantees of internal autonomy, subsequently breached by the French government. From the late nineteenth century, Breton nationalists demand the 'restoration' of the autonomy guaranteed in 1532 (but do not aspire to pre-1532 independence).

Bukovina A small, multi-ethnic territory at the geopolitical meeting-point of Ottoman-Habsburg-Russian imperial expansionism. Annexed from the Ottoman Empire into the Habsburg Empire in May 1775, Bukovina becomes the most easterly duchy of Cisleithania/ Austria within Austria-Hungary after 1867. Though economically underdeveloped, Bukovina (or 'beech-tree country) is granted a measure of autonomy within 'Austria' by the 'Bukovina Compromise' of 1910.

Catalonia/Catalunya Historically, a powerful region centred on the long-established Mediterranean port of Barcelona reduced in the eighteenth century to the most north-easterly province of Spain. Exhibiting growing cultural self-consciousness through the later nine-teenth century, Catalonia is impelled by economic disadvantage to resist central authority in the pursuit of greater autonomy in the early twentieth century. Catalan anarchism precipitates crises in the Spanish state in 1909, 1912 and 1917, when a general strike demanding the independence of Catalonia is launched.

Corsica The fourth largest island in the Mediterranean, strategically located in the conflict zone of competing French, Genoese and even Spanish influence. An independent republic headed by Pasquale Paoli, Corsica is transferred from Genoa to France in 1768 (the year before the birth of its most famous son, Napoleon Bonaparte). Rousseau pays Corsica the compliment of drafting a special constitution tailored to its unique social and political character. An independent Corsica survives with British protection, 1794–1796. After 1796, Corsica becomes a department of 'Greater France' and is permitted no concessions to autonomy during the nineteenth century.

Crete A large island in the eastern Mediterranean which campaigns for independence from the Ottoman Empire and union with Greece. A first Cretan uprising fails over 1866–1869. The Cretans rise again in February 1896. Concessions over autonomy offered by the Ottomans in July 1896 fail to undermine the Cretan desire for union with Greece. Greece declares war in support of Crete in April 1897 and is promptly defeated, inducing the Great Powers to intervene to impose the Treaty of Constantinople between Greece and the Ottoman Empire in December 1897 which grants Crete autonomy within 'Greater Greece'.

Croatia A substantial South Slav 'banat' on the southern periphery of the Habsburg Empire, coinciding approximately to the traditional 'Military Frontier' zone against the Ottoman Turks. The Illyrian Republic established by Napoleon over 1805–1813 plants the beginnings of a new national self-consciousness in Croatia. As a western-looking, Roman Catholic territory, Croatia is pro-Austrian and anti-Hungarian throughout the nineteenth century. In 1848–1849, Croatia (under Jelačić) backs the Habsburgs against the secessionist Hungarians. By the *Ausgleich* of 1867, Croatia is dismayed to find itself allocated not to Cisleithania/Austria but to Transleithania/Hungary. Autonomous status within Hungary is granted to Croatia by the *Nagodba* of 1868, but increasing Magyarisation results in the cancellation of autonomy and the imposition of Hungarian 'direct rule' from 1882. Relatively unscathed in the First World War, Croatia's position between Austria,

Hungary and Serbia is resolved by its unenthusiastic commitment to partnership in the new Kingdom of the Serbs, Croats and Slovenes proclaimed in December 1918.

Cyprus A strategically located island of mixed Greek and Turkish population in the eastern Mediterranean which passes from Ottoman to British jurisdiction. By agreements at Constantinople (July 1878) and Therapia (August 1878), the Ottoman Empire acquiesces to British occupation of Cyprus. Britain annexes Cyprus from the Ottoman Empire in November 1914, a territorial change formally recognised by Turkey in the Treaty of Lausanne in July 1923.

Dobrudja A territory bordering the Black Sea, south of the delta of the river Danube, which looms large in Rumanian-Bulgarian relations.

Northern Dobrudja: ceded by the Ottoman Empire to the new principality of Rumania by the Congress of Berlin in July 1878, remaining part of Rumania from 1878 into the twentieth century (apart from the Austrian-Bulgarian occupation of 1916–1918).

Southern Dobrudja: a territory passing backwards and forwards between Rumania and Bulgaria over the early twentieth century. Granted by the Ottoman Empire to Bulgaria by the Congress of Berlin in July 1878. Defeated in the Second Balkan War, Bulgaria cedes southern Dobrudja to Rumania by the Treaty of Bucharest in August 1913. In the First World War, Bulgaria retrieves southern Dobrudja in 1916; but is compelled to return it to Greater Rumania by the Treaty of Neuilly in November 1919. Southern Dobrudja becomes the 'Alsace-Lorraine of the Balkans', permanently poisoning Bulgarian-Rumanian relations.

Estonia A territory bordering the Baltic Sea and Gulf of Finland annexed from Sweden to the Russian Empire of Peter the Great by the Treaty of Nystadt in 1721. With a distinctive language but slow-developing national consciousness, Estonia is administered as the province of 'Estland' by a Russian Empire increasingly committed to Russification from the mid-nineteenth century onwards. In the First World War, Estonia is occupied by German forces in 1917 and granted independence (as a client-state of Germany) by the Treaty of Brest-Litovsk in March 1918. The independence of Estonia/Eesti is recognised by Bolshevik Russia in the Treaty of Tartu in February 1920 (and supported by the Great Powers in the Paris Peace Settlement).

Euzkadi The national homeland of the Basques, an ancient and autochthonous people settled around the western Pyrenees, partly in three provinces of south-western France but mostly in four provinces (Bizcaya, Guipozcoa, Alana and Navarra) in north-western Spain. The distinctive Basque language and culture is broadly respected by Castile from the fourteenth century until 1839, when the Cortes abrogates many traditional Basque privileges as punishment for supporting the

Carlist claimant in the First Carlist War. With the industrialisation and urbanisation of the Bilbao region towards the end of the nineteenth century, the Basque territory of Euzkadi, combining features of a sub-state with those of an ex-state, begins a campaign to win political recognition within Spain.

Finland The Grand Duchy of Finland is ceded to the Russian Empire by Sweden in the Treaty of Fredericksham, September 1809. The demographic heritage of the imperial Swedish past ensures that throughout the nineteenth century Finland is some 80 per cent Finnish, 15 per cent Swedish and only 5 per cent Russian. Officially, according to the promise given by Tsar Alexander I at the Diet of Borgå/Porvoo in 1809, the Duchy does not become part of the Russian Empire: rather the Duchy retains its traditional privileges in a territorial union justified by the Tsar of Russia being automatically Grand Duke of Finland. The Grand Duchy remains autonomous for most of the nineteenth century, deriving considerable economic benefit from the Russian connection. The tsarist policy of Russification is applied to Finland from the 1890s, leading to the suspension of the Grand Duchy's constitution in 1903. The Russian 'Revolution of 1905' effects a restoration of the constitution but before long the Russification policy is reapplied: the Finnish province of Vyborg/Viipuri is annexed by Russia in 1912 and the Grand Duchy's autonomous status is effectively dissolved on the plea of wartime security in late 1914. Alienated by Russian treatment, Finland proclaims first its autonomy (July 1917), then its independence (December 1917). Finland is the only nation within the tsarist empire to secure permanent independence from Russia after 1917/1918.

Gibraltar The strategic Rock and naval base commanding the narrow straits between Spain and Morocco which connect the Atlantic and Mediterranean. Captured from Spain in 1704, Gibraltar is formally ceded to Britain by the Treaty of Utrecht in 1713. After various attempts at capture, Spain renounces all claims to Gibraltar by the Treaty of Versailles of September 1783. A British crown colony, Gibraltar becomes the principal British naval base for the western Mediterranean over the nineteenth century.

Hungary/Transleithania Hungary is ostensibly a nationalist success story, winning first autonomy (1867) and then independence (1919) over the late nineteenth and early twentieth centuries. The 'Lands of St Stephen' constituting the Kingdom of Hungary are an integral part of the officially unitary Austrian Empire from 1804 until 1867. Hungary demands autonomy within, and then independence from the Austrian Empire in 1848 but is defeated by Austro-Russian military force in 1849. After the *Ausgleich* of 1867, 'Hungary' becomes the junior partner in the Dual Monarchy of Austria-Hungary. The official nomenclature for

Hungary is the geopolitically-depoliticised 'Transleithania', the 'territory across the river Leitha' (as viewed from Vienna). 'Hungary' enjoys considerable autonomy within Austria-Hungary by the terms of the 1867 *Ausgleich*, which encourages a vigorous 'Magyarisation' of its multi-ethnic population but undermines the nationalist urge for independence over the period 1867 to 1914.

Although a reluctant participant in the First World War, Hungary becomes one of the greatest territorial casualties of the Paris Peace Settlement. By the Treaty of St Germain in September 1919, Hungary is endorsed as a sovereign state. Hungary pays the price of independence by the Treaty of Trianon (June 1920), being compelled to cede: Transylvania and half of the Banat to Rumania; Voivodina and Croatia to the Kingdom of the Serbs, Croats and Slovenes; part of northern Slovakia to Poland; the rest of Slovakia and Ruthenia to Czecho-Slovakia; Fiume to Italy and the Burgenland to Austria. Hungary is reduced by two-thirds territorially (ceding to Rumania alone more territory than remains to 'rump Hungary') and suffers a drop in state population from 21 million (1914) to 8 million (1920). The Paris Peace Settlement represents an externally-imposed geopolitical disaster to which the population of 'Trianon Hungary' is never reconciled.

Iceland A large, sparsely-populated island in the Atlantic at the most north-westerly extremity of Europe, part of the empire of Denmark. After a vigorous campaign for autonomy, the Icelanders are granted a local legislature by the Danish crown in 1874. Further concessions in 1903 and 1918 permit Iceland virtual home rule in domestic affairs.

Ireland A large island on the north-western periphery of Europe, comprising part of the United Kingdom. A measure of autonomy enjoyed by Ireland in the eighteenth century is cancelled when, alarmed by Irish rebellion and attempted French invasion, the British government effects the Act of Union in 1800 which incorporates Great Britain and Ireland into the new United Kingdom. A growing campaign for home rule in domestic matters over the later nineteenth century fails to win any constitutional recognition from the British government. In the early twentieth century, the refusal of the northern province of Ulster to accept home rule from Dublin, together with a new nationalist militancy during the First World War, transforms the Irish political situation. By the Irish Treaty of 1920–1921, Ulster remains part of the United Kingdom while the remaining three provinces of southern Ireland are accorded self-governing dominion status within the British Empire as the 'Irish Free State'.

Karelia A large, sparsely-populated region to the east of Finland regarded by Finns as their ethnic heartland, and therefore the principal objective of Finnish nationalists pursuing an irredentist 'Greater Finland' against the Russian Empire.

Kosovo A region of the Balkans at the confluence of Serbian and Albanian territorial expansionism in the early twentieth century. Kosovo is regarded by the Serbs as their historic heartland and also the scene of their greatest national disaster when, at Kosovo Field in 1386, a Serb army was annihilated by the Ottomans. Invested with vibrant emotional resonance, Kosovo is regarded by the Serbs as an essential component of historic 'Greater Serbia'. However, with the majority of the population being Albanian, Kosovo is also viewed as a natural, integral part of 'Greater Albania' by the new Albanian state emerging in 1912–1913.

Latvia A distinctive national territory bordering the Baltic, annexed from Sweden into the Russian Empire by Peter the Great under the Treaty of Nystadt in 1721. Divided into the tsarist provinces of Livonia and Courland, 'Latvia' is accorded no autonomous status or national recognition over the nineteenth century. Opposing the political and social ascendancy of the resident Baltic German landowners, a developing Latvian/Lettish nationalist movement is countered by tsarist Russification in the early twentieth century. Overrun and occupied by German forces in the First World War, Latvia is granted independence (within the German empire) by the Treaty of Brest-Litovsk in March 1918. Supported by the victorious Allies, Latvia is recognised as independent by Bolshevik Russia under the Treaty of Riga in August 1920.

Lithuania A large medieval state, linked to Poland from 1569, Lithuania is annexed by Russia through the Third Polish Partition of 1795. 'Lithuania' is accorded no autonomous status or national recognition over the nineteenth century. A developing nationalist movement is countered by tsarist Russification in the early twentieth century. Overrun and occupied by German forces in the First World War, Lithuania is granted independence (within the German empire and with a German duke as king) by the Treaty of Brest-Litovsk in March 1918. Supported by the victorious Allies, Lithuania survives Russian attack in early 1919 and is recognised as independent by Bolshevik Russia under the Treaty of Moscow in July 1920. The question of territorial jurisdiction over the disputed areas of Vilna and Memel permanently bedevils Lithuania's relations with her larger Russian, German and Polish neighbours.

Macedonia A region of the central Balkans under Ottoman jurisdiction until the Balkan Wars of 1912–1913 but claimed by all emergent neighbouring states as part of 'Greater Serbia', 'Greater Albania', 'Greater Greece' and 'Greater Bulgaria'. The principal arena of conflict between Serbia, Greece and Bulgaria during the First World War, Macedonia becomes the most southerly component of the new Kingdom of the Serbs, Croats and Slovenes after 1918.

Malta An island strategically located in the narrows of the central Mediterranean between Sicily and Africa. With a distinctive history and culture, Malta is held by the Knights of St John of Jerusalem from 1530 to 1798, when it is briefly captured by France. Seized by Britain in 1800, Malta is to be returned to the Knights of St John by the terms of the Treaty of Amiens in March 1802. Malta, however, is retained by Britain and formally annexed as a crown colony in 1814 (with Maltese acquiescence). Over the nineteenth century, Malta becomes the main base of the British Mediterranean fleet.

Moldavia The territory bordering the Black Sea between the rivers Pruth and Danube, and one of the two Danubian Principalities created to reduce Ottoman, Austrian and Russian imperial confrontation in the eastern Balkans. Under Ottoman authority since the fifteenth century, Moldavia is taken under the religious protectorship of Russia by the Treaty of Kutchuk Kainardji in 1774. Occupied by Russia in 1829–1834, Moldavia secures autonomy from the Ottoman Empire. Moldavia is reoccupied by Russia in 1853, then by Austria during the Crimean War (1854–1856). By the Peace of Paris in 1856, Moldavia's autonomy is guaranteed by the Great Powers. In 1858, the Powers sanction separate but identical administrations in Moldavia (centred at Jassy), and in Wallachia (centred on Bucharest). In 1862, the Danubian Principalities of Moldavia and Wallachia are united, adopting the name 'Rumania'. The independence of Moldavia/Rumania is formally conceded by the Ottoman Empire only in 1877.

Moravia A northern province of the Habsburg Empire inhabited by a Czech majority (about 70 per cent of total population). Like its western neighbour the Kingdom of Bohemia, the Margraviate of Moravia benefits from both economic development and growing national self-consciousness over the nineteenth century, contributing to the campaign of the Czech lands for greater autonomy within the Empire. Moravia secures more autonomy within Cisleithania/Austria than Bohemia by the granting of the 'Moravian Compromise' of 1905, but the greater aim of Slav partnership in a tripartite monarchy is never achieved. By the Treaty of St Germain in September 1919, Moravia (together with Bohemia) is ceded by Austria to the new state of Czecho-Slovakia.

Novi Bazar As the most north-westerly Muslim enclave in the Balkans, the Sanjak of Novi Bazar becomes a pawn in the nineteenth-century geopolitical game of carving up the Balkans. Since Novi Bazar constitutes a bridge between Serbia and Montenegro, land-locked Serbia wishes to acquire the Sanjak for 'Greater Serbia', thereby linking up with its ally Montenegro and gaining access to the Adriatic. The Habsburg and Ottoman Empires are equally determined to contain Serbian expansion by denying it the Sanjak. By the Congress of Berlin in 1878, Austria-Hungary is authorised to occupy Novi Bazar (along with Bosnia-Herzegovina). In 1908, alarmed by the Young Turk Revolution, Austria-Hungary formally annexes Bosnia-Herzegovina, securing Ottoman acquiescence by returning Novi Bazar to the Ottoman Empire. Ottoman authority lasts only for five years: by the Treaty of Bucharest in August 1913 at the end of the Balkan Wars, the Ottoman Empire is compelled to cede Novi Bazar jointly to Serbia and Montenegro. The Sanjak is partitioned equally between Serbia and Montenegro, losing its separate political identity. The scene of hard fighting during the First World War, Novi Bazar becomes a part of the Kingdom of the Serbs, Croats and Slovenes in 1918.

Pomerania A territory bordering the southern Baltic relinquished by Sweden to Prussia through the Congress of Vienna in 1815. The transfer symbolises both the northward withdrawal of the declining power of Sweden and the northward advance of the rising power of Prussia to dominate the southern Baltic littoral.

Rumelia A province in the southern Balkans established by the Congress of Berlin in July 1878 to frustrate the 'Big Bulgaria' promoted by Russia through the earlier Treaty of San Stefano (March 1878). The Berlin Congress establishes the independent principality of 'Small Bulgaria' and, on its southern border, a nominally Ottoman entity (with a Christian governor) called eastern Rumelia. The Great Powers' strategy is foiled when, in 1885, Rumelia is annexed by Bulgaria after an existence of only seven years. Despite Great Power concern and Serbian outrage (leading to a brief war), Rumelia is retained by what becomes a 'Biggish Bulgaria'.

Ruthenia A backward territory in the extreme north-east of the Habsburg Empire bordering on Russia, occupied by the Slav Ruthenian people (a sub-group of the Ukrainians). Although claiming historical legitimacy from the thirteenth-century Principality of Halich, Ruthenia experiences little rise in national awareness and remains a social, economic and political backwater throughout the nineteenth century. The Ruthenians are widely settled, with three-quarters within Cisleithania/Austria and one quarter within Transleithania/Hungary after 1867. Uniate by religious confession, the Ruthenians in Hungary suffer severely from Magyarisation. By the Treaties of St Germain (September 1919) and Trianon (June 1920), Ruthenia becomes the most easterly territory of the new state of Czecho-Slovakia (although the majority of Ruthenians find themselves within Poland).

Savoy A classic border region situated between France, Switzerland and Piedmont. Annexed by France in 1792, Savoy is restored to independence (in association with Piedmont-Sardinia) by the Congress of Vienna in 1815. Although providing the royal dynasty of Piedmont-Sardinia (and subsequently Italy), Savoy is transferred to France by

Piedmont in 1860 for services rendered to the Italian cause in the French-Piedmontese-Austrian War of 1859.

Schleswig-Holstein Situated in the most southerly part of the Jutland peninsula, the two Duchies of Schleswig and Holstein (linked since medieval times) become the subject of an argument about national jurisdiction between Denmark and Prussia over the nineteenth century. Although the northern Duchy of Schleswig/Slesvig is partly German by population and the southern Duchy of Holstein is predominantly German (even joining the German Confederation in 1815), both are held by the king of Denmark.

In 1848, Danish nationalists press for the formal annexation of Schleswig-Holstein, provoking resistance from the Duchies' population, backed by Prussia. A Danish-Prussian war ends inconclusively by the Treaty of Berlin in June 1850. In 1863, Denmark incorporates Schleswig but the new King Christian IX of Denmark is rejected by the Duchies, provoking a war between Denmark and Prussia and Austria in 1864. Defeated in war, Denmark cedes the duchies jointly to Prussia and Austria by the Treaty of Vienna in October 1864. By the Convention of Gastein in August 1865, Prussia claims Schleswig and Austria claims Holstein. In 1866, Prussia and Austria quarrel over the division of the duchies. Victorious in the Austro-Prussian Seven-Weeks' War, Prussia annexes both Schleswig and Holstein by the Treaty of Prague in August 1866.

Schleswig and Holstein remain duchies within Prussia and then the German Empire from 1866 to 1918. After the First World War, a plebiscite justifies the return of Slesvig north of the Flensburg Fjord to Denmark in June 1920; the remainder of Schleswig and all Holstein stay in Germany.

Scotland The Kingdom of Scotland is joined with the Kingdom of England and the Principality of Wales to form the United Kingdom of Great Britain by the Union with Scotland Act of 1707. Dynastically linked to England by the Stuarts since 1603, Scotland remains an independent kingdom with its own parliament in Edinburgh until 1707. After the Union, Scotland is granted representation at Westminster but no formal autonomy, and yet retains many unique institutional characteristics, particularly with regard to law, religion and education. Over the late eighteenth and early nineteenth centuries, Scotland experiences a distinctive cultural revival enhancing its traditional sense of national identity. Although in many respects more of an ex-state then a sub-state, Scotland does not embrace the nationalist creed: for the remainder of the nineteenth century, Scottish self-consciousness, already undermined by the Highlander/Lowlander/Uplander divide, is mostly subsumed into a sense of voluntary service to (and exploitation of the opportunities presented by) the British Empire. A politick Scottish/British sense of dual nationality obviates any consistent or effective political campaigns for either independence or autonomy.

Slovakia   A distinctive region of the Habsburg Empire which becomes part of Hungary/Transleithania within the Dual Monarchy of Austria-Hungary after the *Ausgleich* of 1867. No autonomous status or national recognition is accorded Slovakia by Hungary from 1867 to 1918, when a relentless policy of Magyarisation perverts the economic and social development of Slovakia and forces many Slovaks into emigration. After the First World War, under the terms of the Treaty of Trianon (June 1920), Slovakia is transferred from Hungary to become the partner to the Czech lands of Bohemia and Moravia in the new state of Czecho-Slovakia. The unfortunate late nineteenth-century career of Slovakia (within Hungary) may be contrasted with that of Slovenia (within Austria).

Slovenia   A distinctive region of the Habsburg Empire centred on Ljubljana/Laibach which becomes part of Austria/Cisleithania within the Dual Monarchy of Austria-Hungary after the *Ausgleich* of 1867. No autonomous status or national recognition is accorded Slovenia by Austria from 1867 to 1918 but the region experiences impressive economic and social development during the 'late Austrian' period. After the First World War, Slovenia becomes a partner in the Kingdom of the Serbs, Croats and Slovenes proclaimed in December 1918 and endorsed by the Great Powers under the terms of the Treaty of St Germain (September 1919). The progressive late nineteenth-century career of Slovenia (within Austria) may be contrasted with that of Slovakia (within Hungary).

Transylvania   A large region of mixed Hungarian, Rumanian and German settlement within the Austrian Empire until 1867, and within Hungary/Transleithania from 1867 to 1918. Recovered by the Habsburgs from the Ottomans in the late seventeenth century, Transylvania's rural population is mainly Rumanian and its urban population mostly Hungarian and especially German. In 1848–1849, the Rumanian and German populations support the Habsburgs against the rebellious Hungarians. In 1867, the *Ausgleich* allocates the 'Grand Duchy of Transylvania' to Hungary, leading to vigorous Magyarisation of the Rumanian population. A Rumanian National Party is founded in Hungary in 1881 and the emergent state of Rumania across the eastern frontier of Transylvania entertains ambitions for its annexation into a 'Greater Rumania' at Hungary's expense.

During the First World War, Rumania is induced to join the Allied side in August 1916 by the promise of the acquisition of Transylvania after the war, but is soon defeated and occupied by the Central Powers of Germany, Austria-Hungary and Bulgaria over 1917. At the end of the war in November 1918, the Rumanian elements in Transylvania proclaim its union with Rumania. Over autumn 1919 Rumania invades Hungary to seize Transylvania, an acquisition confirmed by the Allies by the Treaty of Trianon (June 1920). The territorial combination of Moldavia and Wallachia (or Regat) with Transylvania in 1919–1920 effects the creation of 'Greater Rumania' at the expense of 'Trianon Hungary'.

Ukraine An extensive, territorially ill-defined region of southern European Russia which becomes, after Russia itself, the single most valuable industrial and agricultural component of the Russian Empire over the nineteenth century. Appreciating the rising value of Ukraine, the tsarist empire concedes no autonomous status or national recognition to the territory, instead pursuing rigorous Russification from the mid-nineteenth century onwards to suppress emergent Ukrainian cultural or political national consciousness. On the fall of the tsarist empire in 1917, Ukrainian nationalists proclaim an independent state (R.A.D.A.), which fails to engage the widespread support of the population of Ukraine. Under the Treaty of Brest-Litovsk in March 1918, Ukraine is detached from Russia and then set up as a German puppet-state under Skoropadsky. Through 1919, Ukraine becomes the arena for blood-letting between the Bolsheviks, the Whites under Denikin, and Ukrainian nationalists under Petlyura. After involuntary involvement in the Polish-Russian War of 1919–1920, 'Greater Ukraine' is effectively subjected to four-way partition and subordination: Bukovina becomes part of Rumania; Ruthenia is taken by Czecho-Slovakia; western Ukraine is annexed by Poland; and eastern Ukraine is retained by Bolshevik Russia.

Ulster The most northerly of the historic four provinces of Ireland. A distinctive Protestant identity, the legacy of a seventeenth-century influx of Scottish Presbyterians, leads to a refusal to join Catholic Ireland in campaigning for home rule within the United Kingdom in the late nineteenth century. By 1914, Ulster militants led by Edward Carson are organising to resist by force the home rule from Dublin decided by the British government. By the Irish Treaty of 1920–1921, the 26 counties of southern Ireland become a dominion called the Irish Free State while the six counties of northern Ireland remain part of a revamped United Kingdom of Great Britain and Northern Ireland.

Vistula Provinces The official tsarist term for the territory of Congress Poland from 1863 to 1914. As punishment for the first Polish Uprising of 1830–1831, the constitution of Congress Poland is abolished in March 1832. As punishment for the second Polish Uprising of 1863, even the name of Poland is expunged from the Russian Empire and the demeaning geographical term 'Vistula Provinces' substituted as part of the wider Russification campaign of the tsarist government.

Wales Dynastically linked to England since the thirteenth century, the

Principality of Wales is attached to the Kingdom of England by the Act of Union with Wales in 1536, subsequently joined to the Kingdom of Scotland (1707) and Ireland (1800) to form the United Kingdom. Although retaining a distinctive cultural, linguistic and (to some extent) religious identity, Wales remains a sub-state rather than an ex-state and mounts no sustained campaign for political acknowledgement and receives neither constitutional autonomy nor national recognition from the British government over the nineteenth century.

Wallachia A region of the eastern Balkans south of the river Danube which becomes one of the two Danubian Principalities and then the southern half of Rumania. Officially under Ottoman authority until 1877, Wallachia is increasingly subject to Russian intervention. Under the pretext of its protectorship of Christians within the Muslim Ottoman Empire (announced by the Treaty of Kutchuk Kainardji in 1774), Russia occupies Wallachia in 1829–1834 to secure its autonomy, and again in 1848–1851 to suppress liberal and nationalist rebellion in Bucharest. During the Crimean War, Wallachia is occupied by Austria from 1854 to 1857. By the Peace of Paris in 1856, the Great Powers guarantee the autonomy of Wallachia to forestall further rival Austrian-Russian expansionism as the Ottoman Empire retreats. In 1858, the Powers sanction separate but identical Danubian Principalities in Wallachia (based in Bucharest) and Moldavia (based in Jassy). In 1862, Wallachia and Moldavia, backed by the Powers, unite territorially under the name 'Rumania'. Finally in 1877, the Ottoman Empire formally concedes the independence of the joint principality of Rumania.

National chronologies

1. The Albanians

Pre-1798
'Albania' a tributary province of the Ottoman Empire

1798–1822
Effective autonomy of 'Albania' under Ali Pasha of Janina

1809
'Albania' impresses the visiting Lord Byron

1878
Assembly at Prizren raises banner of Albanian nation and statehood

1897
Nov. Italian-Austrian agreement over Albania

1903
Death in Italian exile of Girolomo da Rada, 'the Albanian Mazzini'

1908+
Nationalist uprising in 'Albania'

1912
Nov. Ottoman government, under Young Turk pressure, concedes independence to Albania

1913
May London Ambassadorial Conference, ending First Balkan War, agrees on creation of Albania
Aug. Treaty of Bucharest, ending Second Balkan War, establishes independent Muslim principality of Albania
Oct. Austria-Hungary sends Serbia ultimatum over Albania
Dec. The Great Powers approve the accession of Prince William of Wied to the throne of independent Albania

1914
Dec. Italy occupies Valona in Albania

1916
Feb. Austro-Hungarian southern offensive conquers all Serbia, Montenegro and Albania north of Valona

1917
Jun. Albania proclaimed independent under Italian protection

1918
Jul. Allies break through in Albania
Oct. Allies expel Central forces from Serbia and Albania

1921
Nov. Independence of Albania recognised by Greece, Italy and the

Kingdom of the Serbs, Croats and Slovenes after a long territorial wrangle

2. The Armenians

1827
Russian Empire seizes Erivan from Persia

1828
Feb. Peace of Turkmenchai: Russian Empire acquires most of 'Greater Armenia' from Ottoman Empire

1829
Sep. Treaty of Adrianople: Russian acquisitions south of the Caucasus (Armenia and Georgia) formally recognised by Ottoman Empire

1894
Aug. Armenian nationalist rising bloodily suppressed by Ottoman irregular troops: estimates of casualties in the '*Armenian Massacres*' range from 20,000 (Ottoman) to 200,000 (Armenian)

1895
Apr. Great Power protests, backed by the arrival of a British fleet, induce Ottoman Empire to promise reform. Britain publicly reconsiders its traditional support for the territorial integrity of the Ottoman Empire

1896
Armenian nationalists seize Ottoman Bank in Constantinople, prompting three days of slaughter of Armenians. Massacres halted by Great Power intercession but anti-Armenian incidents continue

1896+
Armenian nationalists despair of Great Power patronage, abandon provocation strategy in favour of a wait-and-see policy

1914
In First World War, Armenians find themselves in war zone between Russian and Ottoman Empires on the Caucasian front

1915
Apr.+ '*Armenian Genocide*': Armenians in Ottoman Empire experience up to 1.5 million deaths. According to the Ottomans, a relocation and resettlement exercise that went wrong. According to the Armenians, a deliberate massacre on a scale amounting to an 'Armenian Holocaust' designed to obliterate the Ottoman 'Armenian Question'. Often cited as the first twentieth-century example of attempted genocide

1917

Mar. On fall of tsarism, 'Russian Armenia' joins Georgia and Azerbaidzhan to form independent Transcaucasian Federative Republic
May Ottomans overthrow Transcaucasian Republic, occupy Armenia

1918

May Armenia (and Georgia and Azerbaidzhan) declares its independence, headed by *Dashnaktsutyun* (Armenian Revolutionary Federation)

1919

Armenian delegation to Paris Peace Conference demands recognition of a 'Greater Armenia' stretching from the Black Sea to the Mediterranean
Dec. Britain withdraws forces from Transcaucasus

1920

Dec. Armenia forcibly reincorporated into Bolshevik Russia

1921

Mar. Treaty of Kars: almost half of 'Russian Armenia' is ceded to Ottoman Empire/Turkey

3. The Austrians

1780–1790

Reign of the 'Revolutionary Emperor' Josef II

1789

Oct. Uprising in Austrian Netherlands
Dec. Austrian Netherlands declares its independence as 'Belgium'

1790

Jan. Convention of Berlin between Britain, Prussia and United Provinces over Belgium
Dec. Austrians re-enter Brussels, crush Belgian uprising

1790–1792

Reign of Emperor Leopold II

1792–1835

Reign of Emperor Franz/Francis II

1792

Nov. Austrians defeated at Jemappes by French, who annexe Austrian Netherlands/Belgium

1793

Mar. Austrians defeat French at Neerwinden, retake Austrian Netherlands/Belgium

1794

Jun. Austrians defeated by French at Fleurus, and again lose Austrian Netherlands/Belgium to France

1795

Oct. Third Partition of Poland: Habsburg Empire gets Cracow and western Galicia

1796

May Austrians defeated by Napoleon at Lodi, in northern Italy
Nov. Austrians defeated by Napoleon at Arcola, in northern Italy

1797

Jan. Austrians defeated by Napoleon at Rivoli, in northern Italy
Oct. Peace of Campo Formio: Austria cedes Belgium and Lombardy to France but retains Venetia, Istria and Dalmatia (and the promise of a share in the imminent division of 'Germany')

1799

Mar. Austrians defeat French at Stockach

1800

Jun. Austrians defeated by French at Marengo
Dec. Austrians defeated by French at Hohenlinden

1801

Feb. Austria and France make peace at Lunéville

The Austrian Empire (1804–1867)

1804

Aug. Francis II assumes title of *Emperor of Austria*

1805

Dec. Austria defeated by French at Austerlitz, makes peace at Pressburg

1806

Aug. Francis II renounces crown of Holy Roman Emperor as *Holy Roman Empire abolished*

1809

May Indecisive battle of Aspern between Austrians and French
Jul. Austrians defeated by French at Wagram
Oct. *Metternich appointed Chief Minister (1809–1848).* Treaty of Vienna: Austria forced to cede Trieste and Illyria to France; Galicia divided between Russia and Grand Duchy of Warsaw; and Salzburg ceded to Bavaria

1810

Feb. Execution of Andreas Hofer, leader of Tyrolese Uprising (1809–1810) against Bavaria (and France)

1811
Feb. Official bankruptcy of Austrian Empire
Apr. Civil code introduced into Austrian Empire

1813
Aug. Austrians defeated by French at Dresden
Oct. Austrians ally with Russia and Prussia to defeat Napoleon at battle of Leipzig

1814 Sep.–1815 Jun.
Austrian Empire hosts the *Congress of Vienna*. Austria accepts territorial or jurisdictional losses in 'Belgium' and 'Poland' but is compensated by formal acquisition of Lombardy-Venetia in northern 'Italy'. Austria occupies permanent presidency of new German Confederation

1819
Mar. Kotzebue assassinated by German students
Aug. *Karlsbad Decrees* promulgated, suppressing revolutionary activity in German Confederation

1820
Nov. *Protocol of Troppau* authorising joint intervention to protect the monarchical status quo

1821
May Metternich appointed State Chancellor

1832
Jun. Metternich's Six Acts/Articles

1833
Convention of Münchengrätz

1835–1848
Reign of Emperor Ferdinand I

1846
Nov. Austria annexes Cracow

1848
Mar. 'First Rising' in Vienna forces resignation of Metternich. Piedmont invades Lombardy
Apr. Austria granted constitution, including provision for responsible government. Hungary granted separate autonomous status
May Constitution repealed, provoking 'Second Rising' which forces Emperor to flee from Vienna to Innsbruck
Jun. Windischgrätz bombards Prague into submission
Jul. Reichstag of Austria meets in Vienna to draw up constitution based on universal suffrage. Radetzky defeats Piedmontese at Custozza
Aug. Radetzky reoccupies Lombardy. Emperor Ferdinand returns to Vienna

Sep. Abolition of serfdom and 'robot' in Austria. Jellačić of Croatia invades Hungary

Oct. Austria declares war on Hungary. 'Third Rising' in Vienna forces Emperor to flee to Olmuk. Aided by Jellačić, Windischgrätz bombards Vienna into surrender and submission

Nov. New ministry under Schwarzenberg (1848–1852). Reichstag adjourns to Kremsier in Moravia

Dec. Ferdinand I induced to abdicate, replaced by his 18-year-old nephew Franz Josef

1848–1916
Reign of Emperor Franz Josef

1849
Mar. Austrian Reichstag proclaims *Kremsier Constitution*, providing for a decentralised federal state, then dissolves. Piedmont invades again, beaten decisively at *Novara*

Apr. Kossuth declares Habsburgs deposed in Hungary

May Austria appeals to Russia for aid against Hungarians

Aug. Hungarians defeated by Russians at Világos. Austria rejects Prussian scheme for united Germany

1850
Sep. Insurrection in Hesse-Cassel: Austria supports its Elector, Prussia supports insurgents

Nov. Russia supports Austria over Hesse-Cassel, forcing Prussia to concede to Austria by the *Convention of Olmutz.* Customs union between Austria and Hungary introduced

1851
Dec. Austrian constitution abolished and *Sylvester Patent* restores absolutism

1852
With death of Schwarzenberg, Franz Josef assumes personal command of government

1854
Jun. Austria occupies Danubian Principalities (but keeps out of the Crimean War)

1855
Aug. Austrian Concordat gives Roman Catholic hierarchy control of education and censorship

1856
Jul. Hungarian insurgents of 1848–1849 amnestied

1859
Austro-French-Piedmontese War

Jun. Austrians defeated by French-Piedmontese forces at *Magenta* and *Solferino*

Nov. Treaty of Zurich: Austria cedes Lombardy and Parma to Piedmont

1860

Mar. Powers of Austrian Reichsrat enlarged

Oct. *October Diploma* introduces new Austrian constitution

1861

Feb. *February Patent* centralises Austrian Constitution

Aug. Hungarian Diet dissolved. Hungary to be governed by Imperial Commissions

1864

Austrian-Danish War

Jan. Austrian-Prussian ultimatum to Denmark over Schleswig-Holstein

Feb. Austria and Prussia declare war on Denmark

Oct. Peace of Vienna: Denmark cedes Schleswig and Holstein jointly to Austria and Prussia

1865

Aug. Convention of Gastein: Austria claims Holstein (and Prussia claims Schleswig)

1866

Austro-Prussian-Italian (Seven Weeks) War

Jun. Prussia and Italy declare war on Austria. Austrians defeat Italians at Custozza

Jul. Austrians defeated by Prussians at Sadowa/Königgrätz

Aug. Treaty of Prague: Austria excluded from 'Germany' by Prussia

Oct. Treaty of Vienna: Austria excluded from Italy, ceding Venetia

The Dual Monarchy of Austria-Hungary (1867–1914)

1867

Feb. *Ausgleich* agreed, restoring Hungarian Constitution of 1848

Jun. *Ausgleich* creating the *Dual Monarchy of Austria-Hungary* comes into effect

Dec. New constitution for Austria/Cisleithania formally operative

1868

Jews granted civil liberties in Austria

1873

Apr. Franchise reform to favour Germans

1878

Jul. Congress of Berlin: Austrian Empire authorised to occupy Bosnia-Herzegovina and Sanjak of Novi Bazar

1879

Taaffe becomes Premier, signalling shift from pro-German to 'Iron Ring' policy conciliatory to Slav groups

Oct. *Dual Alliance* of Austria-Hungary and Germany

1889

Jan. Mayerling Scandal: suicide of heir-apparent, Crown Prince Rudolf

1893

Oct. Resignation of Taaffe

1895

Sep. Badeni Ministry attempts to pacify Czech agitation

1897

Oct. Austro-Hungarian Socialist Party splits into six national socialist parties

Nov. Badeni resigns over Czech language policy

1898

Sep. Assassination of Empress Elizabeth in Switzerland

1900

Jan. Von Koerber Ministry makes new attempt to resolve Czech question

1902

Dec. *Ausgleich* formally renewed

1904

Moravian Compromise within Austria/Cisleithania

1905–1906

Hungarian Crisis

1907

Jan. Universal suffrage introduced in Austria/Cisleithania. *Bukovina Compromise* within Austria/Cisleithania

1908

Oct. *Bosnian Crisis*: Austria formally annexes Bosnia-Herzegovina (occupied since 1878), returns Sanjak of Novi Bazar to Ottoman Empire

1912

Feb. Berchtold becomes Foreign Minister (1912–1915)

Jun. Army Bill passed

1913

Oct. New Army Bill passed. Austria-Hungary sends Serbia ultimatum over Albania

1914

Jan. *Polish Compromise* within Austria/Cisleithania

28 Jun. Assassination of Archduke Franz Ferdinand, heir to throne of Austria-Hungary, in Sarajevo

The First World War and the Fall of Austria-Hungary (1914–1919)

1914
23 Jul. Austrian ultimatum to Serbia
28 Jul. Austria-Hungary declares war on Serbia
5 Aug. Austria-Hungary declares war on Russia
10 Aug. France declares war on Austria-Hungary
12 Aug. Britain declares war on Austria-Hungary
Sep. Austro-Hungarian southern offensive against Serbia
Dec. Austrian forces capture Belgrade, then withdraw

1915
Jan. Burian (1915–1916) replaces Berchtold as Foreign Minister
May Italy declares war on Austria-Hungary
Jun. Joint Austrian-German offensive on eastern front captures Lemberg, eastern Galicia and Volhynia from Russia
Oct. Austrian-German-Bulgarian offensive on southern front
Nov. Serbs decisively beaten at Kosovo

1916
Jan.–Feb. On southern front, Austrians occupy all Serbia and northern Albania
Mar.–Sep. On eastern front, Austrians beaten back by Russian counter-offensive ordered by Brusilov
May–Jun. On south-western front, Austrian offensive against Italy unsuccessful
Jul. Czernin (1916–1918) succeeds Burian as Foreign Minister
Aug. Rumania declares war on Austria-Hungary
Nov. *Death of Franz Josef* (Emperor 1848–1916); succeeded by grand-nephew Karl (Charles)
Dec. Successful joint Austrian-German-Bulgarian offensive into Rumania

1916–1918
Reign of Emperor Charles/Karl

1917
Jan. Austrian-German-Bulgarian occupation of Rumania
Mar. Sixtus Affair: Emperor Karl initiates overtures for a separate peace with Allies through Prince Sixtus
Jul. Austrians retreat before Russian offensive, losing Tarnopol
Aug. Austrians lose Czernowitz to Russian advance
Oct. Austrian success on south-western front: rout of Italians at Caporetto
Dec. U.S.A. declares war on Austria-Hungary

1918

Jan. Strikes in Vienna

Mar. *Treaty of Brest-Litovsk*: Austria-Hungary and Germany make massive territorial gains in eastern Europe through separate peace with Bolshevik Russia

Sep. Austria-Hungary sues for peace, refused by Allies

Oct. Austria-Hungary offers Allies separate peace. Austrians defeated by Italians at Vittorio Veneto and expelled by Allied forces from Serbia and Albania. Imperial manifesto offers a federal 'Austria'. Revolution in Vienna

Nov. Austria-Hungary signs Armistice of Padua with Allies. Karl renounces his executive powers as Emperor of Austria-Hungary. Austria proclaims territorial union with Germany

1919

Apr. Habsburg dynasty formally exiled from Austria

Sep. *Treaty of St Germain* between Austria and Allies: Austria cedes South Tyrol and Julian March to Italy; Slovenia, Bosnia-Herzegovina and Dalmatia to new Kingdom of Serbs, Croats and Slovenes; Bohemia and Moravia to new Czecho-Slovakia; Galicia to new Poland; and Bukovina to Rumania. With the recognition of Hungary as an independent state, the Dual Monarchy of Austria-Hungary ceases to exist

4. The Azerbaidzhanis/Azeris

1828

Feb. Treaty of Turkmenchai: Russia acquires part of Azerbaidzhan from Persia

1914+

In First World War, Azerbaidzhan finds itself on the Caucasian front between the Russian and Ottoman Empires

1917

Mar. On fall of tsarism, Azerbaidzhan joins the Transcaucasian Federative Republic (with Georgia and Armenia)

May Azerbaidzhan occupied by Turks

1918

May Azerbaidzhan (with Armenia and Georgia) declares itself independent

Oct. Turks occupy Baku

1919

Dec. Britain quits Transcaucasus, withdraws from Azerbaidzhan

1920

May Ex-Russian Azerbaidzhan forcibly reincorporated into Bolshevik Russia by the Red Army

5. The Basques

Pre-1830
Distinctive language, culture and privileges of the Basques generally respected by Madrid and 'Castilians'

1839
Cortes in Madrid starts to abrogate traditional privileges (*fueros*) of Basque 'exempted provinces' as punishment for support of Carlist claimant in (First) Carlist War (1834–1839)

1876
After the Second Carlist War (1872–1876), most of the remaining Basque *fueros* are revoked, leaving only a degree of economic autonomy (*Concierto Economico*) surviving

1880+
Industrial development of Bilbao region fosters local Basque cultural *renaixenca* and political nationalism

1894
Basque Nationalist Party (*Partido Nacionalists Vasco* or P.N.V.) founded by Sabino de Arana y Goiri to promote separate Basque state of Euzkadi, campaigning for 'God and the Old Laws'

1898
Goiri, founder of Basque *renaixenca*, elected to provincial assembly of Vizcaya

1900+
Only modest growth in Basque movement, although Basque provinces retain unique fiscal structure and a greater degree of autonomy than anywhere else in Spain

1918
For the first time, Basque Nationalist Party puts up candidates for general election to the Cortes, securing seven of the 20 seats for the Basque provinces (five from the 'Basque heartland' of Vizcaya)

6. The Belgians

1789
Oct.   Insurrection in Austrian Netherlands
Dec.   Austrian Netherlands declare independence as 'Belgium'

1790
Dec.   Austrians re-occupy Brussels, suppress Belgian revolution

1792
Nov.   French defeat Austrians at Jemappes, occupying Belgium

1793
Mar. Austrians defeat French at Neerwinden, re-occupy Belgium

1794
Jun. Austrians defeated at Fleurus, losing Belgium back to France

1797
Oct. Peace of Campo Formio: Austria formally cedes Belgium to 'Greater France'

1797–1814
Belgium incorporated as a province of 'Greater France'

1814
May (First) Treaty of Paris: France surrenders Belgium, which is to be united with Holland under the House of Orange as a new independent state

1815
Jun. Congress of Vienna establishes the *United Kingdom of the Netherlands*, which includes 'Belgium' as its southern province, under the sovereignty of the House of Orange

1830
Aug. Belgians rebel against union with Holland
Nov. National Congress proclaims the independence of Belgium. Belgium votes for a monarchy but vetoes the House of Orange
Dec. *Belgian independence* accepted by Great Powers at Conference of London

1831
Jan. Powers' protocol for the separation of Belgium is accepted by the Belgians but rejected by the Dutch
Jun. Louis Philippe of France rejects election of Duc de Nemours as King of Belgium to placate Britain. Leopold of Saxe-Coburg becomes King Leopold I of Belgium, ruling with a liberal constitution (1831–1865). The '18 Articles' proposed by the Conference of London are rejected by the Dutch
Aug. The Dutch invade Belgium but retreat when confronted by the French army
Oct. The revised '21 Articles' of the Conference of London are again rejected by the Dutch
Nov. Great Powers agree a treaty incorporating 24 articles

1832
Nov.–Dec. Capture of Antwerp by French army forces the Dutch to recognise the independence of Belgium

1833
May Belgium and Holland conclude an indefinite armistice

The Kingdom of Belgium (1839–1920)

1839
Apr. Treaty of London effects a final and formal agreement on the dissolution of the 1815 United Kingdom of the Netherlands: Belgium becomes an independent and neutral state, under the collective Great Power guarantee of Britain, France, Prussia, Austria and Russia

1861
Nederduitche Bond to cultivate the Flemish language founded by E. Coremans

1865–1909
Reign of Leopold II

1870
First publication of popular Flemish newspaper *Volksblad* in Ghent

1873
Dec. Flemish language admitted for courts in Belgian Flanders

1878
Flemish made the official language in Flanders

1879
Jun. Secular education introduced in Belgium

1880
Jun. Papal nuncio expelled from Belgium

1883
Secondary schools in Flanders become bilingual

1887
Le Soir founded in Brussels

1893
Reform of the suffrage

1909–1934
Reign of King Albert I

1913
Mar. Army bill

1914
2 Aug. German ultimatum to Belgium demanding free passage and transit for German troops attacking France
4 Aug. Belgium declares war as the German army invades. Britain declares war on Germany in defence of Belgium and the 1839 Treaty of London (notoriously dismissed by Kaiser William II as 'a scrap of paper')

1914 Sep.–1918 Nov.
All but the extreme north-west of Belgium occupied by German army,

administered as part of 'Greater Germany' by governor- general Von der Goltz

1919
Jun. *Treaty of Versailles* formally restores independence and pre-war territorial jurisdiction to Belgium

1920
Sep. Eupen and Malmédy transferred from Germany to Belgium by the Council of the League of Nations

7. The Belorussians

1831
Term 'Belorussia' or 'Belarus' changed to 'West Russia' in official tsarist jargon (in an attempt to inhibit Belorussians following the example of the neighbouring Poles in rebelling against the Russian Empire)

1839
Belorussian language prohibited as a Polish dialect. Uniate Church forcibly incorporated into Orthodox Church

1906
Ban on the Belorussian language (temporarily) lifted

1917
After the fall of tsarism, a political nationalist movement in Belorussia appears for the first time

1918
Mar. Nationalists take advantage of the Treaty of Brest-Litovsk to proclaim an independent Belorussia, tolerated by the German occupying forces

1919
Most of Belorussia forcibly reincorporated into Bolshevik Russia

1921
Mar. Treaty of Riga partitions Belorussia between Lithuania (with 5 per cent of Belorussians), Poland (with 20 per cent of Belorussians) and Bolshevik Russia (with 75 per cent of Belorussians)

8. The Bretons

1793–1795
Royalist risings in the Vendée, encouraged by Britain

1800
Jan. Peace of Montluçon pacifies the Vendée

1898
Aug. Union Regionaliste Bretonne founded

1911
Bleun-Brug (Heather Flower), Breton cultural organisation, founded

1914–1918
Brittany loses 250,000 dead in First World War, one in 14 of the Breton population

1916
Irish Easter Rising inspires Breton nationalists

1920
Foundation of review *Breiz Atao* (Brittany For Ever) and Union of Breton Youth

9. The Bulgarians

1393–1878
Bulgarians under Ottoman rule

1832–1844 Ottoman Empire introduces agrarian reforms, permitting Bulgarians to lease or own land

1835
First Bulgarian school founded at Gabrora

1850+
Bulgarian literary revival

1856
Ottoman Empire promises church reform and recognition of the Bulgarian language in churches and schools

1860
Bulgarian bishops refuse to recognise the authority of the Greek Patriarchate in Constantinople, instead press for autocephalous Bulgarian Church

1866
George Rakovski founds Bulgarian Revolutionary Committee

1870
Ottoman Empire promises to permit a free and national Bulgarian church

1872
Ottoman authority permits establishment of the Bulgarian Exarchate (which encourages nationalist aspirations)

1873
Vasili Levsky (the 'Apostle of Freedom') captured and hanged by Ottomans in Sofia, giving Bulgaria its most famous martyr

1875+
Increase in nationalist agitation and risings

1876
Mar. Bulgarian Atrocities: nationalist risings are suppressed by Ottoman irregular troops, with loss of life estimated at 15,000 Christian Bulgarian men, women and children
Apr. Protests from Great Powers. New Sultan Abdul Hamid promises reforms in Balkans
Aug. William Gladstone takes up cause of oppressed Bulgarians, becoming the 'Bulgarian Champion' in the West
Sep. In his best-selling pamphlet 'The Bulgarian Horrors and the Question of the East', Gladstone demands that the Turks be expelled 'bag and baggage from the province they have desolated and profaned'

1877–1878
Russian-Ottoman War

1878
Mar. Treaty of San Stefano: Russian-sponsored settlement establishing an autonomous principality of 'Big Bulgaria', justified in territorial scope by the medieval Bulgarian Empire, stretching from the Black Sea to the Aegean
Jul. Congress of Berlin: international Great Power settlement contradicting San Stefano and vetoing 'Big Bulgaria', establishing instead a smaller autonomous principality of Bulgaria together with a southern province of Eastern Rumelia still under Ottoman authority

1879
Apr. Prince Alexander of Battenberg elected Prince Alexander I of Bulgaria (rules 1879–1886)

1885
Sep. Nationalist disturbances in eastern Rumelia. Bulgaria (headed by Stambulov) unilaterally defies Great Power settlement of Berlin and occupies eastern Rumelia
Nov. Serbia demands compensation from Bulgaria, declares war and is beaten at the battle of Slivnitza (immortalised in George Bernard Shaw's play *Arms and the Man*)

1886
Mar. Treaty of Bucharest formally ends Bulgarian-Serbian War:

occupation of eastern Rumelia by Bulgaria accepted and Bulgaria recognised as autonomous united principality

Sep.   Prince Alexander I abdicates, Stambulov becomes Regent

1887

Jul.   Ferdinand of Saxe-Coburg ('Foxy Ferdinand') becomes Prince of Bulgaria (1887–1911)

1895

Jul.   Assassination of Stambulov

1896

Mar.   Ferdinand recognised as Prince of Bulgaria by Great Powers

1907

Mar.   Petkov, prime minister of Bulgaria, assassinated

1908

Sep.   Young Turk pressure forces Ottoman Empire formally to recognise Bulgaria as independent

Oct.   Bulgaria formally annexes eastern Rumelia (occupied since 1885)

1911

Bulgaria officially promoted from an autonomous principality to an independent kingdom: Prince Ferdinand becomes Tsar of Bulgaria (1911–1918)

1912

Feb.–Jun.   Bulgaria joins Balkan League against Ottoman Empire

1912 Oct.–1913 May

First Balkan War: Bulgaria suffers more casualties than its Balkan League allies in fighting the Ottoman Empire

1913

May   *Treaty of London* ends First Balkan War: Bulgaria gains territory in Thrace and Macedonia at the expense of the Ottoman Empire

Jun.–Aug.   *Second Balkan War*: Bulgarian demands for extra territory provoke anti-Bulgarian alliance of Serbia, Montenegro, Greece, Rumania and Ottoman Empire

Aug.   *Treaty of Bucharest* ends Second Balkan War: Bulgarian gains from the First Balkan War are confiscated and partitioned between Serbia and Greece, and Bulgaria is forced to cede southern Dobrudja to Rumania

1914–1915

Bulgaria neutral for the first year of the First World War

1915

Sep.   Bulgaria joins the Central Powers in the First World War

Oct.   Allies (including Serbia) declare war on Bulgaria

1916
Sep. Joint Bulgarian-Austrian-German offensive against Rumania
Dec. Bulgaria seizes (back) southern Dobrudja from Rumania

1917
Bulgaria negotiates unsuccessfully for a separate peace with the Allies

1918
Sep. Bulgaria defeated by Allies on the Salonika front and capitulates
Oct. Ferdinand abdicates, succeeded by Boris (Tsar 1918–1943)

1919
Nov. Treaty of Neuilly between Bulgaria and Allies: all wartime gains at the expense of Serbia, Rumania (southern Dobrudja) and Greece (western Thrace) are forfeit; Bulgaria becomes liable for reparations and has its armed forces limited to 20,000 troops

1920
Aug. Provisions of Treaty of Neuilly come into effect

10. The Catalans

1827
Guerra des malcontents in western Catalonia/Catalunya: revolt of the *Agraviados*

1830+
Literary and folklore revival employing the Catalan language

1839+
Spanish government responds to Carlist Wars (1834–39 and 1872–76) by abrogating traditional Catalan privileges in the pursuit of greater centralisation

1880+
Catalan literary and linguistic *renaixanca* centred on Barcelona (with architect Antoni Gaudi as its most famous exponent)

1882
First public manifestations of Catalan nationalism

1892
'Bases of Manresa' published, the first programme of Catalan demands for autonomy

1898
El Desastre, the loss of Cuba and Philippines by the Spanish Empire, loses Catalonia its principal export market, prompting industrial crisis in Barcelona

1901
Catalan autonomist movement led by De La Riba forms *Lliga Regionalista*, which wins the four seats for Barcelona in the 1901 general election to the Cortes

1907
In 1907 general election, 'Catalan Solidarity' (fighting on a platform of 'home rule' not independence) wins 41 of the total 44 seats for Catalonia in the Cortes

1909
Jul. Semana Tragica, a 'Tragic Week' of anarchist-cum-socialist violence in Barcelona, harshly suppressed

1913
Formation of Catalan *Mancomunitat*: the four existing administrative units of 'Catalonia' are united, lending a new sense of Catalan territorial solidarity

1917
Aug. General strike demanding independence for Catalonia/ Catalunya

11. The Croats

Pre-1805
Croatia approximates the 'Military Frontier', the classic border-province of the Habsburg Empire, with the Croatian warrior-nobility defending Vienna against incursions by the Ottoman Empire

1805–1813
Illyrian Republic established by Napoleon at the Peace of Pressburg, exposing much of the Habsburg territory of Croatia to modern Western institutions and ideas

1820+
Stimulated by the Napoleonic experience, an *Illyrian Movement* headed by Ljudevit Gaj and then Josip Strossmayer sows the cultural and linguistic ground for future political union of the South Slavs

1847
Croat *Sabor* (or Assembly) unanimously rejects the substitution of Magyar for Latin in Croatia, condemning Magyar linguistic imperialism and demanding Croatian as the official language of the 'Historic Nation' of Croatia

1848
Apr. Kossuth's speeches on Magyar supremacy within the newly-granted separate Hungary alarm the Croats. Croatian *Sabor* at

Agram/Zagreb demands autonomy, and elects Josip Jelačić as *Ban* (Governor)

Jun. Austria supplies aid to Croatia for future employment against Hungary

Sep. Jelačić, Ban of Croatia, invades Hungary

Oct. Jelačić driven out of Hungary but helps Windischgrätz subdue Vienna

1849

Jelačić participates in military defeat of Hungary

Jul. Hungarian Diet promises equality of treatment to non-Magyars in Hungary but fails to convince the Croats

1851

Sylvester Patent rewards Croatian loyalty by confirming Croatia's privileged territorial separateness from Hungary

1867

Feb. To undisguised Croatian dismay, the *Ausgleich* allocates Croatia to Hungary/Transleithania

1868

Nationalities Law promises fair treatment of non-Magyars within Hungary/Transleithania. *Nagodba* between Hungary and Croatia promises devolved equivalent of *Ausgleich*, favouring Croats as junior partner within Hungary

1873

Nov. Croatia granted self-government within Kingdom of Hungary

1878

Jun. Congress of Berlin authorises Habsburg occupation of Bosnia-Herzegovina, which Croatians view as a natural (and historic) adjunct to 'Greater Croatia'

1880+

Emigration from Croatia to U.S.A. rises dramatically

1883

Croatian *Sabor* lays claim to Bosnia so stridently that Hungary suspends the *Nagodba* of 1868

1883+

Croatia subjected to 'direct rule' of Hungary, in the person of the 'Iron Ban', Count Khuen-Hedérváry (who allies with the Serb minority in Croatia to offset the Croatian majority)

1904

Croatian People's Party presses for federalisation of Austria-Hungary

1905

Rijeka/Fiume Resolution: calls for union of Dalmatia and Croatia. *Zara*

Resolution: 26 Serbian deputies declare that 'Croats and Serbs are one nation by blood and language'

1908–1909

Trial in Zagreb of Croats accused of treason to Austria-Hungary: defending counsel Tomaš Masaryk produces evidence of forgery by Habsburg Foreign Ministry to discredit leaders of South Slav movement

1911

Emigration controls increased to prevent Croatian exodus

1914–1918

Croatian troops are employed on all Austrian fronts against the Allies but Croatia itself does not become a war zone

1917

Jul.   Corfu Declaration: a political blueprint for a South Slav state after the war. Signed by the Serbian Prime Minister Pašić and the leader of the emigré Habsburg South Slavs Trumbić in Corfu (the refuge since late 1915 of the Serbian government-in-exile), the declaration projects a new South Slav kingdom with a democratic constitution and local autonomy under the Serbian Karageorgević dynasty

1918

Oct.   Croatian Diet declares independence of Croatia
Dec.   With the collapse of Austria-Hungary, a Kingdom of the Serbs, Croats and Slovenes is proclaimed

1920

Jun.   Treaty of Trianon between Hungary and the Allies: Hungary officially cedes Croatia to the new Kingdom of the Serbs, Croats and Slovenes

12. The Czechs

1784

Establishment of Royal Bohemian Society of Sciences

1818

Bohemian National Museum founded

1834

Matica Česka cultural society founded

1836

First volume of Palacký's *History of Bohemia* published

1848

Mar. Prague Spring of 1848: Czech and German reformers meet in the 'Assembly of St Wenceslas' to demand autonomy from Vienna on the basis of the historic crownland of Bohemia

Apr. Concessions from Vienna in the 'Bohemian Charter'
May Palacký refuses to attend the Frankfurt Parliament, declaring his support for the Habsburg Empire and faith in 'Austro-Slavism'. Meeting of *Slav Congress* in Prague
Jun. Czech Rising crushed by Windischgrätz's bombardment of Prague

1861
Palacký heads boycott of Imperial Diet after 'February Patent' promulgated

1867
Feb. The *Ausgleich* allocates the Czech lands of Bohemia and Moravia to Cisleithania/Austria

1879–1893
Taaffe Ministry, signalling shift towards more pro-Slav policy

1879
Czechs end boycott of *Reichsrat*

1880
Czech and German languages made equal in administrations of Bohemia and Moravia

1882
University of Prague divided into separate Czech and German sections

1883
Czechs win victories in Bohemian Diet

1890
Establishment in Prague of Czech Academy of Arts and Sciences

1891
Anti-Habsburg riots in Bohemia fomented by Pan-Slavist *Omladina*

1895
Sep. Badeni Ministry attempts to pacify Czech opposition

1897
Apr. Czech language granted equality with German in Bohemia
Nov. Badeni resigns over Czech language issue

1899
Oct. Bohemian language ordinances repealed

1900–1904
Koerber Ministry makes fresh attempt to solve Czech question

1904
Moravian Compromise within Austria/Cisleithania

1906
Publication of Popovici's *The United States of Great Austria* highlights

Czech hopes for a tri-partite monarchy or federation championed by the heir-apparent Archduke Franz Ferdinand

1907
Jan. Universal suffrage introduced in Austria/Cisleithania

1908
Jul. Pan-Slav Congress in Prague
Dec. Revolt in Bohemia

1913
Jul. Constitution of Bohemia suspended

1914–1918
Czech troops are employed by the Habsburgs on all fronts but Bohemia and Moravia never become a war zone

1917
Czech Legion formed by Masaryk from Czech prisoners-of-war in Russia to fight for the Allies on the eastern front

1918
May Pittsburgh Agreement between Masaryk and the leaders of the largest Slovak emigré community in U.S.A., enlisting Slovak support by guaranteeing Slovakia's autonomy within a future Czecho-Slovak state. Lansing Declaration affirming official U.S. sympathy for plans for 'Czecho-Slovakia'
Jun. 'Czecho-Slovakia' recognised by Allies as an Allied power
Oct. New independent state of Czecho-Slovakia proclaimed in Prague
Nov. Masaryk elected President of Czecho-Slovakia

1919
Sep. *Treaty of St Germain* between Austria and the Allies: Bohemia and Moravia are formally (and retrospectively) ceded to the new state of Czecho-Slovakia

1920
Feb. Constitution of Czecho-Slovakia promulgated
Jul. Treaty of St Germain comes into operation

13. The Danes

1788
Denmark invades Sweden but is defeated
Nov. Denmark agrees to withdraw from Sweden by Treaty of Uddevalla

1800
Dec. Denmark joins Sweden and Russia in the Armed Neutrality of the North, a French-inspired anti-British shipping alliance

1801
Denmark occupies Hamburg and Lübeck

1807
Sep.   British bombard Copenhagen and capture Danish fleet
Oct.   Denmark allies with France

1808–1839
Reign of Frederick VI (King of Denmark and Norway, 1808–1814; King of Denmark alone, 1814–1839)

1814
Jan.   Treaty of Kiel: *Denmark cedes Norway to Sweden,* receiving Pomerania from Sweden in compensation

1815
Jun.   Congress of Vienna rewards pro-Allied Sweden by ceding Norway from Denmark to Sweden, but punishes pro-French Denmark by ceding only the small Duchy of Lauenburg to Denmark in compensation

1830
Founding of German *Kieler Korrespondent-Blatt*

1839
Founding of Danish *Dannewirke*

1839–1848
Reign of Christian VIII

1844
Nov.   Estates of Holstein declare independence of the Duchies of Schleswig/Slesvig and Holstein

1846
Jul.   King Christian VIII of Denmark repudiates the independence of Schleswig-Holstein in an 'Open Letter'

1848–1863
Reign of Frederick VII

1848
Mar.   Denmark incorporates Schleswig-Holstein into Danish state. German inhabitants of Holstein organise resistance. *(First) Danish-Prussian War (1848–1850)*
May   Prussia invades Denmark over Schleswig-Holstein issue
Aug.   Denmark and Prussia make temporary peace by Treaty of Malmö

1849
Apr.   Danish-Prussian hostilities resumed
Jun.   Denmark becomes a constitutional monarchy by new liberal constitution

1850
Jul. Under Russian pressure, Denmark and Prussia sign the Peace of Berlin, favouring Denmark: Prussia withdraws. Insurgents in Schleswig-Holstein defeated by Danes at Idstedt

1852
May Territorial integrity of Denmark guaranteed by the Great Powers (including Prussia) by the Treaty of London

1859
Mar. Denmark abolishes the constitution of Holstein

1863
Mar. Schleswig incorporated into Denmark
Oct. German Diet votes for action against Denmark
Nov. Danish Council of State approves a new constitution for Schleswig, which becomes a province of Denmark
Dec. Hanoverian and Saxon forces invade Holstein

1863–1906
Reign of Christian IX

1864
Jan. Austrian-Prussian alliance against Denmark to decide future of Schleswig-Holstein. *(Second) Danish-Prussian War (1864)*
Feb. Joint Austrian-Prussian invasion of Holstein
Apr. Danish forces defeated at Duppel
Jun. Conference in London fails to arbitrate successfully
Jul. Most of Schleswig-Holstein occupied and Danish army defeated
Oct. Peace of Vienna: *Denmark cedes Schleswig and Holstein,* and sells Lauenburg, jointly to Austria and Prussia

1865
Aug. Convention of Gastein: Austria to annexe Holstein, Prussia to annexe Schleswig and Kiel and purchase Lauenburg

1866
Jan. Austrian-Prussian friction over Schleswig and Holstein
Jun. Austrian-Prussian (Seven Weeks) War: Prussia invades Holstein
Aug. Treaty of Prague: Prussia annexes both Schleswig and Holstein
Nov. Danish constitution changed to favour powers of the King and Upper House of Parliament

1872–1894
Ongoing constitutional dispute

1874
Denmark grants limited home rule to Iceland

1906–1912
Reign of Frederick VIII

1912–1947
Reign of Christian X

1914–1918
Denmark neutral in First World War

1920
Feb. Plebiscite in 'first zone' of Schleswig: 74 per cent support transfer
to Denmark
Mar. Plebiscite in 'second zone' of Schleswig: 80 per cent support
existing union with Germany
Jun. Denmark recovers northern Schleswig/Slesvig from Germany

14. The Dutch

1751–1795
Reign of William V of Orange-Nassau, Hereditary Stadtholder of the
United Provinces

1786
Dutch 'Patriot' Party restricts powers of William V

1787
Prussian army defeats the 'Patriots' and restores William V with full
powers as Stadtholder

1788
United Provinces, Britain and Prussia form Triple Alliance to maintain
peace in Europe

1794
Apr. Treaty of the Hague between United Provinces (Holland), Britain
and Prussia
Oct. France invades Holland

1795
Jan. French occupy Amsterdam
May Treaty of Basle: the southern area of United Provinces is annexed
directly into 'Greater France', the northern area is licensed as the
'Batavian Republic', a French client-state which abolishes the Dutch
Stadtholdership

1798
Jan. Directory in France establishes government in Holland

1799
Aug. British land in Holland, seizing Dutch fleet
Oct. British evacuate Holland after Convention of Alkmaar

1801
Sep. A new constitution converts the Batavian Republic into even more of a French puppet-state

1806
Jun. Louis Bonaparte becomes King of Holland

1810
Mar. Louis Bonaparte cedes part of Holland to 'Greater France'
Jul. Louis Bonaparte abdicates. Napoleon annexes Holland into 'Greater France'

1813
Nov. Dutch rebellion against France. Return of William of Orange

1813–1840
Reign of William I

1814
May First Treaty of Paris: Holland and Belgium to be united under the House of Orange in a new independent state

1815
Jun. Congress of Vienna establishes *United Kingdom of Netherlands*, combining 'Holland', 'Belgium' and 'Luxembourg' (which is transferred to the King of the Netherlands in compensation for the loss of Nassau to Prussia). Sovereignty to reside with the House of Orange, currently in the person of the ex-hereditary Stadtholder William I

1830
Aug. Belgians revolt against union with Holland
Dec. Independence of Belgium accepted by London Conference of Great Powers

1831
Jan. Holland rejects London Protocol
Jun. The '18 Articles' proposed by the London Conference are rejected by Holland
Aug. Dutch army invades Belgium to prevent secession but retreats when confronted by French army
Oct. New '21 Articles' proposed by London Conference again rejected by Holland

1832
Nov.–Dec. Capture of Antwerp by French troops compels Holland to recognise the independence of Belgium

1833
May Holland and Belgium conclude indefinite armistice

1839
Apr. *Treaty of London*: final agreement on the Dutch-Belgian frontier;

independent Belgium guaranteed by the signatory Great Powers; Luxembourg to remain a Grand Duchy, with the Dutch King of Orange as hereditary Grand Duke

1840–1849
Reign of William II

1848
Dutch Reformed Church disestablished

1849–1890
Reign of William III

1890
Aug. Princess Wilhelmina becomes Queen of Netherlands
Nov. Grand Duchy of Luxembourg becomes independent (since its current constitution precludes the accession of a woman, the Dutch Queen Wilhelmina, as Grand Duke)

1914–1918
Holland neutral in the First World War

15. The English

1760–1820
Reign of George III

1783
Sep. Britain recognises the independence of U.S.A. by the Treaty of Versailles

1790
Edmund Burke's *Reflections on the Revolution in France*

1791–1792
Thomas Paine's *The Rights of Man*

1793–1795
War of the First Coalition against France

1798
Aug. British destroy French fleet at the Battle of the Nile.
Thomas Malthus's *Essays on the Principle of Population*

1798–1802
War of the Second Coalition against France

1802
Mar. Treaty of Amiens establishes (short-lived) peace between Britain and France

1803
May War between Britain and France renewed

1804–1807
War of the Third Coalition against France

1805
Oct. British defeat the combined French and Spanish fleets at Trafalgar

1806
Nov. Napoleon orders a 'Continental System' to blockade Britain into submission through the closure of all European ports

1808–1814
Peninsular War: Britain fights France in Portugal and Spain

1809
Jan. Moore and British army defeated at Corunna
Jul. Wellesley and British army defeat the French at Talavera

1812
Jul. British victory over French at Salamanca

1813
Jun. British victory over French at Vittoria

1814
Apr. British victory over French at Toulouse

1814 Sep.–1815 Jun.
Congress of Vienna: United Kingdom represented by Lord Castlereagh (and later Wellington too). Britain retains Malta and Heligoland within Europe (and acquires sundry properties from France, Holland and Spain outside Europe)

1815
Jun. Combined British, Prussian and Dutch victory over Napoleon at Waterloo
Nov. Britain retains protectorate of the Ionian Islands

1820–1830
Reign of George IV (previously Regent, 1811–1820)

1820
Oct.–Dec. Congress of Troppau: Britain publicly opposes Troppau Protocol which authorises joint intervention against liberal or nationalist challenges to existing authority

1821
May Congress of Laibach: on hearing that Austria and Russia are preparing to intervene to 'restore law and order' in 'Italy' and 'Greece', Britain withdraws in protest

1822
Dec. Congress of Verona: on discovering that Austria and Russia are supporting French intervention in Spain, Britain withdraws permanently from the 'Congress System'

1827
Jul. Britain, France and Russia agree to support an independent Greece
Oct. British destroy the Ottoman fleet at Navarino

1828
Repeal of Test and Corporation Acts removes last civil disabilities on Protestant dissenters

1829
Catholic Emancipation Act: Roman Catholics become eligible for most offices of state and no oath of supremacy required to sit as either MP in the House of Commons or member of the House of Lords

1830–1837
Reign of William IV

1830
Dec. Britain agrees to the dissolution of the United Kingdom of the Netherlands and the creation of independent Belgium

1832
Jun. Great Reform Act

1837–1901
Reign of Queen Victoria

1839
Apr. Treaty of London: Britain and other Great Powers guarantee the independence and neutrality of Belgium

1840
Jul. Britain intervenes to protect Ottoman Empire against Mehemet Ali
Sep.–Nov. British fleet bombards Beirut and captures Acre

1850
Jan. Don Pacifico Affair: Palmerston orders British fleet to blockade Piraeus in Greece to demonstrate British protection for its citizens abroad

1854–1856
Crimean War (with total British losses of 22,200)

1854
Mar. Britain and France ally with Ottoman Empire against Russia
Sep. British and French armies invade Crimea

Oct. Battle of Balaclava (the occasion of the glorious—if unnecessary—Charge of the Light Brigade immortalised by Tennyson)
Nov. Battle of Inkerman

1855
Sep. British and French armies capture Sebastopol

1856
Mar. Peace of Paris ends the Crimean War

1867
Aug. Reform Act doubles the British electorate

1876
Sep. William Gladstone champions the cause of Bulgaria, demanding in his pamphlet 'The Bulgarian Horrors and the Question of the East' that the Ottoman Turks be expelled 'bag and baggage from the province they have desolated and profaned'

1878
Jul. Congress of Berlin: Disraeli represents the United Kingdom, acquiring Cyprus from the Ottoman Empire

1890
Jul. Britain cedes Heligoland to Germany in exchange for Zanzibar, interpreted as an indicator of Anglo-German rapprochement

1898–1899
Fashoda Incident: clash of British and French imperial ambitions in Sudan embitters Anglo-French relations

1899–1902
Boer War embarrasses and isolates Britain

1901–1910
Reign of Edward VII

1904
Apr. *Entente Cordiale* between Britain and France
Oct. Dogger Bank Incident: British fishing boats are accidentally fired on by the Russian fleet, provoking outrage in Britain

1905
Aug. Anglo-Japanese Alliance

1906
Feb. Britain launches the first *Dreadnought*

1907
Aug. *Anglo-Russian Entente* over spheres of imperial interest in Persia, Afghanistan and Tibet completes the 'Triple Entente' of Britain, France and Russia

1909
Mar. Navy Act

1910–1936
Reign of George V

1912
Sep. Anglo-French naval convention

The United Kingdom in the First World War (1914–1918)

1914
4 Aug. Britain declares war on Germany
9 Aug. British Expeditionary Force lands in France
12 Aug. Britain declares war on Austria-Hungary
Sep. London Declaration: Britain, France and Russia promise no separate peace with Germany. British and French counter-attack at the First Battle of the Marne saves Paris from the German Schlieffen Plan
Nov. Britain declares war on Ottoman Empire

1915
Feb. Britain declares blockade of Germany
Mar.–Apr. Constantinople Agreements: Britain and France secretly promise Russia the Straits at the end of the war
Apr. Treaty of London: Britain and France secretly promise Italy territorial gains on the Adriatic at the end of the war as a reward for joining the Allies. British landings at Gallipoli
May Coalition Government formed under Asquith
Oct. British landings at Salonika. Nurse Edith Cavell shot as a spy by Germans in Brussels
Nov. British troops defeated by Turks at Ctesiphon in Mesopotamia
Dec. Robertson becomes Chief of Imperial General Staff. Haig succeeds French as British Commander-in-Chief

1916
Jan. Final evacuation of Gallipoli
Feb. Military Service Act
Mar. British surrender to Turks at Kut in Mesopotamia
May Conscription introduced. *Sykes-Picot Note*: Sir Mark Sykes (for Britain) and Georges Picot (for France) secretly agree to partition the Ottoman Empire at the end of the war
May–Jun. Battle of Jutland between British and German fleets
Jul. Lloyd George becomes Secretary for War. British offensive on the Somme
Sep. British use tanks for the first time
Dec. New Coalition Government headed by Prime Minister Lloyd George. War Cabinet established

1917

Apr. British offensive in Artois. *Treaty of St Jean de Maurienne:* Britain and her Allies secretly agree to allow Italy to have a share in the partition of the Ottoman Empire at the end of the war
Sep. British offensive near Ypres
Nov. Balfour Declaration affirms British support for the establishment of a Jewish homeland in Palestine. Supreme Allied War Council created. British take Passchendaele. British offensive at Cambrai breaks Hindenburg Line

1918

Mar.–Apr. German offensive on Western Front
May–Jun. Second German offensive
Jul. Third (and last) German offensive on Western Front.
Jul.+ British advance in Balkans against Austria-Hungary
Jul.–Oct. British advance in Palestine against Ottoman Empire
Aug. British victory at Second Battle of the Marne
Sep. British victory at Fourth Battle of Ypres
Oct. General Allied advance on all fronts
11 Nov. Armistice agreed and comes into effect

1919

Jan.+ Allied Peace Conference in Paris: United Kingdom, as one of the 'Big Four' (subsequently 'Big Three'), is represented by David Lloyd George
Jun. Treaty of Versailles between Germany and the Allies includes the surrender to the Allies of all overseas colonies

16. The Estonians

1721

Treaty of Nystadt: at the end of the Great Northern War, Peter the Great of Russia annexes 'Estonia' from Sweden

Mid 1800s

Tsarist government promotes Estonian national self-consciousness in 'Estland' to offset local dominant German minority

1885

Holy Synod forbids mixed-religion marriages in predominantly Lutheran 'Estonia' unless the children are raised in Orthodox faith. Widespread protest at this 'religious Russification'

1890+

Tsarist government switches tactics, now supporting local Germans against fast-developing Estonian nationalism

1917
'Estonia' occupied by advancing German troops

1918
Mar. Treaty of Brest-Litovsk: Estonia to become independent state (within extended German empire)
Apr. Estonia proclaims its independence
Dec. German withdrawal leads to Bolshevik takeover of Estonia

1920
Feb. (First) Treaty of Tartu: Bolshevik Russia recognises the independence of Estonia/Eesti

17. The Finns

1770
Aurora Society founded to foster the Finnish language

1808
Feb. Russia invades and occupies Finland

1809
Mar. Diet of Borgå/Porvoo: Tsar Alexander I makes a Declaration promising to respect the traditional privileges of Finland, ruling not as Tsar of Russia but as Grand Duke of the Grand Duchy of Finland
Sep. Peace of Fredericksham: Russia formally acquires Finland from Sweden

1820
Arwidsson announces that 'Swedes we are no longer, Russians we cannot be, therefore we must become Finns'

1835
Publication of Finnish epic *Kalevala* by Elias Lönnrot

1899
Feb. Tsar Nicholas II starts to abrogate the privileges of Grand Duchy of Finland, signalling the Russification of Finland and its formal incorporation into the Russian Empire. *Finlandia* by Sibelius published as national anthem of Finland under Russian threat

1901+
Finnish campaign of civil disobedience and passive resistance (not paying taxes, not responding to draft, only speaking Finnish) proves successful in embarrassing and frustrating tsarist government in Finland

1904
Jun. Bobrikov, Russian Governor-General of Finland, assassinated

1905
Nov. November Manifesto forced by the '1905 Revolution', cancelling recent Russification legislation against Finland

1907+
Tsarist government of Stolypin returns to assault on the prerogatives of Grand Duchy of Finland

1908
Jun. Nicholas II reserves the right to distribute the affairs of Finland as he sees fit between the Finnish and Russian governments (in practice always favouring the latter)

1910
Jul. Self-government of Finland abolished in State Duma

1912
Finnish province of Vyborg/Viipuri is detached from the Grand Duchy and incorporated as a province of Russia

1914
Nov. All remaining privileges of Finland except its name abrogated under the plea of imperial security in the First World War

1917
Jul. Finland declares its restored autonomy as a Grand Duchy
Dec. *Finland proclaims its independence*

1918
Jan. 'Reds' take control in Finnish capital Helsinki, leading to civil war between Bolshevik-backed left-wing forces and the 'Whites' under Mannerheim
Mar. Treaty between Finland and Germany
Apr. Germans invade Finland, occupy Helsinki
Oct. Germans evacuate Finland at end of First World War

1920
Oct. *(Second) Treaty of Tartu*: Bolshevik Russia recognises the independence of Finland (again)

18. The French

1789
Jun. States-General declares itself the French National Assembly, and refuses to disperse until a constitution is established
Jul. Fall of the Bastille
Aug. *Declaration of the Rights of Man and Citizens* includes the maxim that 'the principle of all sovereignty resides essentially in the nation'. Publication of 'What is the Third Estate?' by Abbe Sièyes

1790

Apr.   National Assembly passes decree of religious toleration
May   Wars of conquest renounced by National Assembly

1791

Sep.   New French constitution. National Assembly becomes Constituent Assembly

1792

Apr.   La Marseillaise composed by Rouget de l'Isle
Sep.   France defeats Prussia at Valmy. Annexation of Nice and Savoy into 'Greater France'. Monarchy abolished and French Republic proclaimed

The First French Republic (1792–1795)

1792

Nov.   France defeats Austria at Jemappes

1793

Jan.   Execution of Louis XVI
Mar.   French defeated at Neerwinden
Jun.   Start of the 'Terror'
Jun.–Dec.   Revolt in La Vendée

1794

Apr.   Execution of Danton
Jun.   French defeat Austrians at Fleurus, take Belgium
Jul.   Execution of Robespierre
Dec.   French invade Holland

1795

Apr.   Peace of Basle: Prussia concedes Rhine frontier to France
Jun.–Oct.   Risings in Brittany, encouraged by Britain
Aug.   Third French Constitution (includes freedom of worship)

The French Directory (1795–1799)

1795

Nov.   Convention replaced by the Directory (of five Directors)

1796

May   Peace of Cherasco: France gains Nice and Savoy formally from Piedmont-Sardinia. Napoleon defeats Austrians at Lodi in northern Italy
Nov.   Napoleon defeats Austrians again at Arcola

1797

Jan.   Third defeat of Austrians by Napoleon in Italy at Rivoli
Oct.   *Peace of Campo Formio*: France receives Lombardy and Belgium in political land-deal with Austria

1798

Mar.   France annexes left bank of Rhine
May-1799 September   Napoleon in Egypt
Oct.   French attempt to invade Ireland fails

1799

Mar.   French defeated by Austrians at Stockach
Sep.   Napoleon returns from Egypt to France
Nov.   Napoleon overthrows the Directory, becomes First Consul

The French Consulate (1799–1804)

1800

Feb.   Centralisation of administration of France initiated
Jun.   Napoleon inflicts stunning defeat on Austrians at Marengo

1801

Feb.   Treaty of Lunéville: 'Greater France' is again conceded left bank of Rhine
Jul.   Concordat with Pope Pius VII

1802

Jan.   Napoleon becomes President of the Italian Republic
Mar.   Peace of Amiens between France and Britain
Aug.   Napoleon becomes Consul for life

1803

May   France again at war with Britain

1804

Mar.   Promulgation of civil *Code Napoléon*
May   Napoleon becomes Emperor

The (First) French Empire (1804–1814 and 1815)

1804

Dec.   Napoleon crowns himself *Emperor of the French*

1805

May   Napoleon becomes *King of Italy*
Oct.   French and Spanish fleets beaten by British at Trafalgar
Dec.   Napoleon defeats Austrians and Russians at Austerlitz. Peace of Pressburg

1806

Jul.   Napoleon establishes *Confederation of the Rhine*
Oct.   Prussia defeated at Jena
Nov.   Berlin Decree establishes the 'Continental System' designed to blockade Britain into submission

1807
Jul.   *Treaty of Tilsit:* France and Russia divide Europe

1808
Jan.   Napoleon annexes Etruria
Apr.   Napoleon annexes Papal Legations

1809
May   Napoleon annexes Papal States
Jun.   Pius VII excommunicates Napoleon
Jul.   Pius VII imprisoned at Savona. French defeat Austrians at Wagram

1810
Jul.   Holland annexed to 'Greater France'
Nov.   Valais annexed
Dec.   Northern Hanover, Bremen, Hamburg, Lauenberg and Lübeck all annexed

1811
Jan.   Oldenburg annexed

1812
French invasion of Russia ends in disaster
Sep.   French defeat Russians at Borodino, occupy Moscow
Oct.   Start of French retreat from Moscow

1813
May   French victories at Lützen and Bautzen
Jun.   French defeated by British at Vittoria
Oct.   Napoleon defeated by Austria, Prussia and Russia at Leipzig

1814
Mar.   Allies enter Paris
Apr.   Napoleon abdicates and goes into exile on Elba
May   (First) Treaty of Paris: France keeps her borders of 1792

The Restored French Monarchy (1814–1848)

1814–1824
Reign of Louis XVIII

1815
Mar.–Jun.   Napoleon's 'One Hundred Days'
Jun.   Napoleon defeated by British, Dutch and Prussians at Waterloo. Congress of Vienna concludes settlement of post-Napoleonic Europe
Jul.   Allies occupy Paris (again). Return of Louis XVIII (again)
Aug.   Napoleon banished to St Helena
Nov.   *Second Treaty of Paris:* France reduced from her 1792 to her 1789 frontiers

1818

Sep.–Nov. *Congress of Aix-la-Chapelle.* Allied troops withdrawn from France, which is re-admitted (early) to the Great Powers

1820

Feb. Duc de Berry's assassination is made the pretext for introduction of repressive measures against freedom of press and elections

1821

May Death of Napoleon on St Helena

1823

Apr.–Aug. French army, backed by Austria and Russia under Troppau Protocol, invades Spain and restores King Ferdinand VII

1824–1830

Reign of Charles X

1827

Apr. National Guard disbanded
Nov. Elections prompt riots and barricades in Paris

1830

May Dissolution of Chamber of Deputies
Jul. Ordinances of St Cloud provoke street disturbances. Charles X abdicates
Aug. Louis Philippe, Duc d'Orleans, persuaded to accept crown. Constitutional Charter published

1830–1848

Reign of Louis Philippe

1832

Jun. Republican insurrection in Paris suppressed

1836

Oct. Louis Napoleon fails to seize Strasbourg, and is exiled to U.S.A.

1840

Aug. Louis Napoleon again fails to seize power
Dec. Napoleon Bonaparte reburied in Les Invalides in Paris, boosting Napoleonic cult

1847

Reform banquet campaign throughout France

1848

Jan. Guizot bans 71st reform banquet
Feb. Popular demonstrations fired on. Louis Philippe abdicates. Lamartine leads Provisional Government promising liberal reform. Republic proclaimed

The Second French Republic (1848–1852)

1848
Apr. Elections to Constituent Assembly return a moderate republican majority
May National Assembly meets but is invaded by mob. National Guard restores order
Jun. Widespread demonstrations in Paris suppressed by General Cavaignac
Nov. Constitution of Second Republic announced
Dec. Louis Napoleon elected President of French Republic by massive majority

1849
May National Assembly dissolved, one among many measures of repression by government

1850
May Universal suffrage abolished
Sep. Freedom of press curtailed

1851
Jul. Louis Napoleon fails to gain two-thirds majority necessary to change the constitution and extend his presidency
Dec. Coup d'état by Louis Napoleon encounters little resistance. Plebiscite ratifies Louis Napoleon as President for ten years

1852
Jan. New constitution grants President quasi-monarchical powers
Nov. Plebiscite favours imperial constitution
Dec. Louis Napoleon proclaimed Emperor Napoleon III

The Second French Empire (1852–1870)

1854–1856
Crimean War (claiming 93,600 French casualties)

1854
Mar. France allies with Britain and declares war on Russia
Sep. French and British forces land in Crimea
Nov. French and British forces defeat Russians at Inkerman

1855
Sep. French and British occupy Sebastopol. Paris World Exhibition

1856
Feb. *Peace of Paris* concludes Crimean War: Napoleon III hosts conference and attempts to introduce question of Italian unification onto agenda

1858

Jan.   Orsini plot to assassinate Napoleon III fails

Jul.   *Pact of Plombières*: Napoleon III and Count Cavour of Piedmont-Sardinia agree to join forces against Austrian Empire to create 'Upper Italy'

1859

May   France supports Piedmont in war against Austria

Jun.   French/Piedmontese victories at Magenta and Solferino

Jul.   *Peace of Villafranca* ends Franco-Austrian War

Aug.   Amnesty and extension of political rights within France

1860

Mar.   France acquires Nice and Savoy (as price agreed at Plombières for aiding Piedmont against Austria)

1862

Feb.   France acquires Menton and Roquebrune from Monaco

1862–1867

Unsuccessful French promotion of Mexican Empire under Maximilian

1865

Oct.   Napoleon III and Bismarck meet at Biarritz; agree on need for Prussian ascendancy in Germany, and a unified Italy

1866

Jun.–Jul.   France facilitates transfer of Venetia from Austria to Italy following Austro-Prussian-Italian War

1868

Jun.   Freedom of press and assembly granted

1869

Jul.   Parliamentary system adopted

1870

Apr.   New liberal constitution introduced

May   Plebiscite supports new 'liberal empire'

1870–1871

Franco-Prussian War (claiming 580,000 French casualties)

1870

Jul.   Quarrel over Hohenzollern candidacy for throne of Spain. France declares war on Prussia over 'Ems Telegram'

Sep.   French defeated at Sedan, Napoleon III captured. New (Third) Republic proclaimed. Prussian army commences siege of Paris

The Third French Republic (1870–1940/1946)

1870

Oct.   Surrender of French army at Metz

1871
Jan. Franco-Prussian armistice. Paris capitulates
Feb. National Assembly elected, convenes in Bordeaux and elects Thiers as head of executive
Mar. Prussians enter Paris. National Guard takeover. Communes proclaimed in Lyons, Marseilles then Paris
Apr. Civil war between Paris Commune and National Government
May Treaty of Frankfurt formally ends Franco-Prussian War: France to suffer military occupation until payment of 5 million francs reparations, and surrender Alsace-Lorraine to new German Empire. Communards in Paris bombarded and beaten on the barricades
Aug. Thiers elected first President of Third Republic

1872
Jan. Comte de Chambord makes 'Antwerp Declaration', calling for a legitimist 'Revolutionary Monarchy' in France
Nov. Leading Communards executed

1873
Sep. German army evacuates France
Oct. Comte de Chambord refuses to recognize the tricolour as national flag, dashing monarchist hopes for restoration

1875
Jan. Republican constitution formally established

1879
Jan. Amnesty for Communards

1880
Nov. Roman Catholic orders expelled

1887
Oct. Boulanger Coup fails

1889
Jan. Second Boulanger attempt also fails
Apr. Boulanger flees from France, committing suicide in 1891.
Eiffel Tower constructed in Paris by Gustave Eiffel

1891
Aug. Franco-Russian Entente

1892
Aug. Franco-Russian military convention agreed

1893
Mar. Panama Scandal: trial and imprisonment of directors of bankrupt Panama Canal Company prompts rise in anti-Semitism
Jun. Franco-Russian commercial treaty
Dec. Franco-Russian military convention operative

1894–1906
Dreyfus Affair: protracted scandal of official anti-Semitism which polarises French public opinion and society

1898–1899
Fashoda Incident: a clash of rival French and British imperial expansionism in Sudan sours relations between France and Britain

1899
First appearance of *Action Française*

1902
Nov. Franco-Italian Entente: Italy agrees to remain neutral in the event of war between France and Germany

1904
Apr. Entente Cordiale established between France and Britain

1905
Dec. Roman Catholic Church and French State separated

1905 Apr.–1906 Apr.
First Moroccan Crisis

1911
Jul.–Nov. Second Moroccan Crisis

1913
Aug. Army Bill

France and the First World War (1914–1918)

1914
3 Aug. Germany declares war on France
12 Aug. France declares war on Austria-Hungary
Sep. London Declaration: France, Britain and Russia promise no separate peace with Central Powers. First Battle of the Marne saves Paris from German Schlieffen Plan. French and British counter-offensive in Battle of the Aisne withstood by Germans, establishing trench-line
Nov. Ottoman Empire declares war on France

1915
Succession of battles against Germans in Champagne and Artois
Oct. French troops land at Salonika. Briand becomes new Premier
Dec. Joffre appointed French Commander-in-Chief

1916
Feb.+ Battle of Verdun
Jul.+ Battle of the Somme
Dec. Nivelle new French Commander-in-Chief. Castelnau appointed Chief of French General Staff

1917

Apr.+ French offensive on Aisne in Champagne
May First mutinies in French army. Pétain new French Commander-in-Chief
Jun. First American troops arrive in France
Nov. Supreme Allied War Council established. Clemenceau becomes new Premier

1918

Mar. Foch appointed Commander-in-Chief of Allied forces in France
Mar.–Apr. First German offensive captures Rheims
May–Jun. Second German offensive
Jul. Third (and last) German offensive
Jul.–Aug. Second Battle of the Marne halts German offensive
Sep. Germans retreat to Siegfried Line
Oct. General Allied advance
3 Nov. Armistice between Allies and Austria-Hungary
11 Nov. Armistice between Allies and Germany signed at Compiègne

1919

Jan. Start of *Paris Peace Conference.* France one of the 'Big Four' (subsequently 'Big Three'), represented by Georges Clemenceau
Jun. *Treaty of Versailles* between Germany and Allies: France recovers Alsace-Lorraine

19. The Georgians

1783

Heraclius/Irakli II of Georgia recognises switch of sovereignty over Georgia from Ottoman Empire to Russian Empire by treaty of Georgievsk

1801

Sep. Russian Empire formally annexes Georgia

1810

Russia annexes Sukhumi

1864

Russia annexes Abkhazia

1914–1917

In First World War, Georgia finds itself in the war zone of the Caucasian front between the Russian and Ottoman Empires

1917

Mar. On fall of tsarism, Georgia joins Armenia and Azerbaidzhan in the Transcaucasian Federative Republic

Jun. German troops occupy Georgia

1918
May Georgia proclaims its independence, seeking first German and later British recognition and support

1919
Dec. British withdraw from Caucasus area

1920
Georgian independence precariously maintained by Polish support and the distracting Polish-Soviet War

1921
Apr. Georgia forcibly reincorporated into Bolshevik Russia by the Red Army

20. The Germans

1786
Aug. Death of Frederick the Great; succeeded as King of Prussia by Frederick William II (1786–1797)

1787
Prussia intervenes in United Provinces to reinstate Stadtholder

1791
Completion of Brandenburg Gate in Berlin (by Langhans)
Aug. Declaration of Pillnitz: Prussia and Austria are prepared to attack revolutionary France if other Great Powers agree

1792
Jul. Prussia declares war on France
Aug. Prussia and Austria invade France
Sep. Prussians defeated by French at Valmy

1793
Feb. Prussia joins First Coalition against France
May Second Partition of Poland between Prussia and Russia: Prussia gains Danzig, Thorn, Posen, Griesen and Kalisz

1794
Apr. Treaty of the Hague between Prussia, Britain and Holland
Oct. Prussia withdraws from Treaty of the Hague

1795
Oct. Third Partition of Poland between Prussia, Austria and Russia: Prussia gains Warsaw and territory between rivers Bug and Niemen

1796
Aug. Prussia concedes France the left bank of the Rhine

1797–1840

Reign of Frederick William III of Prussia

1803

Feb. Diet of Ratisbon reconstructs 'Germany': most ecclesiastical princedoms and imperial cities abolished; four new Electorates created. Ernst Arndt publishes *Germany and Europe,* championing a 'Big Germany' uniting territory 'as far and as wide as the German tongue is heard'. Schiller publishes *William Tell,* a story of heroic German resistance against alien (specifically Habsburg) oppression

1804

Oct. Stein appointed Prussian Minister of Trade

1805

Dec. Prussia signs Treaty of Schönbrunn with France, acquiring Hanover but ceding Neuchâtel to France and Ansbach to Bavaria. By *Peace of Pressburg,* Austria recognises the southern German states of Bavaria and Württemberg as Kingdoms and Baden as a Grand Duchy; Austria also cedes the Tyrol to Bavaria and its Swabian territories are divided between Baden and Württemberg.

1806

Jul. Confederation of the Rhine established by Napoleon as an anti-Prussian, anti-Austrian client state of western 'Germany', dominated by Bavaria, Württemberg and Baden

Dec. Saxony created a Kingdom, joins Confederation of the Rhine

1807

Jul. Treaty of Tilsit between Prussia and France: after defeat at Jendh, Prussia loses her territories west of river Elbe

Oct. Stein reforms Prussian administration, emancipates Prussian peasantry and introduces conscription

Nov. Town councils instituted in Prussia

1808

Formation of *Tugenbund* to foster the spirit of German resistance to the domination of Napoleon

1810

Founding of Krupp Works at Essen. *Seehandlung* becomes the Bank of Prussia. Foundation of University of Berlin

Dec. Napoleon annexes northern Hanover, Bremen, Hamburg, Lauenberg and Lübeck from Prussia

1811

Jan. Napoleon annexes Oldenburg from Prussia. Hardenberg continues Stein's reforms in Prussia

1812

Feb. Prussia allies with France

Dec. After Napoleon's disastrous Moscow campaign, Prussia switches sides, allying with Russia by the Convention of Tauroggen

1813

Feb. Formal alliance of Kalisz between Prussia and Russia against France

May Prussians and Russians defeated by Napoleon at Lützen and Bautzen

Oct. Joint Prussian-Russian-Austrian armies defeat Napoleon at *Leipzig* ('The Battle of the Nations'). The Confederation of the Rhine evaporates

1815

May Frederick William III of Prussia promises a liberal constitution.

Jun. Prussians under Blücher help in defeat of Napoleon at Waterloo. Congress of Vienna: Prussia (represented by Hardenberg) acquires or re-acquires Posen, Danzig, most of Saxony and Westphalia, Pomerania (from Sweden) and Nassau (from Holland)

The German Confederation (1815–1866)

1815

Jun. Congress of Vienna: *'German Confederation'* of 39 states under permanent Austrian presidency established

Aug. Prussia joins Austria and Russia in Holy Alliance

1816

May Karl-August of Saxe-Weimar grants the first constitution in 'Germany'

Nov. First meeting of the Diet of the German Confederation, in Frankfurt

1817

Oct. *Wartburg Festival* to celebrate 300th anniversary of the Reformation reveals the new militancy of nationalist youth in the *Burschenschaften*

1818

May Constitution granted in Bavaria

Aug. Constitution granted in Baden

1819

Mar. Murder of Kotzebue, a Russian reactionary, by German students

Sep. *Karlsbad Decrees* promulgated by delegates of the states of the German Confederation under the presidency of Metternich: suppression of free press and free association to prevent opposition activity, setting the tone for 'Germany' for the next 30 years

Oct. Prussian trade treaty with Schwarzburg-Sonderhausen lays the foundation for the *Zollverein*

1820
May 'Final Act' of Vienna authorises the larger states of 'Germany' to intervene in the affairs of the smaller states (setting up the rivalry of Prussia and Austria)

1823
Dec. Establishment of provincial diets in Prussia

1826
Start of publication of the *Monumenta Germaniae Historica*, a multi- volume collection of primary sources for medieval German history edited by Baron vom Stein. Each volume carries the same motto: *'Sanctus amor patriae dat animum'* (the holy love of the fatherland inspires us)

1830
Sep. Revolts in Hesse, Brunswick and Saxony dethrone their kings and occasion new liberal constitutions

1831
Jan. Hesse-Cassel granted a constitution
Sep. Saxony granted a constitution

1832
May Hambach Festival demands revolt against Austrian rule

1833
Mar. Establishment of *Zollverein*, with Austria pointedly excluded. Convention of Münchengrätz

1834
Launch of *Young Germany* movement

1835
May Baden joins *Zollverein*

1837
Jun. Constitution granted in Hanover in 1833 is suspended. Struggle between state and Roman Catholic Church in Prussia is forerunner of the *Kulturkampf* of the 1870s

1840–1858/1861
Reign of Frederick William IV of Prussia

1840
French expansionist ambitions provoke the 'Rhine Crisis'

1841
Friedrich List's *National System of Political Economy* published, advocating the economic nationalism of a united Germany

1842
Sep. Consecration (and commitment to completion) of Cologne/Köln Cathedral, attended by Frederick William IV: 'The Rhine is German'

1846
Meeting of German professors at Frankfurt (billed as the 'Intellectual Diet of the German People')

1847
Feb. Frederick William IV of Prussia summons a united Diet

1848
Mar. Uprising in Berlin forces Frederick William IV to grant Prussia a constitution. *Vorparlament* convenes in Frankfurt
May Prussia invades Denmark over Schleswig-Holstein. German National Assembly meets in Frankfurt, and suspends the German Confederation. Prussian National Assembly meets in Berlin
Aug. Prussia and Denmark make peace by the Treaty of Malmö
Dec. Dissolution of Prussian National Assembly. German National Assembly proclaims fundamental rights

1849
Jan. Prussia demands a united Germany excluding Austria
Mar. German National Assembly in Frankfurt passes a constitution, and offers Frederick William IV of Prussia the title of 'Emperor of the Germans'
Apr. Frederick William refuses the crown of Germany
May Prussian forces suppress revolt in Dresden. 'Three Kings' League' of Prussia, Saxony and Hanover formed
Jun. German National Assembly moves from Frankfurt to Stuttgart, where it is forcibly dissolved by troops
Jul. Rebels in Baden surrender to Prussians at Rastatt

1850
Jan. Prussia granted a liberal constitution
Mar. Frederick William IV summons a German Parliament to Erfurt
Apr. Erfurt Parliament opens
May Schwarzenburg revives old Confederation Diet of Frankfurt, inviting all German states to send delegates to discuss revision of the German Confederation to establish a new authority for 'Germany'
Jul. Under pressure from Russia, Prussia and Denmark sign the Peace of Berlin (favouring Denmark)
Sep. Diet of German Confederation convenes, pointedly not attended by Prussia. Rising in Hesse-Cassel: Austria supports the Elector, Prussia supports the insurgents
Nov. *Convention of Olmütz:* a humiliation of Prussia imposed by Austria (and supported by Russia). Prussia agrees to back down over Hesse-Cassel, abandon its 'Erfurt Union' and accept the authority of the German Confederation
Dec. Dresden Conference: Schwarzenberg forced to abandon his plan to include the Habsburg Empire in the Confederation

1851

May Prussia formally rejoins German Confederation

1852–1853

Foundation of Germanic National Museum in Nuremberg

1853

German customs union (*Zollverein*) renewed for another 12 years and joined by Hanover and Oldenburg. Austria only secures a commercial treaty with Prussia (not the Austro- German customs union wanted by Bruck, Austrian Minister for Commerce)

1854

Oct. Prussian Upper House (*Herrenhaus*) established

1855

Jan. Bismarck, Prussian minister at Frankfurt, persuades Diet that German Confederation should keep out of the Crimean War (to Austria's annoyance)

1858–1861

Regency occasioned by insanity of Frederick William IV

1859

Sep. Foundation of German National Association
Dec. Albert von Roon becomes Prussian Minister of War

1860

Feb. Von Roon presents his military reform plan to Prussian *Landtag*

1861–1888

Reign of William I of Prussia

1861

Oct. Saxony proposes tripartite reorganisation of German Confederation
Dec. Prussia rejects 'Saxon proposal': Confederation is unreformable, making necessary the unification of Germany under Prussian leadership

1862

Feb. Austria advances revised version of the 'Saxon proposal', again rejected by Prussia. *Reformverein* is founded, a 'reform union' promoting the unification of Germany under Austrian leadership
Sep. *Bismarck appointed Minister-President of Prussia*
Oct. Prussian Diet rejects proposed increase of military budget. Bismarck delivers his 'Blood and Iron' speech on German unification and governs without a formal budget until 1866
Dec. Bismarck warns Austria of the danger of not recognising Prussia as its equal within Germany

1863

Jan. Austrian proposals for revamped Confederation finally defeated in the Diet after Prussia threatens to walk out

Feb. Polish Uprising: Bismarck enters into alliance with Russia to effect a joint suppression of Polish nationalism

Mar. Denmark incorporates Schleswig

Aug. Bismarck persuades William I not to attend an Austrian-organised meeting of the German princes at Frankfurt to reform the German Confederation

Oct. German Diet votes for action against Denmark

Dec. Hanoverian and Saxon forces invade Holstein

1864

Jan. Prussian-Austrian alliance: joint action against Denmark and joint agreement over the future of Schleswig

Feb. *Prussian-Austrian-Danish War 1864:* Joint Prussian-Austrian invasion of Schleswig

Apr. Danish army defeated at Duppel

Jul. Danish army finally beaten

Oct. *Peace of Vienna:* Denmark cedes Schleswig-Holstein and Lauenberg jointly to Prussia and Austria

Nov. Bismarck persuades the Diet into leaving the Prussian and Austrian forces in sole charge of Schleswig-Holstein

1865

Aug. *Convention of Gastein:* Austria receives Holstein, Prussia receives Schleswig and Kiel (and purchases Lauenberg)

Oct. Bismarck and Napoleon III meet at *Biarritz,* and agree on Prussian ascendancy in Germany and the need for a unified Italy

1866

Jan. Prussian-Austrian friction over Schleswig-Holstein

Feb. Prussian Crown Council agrees to accept Austria's challenge even at the risk of war

Apr. Secret military alliance between Prussia and Italy. Rumours of Italian troop movements induce Austria to mobilise her forces in Venetia. Prussian mobilisation ordered

Jun. Prussian invasion of (Austrian) Holstein. Bismarck announces plans for the dissolution of the German Confederation and the creation of a new German state excluding Austria. Secret treaty between Austria and France. Prussia and Austria break off diplomatic relations. German Diet votes to mobilise against Prussia, and this prompts a Prussian invasion of Saxony, Hanover and Hesse-Cassel. Hanover defeats Prussia at Langensaza, then capitulates. *Prussian-Austrian-Italian (Seven Weeks) War:* Italy declares war on Austria

Jul. Prussian victory over Austrians at *Sadowa*/Königgrätz. Austria seeks mediation of Napoleon III, agreeing to cede Venetia to France, and through France to Italy, in order to free 100,000 Austrian troops for transfer from Italy to the Prussian front. Rapid Prussian advance towards Vienna forces Austria into preliminary peace negotiations at Nikolsburg

Aug. Prussia signs peace treaties with Bavaria, Württemberg and Baden. *Treaty of Prague:* German Confederation dissolved and Austria excluded from Germany; Prussia annexes Schleswig-Holstein, Hanover, Hesse-Cassel, Nassau and Frankfurt; Austria cedes Venetia to Italy and pays reparations of 40,000 thalers

The North German Confederation (1866–1871)

1866

Aug. Treaty of Prague: North German Confederation (dominated by Prussia) replaces German Confederation (dominated by Austria). Secret agreement between Prussia and south German states: reciprocal guarantee of territorial integrity but, in the event of war, all southern states to place their forces under the command of Prussia

Sep. Peace signed between Prussia and Hesse

Oct. Peace signed between Prussia and Saxony

1867

Feb. First Diet of the North German Confederation agrees the constitution of the Confederation (operative from April 1867): the presidency of the Confederation is united with the crown of Prussia, which represents the Confederation in international relations, diplomacy, war and peace. Bismarck becomes Chancellor of the Confederation

May Luxembourg Question: Bismarck prevents Napoleon III acquiring Luxembourg from Holland by agreeing to withdraw his Prussian garrison in exchange for international Great Power guarantee of the neutrality of Luxembourg by the London Conference

Jul. Customs treaties between the North German Confederation and the south German states

1868

Mar. Prussia confiscates the property of the King of Hanover

1870

Jul. Hohenzollern candidacy for the Spanish throne increases Prussian-French tensions. 'Ems Telegram' incident inflames French public opinion against Prussia. War fever in France prompts French declaration of war. *Franco-Prussian War 1870–1871.* Confederation *Reichstag* votes war credits unanimously

Sep. Prussian victory over French at Sedan. Surrender of Sedan and Napoleon III. Siege of Paris begins

Oct. French forces at Metz capitulate

Nov. Southern German states of Bavaria and Württemberg ally with North German Confederation (22nd and 23rd to do so)

Dec. Deputation of North German Confederation offers William I of Prussia the crown of a new German Empire, which he accepts

The (Second) German Empire (1871–1914)

1871
Jan. Proclamation at Versailles of William I, King of Prussia, as German Emperor
Mar. First German Imperial Parliament convenes
Apr. German Imperial Constitution adopted: King of Prussia automatically to be German Emperor (*Kaiser*), representing the German Empire diplomatically and heading the Empire militarily. Federal Council (*Bundesrath*) composed of representatives of the 25 constituent governments of the Empire, under the presidency of the Imperial Chancellor (Bismarck). Imperial Parliament *Reichstag* composed of 382 members elected by universal manhood suffrage
May Peace of Frankfurt ends the Franco-Prussian War: France cedes Alsace (except Belfort) and Lorraine to Germany and suffers German military occupation until reparations of 5,000 million francs are paid
Jul. Start of *Kulturkampf* when government of Prussia refuses the demand of the Archbishop of Cologne/Köln to dismiss 'Old Catholics' (those refusing to acknowledge the recently-promulgated doctrine of Papal Infallibility) from schools and universities

1872
Jun. Bismarck seeks to subordinate the Roman Catholic Church in Germany to the state: Germany expels the Jesuits and severs diplomatic relations with the Vatican

1873
May May Laws passed in Prussia, increasing state power over education and the appointment of clergy
Sep. German army withdraws from France on payment of reparations

1874
May Registration of births, deaths and marriages secularised

1875
May Kulturkampf reaches its peak: Pope Pius IX condemns the German government for its persecution of the Roman Catholic Church. Erection of the Arminius Monument or *Hermannsdekmal*, commemorating the ancient battle of the Teutoburg forest between the Teuton tribes and the Romans. Creation of the *Reichsbank*

1876
Fearing permanent religious division within the new Germany, Bismarck makes moves towards reconciliation with the Catholic Church

1877

Administration and procedure of justice unified and standardised throughout Germany

1878

Feb. Pope Pius IX dies. His successor, Pope Leo XIII, advances a more conciliatory line, resulting in Bismarck and a papal envoy meeting for talks at Bad Kissingen

May–Oct. Two assassination attempts on the Emperor provide Bismarck with the pretext for introducing anti-socialist legislation, including a ban on trade union activity

1879

Jul. Passage of a general tariff bill cements a new 'alliance of steel and rye' between industrialists and landowners on the basis of self-interested protection, solidifying Bismarck's power-base. 'Exceptional Law' passed to suppress Social Democratic Party (only founded in 1875). Agreement with the Papacy leads to the start of repeal of recent anti-Catholic, anti-clerical legislation

Aug. Alsace-Lorraine declared a *Reichsland*

1880

Oct. Completion and re-consecration of Cologne/Köln Cathedral

1881

Bismarck announces to the Reichstag a comprehensive welfare system for the German working classes, to be phased in over the 1880s

1882

Apr. Anti-Semitic League founded in Prussia

May Germany, Austria-Hungary and Italy form *Triple Alliance*

1883

Niederwald Monument at Rudesheim consecrated

1886

Apr. Prussian laws expropriating Polish landowners in Posen

1887

Jan. Bismarck's demands for increased military expenditure countered by Reichstag's demand for greater control over military budget. Bismarck dissolves the Reichstag. General election produces a new Reichstag favourable to Bismarck

Jun. *Reinsurance Treaty* with Russia

1888

Mar. Crown Prince Frederick succeeds as Emperor on death of William I

Jun. Frederick III dies, succeeded as German Emperor by William II (1888–1918)

1889
Bismarck and William II clash over social policy

1890
Jan.–Feb. Reichstag rejects Bismarck's anti-socialist legislation and is dissolved. The general election produces a new Reichstag with a substantially-increased socialist and radical representation. With his political position badly weakened, Bismarck revives a Prussian cabinet order of 1852 which stipulates that ministers may communicate with the Emperor only through the Minister-President (Bismarck himself). William II is outraged and demands the repeal of the order
Mar. William II accuses Bismarck of dereliction of duty in not warning Austria of Russian troop movements in the Balkans. *Bismarck resigns,* and is replaced as Minister-President by Caprivi
Jun. Germany allows Reinsurance Treaty with Russia to lapse

1891
Apr. Pan-German League formed. Count Schlieffen becomes Chief of German General Staff

1892
Nov. Caprivi introduces Army Bill involving expansion of the army by 84,000 men, which is rejected by the Reichstag

1893
Jul. Caprivi dissolves Reichstag. General election produces a more nationalist Reichstag which (narrowly) passes the Army Bill

1894
Oct. William II demands anti-socialist legislation. Caprivi refuses and resigns; succeeded as Chancellor by Prince Hohenlohe

1895
Jun. Kiel Canal opened, effecting for the first time direct German-controlled access between the Baltic and North Seas. Subversion Bill (which includes making 'disparagement of the state' a punishable offence) rejected by Reichstag

1896
Jan. William II sends the *Kruger Telegram*, antagonising Britain

1897
Jun. Admiral von Tirpitz becomes Secretary of State for the Navy
Oct. Move in Prussian *Landtag* to give police power to dissolve all societies 'threatening law, order and the state' is defeated
Nov. New Foreign Minister Bülow asserts Germany's imperial ambitions: 'We do not wish to put anyone in the shade but we do demand our place in the sun.' Kyffhauser Monument in Thuringia completed

1898

Mar. Naval Bill for the expansion of the German fleet, proposed by Tirpitz, passed by Reichstag

Apr. Tirpitz sponsors the founding of the German Navy League (*Flotterverein*) to campaign for further expansion, supported by industrialists like Krupp

1900

Jul. Second Naval Bill passed by Reichstag: Tirpitz's proposal to increase number of German capital ships to 36 accepted by large majority

1901

Oct. Bülow becomes Chancellor (1901–1909)

1903

May Polish school strike in Prussian province of Posen. Sickness and accident insurance for workers extended

1905

Tangier Incident. Schlieffen Plan devised, committing future German wartime strategy to a swift knock-out blow against France

1906

Jun. Third Naval Bill proposes further expansion of fleet

Dec. Reichstag dissolved for opposing increased expenses of maintaining overseas empire

1907

Jun.–Oct. At Second Hague Peace Conference, Germany rejects any scheme for disarmament

Jul. Triple Alliance renewed for a further six years

1908

Jun. Fourth Naval Bill

Oct. Daily Telegraph Affair: William II's feisty press interview glorifying German *Weltpolitik* outrages British public opinion

1908–1909

Bosnian Crisis: Germany backs Austria-Hungary in the Balkans, to the anger and frustration of Russia

1909

Jul. Bülow's finance bill (raising indirect taxation and death duties) is rejected by Reichstag. Bülow resigns; succeeded by Bethmann-Hollweg (Chancellor 1909–1917)

1911

Feb. German Army Bill is passed by Reichstag

May A degree of autonomy permitted to Alsace-Lorraine

Jul. Agadir Incident

1912

Jan. Socialists become the largest party in the Reichstag (with 110 seats) for the first time

May Army and Naval Bills demanding further expansion are passed by Reichstag

1913

Jan. Another Army Bill increases the size of the German Army

Jun. Germany makes financial provision for doubling the strength of the German armed forces

Nov. 'Zabern Incident' shows that the Army High Command is operating in virtual defiance of formal constitutional constraints

1914

Jun. Enlarged Kiel Canal is opened. Assassination of Archduke Franz Ferdinand

The First World War and the Fall of the Second German Empire (1914–1920)

1914

1 Aug. Germany declares war on Russia. German-Ottoman Treaty signed

2 Aug. Germany occupies Luxembourg and demands transit through Belgium to attack France

3 Aug. Germany declares war on France

4 Aug. Britain and Belgium declare war on Germany

Aug. In the West, German invasion of Belgium and Luxembourg to implement the (modified) Schlieffen Plan. In the East, Hindenburg (appointed Commander in East Prussia, with Ludendorff as Chief-of-Staff), defeats Russians at Tannenburg

Sep. On the Western Front, the Schlieffen Plan objective of the capture of Paris is frustrated by French and British action at the First Battle of the Marne. On the Eastern Front, the Russians are roundly defeated at the Masurian Lakes. Falkenhayn replaces Moltke as German Commander-in-Chief

Oct. Germans advance into Russian Poland

Nov. Hindenburg appointed Commander-in-Chief on the Eastern Front

1915

Feb. Start of 'War at Sea': Germany declares blockade on Britain (including submarine warfare against merchant shipping)

Mar. Start of 'War in the Air': first air raid as German Zeppelins bomb Yarmouth

Apr.–Sep. Western Front: succession of inconclusive trench-warfare battles in Artois and Champagne against France and Britain. Eastern Front: steady German advance into Russia, capturing Warsaw (in August) and Vilna (in September)

Sep.–Nov. Southern Front: German-Austrian-Bulgarian attack on Serbia; Serbs beaten at Kosovo and Serbia occupied

1916

Feb.+ Battle of Verdun

Jul.+ Battle of the Somme

Aug. Hindenburg appointed Chief of General Staff, with Ludendorff as Quartermaster-General. *Germany declares war on Rumania*

Sep. Supreme War Council of the Central Powers established

Dec. Joint German-Austrian-Bulgarian offensive into Rumania

1917

Jan. German-Austrian occupation of Bucharest and most of Rumania

Feb.+ German army on defensive on Western Front

Apr. *U.S.A. declares war on Germany.* William II promises universal suffrage in Prussia

Jul. Bettmann-Hollweg replaced as Chancellor by Michaelis (July to November 1917). Mutiny in the German fleet. Reichstag passes motion for peace

Aug. Kühlmann becomes Foreign Minister

Sep. On the Eastern Front, the Germans resist a Russian summer offensive and advance to capture Riga

Oct. German offensive on the Western Front

Nov. On the Western Front, the Hindenburg line is broken by a British offensive; on the Eastern Front, the new Bolshevik government in Russia sues for peace

Dec. Hostilities are suspended on the Eastern Front during negotiations for a separate peace between Germany and Bolshevik Russia. Michaelis replaced as Chancellor by Hertling (December 1917–September 1918)

1918

Jan. Strikes in Berlin

Feb. German advance on Eastern Front, capturing Minsk, Reval, Kiev and Odessa

Mar. *Treaty of Brest-Litovsk:* Bolshevik Russia secures peace at the price of enormous losses in territory to the Greater German Empire and its client-states

Mar.–Apr. First German offensive on the Western Front during 1918

May Prussian Diet rejects universal suffrage

May–Jun. Second German offensive on the Western Front

Jul. Third (and last) German offensive on the Western Front

Sep. Germans retreat to Siegfried Line. Hindenburg proposes armistice. Hertling replaced as Chancellor by Prince Max of Baden (September–November 1918)

Oct. Germany asks President Wilson of U.S.A. for armistice. Ludendorff dismissed. William II publishes democratic reform of the constitution of the German Empire

Nov. Bavarian Republic proclaimed in Munich. Revolutionary disturbances in Berlin. William II abdicates as German Emperor, flees to Holland. *Armistice* between Germany and the Allies signed at Compiègne. Transitional republican government headed by Ebert announced

1919

Jan. *Spartacist Revolt* in Berlin bloodily suppressed by *Freikorps*. Election of German National Constituent Assembly.

Feb. National Constituent Assembly meeting at Weimar appoints the *Weimar Republic*, headed by Ebert

Apr. Socialist Republic of Bavaria overthrown

Jun. German fleet scuppered at Scapa Flow. *Treaty of Versailles* signed between Germany and the Allies, including Clause 231, the 'war guilt clause'

1920

Jan. Terms of Treaty of Versailles come into force

21. The Greeks/Hellenes

1810s

Greek cultural renaissance, increasingly backed by Russia, activates Greek nationalists in the Danubian Principalities

1821

Apr. Greeks attack Turks in the Morea, prompting Ottoman reprisals

Jun. Ottomans defeat Greeks at Dragashan

Oct. Greek rebels in the Morea capture Tripolitza

1822

Jan. *Greeks declare independence* at Epidauros

Apr. Ottomans capture Chios and massacre Greeks

Jul. Ottoman invasion of 'Greece'

1824

Apr. Lord Byron dies at the siege of Missolonghi fighting 'for Freedom's Battle', exciting Western Philhellenic sentiment

1826

Apr. *St Petersburg Protocol*: Britain and Russia agree on autonomy for Greece (subsequently accepted by France). Capodistrias elected President of Greek National Assembly

1827

Jun. Ottoman forces enter Athens

Jul. *Treaty of London*: Britain, Russia and France recognise the autonomy of Greece

Aug. Ottomans reject Treaty of London
Oct. Ottoman fleet destroyed by British fleet at *Navarino*

1828
Apr. Russia declares war on Ottomans
Jul. London Protocol signed
Aug. Ottoman forces under Mehemet Ali agree to withdraw from Greece
Oct. Russian forces occupy Varna
Nov. Greece recognised as an independent state

1829
Sep. *Treaty of Adrianople* ends Russo-Ottoman War

1830
Feb. *Conference of London*: independence of Greece guaranteed by Britain, Russia and France

1831
Oct. Capodistrias assassinated

The Kingdom of Greece (1832–1914)

1832
Aug. Greek National Assembly elects Prince Otto of Bavaria as King of the Hellenes

1833–1862:
Reign of Otto

1844
Mar. Greek constitution

1850
Jan. Don Pacifico Affair: British fleet blockades the Piraeus to demonstrate international protection of British citizens

1852
Nov. London Agreement between Britain, Russia, France, Bavaria and Greece about the Greek succession

1854
May Greece promises neutrality in the Crimean War

1862
Oct. Military revolt in Athens forces King Otto to abdicate

1863
Mar. Prince George of Denmark becomes King George I of Greece

1863–1913:
Reign of George I

1864

Mar. London Agreement between Britain, Russia, France and Greece: Britain quits Ionian Islands and permits their union with Greece

1866–1869

(*First*) *Revolt in Crete:* assisted by Greek volunteers, the Cretans rebel against Ottoman rule and demand union with Greece. The Great Powers forbid Greece to support Crete and the revolt gradually peters out

1878

Jan. Rebellion against the Ottomans in Thessaly

Feb. Greece declares war on Ottoman Empire

Mar. Treaty of San Stephano promotes a 'Big Bulgaria' occupying territories in Thessaly and Thrace regarded by Greeks as part of 'Greater Greece'

Jul. Congress of Berlin prevents a 'Big Bulgaria' but allows Greece no territorial gains

1881

Jul. Greece acquires Thessaly and Anta (part of Epirus) from Ottomans

1896

Feb. (*Second*) *Revolt in Crete* launched

Jul. Concession of self-government for Crete from Sultan Abdul Hamid II fails to satisfy Cretans

1897

Feb. Crete proclaims its union with Greece

Mar. Great Powers blockade Crete

Apr. Greece declares war on Ottoman Empire

May Greeks defeated by the Ottomans in Thessaly, forcing the Great Powers to intervene and impose Greek-Ottoman armistice

Dec. Peace of Constantinople between Greece and Ottoman Empire

1898

Dec. Last Ottoman troops finally withdraw from Crete

1899

Mar. Prince George of Greece appointed High Commissioner of Crete by the Great Powers

1903

Oct. Austrian-Russian Agreement of Murzsteg over Macedonia

1905

Mar. Union of Crete with Greece announced by President of Cretan Assembly, Venizelos

1905

Jun. Delyanni, Prime Minister of Greece, assassinated

1908
Oct. Crete again proclaims its union with Greece

1910
Oct. Venizelos becomes Prime Minister, introduces reform of financial and military administration of Greece

1911
Jun. Constitution revised

1912
Feb.–Jun. Balkan League against Ottoman Empire created, comprising Greece, Bulgaria, Serbia and Montenegro

1912 Oct.–1913 May
First Balkan War. Greece joins Serbia, Montenegro and Bulgaria in successful war against Ottoman Empire

1913
Mar. Assassination of King George I

1913–1917:
Reign of Constantine I

1913
May Ambassadorial Treaty of London ends First Balkan War: Greece receives territory at Ottoman expense (including formal recognition of the transfer of Crete to Greece)

1913
Jun.–Aug. Second Balkan War. Greece joins Serbia, Montenegro, Rumania and Ottoman Empire in successful war against Bulgaria

1913
Aug. Treaty of Bucharest ends the Balkan Wars: Greece gains Macedonia, western Thrace (including Salonika) and almost all the Aegean Islands

The First World War and 'Greater Greece' (1914–1923)

1914
Aug. Venizelos pro-Allies, King Constantine pro-Central Powers in First World War

1915
Mar. When Venizelos tries to commit Greece to the Allies, King Constantine (married to the Princess Sophia, sister of Kaiser William II) replaces him as Prime Minister with Gounaris
Jul. Allied reprisals against Greece
Aug. Venizelos back as Prime Minister, again tries to commit Greece to the Allies
Oct. Britain and France land troops at Salonika. Constantine replaces Venizelos as Prime Minister with Zaimis

1916
Jun. Allies blockade Greece
Sep. Venizelos establishes pro-Allied Greek government-in-exile in Crete
Oct. Allied ultimatum to Greece. Greek fleet surrenders and British troops enter Athens. Venizelos moves his pro-Allied government to Salonika
Nov. In the name of his government, Venizelos declares war on the Central Powers

1917
Jun. King Constantine forced to abdicate in favour of son Alexander. Greece formally joins the Allies

1917–1920
Reign of Alexander I

1918:
100,000 Greek troops participate in campaign on southern front

1919
Nov: Treaty of Neuilly: Bulgaria is forced to relinquish her wartime territorial gains. Greece has pre-war jurisdiction restored with the addition of territory in western Thrace

1920
Aug. Treaty of Sèvres: Ottoman Empire cedes all Thrace to Greece and grants Smyrna and its Anatolian hinterland to Greece for a trial period of five years
Oct. Death of King Alexander (from a monkey bite)
Nov. Venizelos defeated in elections
Dec. Plebiscite overwhelmingly approves return of King Constantine

1920–1922:
Second reign of Constantine I

1920–1923
Greek-Turkish War: Turkish nationalist forces under Kemal resist Greek 'military occupation' of Anatolia

1922
Sep. Kemal attacks Greek settlements in Anatolia/Asia Minor, massacring the Greeks of Smyrna. Blamed for the Smyrna disaster, Constantine abdicates (again)

1922–1923
Reign of King George II

1923
Jul. Treaty of Lausanne: Greek expulsion from Asia Minor recognised, puncturing ambitions for 'Greater Greece' and provoking ongoing political crisis within Greece

22. The Gypsies/Roma

Pre-1770
Gypsies regarded as sub-human throughout Europe: reputation for child-stealing and cannibalism serves as justification for ferocious suppression, abject slavery and the 'sport' of Gypsy-hunting

1770s
Catherine II makes all Russian Gypsies 'crown serfs'. Maria Theresa implements programme to sedentarise and educate Gypsies of Habsburg Empire

1782
Gypsies tried and found guilty of cannibalism in Hungary

1785
Moldavian law prohibits marriage between Gypsies and non-Gypsies

1811
Von Arnim's *Isabella of Egypt* published, an early romanticisation of Gypsy life

1818
Wallachian penal code: Gypsies are born slaves

1833
Moldavian penal code: Gypsies are slaves, may not marry non-Gypsies and may only marry other Gypsies with their owner's consent

1841
George Borrow's *The Zincali: The Gypsies of Spain* published, promoting both the romanticisation of Gypsy life and scientific study of Gypsy language, folklore and history

1844
First scientific, historical and comparative study of Romani language published by Augustus Pott in Germany

1855
Gypsy slavery abolished in Moldavia

1856
Gypsy slavery abolished in Wallachia

1864
Gypsies formally liberated as slavery abolished in united Danubian Principalities

1864+
Gypsy exodus from Rumania throughout Europe, then to U.S.A.

1879

First pan-European Gypsy Congress in Kisfalu in Hungary demands full civil rights for Gypsies

1880s

Gypsy immigration banned by U.S.A.

1899

Establishment in Munich of 'Central Office for Fighting the Gypsy Nuisance'

1900s

First stirrings of Roma nationalism: territorial ambition for a Gypsy nation-state of 'Romanestan' in the Balkans, probably located in Macedonia

23. The Hungarians/Magyars

1784

Emperor Josef II outrages the Hungarian aristocracy by removing the crown of Hungary to Vienna, then ordering the replacement of Latin by German as the official language of Hungary

1795

Habsburg fear of the spread of French Revolutionary ideas demonstrated by execution of Martinovics and other 'conspirators'

1802

Count Francis Széchenyi founds Hungarian National Museum

1809

Napoleon considers establishing a client-state of Hungary to reduce the geopolitical weight of the Austrian Empire

1825

Foundation of Hungarian Academy by Count Stephen Széchenyi

1840

Magyar Diet succeeds in having Hungarian (not German) substituted for Latin as the new official language of Hungary. Foundation of patriotic journal *Pesti Hirlap*, under the crusading editorship of Louis/ Lajos Kossuth (1840–1844)

1848

Mar. Kossuth demands change in the government of Hungary. Hungarian Diet passes liberal constitutional reform plans

Apr. Emperor concedes separate constitutional status of Hungary. Feudalism in Hungary abolished. Kossuth's call for Magyarisation alarms non-Magyar minorities within Hungary, who prefer Habsburg rule

Jun. Habsburgs prepare to reincorporate Hungary, supplying aid to Jelačić of Croatia for future use against Hungary
Sep. Jelačić invades Hungary. Kossuth proclaimed President of Committee for the National Defence of Hungary
Oct. Austria formally declares war on Hungary. Jelačić driven out of Hungary
Dec. Franz Josef becomes Emperor

1849
Apr. Hungarian army under Gorgei defeats Habsburg forces under Windischgrätz. Hungarian Diet issues a Declaration of Hungarian Independence. Emperor Franz Josef appeals to Russia for aid against Hungary
May Gorgei retakes Budapest after its capture by Habsburgs
Aug. Austrian and Russian forces defeat Hungarians at *Világos*. Hungarians surrender, Kossuth flees into exile

1850
Customs union between Austria and Hungary imposed

1861
Feb. February Patent centralises the constitution of Habsburg Empire
Aug. Dissolution of Hungarian Diet. Government by Imperial Commissions introduced

1865
Dec. Transylvania incorporated into Hungary

1866
Austro-Prussian (Seven Weeks) War damages Habsburg morale

Hungary under the Dual Monarchy (1867–1914)

1867
Feb. *Ausgleich* (or 'Compromise') agreed between Austria/Cisleithania and Hungary/Transleithania, establishing the Dual Monarchy of Austria-Hungary (by effectively restoring the autonomist Hungarian Constitution of April 1848)
Jun. Ausgleich comes into effect, giving Hungary self-rule in all areas other than the dynastic, diplomatic and military (which are reserved as an Imperial Habsburg monopoly)

1868
Nationalities Law promises fair and equal treatment for all Magyars and non-Magyars within Transleithania/Hungary. *Nagodba* agreed with Croatia: Croatia promised the same autonomy/devolution within Hungary as Hungary itself has just received within the Dual Monarchy

1873
Nov. Croatia granted self-government within Kingdom of Hungary

1881
Foundation of Rumanian National Party in Hungary, demanding autonomy for Transylvania

1883
Hungary suspends *Nagodba*

1883+
Croatia subjected to 'direct rule' by Hungary in the person of the 'Iron Ban', Count Khuen-Hedérváry

1886
'Jansky Affair' exacerbates deteriorating Hungarian-Austrian relations

1890s
Official Magyarisation of non-Magyar minorities fully operative, contributing to mounting emigration to U.S.A. and increasing condemnation of the Magyar establishment in the West

1896
Millennial celebrations of 1000 years of the Hungarian state boost nationalist ambitions in Hungary

1905–1906
'Hungarian Crisis': new Hungarian Diet has nationalist majority (led by Kossuth's son Ferenc), and demands a Hungarian army (*Honvéd*) in breach of the *Ausgleich*. Hungarians back down when confronted by Habsburg military occupation and the threat of imposed manhood suffrage

1913
Mar. Suffrage adjusted to favour Magyars even more

The First World War and 'Lesser Hungary' (1914–1920)

1914
Aug. Hungary is a reluctant combatant but bound by the terms of the *Ausgleich* to follow Austria into the First World War

1914–1918
With the general success of Austria-Hungary on the eastern and southern fronts, Hungarians are heavily invested in the war effort of the Central Powers, but Hungary itself never becomes a military combat zone

1918
Oct. Revolution in Hungary. Hungarian premier, Tisza, assassinated
Nov. Emperor Charles/Karl quits the throne of Hungary

1919
Mar.–Aug. *Hungarian Soviet Republic*, headed by Béla Kun

1919
May–Nov   Hungarian-Rumanian War

1919
Aug.   Favoured by the Allies, Rumania invades Hungary to seize Transylvania, occupying Budapest and toppling the Kun Government
Sep.   *Treaty of St Germain*: Austria-Hungary is formally dissolved and Hungary becomes independent from Austria
Nov.   Under Allied pressure, Rumania withdraws from Hungary

1920
Feb.   New Hungarian constitution
Mar.   Admiral Horthy becomes Regent of Hungary
Jun.   *Treaty of Trianon*: punishes Hungary for being on the losing side in the First World War: pre-1914 Transleithania is reduced by two-thirds to a 'Lesser Hungary', and obliged by the Allies to surrender territory to all its neighbouring states. 'Trianon Hungary' represents an externally-imposed geopolitical disaster to which humiliated Hungarians both outside and inside the reduced state are never reconciled

24. The Icelanders

1815+
Growing movement for Icelandic autonomy under the Danish crown, focussed on restoration of the *Althing*, the historic popular assembly of the Icelanders

1838
Icelanders petition for separate assembly

1840
New Danish King Christian VIII appoints a special commission to consider a separate Icelandic assembly

1843
Christian VIII concedes an advisory Icelandic assembly of 26 (20 elected, 6 appointed by the crown), termed the Althing

1845
New Althing convenes in Reykjavik: Jon Sigurdsson leads campaign for greater powers and broader suffrage

1848
Jun.   *Assembly at Thingvellir* (historical venue of Althing) demands broader franchise and an assembly of 48 seats
Sep.   Rescript from new Danish King Frederick VII: no constitutional decisions will be made affecting Iceland without consultation with the Icelandic Althing

1849
Sep. Frederick VII accepts Thingvellir demands

1850
May New expanded Althing elected but convening postponed because of Danish-Prussian War: Denmark reluctant to concede to Iceland in case Schleswig-Holstein demands similar treatment

1851
Jul. Danish government adopts hard line: by a new constitution, the Althing is sidelined and Iceland is once again subordinated to the King of Denmark and the Danish Rigsdag

1855
Sep. Icelanders' petition for restoration of the Althing refused
Oct. New unitary Constitution for Denmark: Iceland reduced to a Danish colony, with no constitutional representation

1864
· Second Danish-Prussian War: Denmark loses Schleswig, Holstein and Lauenberg

1867
Danish government reverts to softer line and promises concessions to Iceland

1871
Jan. Danish Rigsdag decides that while Iceland is an inalienable part of Denmark, it will now be allowed self-government in purely domestic affairs

1872
New office of Governor of Iceland created without consultation with the Althing, arousing fresh suspicion of Denmark among Icelanders

1874
Jun. Christian IX formally grants Iceland a constitution: the Althing is granted legislative power over all domestic affairs
Aug. Millenial celebrations of 1,000 years of Icelandic history: Christian IX attends in person to sanction the transition of Iceland from colonial to autonomous status within the jurisdiction of Denmark

25. The Irish

1782–1800
'Grattan's Parliament' operates on the basis of the 'Constitution of 1782', giving the Irish parliament greater autonomy from Westminster

1791
United Irishmen founded in Belfast by Wolfe Tone

1795

British government establishes college at Maynooth to train Catholic priests 'under licence'. Foundation of Protestant 'Orange Society'

1796

Insurrection Act by British government to secure Ireland

1798

Jun. Rebellion of the United Irishmen defeated at Vinegar Hill after seizure of Wexford

Aug.–Sep. 'The Year of the French': French landing in Ireland fails but further alarms Britain about its vulnerability

Nov. Suicide of Wolfe Tone awaiting execution after death sentence

1799

Virtual martial law in Ireland

Ireland under the Union (1800–1870)

1800

Jul. *Act of Union* incorporates Ireland into the new United Kingdom of Great Britain (England, Wales and Scotland) and Ireland. Ireland is promised commercial concessions, retention of its own legal system and representation at Westminister (4 spiritual and 24 temporal peers in the House of Lords and 100 MPs in the House of Commons). Passed by Irish Parliament through British political pressure and bribery

Aug. Act of Union receives Royal Assent

1801

Jan. Act of Union becomes law

Feb. Pitt resigns as Prime Minister when Catholic Emancipation, promised as part of the Act of Union, is blocked by George III (on the grounds that it contradicts his coronation oath)

1802

Break-up of Despard conspiracy

1803

Jul.–Sep. Insurrection of Robert Emmett suppressed

1814

Dissolution of élite pro-Emancipation Catholic Board

1823

Catholic Association founded by Daniel O'Connell ('The Liberator') to campaign as a mass movement for Catholic emancipation

1828

O'Connell elected as M.P. for Co. Clare but, as a Catholic, he is unable to take his seat at Westminster. *Repeal of Test and Corporation Acts* removes last civil disabilities on Protestant dissenters (introduced by Peel and Wellington to undercut Irish unrest)

1829

Catholic Emancipation Act makes Catholics eligible for almost all offices of state, and no oath of supremacy required to sit in either House of the British Parliament. *Irish Franchise Act* removes poorest and most numerous class of Irish Catholic voters

1832

Aug. Irish Reform Act. National Repeal Association established by O'Connell

1842

'Young Ireland' nationalist group formed

1843

O'Connell's attempt to organise a mass campaign for repeal of the Union fails, partly because of his cancellation of the Clontarf meeting, partly because of the appeal of the more militant 'Young Ireland' movement. O'Connell arrested and imprisoned

1844–1845

Maynooth Grant issue divides British cabinet

1845

Oct.+ Blight ruins three-quarters of the Irish potato crop

1846–1851

Irish Famine: up to one million die of starvation, prompting extensive emigration to the U.S.A. by the surviving, embittered population. ('A million dead, a million fled')

1848

Attempts at insurrection by 'Young Ireland' fail and its leaders, Mitchel and O'Brien, are transported to Australia

1850

Oct. Irish Franchise Act expands the electorate

1858

Irish Republican Brotherhood (*Fenians*) founded among Irish emigrants in U.S.A. by James Stephens

1866

Feb. Habeas Corpus Act suspended in Ireland
May American Fenians stage a raid across Canadian border

1867

Feb. Fenians in England attempt to seize Chester and blow up Clerkenwell Jail, killing 12 people

1868

May Michael Barnett of the Fenians is hanged for Clerkenwell outrage (the last public execution in Britain)

1869

Mar. Anglican Church in Ireland disestablished (effective from 1871)

Nov. Last Fenian rising (in western Canada)

1870

Aug. Irish Land Act

The Irish Home Rule Campaign (1870–1914)

1870

Irish Home Government Association formed by Isaac Butt

1873

Nov. Irish Home Rule League established in Dublin

1874

In General Election, Home Rule Party wins 60 of Irish total of 103 seats, and initiates a policy of parliamentary obstruction

1880–1890

Home Rule Party led by Charles Stuart Parnell

1881

Irish Land League founded by Michael Davitt

1882

Apr. 'Kilmainham Treaty' deal between Parnell and British government

May Phoenix Park Murders: Thomas Burke (Permanent Under-Secretary for Ireland) and Lord Frederick Cavendish (newly-appointed Chief Secretary for Ireland) hacked to death in Dublin by the 'Invincibles', a gang of fanatical nationalists. Government passes a Prevention of Crimes Act (valid for three years) abolishing trial by jury and giving the police exceptional powers. Hardens both British public opinion against Ireland and Irish public opinion against Britain

1885

In General Election, Home Rule Party wins 86 seats, holding the balance in the Commons

Dec. Gladstone decides to favour Home Rule for Ireland

1886

Jun.

Gladstone's *(First) Home Rule Bill* defeated by 30 votes in House of Commons

1888

Papal decree forbidding boycotting antagonises Irish MPs

1890

Parnell cited in O'Shea divorce, with ensuing scandal splitting Home Rule Party

1892

Jun. Duke of Abercorn tells Belfast 'We will not have Home Rule'

1893

Gaelic League founded. *Ulster Defence Union* founded. Gladstone's *(Second) Home Rule Bill* passes House of Commons but is defeated in House of Lords

1900

Home Rule Party reunited under John Redmond

1902

Sinn Fein Party founded in Dublin by Arthur Griffith (becoming *Sinn Fein League* over 1907–1908)

1905

Ulster Unionist Council established

1910

Edward Carson rallies Ulster opposition to Home Rule

1911

Parliament Act limits the power of House of Lords to block bills passed by House of Commons, clearing the way for another Home Rule bill. Ulster Unionist Council plans to take over in the event of imposed Home Rule

1912

Apr.+ (Third) Home Rule Bill prompts opposition in Protestant Ulster, where Carson threatens armed resistance to 'Dublin Rule'
Sep. 'Solemn League and Covenant' signed by Ulster Protestants and Ulster Volunteer Force formed

1913

Jan. & Jul. House of Lords rejects (Third) Home Rule Bill. 'Citizen Army' formed in southern Ireland

1914

Mar. 'Curragh Incident': British officers in Ireland refuse to impose Home Rule on Ulster
May Conservatives and Liberal Unionists unite. *(Third) Home Rule Bill passes third reading*
Jun. Buckingham Palace Conference fails to reach compromise: Redmond is persuaded to accept the exclusion of Ulster from Irish Home Rule for six years; but Carson refuses to 'surrender'

The First World War and the Partition of Ireland (1914–1922)

1914–1918
Implementation of Home Rule is suspended for the duration of the First World War. Ireland never becomes a combat zone in the First World War but Irish casualties in the British Army are high

1916
Apr. *Easter Rising* in Dublin, seeking immediate independence for Ireland, led by Patrick Pearse of the Irish Republican Brotherhood and James Connolly of Sinn Fein. The Rising is suppressed and 14 of its ringleaders executed, antagonising large sectors of southern Irish public opinion
Jul. Battle of the Somme: very heavy Irish, especially Ulster, casualties
Aug. Roger Casement executed for treason

1917
Jun. Amnesty for all participants in Easter Rising, as British government attempts to defuse the Irish crisis. *Irish Convention* organised by Lloyd George. 'Unification' of Sinn Fein

1918
Attempts to extend conscription to Ireland deeply unpopular
Dec. Sinn Fein wins 73 seats in General Election

1919
Jan. Formation of *Irish Republican Army (I.R.A.)* by Michael Collins to fight for a free Ireland against the British. *Dail Eireann* established in Dublin as alternative parliament for Ireland
Apr. Eamonn de Valera elected President of Sinn Fein Executive
Sep. Dail Eireann proscribed by British government

1920
Mar.+ 'Black and Tans' active against Irish insurgents
Sep. Black and Tan reprisal at Balbriggan, near Dublin, causes outcry in Ireland, Britain and U.S.A.
Dec. *Government of Ireland Act* provides for a northern Irish parliament at Belfast and a southern Irish parliament at Dublin

1921
Jun. I.R.A. assassinates Sir Henry Wilson, Chief of the Imperial General Staff, outraging British public opinion
Dec. *Anglo-Irish Treaty*: southern Ireland granted dominion status as 'Irish Free State', six of the nine counties of Ulster granted limited self-government as 'Northern Ireland' within the revamped United Kingdom by agreement signed between David Lloyd George and Irish representatives, Michael Collins and Arthur Griffith. The Treaty and its Irish signatories are denounced by the Republicans headed by de Valera, leading to civil war in Ireland

1922
Jan.   Provisional Government for Irish Free State formed
Oct.   Constitution of Irish Free State adopted
Dec.   *Irish Free State* officially proclaimed on the first anniversary of the Anglo-Irish Treaty

26. The Italians

Pre-1789
Ancien régime 'Italy' comprises an agglomeration of separate states of various sizes, most ruled by reactionary, usually non-Italian legitimist dynasties

Napoleonic 'Italy' (1796–1815)

1796
Mar.   Napoleon Bonaparte appointed to command French army in Italy
Apr.   Napoleon defeats Piedmont-Sardinia. Armistice of Cherasco: Victor Amadeus III of Piedmont-Sardinia makes peace with France, surrenders Nice and Savoy
May   After Napoleon's defeat of Austrians at Lodi, Lombardic Republic established as French client-state
Oct.   Cispadane Republic established

1796–1802
Reign of Charles Emmanuel IV as King of Piedmont-Sardinia

1797
May   Venetian constitution altered
Jun.   Ligurian Republic established
Jul.   Cisalpine Republic established, subsequently subsuming the Cispadane Republic

1798
Feb.   Roman Republic established
Nov.   Ferdinand IV of Naples enters Rome
Dec.   France declares war on Naples, annexes Piedmont-Sardinia

1799
Jan.–Jun.   Parthenopaean Republic (Naples) established

1799 Jun.–1800 Jun.
Sardinia occupied by Austrian and Russian forces

1800
Jun.   Victory at Marengo re-establishes Napoleonic control over northern 'Italy'. Cisalpine Republic re-established

1801
Republic of Italy founded by Napoleon

1802
Jan. Napoleon appoints himself President of Italian Republic
Aug.–Sep. Napoleon annexes Elba, Piedmont- Sardinia (again), Parma and Piacenza

1802–1821
Reign of Victor Emmanuel I as King of Piedmont-Sardinia

1805
May Napoleon crowned *King of Italy* in Milan
Jun. Napoleon annexes Ligurian Republic (Genoa)

1806
Mar. Joseph Bonaparte becomes King of Naples

1807
Carbonari (charcoal-burners), a secret society, founded in Calabria

1808
Jan. Napoleon annexes Etruria
Apr. Napoleon annexes Papal Legations
Jun. Joseph Bonaparte switched from King of Naples (1806–1808) to King of Spain. Replaced as King of Naples by Murat

1809
May Napoleon annexes Papal States, imprisoning the protesting Pope Pius VII in Savona

1815
Murat deposed as King of Naples

Restoration 'Italy' (1815–1847)

1815
Jun. Congress of Vienna: restoration of legitimate dynasties in Kingdoms of Naples/Two Sicilies and Piedmont-Sardinia, and in Grand Duchies of Tuscany and Modena; creation of subject Kingdom of Lombardy-Venetia, ruled by Emperor of Austria. 'Italy' remains 'a geographical expression' (Metternich), comprising eight principal states (only two of which are ruled by Italians)

1817
Jun. Rising at Macerata collapses

1820
Jul. Uprising in Naples leads to promise of a constitution
Aug. Membership of *Carbonari* declared treasonable in Lombardy-Venetia

1821
Feb. Austria sends military aid to hard-pressed Ferdinand of Naples
Mar. Austrian troops enter Naples, defeating the rebels. Uprising in Piedmont-Sardinia forces Victor Emmanuel I to abdicate in favour of regency of Charles Felix (1821–1824), who grants a liberal constitution
Apr. Austrian intervention in Piedmont: Austrian troops defeat insurgents at Novara, enter Turin and Alessandria

1823–1829
Pope Leo XII continues reactionary misrule of the Papal States

1824–1849
Reign of Charles Albert I as King of Piedmont-Sardinia

1830–1859
Reign of Ferdinand II as King of Naples

1831–1846
Papacy of Gregory XVI

1831
Young Italy ('Giovine Italia') founded by Guiseppe Mazzini (in Marseilles) with the motto 'Freedom, Equality, Humanity, Independence and Unity'
Feb. Risings in Modena, Parma and Papal States
Mar. In response to an appeal by Pope Gregory XVI, Austrian troops intervene in Papal States, entering Bologna
May Ambassadors of Great Powers produce a memorandum proposing reform of the Papal States. Ignored by Gregory XVI

1832
Jan. Austrians suppress uprisings in Romagna. Louis Philippe sends French forces to occupy Ancona

1834
Young Europe founded by Mazzini (in Berne, Switzerland)

1838
Oct. Austria evacuates Papal States (except Ferrara)

1839
Italian Scientific Congress discusses unification of Italy

1843
Vincenzo Gioberti publishes *The Moral and Civil Supremacy of Italy*, advocating an Italy united under the Papacy

1844
Jul. Bondiero brothers shot as rebels in Calabria

1846–1878
Papacy of Pius IX ('Pio Nono')

1846

Jun. New Pope Pius IX introduces liberal reforms in Papal States, alarming Metternich ('We had foreseen everything but a liberal Pope'). Charles Albert of Piedmont-Sardinia launches anti-Austrian crusade

1847

Il Risorgimento ('The Resurrection'), a newspaper demanding a liberal unified Italy, is founded by Camillo Cavour and others

Risorgimento 'Italy' (1848–1861)

1848

Jan. 'Tobacco Riots' against Austrian rule in Lombardy. Revolt and proclamation of independence in Sicily

Feb. King Ferdinand II concedes liberal constitution in Naples. Liberal constitution conceded in Tuscany

Mar. Charles Albert proclaims liberal constitution in Piedmont. Pius IX reluctantly grants constitution in Papal States. Daniele Manin leads revolt in Venice, proclaiming the 'Venetian Republic of St Mark'. Uprising in Milan forces Austrians under Radetzky to withdraw. Charles Albert of Piedmont issues proclamation sympathising with Lombardy and Venetia, and orders troops into Lombardy

Apr. Austrians defeated by Piedmontese at Gioto and Pastrengo. Pius IX first approves the war against Austria, then withdraws his support. Sicily declares independence from Naples

May Collapse of uprising in Naples. Austrians defeat rebels in Tuscany at Curtatone

Jun. Austrian victory at Vicenza

Jul. Battle of *Custozza*: Radetzky defeats and expels Piedmontese from Milan and then all Lombardy

Aug. Piedmont and Austria sign Armistice of Vigevano

Sep. Kingdom of Naples recovers Sicily. Venice expels Piedmontese troops

Nov. Anti-Papal nationalist sentiment grows: Count Rossi (Premier of Papal States) assassinated and Pius IX flees from Rome to Gaeta

1849

Feb. Grand Duke of Tuscany also flees to Gaeta for sanctuary. Mazzini proclaims the 'Roman Republic'

Mar. Piedmont breaks truce and attacks Austrians. Battle of *Novara*: Austrians crush Piedmontese army. *Charles Albert abdicates* as King of Piedmont-Sardinia in favour of son, Victor Emmanuel II

Apr. French troops land in Papal States to restore Pius IX

May Guiseppe Garibaldi enters Rome. Troops from Naples occupy Palermo in Sicily

Jul. French troops enter Rome to restore Pius IX. Austrians restore Grand Duke Leopold II of Tuscany

Aug. *Peace of Milan* formally ends Piedmontese-Austrian War of 1848–1849. Venice surrenders to Austrians after five-week siege

1849–1878
Reign of Victor Emmanuel II as King of Piedmont-Sardinia (and as King of Italy, 1861–1878)

1850
Apr. Pius IX returns to Rome
Oct. Cavour appointed minister of agriculture and commerce in Piedmont-Sardinia

1851
Cavour appointed minister of finance in Piedmont- Sardinia

1852
May Grand Duke Leopold II of Tuscany abolishes constitution
Nov. *Cavour appointed Prime Minister of Piedmont-Sardinia*

1855
Jan. Cavour commits Piedmont to joining Britain and France in the Crimean War against Russia
May Piedmontese contingent under General La Marmora joins Allies in Crimea and acquits itself well

1857
Aug. Association for the Unification of Italy formed by Garibaldi, with Piedmontese backing

1858
Jan. *Orsini Bomb Plot:* failed assassination attempt on Napoleon III publicises the Italian cause and engages sympathy in France
Jul. *Pact of Plombières:* Cavour and Napoleon III secretly agree to cooperate in military expulsion of Austrians from Lombardy and Venetia to establish an independent Piedmont- led 'Upper Italy'
Sep. Victor Emmanuel's daughter Clotilde marries Napoleon III's cousin Jerome

1859
Jan. Formalisation of Pact of Plombières. Victor Emmanuel provokes Austria by troop movements on border
Apr. Austrian ultimatum to Piedmont to demobilise rejected, prompting Austrian attack
May France declares war on Austria
Jun. Battles of *Magenta* and *Solferino:* Austria heavily defeated by combined French and Piedmontese forces
Jul. *Peace of Villafranca:* to Piedmontese dismay, Napoleon III decides to end the hostilities (prematurely), insisting that Austria cede Lombardy and Parma to an enlarged Piedmont but permitting Austria to retain Venetia. Cavour resigns in protest

Aug. Assemblies meet in Modena, Parma, Romagna and Tuscany to form a military alliance and hail Victor Emmanuel as their King

Nov. Treaty of Zurich formally confirms the terms of the Peace of Villafranca, ending the Franco-Piedmontese-Austrian War of 1859

1860
Jan. Cavour returns as Prime Minister of Piedmont-Sardinia

Mar. Piedmont cedes Nice and Savoy to France (as price agreed at Plombières for French aid against Austria in War of 1859). Near-unanimous vote in plebiscites in Modena, Parma, Romagna and Tuscany for union with Piedmont

Apr. Meeting of the first 'Italian Parliament' in Turin. Rising in Sicily against Francis II of Naples

May One Thousand Redshirts' Expedition of Garibaldi sails from Genoa to emancipate Sicily

Jun. Redshirts land in Sicily and take Palermo

Aug. Garibaldi and his Redshirts land on Italian mainland

Sep. Fall of Naples to Garibaldi. To forestall Garibaldi, Cavour despatches Piedmontese troops to the Papal States, but Garibaldi defeats the Papal forces at Castelfidardo

Oct. Naples and Sicily opt for union with Piedmont. Garibaldi proclaims Victor Emmanuel King of Italy

Nov. Umbria votes for union with Piedmont

1861
Feb. Francis II of Naples formally surrenders to Garibaldi at Gaeta. Victor Emmanuel II of Piedmont-Sardinia proclaimed King of Italy by the Italian Parliament

The Kingdom of Italy (1861–1914)

1861
Mar. Formal proclamation of the Kingdom of Italy, based upon Piedmontese liberal constitution of 1848

Jun. Death of Cavour

1862
Mar. Garibaldi incited by Ratazzi Ministry in Turin to mount a campaign to overthrow Papal temporal power

Aug. Garibaldi invades Italy from Sicily, is defeated at Aspromonte and imprisoned at Spazzia

1864
Sep. By 'September Convention', Napoleon III agrees to withdraw French troops from Rome in return for the renunciation of Rome as the new capital of Italy

1865
Apr. Florence/Firenze proclaimed as (compromise) capital of Italy, prompting Napoleon III to withdraw his troops from Rome

1866
Jan. Military lobby at Habsburg court frustrates Italian offer to buy Venetia from Austrian Empire
Apr. Secret alliance between Italy and Prussia against Austria.
Austro-Prussian-Italian (Seven Weeks) War
Jun. Italian forces under La Marmora defeated by Austrians under Archduke Albrecht at *Custozza*. Garibaldi defeated and wounded at Monte Suello
Jul. Italy's ally Prussia defeats Austrians at *Sadowa*. Italian fleet destroyed by Austrian fleet at Lissa in Adriatic
Aug. Italians sign armistice with Austrians
Oct. Treaty of Vienna: at Prussian insistence, Austria cedes Venetia to Italy (through the good offices of France). Venetia formally votes for union with Italy

1867
Oct. Garibaldi raises volunteers for a march on Rome, prompting Napoleon III to intervene to protect Pope
Nov. French troops defeat Garibaldi at Mentana and invest Rome. Garibaldi arrested by Italian government

1868
La Stampa newspaper founded in Turin

1870
Sep. Defeat of France in Franco-Prussian War leads to fall of Napoleon III and withdrawal of French troops from Rome. Victor Emmanuel announces march on Rome. Italian forces enter Rome despite resistance from Papal troops
Oct. Plebiscite in Papal States approves union with Italy. Papacy permitted to retain temporal authority over Vatican City. Italian Assembly votes to transfer capital of Italy from Florence (1865–1870) to Rome

1871
May Law of Guarantees for Papacy (though Pius IX still considers himself the 'Prisoner in the Vatican')
Jul. Victor Emmanuel takes up residence in Quirinal Palace in Rome as first King of United Italy

1876
Corriere della Sera newspaper founded in Milan

1878
Jan. Death of Victor Emmanuel II

1878–1900
Reign of Umberto I as King of Italy

1878
Feb. Death of Pope Pius IX

1878–1903
Papacy of Leo XIII

1882
Jan. Electoral reform passed
May Italy joins Germany and Austria in Triple Alliance

1896
Mar. Battle of Adowa: Italians defeated by Abyssinians, a humiliating setback to ambitions for Italian North African Empire

1900
Jul. Assassination of Umberto I

1900–1946
Reign of Victor Emmanuel III as King of Italy

1902
Nov. Treaty between Italy and France, publicly over spheres of influence in north Africa, secretly promising that Italy will be neutral in any war involving France

1911–1912
Italian-Ottoman War

1912
May Italy seizes Dodecanese Islands from Ottoman Empire
Oct. Treaty of Ouchy: Italy secures Rhodes, Dodecanese Islands, Tripoli and Cyrenaica from Ottomans, realising ambitions for Italian North African Empire

The First World War and 'Italia Irredenta' (1914–1920)

1914
Aug. Italy neutral, invoking 1902 treaty with France against its obligations to Triple Alliance of 1882
Dec. Italy occupies Valona in southern Albania, exploiting Austrian-Serb conflict

1915
Apr. Treaty of London: secret agreement between Italy and Britain, France and Russia promising extensive territorial *Italia Irredenta* gains at Austrian expense in return for Italy joining the Allied war effort
May Italy quits Triple Alliance, declares war on Austria-Hungary
Aug. Italy declares war on Ottoman Empire (in hope of a share in the future territorial partition of Asia Minor)

Nov. Italy accedes to Declaration of London of 1914: no separate peace with Austria-Hungary

1916
Aug. Italy declares war on Germany

1917
Apr. Treaty of St Jean de Maurienne: Italy promised its share (the western littoral of Asia Minor and hinterland of Smyrna) in the post-war Western partition of the Ottoman Empire
Oct. Caporetto: Italian army routed by combined Austrian and German offensive
Nov. Italian rout only stemmed by British and French reinforcements. The ultimate military humiliation for the Italians: 300,000 captured, another 300,000 desert

1918
Oct. Vittorio Veneto: Italian victory over Austrians in last month of war, partial compensation for Caporetto

1919
Jan. Paris Peace Conference opens, with Prime Minister Vittorio Orlando representing Italy as one of the 'Big Four'
Apr. Italy seizes Adalia in southern Asia Minor to stake its claim to a share in partitioned Ottoman Empire
Jun. Prime Minister Orlando sidelined by the 'Big Three'; resigns when full *Italia Irredenta* claims dismissed
Sep. Treaty of St Germain between Austria and the Allies: Italy receives South Tyrol and Julian March but other *Italia Irredenta* territories on the Adriatic littoral (promised by the 1915 Treaty of London) are instead ceded to the new Kingdom of the Serbs, Croats and Slovenes. Italian public opinion outraged, prompting D'Annunzio's seizure of Fiume/ Rijeka to demonstrate Italian commitment to *Italia Irredenta* (but withdrawing in January 1921)

1920
Jun. Treaty of Trianon between Hungary and the Allies: Italy receives Fiume/Rijeka
Aug. Treaty of Sèvres between Ottoman Empire and Allies: Italy only confirmed in her 1912 acquisition of Rhodes and Dodecanese, with no extra share of the Western partition of Asia Minor (which is instead transferred to Greece)
Nov. Treaty of Rapallo between Italy and Kingdom of the Serbs, Croats and Slovenes: in a temporary settlement of Adriatic littoral disputes, Italy gets Zara, 'Yugoslavia' gets Split and Sebenico, and Fiume/Rijeka becomes independent; a joint pledge is signed to observe all the peace treaties to prevent a Habsburg restoration

27. The Jews

1782
Edict of Tolerance for Jews issued by Emperor Josef II of Austria

1791
Removal of civic disabilities on Jews in France

1804
'Constitution of the Jews' issued by Tsar Alexander I to integrate Jews into Russian state and society

1806–1807
Napoleon convenes 'Sanhedrin' to integrate Jews into French state and society

1812
Emancipation of Jews in Prussia

1815
Congress of Vienna promotes emancipation of Jews, especially within German Confederation. Jewish *Pale of Settlement* formally established in western borderlands of Russian Empire

1848–1849
Jewish emancipation effected in most states of central Europe

1858
Baron Lionel de Rothschild becomes the first professing Jew to take seat as M.P. in British House of Commons

1860
Alliance Israelite Universelle founded in Paris. Term 'anti-Semitism' first appears

1860s
Tsar Alexander II introduces concessions to Jews in Russia

1868
Jews receive civil liberties in Austria/Cisleithania

1871
'Anglo-Jewish Association' founded in London

1878
Prussian court preacher Adolf Stoecker launches attacks on Jews in Germany

1881
Pogroms against Jews in southern Russia, blamed for assassination of Tsar Alexander II

1882

Anti-Semitic League founded in Prussia. 'May Laws' in Russia: Jews restricted geographically (to the Pale of Settlement) and professionally (excluded from civil service). Prompts first wave of Jewish emigration from Russia. Jewish ritual murder trial at Tisza-Eszlar in Hungary

1889–1893

Panama Scandal: Jewish directors of bankrupt Panama Canal Company brought to trial, occasioning wave of anti-Semitic sentiment throughout France

1891

Expulsion of many Jews from Moscow and St Petersburg into the Pale of Settlement prompts second wave of emigration from Russia to U.S.A.

1894–1905

Dreyfus Case: official persecution of French Jewish army officer on espionage charges polarises France into liberal Dreyfusards and reactionary, anti-Semitic anti-Dreyfusards. Converts many assimilated Jews to Zionism (notably Theodor Herzl)

1896

Herzl publishes *The Jewish State*

1897

First Zionist Congress meets in Basle, organised by Herzl, 'to secure for the Jewish people a home in Palestine guaranteed by public law'. The majority of assimilated Jews oppose Zionism. 'Jewish Bund' (League of Jewish Workers of Lithuania, Poland and Russia) founded in Vilna

1901

'Hilfsverein der Deutschen Juden' founded in Germany

1903–1906

Succession of anti-Jewish pogroms in Russia (often fomented by anti-Semitic 'Black Hundreds' with government connivance), claims up to 50,000 Jewish lives, again boosting emigration

1904–1905

'Uganda Dispute' between Zionists and Jewish 'territorialists' about a British offer of a homeland other than in Palestine

1908

First Zionist office set up in Palestine, in Jaffa

1912–1913

Beilis Case: trial in Russia of Mendel Beilis, accused of Jewish ritual blood-sacrifice of a Christian child

1914–1918

First World War affects Jews disproportionately, inflicting great damage, displacement and death across eastern Europe

1917

Balfour Declaration: British Foreign Secretary Sir Arthur Balfour declares British Government support for a Jewish homeland in Palestine (provided that the rights of resident non-Jewish communities are safe-guarded)

1920

San Remo Conference: Balfour Declaration supported by Allies, forms basis for League of Nations' mandate over Palestine assigned to Britain (formally in 1923)

28. The Latvians/Letts

1721

'Livland' or 'Livonia' transferred from Sweden to Russian Empire by Treaty of Nystadt

1795

By Third Partition of Poland, Russia acquires 'Courland'. The future 'Latvia', comprising most of the tsarist provinces of Livonia and Courland, is dominated politically and socially by German land-owning 'Baltic Barons' throughout the nineteenth century

1880s

Tsarist Russification targets Latvian/Lettish self- consciousness

1885

Holy Synod forbids mixed-religion marriages in largely-Lutheran 'Latvia' unless children are raised in Orthodox faith. Widespread Latvian protest at this 'religious Russification'

1914–1918

'Latvia' in war zone of Eastern Front between Russia and Germany

1915

German advance captures south-western 'Latvia'

1917

Sep. German forces occupy Riga
Oct.+ New Bolshevik Regime supported (almost solely) by Lettish regiments of Russian Army

1918

Mar. Treaty of Brest-Litovsk: 'Latvia' detached from Russian jurisdiction and comes within 'Greater German Empire'
Apr. Latvia proclaims its independence
Dec. Bolsheviks take over Latvia

1919

May Latvia freed from Bolsheviks

Dec. Germans evacuate Latvia

1920
May Treaty of Berlin between Latvia and Germany: Germany recognises independence of Latvia
Aug. *Treaty of Riga* between Latvia and Russia: Bolshevik Russia recognises independence of Latvia

1921
Jan. International recognition for independent Republic of Latvia

29. The Lithuanians

1569–1795
Lithuania united territorially and politically to Poland

1795
By the Third Partition of Poland, Russian Empire acquires territory of 'Lithuania', subsequently divided into the tsarist provinces of Kovno and Vilna

1815–1917
Establishment of 'Pale of Settlement', to which Russian Jews are confined by law, includes 'Lithuania'

1880s+
Lithuanian cultural and national movement begins

1914–1918
'Lithuania' in the war zone of the Eastern Front between Russia and Germany

1915
Jan.–Oct. All 'Lithuania' occupied by advancing German forces

1917
Mar. Fall of tsarist empire. Lithuanians encouraged to entertain ambitions for autonomy under Germany

1918
Mar. *Treaty of Brest-Litovsk:* 'Lithuania' (already occupied since 1915) is formally detached from Russian jurisdiction to become part of the 'Greater German Empire'. Kingdom of Lithuania proclaims its independence (tolerated by Germany as a client-state with a German duke as king)
Nov. At end of First World War, a republican government assumes power in Lithuania
Dec. Bolshevik Russian invasion

1919
Jan. Russians occupy Vilna, establishing Lithuanian Soviet Republic
Apr. Poles seize Vilna area from Russians as part of Poland
Dec. Germans finally evacuate remainder of Lithuania

1920
Jul. Treaty of Moscow: independence of Lithuania (without Vilna) recognised by Bolshevik Russia. Bolsheviks seize Vilna area from Poland during Polish-Russian War of 1919–1920
Oct. Poles seize Vilna area back from Russians, never returning it to Lithuania

1922
Independent Lithuania recognised by the Great Powers

30. The Montenegrins

15th century
Principality engulfed by Ottoman Empire but retains practical autonomy through its guerrilla warfare terrain

1799
Autonomy of Montenegro acknowledged by Ottomans

1830–1851
Reign of Petar Njegos, Prince-Bishop of Montenegro

1852
Mar.
Montenegro made a secular hereditary principality under the native Petrović dynasty

1852–1860
Reign of Prince-Bishop Danilo I

1852–1853
Montenegrin-Ottoman War over seizure of adjoining territory

1858
Feb.–Jul. Montenegrin-Ottoman War over territory and status
Nov. Formal independence and frontiers of Montenegro established by Sultan of Ottoman Empire

1860
Aug. Assassination of Danilo I

1860–1918
Reign of Nicholas I (Prince, 1860–1910; King, 1910–1918)

1876
Jul. Montenegro allies with Serbia against Ottomans

1880

Nov. Montenegrin occupation of Dulagno accepted by Ottomans

1905

Formal constitution granted

1908–1909

Bosnian Crisis: Montenegro angered by Austrian annexation of Bosnia-Herzegovina and return of Sanjak of Novi Bazar to Ottoman Empire. Both developments frustrate ambitions of Montenegro (and Serbia) for territorial expansion

1910

Aug. Montenegro elevated from Principality to Kingdom

1912

Jun. Montenegro joins Balkan League of Serbia, Bulgaria and Greece against the Ottoman Empire

1912–1913

First Balkan War

1913

May Treaty of London concludes First Balkan War: Montenegro doubles her territory at Ottoman expense but is angered at proposed new state of Albania blocking her southward expansion

1913

Aug. Treaty of Bucharest concludes Second Balkan War: Montenegro is confronted by new state of Albania as unwelcome southern neighbour

1914

Aug. Montenegro declares war on Austria-Hungary in act of solidarity with its traditional ally Serbia

1915

Nov. Montenegro finally defeated by Austrian army after determined resistance

1916

Jan. Cetinje, the Montenegrin capital, and then all the remainder of Montenegro overrun and occupied by Austrian army. King Nicholas flees into exile amid rumours of collusion with the Austrians

1918

Nov. Packed Assembly at Podgorica deposes King Nicholas and the Petrović dynasty and votes for the union of Montenegro with Serbia under the Serbian Karageorgević dynasty. Montenegro becomes an integral part of the new 'Kingdom of the Serbs, Croats and Slovenes'

31. The Norwegians

1397–1814
Norway part of Denmark

1807
Norwegians secure the concessions of a national assembly, the *Storting*, and own university from Denmark

1814
Jan.   *Peace of Kiel:* Denmark cedes Norway to Sweden
Apr.   Norwegian constitution drawn up
Nov.   Under Swedish pressure, Norwegian Assembly declares Norway a free and independent state now united with Sweden in the *Kingdom of Sweden and Norway.* In return, Sweden promises to respect the Norwegian constitution and Storting

1815
Jun.   Congress of Vienna confirms the transfer of Norway from Denmark to Sweden and the guarantee of Norwegian privileges and rights

1840+
Norwegian cultural nationalism develops, producing later nineteenth-century generation of Grieg, Ibsen, Munch and Hamsun

1855
Nov.   Agreement at Stockholm of Britain, France and Sweden to preserve united Kingdom of Sweden and Norway

1860
Aftenposten newspaper founded in Christiania/Oslo

1884
Jul.   Democratic reforms in constitution

1898
Adoption of universal manhood suffrage fuels campaign for independence of Norway

1905
Jun.   Storting votes for dissolution of union with Sweden
Sep.   Plebiscite in Norway approves vote for independence
Oct.   *Sweden accepts and concedes independence of Norway*

1905–1957
Reign of King Haakon VII (formerly Prince Karl of Denmark)

1907
Jun.   Suffrage for women introduced

1914–1918
Norway neutral in First World War

32. The Poles

1772
Aug. First Partition of Poland: Polish Commonwealth loses territory to neighbouring Russia, Austria and Prussia

1791
May New Polish constitution on the French model proclaimed

1792
May Russia invades Poland, abrogating the Polish Constitution

1793
Jan. Russia and Prussia decide on second partition of Poland
May Second Partition of Poland: Russia gains Poland east of rivers Duna and Dniepr; Prussia gains Danzig, Thorn, Posen/Poznan, Gresen and Kalisz, leaving rump state of Poland

1794
Mar. Polish Rising under Kościuszko
Nov. Rising crushed and Russians occupy Warsaw

1795
Jan. Secret treaty between Russia and Austria for final partition
Aug. Treaty joined by Prussia
Oct. Third Partition of Poland: Prussia gains Warsaw and territory between rivers Bug and Nieman; Austria gains Cracow and western Galicia; Russia takes the remainder. Poland disappears as a unified state
Nov. Stanislaw (Poniatowski) of Poland abdicates (King, 1764–1795)

1797
Jan. Final treaty of Polish Partition

1800s
Polish emigrés join Napoleon as only hope for a revived state, persuading Napoleon to champion the cause of a revived Poland for tactical reasons

1807
Jul. Grand Duchy of Warsaw set up by Napoleon after Treaty of Tilsit between France and Prussia as a geopolitical wedge undermining Prussia and Austria (and implicitly Russia too)

1812
Napoleon invades Russia with *Grande Armée* (including 85,000 Poles) to forestall Russian attack on Grand Duchy of Warsaw

1813
Nov. Grand Duchy of Warsaw collapses with the defeat of Napoleon at the battle of Leipzig

The Stateless Nation of Poland (1815–1914)

1815
Jun. Congress of Vienna: all 'Poland' (except Cracow) is redivided between Prussia (regaining Posen/Poznan), Austria (regaining Galicia) and Russia (acquiring most of pre-1772 Poland, now established as a new 'Kingdom of Poland' under the Tsar of Russia). Cracow becomes an independent city-state under the joint protection of Austria, Prussia and Russia
Nov. Kingdom of Poland (or 'Congress Poland') granted a constitution by Tsar Alexander I

1815–1849
Grand Duchy of Posen/Poznan retains a measure of autonomy within Prussia (much reduced after 1831)

1825+
New Tsar Nicholas I starts to prune Polish privileges

1830
Nov. (First) Polish Uprising: Poles rebel and expel Russian garrison from Warsaw

1831
Jan. Declaration of independence by Polish Diet
May Polish forces defeated at Ostrolenka
Sep. Russians recapture Warsaw. Uprising collapses and aristocratic leaders flee to France

1832
Feb. Constitution of Congress Poland abolished by Nicholas I as punishment for the Polish Uprising

1833
Treaty of Münchengrätz: Russia, Austria and Prussia agree to cooperate to maintain order and stability in their respective Polish territories

1834
Adam Mickiewicz publishes *Pan Tadeusz*

1840s
Cracow becomes centre of local Polish nationalism

1846
Polish insurrection in Austrian Galicia
Nov. Austrian Empire annexes Cracow (the last territorial remnant of independent Poland)

1847

May Ex-Congress Poland converted into provinces of Russian Empire

1848

Apr. Prussia helps Russia suppress Polish insurrection in Warsaw

May Austria suppresses insurrection in recently-incorporated Cracow

1849+

Grand Duchy of Posen integrated into Prussia

1856

May New Tsar Alexander II amnesties Polish insurgents as start-of-reign gesture of Russian goodwill

1861–1864

Second Polish Uprising against Russia

1861

Widespread Polish discontent, more 'popular' than in 1830–1831

1863

Jan. Start of overt Polish guerrilla warfare

1864

Aug. Final Russian military suppression of Polish Uprising, aided by Prussia and Austria

1864+

Rebels deported to Siberia, Roman Catholic institutions repressed. Territory of ex-Congress Poland subdivided into ten 'Vistula Provinces' of Russian Empire

1886

Apr. In Germany, Prussian law expropriates Polish landowners in Posen and western Prussia

1892

Dec. Pan-Slav Congress in Cracow

1901

May Polish school strike in Prussian province of Posen

1905

Attempted revolution in Russia prompts general strikes and political demonstrations in Russian Polish provinces, though no concerted (Third) Uprising

The First World War and the Re-creation of Poland (1914–1921)

1914–1918

In the First World War, 'Poland' is situated in the war zone of the Eastern Front between Russia and the Central Powers of Germany and Austria-Hungary

1914

Sep. Grand Duke Nicholas, Commander-in-Chief of Russian Forces, issues a proclamation promising a degree of autonomy to Russian Poland
Oct.–Dec. Western part of Russian Poland captured by Germany but much of Austrian Poland captured by Russia

1915

Jan.–Nov. Almost all Austrian Poland retrieved by Austrians and all Russian Poland (and much more) captured by Germans

1916

Jun.–Aug. Russia retrieves part of Austrian Poland (by the 'Brusilov Offensive')
Nov. Central Powers announce creation of Kingdom of Poland (as projected 'tributary-state' under German control)

1918

Mar. Treaty of Brest-Litovsk: Russian Poland is formally detached from Russian jurisdiction and permitted to exist as a client-state within the 'Greater German Empire'
Nov. End of First World War. *Independent state of Poland proclaimed*

1918–1922

Jan Pilsudski President of Poland

1919

State of Poland endorsed by patronage of Allies at the Paris Peace Conference
Apr. Poles seize Vilna area from Russia
Jun. Treaty of Versailles: Germany cedes parts of Prussian Posen, East Prussia and Upper Silesia to new Polish state (constituting the 'Polish Corridor' to the Baltic Sea)
Sep. Treaty of St Germain: Austria cedes Galicia to Poland

1920

Apr.–Oct. Polish-Russian War intensifies
Apr. Polish offensive into Bolshevik Russia (following Treaty of Warsaw with Ukraine)
Jun. Treaty of Trianon: Hungary cedes part of northern Slovakia to Poland. Polish offensive reaches Kiev
Jul. Russian counter-offensive
Aug. 'Miracle on the Vistula': Russian armies are defeated on Polish territory and retreat
Oct. Preliminary armistice between Poland and Russia at Riga. Poland annexes Vilna area from Lithuania

1921

Mar. Treaty of Riga: Polish-Russian War formally ended; Bolshevik Russia recognises the independence of Poland; the border between

Poland and Russia is established (to Polish advantage and Russian, Belorussian and Ukrainian disadvantage)

33. The Portuguese

1777–1816
Reign of Queen Maria I of Portugal

1807
Nov. Portuguese royal dynasty of Braganza dethroned by Napoleon

1808
Aug. British expeditionary force under Sir John Moore lands and expels French from Portugal

1809
Jan. Moore killed in British retreat at Corunna
Apr. Sir Arthur Wellesley (later Wellington) assumes command of British forces in Peninsular War

1811
Apr. British expel French forces from Portugal

1816–1826
Reign of John VI (already Regent of Portugal since 1792)

The Portuguese Constitutional Monarchy (1820–1910)

1820
Aug. Portuguese garrisons in Lisbon and Oporto revolt against British influence and force a convening of the *Cortes*, which produces a liberal constitution

1822
Sep. *Liberal constitution introduced.* Brazil declares itself independent from Portugal

1824
Feb. John VI recalls the Cortes (parliament). Coup by John's brother Dom Miguel and his *miguelista* forces John to flee, but he regains the throne with British aid

1826
May John VI succeeded by Dom Pedro (or Pedro IV) of Brazil, who nominates his daughter Maria, agreeing to rule by a modest charter providing for limited parliamentary government (broadly on the model of the British constitutional monarchy)

1826–1828
Reign of Queen Maria II

1828
Feb. Dom Miguel becomes Regent of Portugal
Jun. Dom Miguel proclaims himself King of Portugal and revokes liberal constitution of 1822

1828–1834
Reign of King Miguel

1833
Queen Maria reclaims throne

1834
May Miguel defeated, surrenders and abdicates at Evaromonte
Sep. Dom Pedro dies, formally succeeded by Queen Maria

1834–1853
(Second) Reign of Queen Maria II

1836
Sep. New 'Septembrist' constitution, a more middle-class compromise between the liberal constitution of 1822 and the moderate conservative constitution of 1826

1839–1842
A more conservative liberal 'Chartism' emerges

1846
May Risings in Portugal

1847
Feb. Royal troops suppress insurgents

1851–1878
Era of 'Regenerationism' and 'Rotativism'

1852
Constitution amended

1853–1861
Reign of King Pedro V

1861–1889
Reign of King Luiz I

1885
Constitution amended again

1889–1908
Reign of King Carlos I

1892
Jun. State bankruptcy announced

1895
Constitution amended twice

1899
Oct. Treaty of Windsor: Portugal and Britain renew treaties of 1642 and 1661

1902
May State bankruptcy again announced

1908
Feb. King Carlos and Crown Prince assassinated

1908–1910
Reign of King Manuel/Manoel II

The Portuguese Parliamentary Republic (1910–1926)

1910
May Insurrection in Lisbon
Oct. King Manuel/Manoel II flees into exile (in England). *Republic of Portugal proclaimed*

1910–1926
Twenty-four revolutions and coups d'état occur within lifetime of the Republic, with the weakening, anti-clerical but pro-liberal Republic increasingly dependent on support from the military

1911
Apr. Separation of Church and State in Portugal
Aug. Republican constitution passed

1915
Jan.–May Pimenta de Castro Government ('The First Reaction')

1916
Feb. Portugal enters First World War on Allied side
Mar. Germany declares war on Portugal

1917
Jan. Portugal sends troops to Western Front
Dec. Sidonia Pais seizes power

1917–1918
Republica Nova of Sidonia Pais ('The Second Reaction')

1918
Dec. Murder of Pais brings 'Presidentialism' to an end

34. The Rumanians

15th century+
Moldavia and Wallachia (the future 'Rumania') comprise tributary territories of the Ottoman Empire

1812
May Treaty of Bucharest: Russian Empire, expanding southwards, claims Bessarabia from Ottoman Empire. Prospect of further Russian advance into Moldavia and then Wallachia

1821
Mar. Rebels in Moldavia and Wallachia led by Tudor Vladimirescu appeal to Tsar of Russia for support against Ottoman rule

1826
Oct. Ackerman Convention: Russia gains the Danubian Principalities (Moldavia and Wallachia) from Ottomans

1829
Sep. Treaty of Adrianople: Ottoman Sultan recognises the *autonomy of the Danubian Principalities*

1829–1834
Russia occupies Principalities to forestall Ottoman revanche

1831
Constitutions proclaimed in Principalities

1845
Customs union between Moldavia and Wallachia

1848
Jul. Russia invades Principalities to suppress attempted revolutions

1849
May Convention of Balta Liman: joint Russian-Ottoman occupation of the Principalities for seven years agreed to combat rebellion

1854
Jun. Treaty of Boyadjii-Keuy: Ottoman Empire permits Austria to occupy Principalities (to deny them to Russia)

1856
Mar. Treaty of Paris concludes the Crimean War: most of Bessarabia ceded back to Ottoman Empire, separating Russia from Principalities. Russia cedes mouth of Danube and part of Bessarabia to the Danubian Principalities, which are guaranteed by the signatory Great Powers

1858
Aug. Paris Agreement of the Great Powers to sanction the creation of separate but identical administrations in Moldavia (at Jassy) and Wallachia (at Bucharest) as the 'United Danubian Principalities'

The Principality and Kingdom of Rumania (1861–1914)

1861

Dec. Danubian Principalities of Moldavia and Wallachia united as a joint principality under Alexander Cuza

1862

International recognition of the autonomous united Principality of 'Rumania'

1864

Rumanian Church proclaimed national and independent of the Patriarchate in Constantinople

1866

Feb. Alexander Cuza dethroned, replaced by Charles/Carol, Prince of Hohenzollern-Sigmaringen

1866–1914

Reign of Charles/Carol I (Prince, 1866–1881; King, 1881–1914)

1877

May Rumania declares war on Ottoman Empire

1878

Jul. *Congress of Berlin* formally acknowledges the independence of 'Rumania' but demands abolition of Article 7 of the Rumanian Constitution: non-Christians (specifically Muslims and Jews) cannot become Rumanian citizens. Rumania is granted northern Dobrudja in return for ceding Bessarabia to Russia

1881

Mar. Prince Charles/Carol I proclaimed King as Rumania is promoted from a principality to a kingdom

1883

Oct. Alliance between Rumania and Austria, later extended to Germany and Italy. Renewed in 1892, 1896, 1902 and 1913

1885

Patriarchate in Constantinople accepts Rumanian Church as auto-cephalous

1893

Rumanian Church maintained by the state and its priests converted into government employees

1912 Oct.-1913 May

First Balkan War: Rumania keeps out, missing out on a share of ex-Ottoman territory at the Treaty of London

1913

Jun.–Jul. Second Balkan War: Rumania joins Serbia, Montenegro, Greece and the Ottoman Empire against Bulgaria

Aug. Treaty of Bucharest: *Rumania gains southern Dobrudja* from defeated Bulgaria. Renewal of alliance between Rumania and Austria-Hungary, Germany and Italy

The First World War and 'Greater Rumania' (1914–1920)

1914

Sep. Despite the obligations of its recently renewed alliance with Austria-Hungary and Germany, *Rumania remains neutral*, then seals agreement with Russia

Oct. Death of King Charles/Carol I

1914–1927

Reign of King Ferdinand I

1916

Aug. *Rumania declares war on Austria-Hungary* and invades Transylvania. Germany declares war on Rumania

Dec. Austrian-German-Bulgarian offensive against Rumania. Bucharest captured

1917

Jan. Rumanian army routed at battle of Focsani. Austrians and Germans take Braila and mouth of Danube. Bulgaria occupies southern Dobrudja (again)

Jul. Joint Rumanian-Russian offensive briefly successful

Dec. Rumanians suspend hostilities during negotiations for a separate peace with Germany and Austria-Hungary

1918

Apr. Bessarabia proclaims its secession from Russia and union with Rumania

May Treaty of Bucharest: *Rumania makes peace with Central Powers* and leaves the war (the Rumanian equivalent of the Russian Treaty of Brest-Litovsk)

Nov. Rumania re-declares war on the Central Powers. On collapse of Austria-Hungary, Transylvania proclaims its union with Rumania

Dec. Mass meeting at Alba Iulia proclaims the unity of all Rumanians

1919

Aug.–Nov. Rumanian-Hungarian War: Rumanian army occupies Budapest to press its claim to Transylvania

Sep. Treaty of St Germain: *Austria cedes Bukovina to Rumania*

Nov. Treaty of Neuilly: Bulgaria cedes wartime acquisition of southern Dobrudja back to Rumania

1920

Jun. Treaty of Trianon: *Hungary cedes Transylvania and half of the Banat to Rumania.* The 'Greater Rumania' precipitated by the cumulative treaties of the Paris Peace Settlement is—through the addition of

Transylvania, Bessarabia and Bukovina—almost double the size of pre-1914 Rumania

35. The Russians

1772

Aug. First Partition of Poland: Russia, together with Austria and Prussia, acquires territory at Poland's expense

1773–1775

Pugachev Uprising threatens stability of southern Russia

1774

Jul. Treaty of Kutchuk-Kainardjii: Russia gains the Crimea and Black Sea littoral as far south as the Dniepr from Ottoman Empire

1783

Transfer of Georgia from Ottoman Empire to Russia agreed

1784

Jan. Convention of Constantinople: Ottomans formally accept their territorial losses to Russia effected in 1774

1792

Jan. Treaty of Jassy: Russian and Ottoman Empires establish river Dniepr as their mutual border

May Russia invades Poland, abrogating new Polish constitution

1793

May Second Partion of Poland between Russia and Prussia: Russia acquires all Poland east of rivers Duna and Dniepr

1794

Mar.–Nov. Polish Uprising led by Kościuszko suppressed by Russian forces

1795

Oct. Third Partition of Poland: remainder of 'rump Poland' distributed between Russia, Austria and Prussia

1796

Nov. Death of Catherine the Great, Tsarina of Russia (1762–1796)

Tsar Paul (1796–1801)

1796

Paul revokes the Charter of the Nobility and limits serf-labour

1798

Dec. Russia joins Second Coalition against France

1799
Apr. Russians under Suvorov defeat French at Cassano, and enter Milan
Jun. Suvorov defeats French at Trebbia, and enters Naples
Aug. Suvorov defeats French at Novi
Sep. Suvorov defeated by French at Zurich; withdraws from Switzerland
Oct. Russia withdraws from Second Coalition

1800
Russian-French *rapprochement*
Dec. Russia, Prussia, Sweden and Denmark form (Second) Armed Neutrality of the North against Britain

1801
Mar. Tsar Paul murdered in aristocratic palace revolution in St Petersburg

Tsar Alexander I (1801–1825)

1801
Sep. Russia formally annexes Georgia

1804
Nov. Secret Russian-Austrian treaty to maintain status quo in 'Italy'

1805
Apr. Russian-British alliance against France signed
Dec. Combined Russian and Austrian armies defeated by Napoleon at Austerlitz, shattering the Third Coalition

1806–1812
Russian-Ottoman War

1807
Feb. Napoleon defeats Russians at Eylau
Jun. Napoleon defeats Russians at Friedland
Jul. *Treaty of Tilsit:* division of Europe between Napoleon and Alexander I into French and Russian spheres of influence (including French support for Russian acquisition of Finland from Sweden, and Moldavia and Wallachia from Ottoman Empire)
Oct. Russia declares war on Britain

1808
Sep. Erfurt Congress between Russia and France

1808–1809
Russian-Swedish War

1809
Sep. Treaty of Fredericksham: *Russia acquires Grand Duchy of Finland from Sweden*

1810
Sukhumi (in Caucasus) annexed by Russia
Dec. Alexander I authorises trade with Britain, thereby breaching the Napoleonic 'Continental System'

1812
Apr. Treaty of Åbo: Sweden accepts transfer of Finland to Russia in return for Russian support for Sweden acquiring Norway
May Treaty of Bucharest ends Russian-Ottoman War: *Russia takes Bessarabia from Ottoman Empire*
Jun. *Napoleon launches invasion of Russia*
Jul. Treaty of Örebro: Britain ends war with Russia and Sweden, promising aid against France
Sep. Inconclusive battle of Borodino between Russians and French. Napoleon enters Moscow
Oct.–Dec. *Napoleon's retreat from Moscow*

1813
Treaty of Gulistan: Russia takes most of 'Azerbaidzhan' from Persia
Feb. Treaty of Kalisch: Russia and Prussia ally against France
May Russians defeated by Napoleon at Lützen and Bautzen
Jun. Treaty of Reichenbach: Russia, Prussia and Austria agree on abolition of Grand Duchy of Warsaw and Confederation of the Rhine
Sep. Treaty of Teplitz between Russia, Austria and Prussia establishes terms and objectives of anti-French alliance
Oct. Russians participate in defeat of Napoleon at Battle of Leipzig

1814
Victory parade by Russian army through Paris

1814–1818
Russian occupying forces in France

1815
Jun. *Congress of Vienna:* Russian acquisitions of Finland and Bessarabia confirmed. 'Poland' redivided to Russian advantage, with 'Russian Poland' or 'Congress Poland' established as a kingdom within the Russian Empire
Sep. *Holy Alliance* created by Alexander I as a Christian monarchical compact to support the status quo. Signed by Russia, Austria and Prussia
Nov. Quadruple Alliance: Russia, Austria, Prussia and Britain agree to guarantee each other's possessions and meet periodically to resolve challenges to 'the maintenance of the peace of Europe'. Alexander I grants 'Congress Poland' a constitution

1818
Congress of Aix-la-Chapelle: France readmitted to Great Power club, Russian occupying forces withdrawn from France

1820

Mutiny of Semenovsky Regiment alarms Alexander I

Oct.–Dec. Congress of Troppau: Alexander agrees to Troppau Protocol authorising Great Power intervention to re-establish legitimist government

1823

Formation of Society of United Slavs

Tsar Nicholas I (1825–1855)

1825

Dec. Decembrist Revolt: aristocratic rebels exploit confusion over the dynastic succession to Alexander I to stage an attempted revolution in St Petersburg, but are shot down by the new Tsar Nicholas I

1826

Jan. Mutiny of Chernigov Regiment in Ukraine in support of the Decembrists is suppressed. Nicholas I establishes 'Third Section' of Imperial Chancellery to combat internal revolution and rebellion

1826–1828

Russian-Persian War

1827

Russia seizes Erivan (in Armenia) from Persia

1828

Feb. Peace of Turkmenchai: Russia acquires more of 'Armenia' from Ottomans and more of 'Azerbaidzhan' from Persia

Apr. Russia declares war on Ottoman Empire in support of Greece

Oct. Russians take Varna and defeat Ottoman army

1829

Sep. Treaty of Adrianople: Russia formally acquires territory south of the Caucasus mountain range ('Armenia' and 'Azerbaidzhan') from Ottoman Empire

1830

Nov. Polish Uprising expels Russians from Warsaw

1831

Sep. Polish Uprising finally suppressed by Russian army

1832

Constitution of 'Congress Poland' abrogated by Nicholas I as punishment for Polish Uprising

1833

Jul. Treaty of Unkiar-Skelessi: defensive accord between Russian and Ottoman Empires over control of the Straits

Sep. Nicholas I and Metternich sign reactionary *Münchengrätz Agreement* pledging mutual aid against internal threat

Oct. Agreement of Berlin: Russia, Austria and Prussia reaffirm the interventionist Troppau Protocol of 1820

1841

Jul. *Straits Convention:* Russia has to agree to closure of Dardanelles to all but Ottoman warships (a strategic reversal of the advantageous 1833 Treaty)

1848

Jul. Russians invade Danubian Principalities to suppress revolts

1849

Apr. Nicholas I receives appeal from Emperor Franz Josef of Austria for aid against the rebel Hungarians (in the spirit of the Münchengrätz Agreement of 1833). Nicholas I is eager to respond as the 'Gendarme of Europe'

May Convention of Balta-Liman: joint Russian-Ottoman occupation of the Danubian Principalities for seven years to forestall revolution

Aug. *Russian military intervention in Hungary* crowned by defeat of Hungarians at Világos

1853

Russia annexes Khiva (in central Asia)

Apr. Russia declares its protectorship over Christian subjects in the Ottoman Empire

Jul. Russia invades Danubian Principalities

1854

Mar. *France and Britain declare war on Russia*

Sep. French and British forces land in Crimea

Nov. French and British armies defeat Russians at Inkerman

1855

Sep. French and British take Sebastopol

Tsar Alexander II (1855–1881)

1856

Mar. *Treaty of Paris* ends the Crimean War: Russia cedes part of Bessarabia back to Ottoman Empire and the remainder to the Danubian Principalities. The Black Sea is neutralised

1857

Russia annexes Mingrelia in Trans-Caucasia

1861–1874

The Emancipation of the Serfs initiates a complex package of fundamental reforms sponsored by Alexander II to modernise Russian society and secure the Great Power status of the Russian Empire without prejudicing the autocratic authority of tsarism

1861–1864
Second Polish Uprising eventually suppressed after military and political measures by Russia (and Prussia)

1864
Russia annexes Abkhazia in Trans-Caucasia

1865
Russia annexes Tashkent in central Asia

1866
Relations between Russia and Papacy broken off (over Russian suppression of the Roman Catholic Poles after 1863)

1867
Mar. Russia sells Alaska to U.S.A.
Jul. Russia establishes Governor-Generalship of Turkestan. Slavonic Ethnographic Exhibition in Moscow boosts Pan-Slavist sentiment in Russia and eastern Europe

1868
Russia occupies Samarkand in central Asia

1873
Aug. Russia claims suzerainty over Khiva and Bokhara in central Asia

1877–1878
Russian-Ottoman War

1877
Mar. London Protocol: Russia and other Great Powers demand reforms from Ottoman Empire
Apr. Russia invades Ottoman Empire to protect fellow Slavs
Dec. Strategically-crucial Ottoman fort of Plevna falls to Russians

1878
Jan. Adrianople falls to Russians, leading to armistice
Mar. *Treaty of San Stephano*: Russia imposes settlement stipulating a 'Big Bulgaria' as a Russian client-state and Russian territorial gains from the Ottoman Empire in Trans-Caucasia (notably Kars)
Jul. *Congress of Berlin* thwarts Russian imperialist strategy, reducing the size of Bulgaria and limiting Russian territorial gains to the recovery of Bessarabia

1879+
Campaign of Russian terrorist group *Narodnaya Volya* ('People's Will') to kill Alexander II

1881

Mar. Alexander II assassinated by *Narodnaya Volya*

Tsar Alexander III (1881–1894)

1881

Mar.+ Alexander III institutes a new hard, repressive régime. Pogroms against Jews in southern Russia, who are blamed for the assassination of 'Tsar-Liberator' Alexander II. Russia annexes Ashkhabad in central Asia

1882

May 'May Laws' increase geographical and professional restrictions against Jews, prompting first wave of Jewish emigration

1884

Jan. Russia annexes Merv in central Asia

1885

Headed by Konstantin Pobedonostsev, Holy Synod forbids mixed-religion marriages in Baltic provinces unless children are raised in Orthodox faith. Widespread protest among Estonians, Latvians and Lithuanians

Mar. Russia occupies Penjdeh on Afghan-Turkestan border, inflaming British fears of Russian encroachment on Afghanistan and India

1887

Jul. Russian-British detente over Afghanistan

1891

May Construction of Trans-Siberian Railway started

1892

Expulsion of Jews from Moscow and St Petersburg to the Pale of Settlement promotes second wave of Jewish emigration to U.S.A.

1893

Dec. Russian-French military convention comes into effect, identifying new *'Entente' alliance of Russia and France* against Germany and Austria-Hungary

Tsar Nicholas II (1894–1917)

1897

First Imperial Russian Census reveals that the Russians constitute only 40 per cent of the state population, encouraging the non-Russian nationalities to undertake nationalist campaigns and alarming the tsarist government into greater Russification

1899+

Nicholas II starts to abrogate privileges of Grand Duchy of Finland

1904–1905
Russo-Japanese War over Manchuria

1905
'Revolution of 1905' forces concessions from Nicholas II towards non-Russian nationalities, including the (temporary) suspension of recent Russification measures. Despite tsarist fears of a 'Romanov 1848', the non-Russians generally neglect to exploit the situation to their own nationalist advantage
Sep.   Treaty of Portsmouth, New Hampshire ends Russo-Japanese War
Oct.   'October Manifesto' concedes an elected imperial parliament (*Duma*)

1906
Apr.   New 'Fundamental Laws' establish an ostensibly constitutional 'Duma Monarchy'
May–Jul.   (First) *Duma* convenes, and is dissolved by Nicholas II for oppositional intransigence

1907
Feb.–Jun.   Second *Duma* even more intransigent; dissolved
Jun.   Prime Minister Peter Stolypin alters electoral system to favour Russians over non-Russians (and landowners over proletariat)
Aug. Russian-British Convention over division of spheres of interest in Persia, Afghanistan and Tibet effectively completes the *Triple Entente of Russia, France and Britain*

1907–1912
Amenable Russian-dominated Third *Duma* collaborates with government of Stolypin in returning to Russification campaign with greater sense of urgency and renewed vigour

1908–1909
Bosnian Crisis: Russian and Pan-Slavist sentiments outraged by Austrian seizure of Bosnia-Herzegovina (and Austrian Foreign Minister Aehrenthal's deception of Russian Foreign Minister Izvolsky), pressuring tsarist government to adopt a more militant and interventionist stance in the Balkans

1910
Oct.   Sergei Sazonov becomes Russian Foreign Minister (1910–1916)

1911
Sep.   Stolypin assassinated in Kiev Opera House

1912
'Great Programme' of five-year overhaul and modernisation of Russian armed forces agreed and introduced

1912–1913
First and (especially) Second Balkan Wars further increase popular

pressure on tsarist government to adopt a stronger, interventionist policy in the Balkans

1912–1917
Fourth *Duma* continues collaboration with tsarist government

The First World War and the Fall of Tsarist Russia (1914–1917)

1914
28 Jun.   Assassination of Archduke Franz Ferdinand in Sarajevo
23 Jul.   Austrian ultimatum to Serbia
24 Jul.   Russia declares that it will defend Serbia against any attack from Austria-Hungary
25 Jul.   Austria-Hungary mobilises against Serbia
26 Jul.   Austro-Hungarian forces mobilise on frontier with Russia
28 Jul.   Austria-Hungary declares war on Serbia
30 Jul.   Russia declares general mobilisation
31 Jul.   Germany demands that Russia cease mobilisation
1 Aug.   *Germany declares war on Russia*
5 Aug.   *Austria-Hungary declares war on Russia.* Russians invade East Prussia; disastrously defeated at Battle of Tannenberg. Imperial capital of St Petersburg renamed Petrograd
Sep.   Declaration of London: *Russia, France and Britain promise no separate peace with Germany.* Russian-Rumanian agreement about Rumania's benevolent neutrality. Russians badly beaten at Battle of the Masurian Lakes
Oct.   Russians rally, forcing Germans and Austrians into retreat
Nov.   *Ottoman Empire declares war on Russia*

1915
Mar.+   Russian retreat before steady German-Austrian offensive
Apr.   *Constantinople Agreements*: Russia is promised Constantinople and the Straits at the end of the war by Britain and France
Jun.   Austro-Hungarian forces take Lemberg
Aug.   German forces capture and occupy Warsaw. A *'Progressive Bloc'* of moderate parties forms in Fourth Duma to improve Russian war effort by deal with tsarist government
Sep.   German forces take Vilna. Grand Duke Nikolai Nikolaievich replaced as Russian Commander-in-Chief by Tsar Nicholas II
Nov.   All Russian Poland and parts of Baltic provinces lost to German and Austro-Hungarian occupying forces

1916
Jan.   Russian offensive on Caucasian front against Ottoman Empire
Feb.   Russians capture Erzerum in Ottoman Armenia
Mar.   Russian 'Brusilov offensive' against Austrian-Hungarian front
Apr.   Russians capture Trebizond from Ottomans
Jul.   Russians capture Czernowitz from Austrians

Aug. *Rumania joins Allies against Austria-Hungary*
Sep. Russian-Rumanian offensive against Austria-Hungary
Oct.–Dec. Austrian-German-Bulgarian counter-offensive against Rumania

1917
Jan. Russians and Rumanians defeated at Focsani
Feb. Collapsing standard of living in Petrograd prompts food riots and demonstrations
Mar. *Revolution in Petrograd*: Tsar Nicholas II abdicates, and his chosen heir Grand Duke Michael declines the crown. Romanov dynasty and tsarist government come to an end

Revolutionary Russia (1917–1921)

1917
Mar. *Provisional Government*, headed by George Lvov, Paul Miliukov and other leading representatives of the Progressive Bloc, assumes 'caretaker' power until the convening of a democratically-elected Constituent Assembly. Rival Petrograd Soviet formed
May Second Provisional Government, with Alexander Kerensky as Minister of War
Jun. Kerensky launches Russian offensive
Jul. Kerensky becomes Premier of Provisional Government. Russian offensive claims Tarnopol
Aug. Russians recapture Czernowitz from Austrians
Sep. Kerensky proclaims Russian Republic. German offensive captures Riga
Nov. *Bolshevik Revolution in Petrograd*: Provisional Government falls, replaced by Bolshevik government headed by Lenin and Trotsky. Trotsky negotiates immediate armistice on eastern front
Dec. Hostilities suspended during Russian-German negotiations for a separate peace at Brest-Litovsk

1918
Jan. Constituent Assembly suppressed on its opening day
Mar. *Treaty of Brest-Litovsk*: Bolshevik Russia loses all its western borderlands of Poland, Finland, the Baltic provinces, Belorussia and Ukraine as the price of a separate peace
Jul. Nicholas II and family murdered during Russian Civil War
Nov. With the end of the First World War, Bolshevik Russia formally renounces the Treaty of Brest-Litovsk

1919
Mar. *Komintern* (or Third Communist International) founded in Moscow as Bolshevik-based international agency for promoting worldwide communist revolution

not part of revolution :)

Oct. British evacuate Murmansk (indicating Western abandonment of intervention against Bolshevik power)
Nov. Defeat of Yudenitch's White Army (indicating future Red victory in Russian Civil War)
Dec. Ukraine reincorporated into Bolshevik state

1920
Feb. Treaty of Tartu: Russia recognises independence of Estonia
Jun. Azerbaidzhan reincorporated into Bolshevik state
Jul. Treaty of Moscow: Russia recognises independence of Lithuania
Aug. Treaty of Riga: Russia recognises independence of Latvia. *Belorussia reincorporated into Bolshevik state*
Oct. Preliminary treaty of Riga: Russia preparing to recognise independence of Poland. Treaty of Tartu: Russia recognises independence of Finland
Nov. Last White army of Wrangel expelled from Russia, marking Bolshevik victory in the Russian Civil War
Dec. Armenia reincorporated into Bolshevik state

1921
Mar. Georgia reincorporated into Bolshevik state. Treaty of Riga: Bolshevik Russia formally recognises the independence of Poland. The Riga Treaty represents a territorial and geopolitical watershed, marking the jurisdictional stabilisation of the Bolshevik Russian state in Europe

36. The Ruthenians

1840s
Ruthenians in eastern Galicia favoured by Habsburgs to offset dominance of Poles in western Galicia

1848
May At the Slav Congress in Prague, Ruthenian delegates demand autonomy from the Poles within an 'Austro-Slav' state

1867
Feb. By the terms of the *Ausgleich* establishing the Dual Monarchy of Austria-Hungary, 'Ruthenia' falls partly within Hungary/ Transleithania, mostly within Austria/Cisleithania

1870+
Russia claims Ruthenians as 'Habsburg Ukrainians' while Habsburgs foster Ruthenian self-consciousness to combat Russian expansionist Pan-Slavism

1890+
'Ruthenia' acquires the hopeful reputation of the 'Ukrainian Piedmont', cynically tolerated by the Habsburgs to embarrass the tsarist

government in its suppression through Russification of Ukrainian nationalism

1914–1918
'Ruthenia' and the Ruthenians are in the combat zone of the eastern front in the First World War

1914
Nov.–Dec. 'Ruthenia' is (briefly) occupied by the Russian forces, who antagonise the Ruthenians by harsh Russifying treatment

1915
'Ruthenia' recaptured by Austria-Hungary

1916
'Ruthenia' again in combat zone of Russian-Austrian conflict

1917
Jun. American Ruthenian Congress demands freedom for Ruthenia from Hungary

1918
Oct. Philadelphia Agreement between Czech leader Tomaš Masaryk and Gregory Žatković (spokesman for emigrant Ruthenian community in U.S.A.) promises 'Ruthenia' autonomy within the projected federal state of 'Czecho-Slovakia'

1919
Sep. Treaty of St Germain: *'Ruthenia' to receive autonomy within new state of Czecho-Slovakia*

1920
Jun. Treaty of Trianon: Hungary formally (and retrospectively) cedes 'Ruthenia' to Czecho-Slovakia

1920+
'Ruthenia' becomes the most easterly province of Czecho-Slovakia (with Ruthenians comprising 3.9 per cent of its population); but the great majority of Ruthenians (in Galicia) are incorporated into the new Polish state (comprising 14.3 per cent of its total population and constituting Poland's largest national minority)

37. The Scots

1770s–1830s
Scottish cultural 'Golden Age'

1759–1796
Robert Burns recognised as national poet of Scotland

1760–1763

MacPherson brothers publish *Ossian's Poems*, pioneering a long line of nationalist epic literary fakes

1771–1832

Walter Scott recognised as national novelist of Scotland

1828

Repeal of Test and Corporation Acts removes last civil disabilities on Protestant dissenters

1829

Catholic Emancipation Act makes Roman Catholics eligible for most offices of state, with no oath of supremacy required to sit as M.P. in House of Commons

1830–1842

Scotland is 'discovered' musically by Mendelssohn: *Hebrides Overture* and *'Scotch Symphony'*

1843

Disruption of Scottish Church. Establishment of Free Church of Scotland

1848–1852

Purchase of Balmoral, marking the beginning of royal identification with the Highlands

1853

Association for the Vindication of Scottish Rights founded

1885

Office of Secretary of State for Scotland created within government of United Kingdom

1886

Scottish Home Rule Association founded

1900

Glasgow recognised as both 'Second City of the British Empire' and sixth largest city in Europe (with a population of 1,052,000)

1907

Programme for a proposed 'Scottish Party' demands a compulsory qualification in the Gaelic language for all public office-holders in Scotland

38. The Serbs

1789

Austrians take Belgrade, capital of 'Serbia', during the Austrian-Russian-Ottoman War of 1787–1792

1804–1807
(First) Serb Insurrection

1811
Feb. In Russian-Ottoman War of 1806–1812, Russian forces capture Belgrade

1812
May Treaty of Bucharest: anticipating a French invasion, Russia settles with Ottoman Empire, evacuating Serbia

1815–1817
Second Serb Insurrection

1817
Nov. Ottoman Empire grants Serbia partial autonomy

1826
Oct. Ackerman Convention: Russia gains recognition of independence of Serbia and Danubian Principalities from Ottoman Empire

1858
Dec. Serbian Diet deposes Prince Alexander Karageorgević, installs Milan Obrenović

1862
Jun. Serb Rising in Belgrade. Ottomans bombard Belgrade

1868
Jun. Assassination of Prince Michael Obrenović

1868–1889
Reign of Milan IV (Prince, 1868–1882; King, 1882–1889)

1876
Jun. Serbia declares war on Ottoman Empire
Oct. Ottoman victory over Serbs at Alexinatz

1877
Feb. Peace treaty between Serbia and Ottoman Empire
Dec. Serbia redeclares war on Ottoman Empire (joining Russia)

1878
Mar. Treaty of San Stefano: Serbia enlarged territorially, with its independence recognised by the Ottoman Empire
Jul. Congress of Berlin: Serbia still enlarged territorially, with its independence recognised by the Ottoman Empire

1881
Jun. Serbia enters alliance with Austria-Hungary

1882

Jan. Prince Milan assumes title of King Milan IV (promoting Serbia from a principality to a kingdom)

1885

Nov. Serbia declares war on Bulgaria, suffering defeat at Slivnitza

1886

Mar. Austrian ultimatum brings end to *Serbian–Bulgarian War* by the Treaty of Bucharest

1889

Mar. Abdication of Milan IV in favour of son Alexander

1893

Apr. Alexander I declares himself of age as King of Serbia

1903

Jun. Assassination of King Alexander I and Queen Draga. Succeeded by Peter Karageorgević

1903–1921

Reign of King Peter Karageorgević

1904

Mar. Treaty of Sofia establishes alliance between Serbia and Bulgaria

1905

Rijeka Resolution: Serb and Croat leaders attempt a joint campaign against Austria-Hungary. *Zara Resolution*: 26 Serb deputies declare that 'Croats and Serbs are one nation by blood and language'.

1906

Customs war with Austria-Hungary ('Pig War')

1908–1909

Bosnian Crisis: Serbia is outraged by Austro-Hungarian annexation of Bosnia-Herzegovina (which it regards as the next component of 'Greater Serbia') and return of the Sanjak of Novi Bazar to Ottoman Empire (which prevents Serbia linking up with Montenegro to gain access to the Adriatic)

1912

Feb.–Sep. *Balkan League* headed by Serbia and Bulgaria, joined by Greece and Montenegro, against the Ottoman Empire

1912 Oct.–1913 May

First Balkan War: Serbia leads Montenegro, Greece and Bulgaria in successful campaign against Ottoman Empire

1913

May *Treaty of London* ends First Balkan War: Serbia receives territory at the expense of the retreating Ottoman Empire. Serbia and Greece sign secret military convention against Bulgaria

Jun.–Jul. Second Balkan War: Serbia joins Montenegro, Greece, Rumania and Ottoman Empire against Bulgaria

Aug. Treaty of Bucharest: Serbia receives more territory in Macedonia, this time at the expense of Bulgaria

1914

28 Jun. Assassination of Archduke Franz Ferdinand in Sarajevo

23 Jul. Austrian ultimatum to Serbia

25 Jul. Serbian reply

28 Jul. Austria-Hungary declares war on Serbia

6 Aug. Serbia declares war on Germany. Austrian attack on Serbia checked at Jadar

Sep. Second Austrian attack again checked by Serbs

Nov. Third Austrian attack repulsed by Serbs

Dec. Austrians capture Belgrade, then withdraw

1915

Estimated 300,000 Serbs die in typhus epidemic

Oct. Combined Austrian-German-Bulgarian offensive against Serbia. Landing of Allied troops at Salonika to support Serbs

Nov. Serbs beaten at Kosovo. *Serbia occupied by Austrian and Bulgarian forces*

1916

Jan.–Feb. Serbian army evacuated to Corfu after losing 70,000 of its 200,000 troops during winter retreat through Albania

Mar.+ Serbian troops transferred to Salonika front by Allies, contributing to the capture of Monastir (in November)

1917

Jul. Pact of Corfu: declaration of intent to establish a democratic and federal South Slav state, signed by Pašić (Prime Minister of Serbia) and Trumbić (President of Yugoslav Committee)

1918

Oct. Allied forces expel Austrian-German-Bulgarian forces from Serbia

Nov. Assembly at Podgorica deposes King Nicholas of Montenegro and votes for union of Montenegro with Serbia

Dec. Proclamation of the new Kingdom of the Serbs, Croats and Slovenes (under the Serbian Karageorgević dynasty)

1918–1920

The fundamental territorial jurisdiction and geopolitical shape of the Kingdom of the Serbs, Croats and Slovenes (subsequently rechristened *Yugoslavia*) is established

1919

Sep. Treaty of St Germain: Austria cedes Slovenia, Dalmatia and

Bosnia-Herzegovina to the Kingdom of the Serbs, Croats and Slovenes
Nov. Treaty of Neuilly: Bulgaria cedes all wartime territorial conquests
from Serbia to Kingdom of Serbs, Croats and Slovenes

1920
Jun. Treaty of Trianon: Hungary cedes Croatia and Voivodina to
Kingdom of Serbs, Croats and Slovenes
Nov. Treaty of Rapallo: Italy and the Kingdom of the Serbs, Croats and
Slovenes reach a (temporary) accommodation over the Adriatic littoral

39. The Slovaks

Pre-1848
The Slovaks, located within the Hungarian sphere of influence in the
Austrian Empire, are increasingly attracted to Pan-Slavism as protection
against the threat of cultural Magyarisation

1848–1849
Fearing the repressive nationalism of the Hungarians, Slovaks ally with
the Habsburgs against the Hungarian campaign for independence

1867
Under the *Ausgleich* establishing the Dual Monarchy of Austria-
Hungary, Slovakia falls within Hungary/Transleithania

1868
Nationalities Law promises equality for all nationalities within
Transleithania. Slovak National Party tolerated

1875
Matica Slovenská, institutional centre of Slovak cultural nationalism
since 1863, is closed down by the Hungarian government 'for
promoting Pan-Slavism'

Late 1870s+
Increasing Magyarisation of Slovak institutions and culture

1890s+
Slovak emigration to U.S.A. mounts to proportionately massive levels

1905
Slovak People's Party tolerated

1907
Černová Affair. Slovak priest Hlinka jailed for 'seditious agitation' after
protesting against Magyarisation. Fifteen Slovaks killed by police in
subsequent demonstrations

1914–1918
Slovakia initially close to combat zone of the Eastern Front between

Austria-Hungary and Russia, then increasingly remote as the Central Powers advance eastwards

1915
Oct. Emigrant Slovak League and Czech National Association in Cleveland, U.S.A. agree to campaign for a federal Czecho-Slovak state

1918
May Pittsburgh Agreement: Czech leader Masaryk and spokesmen for Slovak organisations in U.S.A. jointly demand a new federal state of Czecho-Slovakia, in which Slovakia is guaranteed full autonomy and its own Diet
Oct. Declaration of Turciansky Svaty Martin: Slovaks express willingness to join the Czechs in a common independent state of 'Czecho-Slovakia'

1919
Aug. Slovak Soviet Republic established (briefly) by invading Hungarian forces

1920
Jun. Treaty of Trianon: Hungary (retrospectively) cedes a small part of northern Slovakia to the revived state of Poland, the remainder of Slovakia to the new state of Czecho-Slovakia. Slovaks comprise 16 per cent of the population of the new state of Czecho-Slovakia

40. The Slovenes

Pre-1805
Slovenia a subject territory of the Habsburg Empire

1805–1813
Illyrian Republic established as a Napoleonic client-state, exposing Slovenes to Western influences and encouraging early nationalist ambitions for greater freedom

1814–1866
Slovenia reverts to a subject territory of the Habsburg Empire

1867
Under the *Ausgleich* creating the Dual Monarchy of Austria-Hungary, Slovenia is included within Cisleithania/Austria

1870+
Jernej Kopitar develops Slovene language

1880+
As a Roman Catholic area bordering upon German Austria, Slovenia receives benevolent treatment from Vienna, making substantial economic and social progress

1900+
Development of Slovene nationalist ambitions, legitimised by historical claims of tenth-century Freising Manuscripts

1912
Resolution of Ljubljana/Laibach confirms Slovene 'Austro-Slav' preference for greater autonomy for Slovenia within Austria-Hungary (not independence)

1915
Apr. Treaty of London promises Italy large tracts of Slovenia claimed as part of *Italia Irredenta* in return for joining the Allies in the First World War

1918
Dec. *Kingdom of the Serbs, Croats and Slovenes proclaimed* (accepted by Anton Korošec, anti-Italian Slovene leader)

1919
Sep. Treaty of St Germain: Austria cedes Slovenia to the Kingdom of the Serbs, Croats and Slovenes. Slovenes comprise 8.1 per cent of the population of the new state of the Kingdom of the Serbs, Croats and Slovenes

1920
Nov. Treaty of Rapallo between Italy and Kingdom of the Serbs, Croats and Slovenes agrees a (temporary) accommodation over territorial claims to the Adriatic littoral, including the establishment of an independent Fiume/Rijeka

41. The Spanish

1788–1808
Reign of Charles/Carlos IV of Spain

1793
Feb. Spain joins First Coalition against France

1795
Jul. Spain quits First Coalition, makes peace with France

1796
Aug. Alliance of San Ildefonso between Spain and France
Oct. Spain declares war on Britain

1797
Feb. Spanish fleet defeated by British at Cape St Vincent

1804
Dec. Spain (again) declares war on Britain

1805
Oct. Spanish-French combined fleet defeated by Nelson at Trafalgar

1808
Mar. Spanish military revolt against Napoleon at Aranjuez, demanding succession of Crown Prince Ferdinand
May Spanish revolt against Napoleon in Madrid, initiating 'War of Spanish Independence'
Jun. King Charles/Carlos and Crown Prince Ferdinand of Spain forced to abdicate. Joseph Bonaparte proclaimed new King of Spain
Jul. Spanish defeat French at Baylen, puncturing French reputation for military invincibility. Constitution of Bayonne proclaimed

1808–1812
Bonapartist Spain. Reign of Joseph Bonaparte as King of Spain

1808–1809
Sieges of Saragossa and Gerona

1810
Start of attempt at constitutional régime

1812
Jan.–Aug. Succession of victories by British expeditionary force in Spain, led by Wellington, against French
Mar. Liberal *Constitution of Cadiz* drawn up by the *Cortes* (parliament)

1813
Jun. Wellington defeats French at Vittoria, expelling French forces from Spain
Dec. Napoleon forced to reinstate exiled Ferdinand VII as King of Spain

1813–1833
Reign of King Ferdinand/Fernando VII

1814
May 'Constitution of Cadiz' of 1812 abolished by newly-returned King Ferdinand VII

1814–1820
The 'Fernandine Reaction'

1820
Jan. Pro-liberal mutinies in Cadiz led by Riego and Quiroga. 'Constitution of Cadiz' of 1812 restored under military duress

1820–1823
The 'Liberal Triennium'

1821
Jul. Peru proclaims independence from Spain

Nov. Panama proclaims independence from Spain

1822

Oct.–Dec. Congress of Verona discusses intervention in the spirit of the Troppau Protocol to restore legitimist stability in civil war-torn Spain

1823

Apr. French forces intervene in Spain

Aug. French forces restore Ferdinand VII, who institutes harsh 'Second Fernandine Reaction' and re-abolishes Constitution of 1812/1820

1824–1833

Fernandine Absolutism between Ultra-Royalism and Liberalism

1825

Aug. Bolivia and Uruguay proclaim independence from Spain

1825–1827

Revolt of *Agraviados* in Catalonia

1830

Ferdinand VII reaffirms Carlos IV's decree of 1789, declaring Spain no longer bound by the Salic Law (excluding women from the succession), thereby legitimising the imminent accession to the throne of his young daughter Isabella

1833

Sep. On his deathbed, Ferdinand VII declares his daughter Isabella Queen of Spain

1833–1868

Reign of Queen Isabella II

1834

Estatuto Real (Royal Statute) introduces a liberal constitution. Ferdinand's brother Don Carlos contests his niece's succession, backed by conservative/aristocratic/northern interests in Spain

1834–1837

(First) Carlist War divides and damages Spain

1837

Don Carlos defeated and leaves Spain, ending Carlist War. Liberal constitution proclaimed

1841

Jul. Espartero appointed Regent of Spain

1843

Jul. Narvaez defeats Espartero, who leaves Spain

Nov. Isabella II declared of age as Queen of Spain

1847
Sep. Espartero recalled from exile to Spain

1851
Spain signs concordat with Papacy: Roman Catholicism declared the religion of the Spanish state 'to the exclusion of all others'

1854
Jul. Liberal revolt: Regent Maria Christina exiled

1854–1856
The 'Progressive Biennium'

1864
Sep. Maria Christina returns to Spain

1868
Sep. 'September Revolution': *Cortes* proclaims liberal principles. Queen Isabella II flees into exile in France

1868–1874
Interregnum

1869
New government headed by Marshal Prim introduces liberal constitution

1869–1873
The Elective Monarchy

1870
Jun. Isabella formally abdicates in favour of her son Alfonso XII
Jul. Succession crisis: candidacy of Leopold of Hohenzollern antagonises Spain (and triggers Franco-Prussian War)
Nov. A second Don Carlos (grandson of the original) claims Spanish throne when Amadeo, Duke of Aosta, is chosen as successor to Isabella II
Dec. Marshall Prim assassinated in Madrid

1871–1872
Reign of (elected) King Amadeo I

1872–1876
Second Carlist War

1872
Apr. Don Carlos recognised by Pope as Charles/Carlos VII, but defeated militarily
May Convention of Amorebeita

1873
Feb. Amadeo abdicates and leaves Spain. 'First Republic' proclaimed by *Cortes*, provoking Carlist opposition

1874
Jan.   Marshal Serrano becomes dictator of Spain. Carlists again beaten
Sep.   Restoration of Bourbon monarchy with accession of Alfonso XII

1874–1885
Reign of King Alfonso XII

1875
Jan.   Alfonso XII returns from exile, lands in Barcelona, becomes generally recognised as King of Spain

1875–1899
The Restored Constitutional Monarchy

1876
Feb.   Don Carlos forced into exile in France. New Spanish constitution

1876+
Second Carlist War over but sporadic Carlist disorders continue throughout 1880s and into 1890s

1885
Death of King Alfonso XII and birth of his son Alfonso XIII

1885–1902
Regency of Alfonso XIII's mother, Queen Maria Christina

1885–1890
Reform Ministry of Sagasta

1888
First public manifestations of Catalan nationalism

1890
Mar.   Universal male suffrage introduced

1890s
Stagnation of Restoration politics. Maura and the 'Revolution from Above'

1898
El Desastre: loss of north American colonies of Cuba, Puerto Rico and Philippines (to U.S.A.) precipitates economic and political crisis in Spain

1899+
Crisis and Collapse of Spanish Liberalism

1902–1931
Reign of King Alfonso XIII

1911
Dec.   Spanish premier Canalejas murdered

1913–1915
Breakdown of Party System

1914–1918
Spain remains neutral throughout First World War

1917
Aug. Political crisis triggered by general strike supporting independence for Catalonia

42. The Swedes

1771–1792
Reign of Gustavus III

1772
Gustavus III establishes absolutist monarchy by bloodless palace revolution, and becomes reforming 'Enlightened Despot'

1788–1790
Swedish-Russian War

1788
Jun. Gustavus III exploits Russian-Ottoman War to declare war on Russia
Nov. Treaty of Uddevalla: invading Danes defeated by Gustavus III and agree to withdraw from Sweden

1789
Gustavus suppresses internal mutinies and opposition

1790
Sweden routs the Russian fleet at Svenskund
Aug. Treaty of Varela: Gustavus settles for peace with Russia on pre-war basis

1792
Mar. Gustavus III assassinated

1792–1809
Reign of Gustavus IV Adolphus

1800
Dec. Armed Neutrality of the North (comprising Sweden, Denmark and Russia) revived by France as anti-British shipping alliance

1807
Jul. Treaty of Tilsit: Napoleon promises to support Tsar Alexander I's proposed annexation of Finland from Sweden

1808–1809
Swedish-Russian War

1809
Mar. Gustavus IV forced to abdicate
Sep. *Peace of Fredericksham: Sweden cedes Finland to Russia*

1809–1818
Reign of Charles/Karl XIII (King of Sweden, 1809–1814; King of Sweden and Norway, 1814–1818)

1810
Aug. Charles XIII recognises Marshal Jean-Baptiste Bernadotte as elected Crown Prince and heir to the throne of Sweden

1812
Jan. Napoleon seizes Swedish Pomerania
Apr. Secret Treaty of Åbo between Sweden and Russia against France: Sweden accepts loss of Finland to Russia in return for Russian aid in acquiring Norway from Denmark
Jul. Treaty of Örebro: Sweden and Russia make peace with Britain against France

1813
Feb. Alliance of Kalisz between Russia and Prussia joined by Sweden
Mar. Treaty between Sweden and Britain: Britain subsidises Swedish war effort against Napoleon and agrees to support Sweden's acquisition of Norway
May Swedish troops enter Swedish Pomerania

1814
Jan. *Treaty of Kiel*: Denmark cedes Norway to Sweden
Nov. Kingdom of Sweden and Norway formally agreed by Norwegian Assembly

1815
Jun. *Congress of Vienna* confirms Sweden's acquisition of Norway from Denmark

1818–1844
Reign of Charles/Karl XIV (Bernadotte)

1844–1859
Reign of Oscar I

1855
Nov. Agreement at Stockholm between Britain, France and Sweden to preserve the united Kingdom of Sweden and Norway

1859–1872
Reign of Charles/Karl XV

1859
Members of non-Lutheran faiths permitted full toleration

1866
Jun. New constitution replaces four Estates with two parliamentary Chambers

1872–1907
Reign of Oscar II (King of Sweden and Norway, 1872–1905; King of Sweden, 1905–1907)

1873
Swedes now permitted to leave Lutheran Church to join any other Christian church

1905
Jun. Norwegian Assembly votes for dissolution of union with Sweden
Sep. Plebiscite in Norway approves vote for independence
Oct. *Sweden accepts and concedes loss of Norway*

1907–1950
Reign of Gustavus V

1910
Feb. Revision of constitution

1914–1918
Sweden neutral in First World War

43. The Swiss

Pre-1798
Aristocracy and oligarchy-dominated traditional Swiss Confederation finds its internal unity, territorial integrity and international neutrality increasingly challenged

1798
Jan. Lemanic Republic (based on Geneva) proclaimed
Mar. French seize Berne and exact reparations
Apr. Annexation of Geneva and Helvetic Republic proclaimed
Aug. Alliance between Helvetic Republic and France

1799
Sep. Defeated Russian army retreats through Switzerland

1802
Oct. Napoleon intervenes in civil war between town and country cantons as 'Mediator of the Helvetic League'

1803
Feb. French Act of Mediation: federal government weakened and the constituent cantons regain much of their independence

1814
May First Treaty of Paris: France must withdraw from all territories annexed from Switzerland since 1789
Jun. *Congress of Vienna* re-establishes Swiss Confederation, which is increased from 19 to 22 cantons by the addition of Geneva, Wallis and Neuchâtel. The neutrality of the Swiss Confederation is guaranteed by the signatory Great Powers

1823
Jul. Switzerland refuses right of asylum to foreign refugees

1845
Sep. *Sonderbund* of Roman Catholic Swiss cantons formed

1847
Oct.–Nov. *'Sonderbund' War*: secessionist ambitions of Catholic cantons defeated and the *Sonderbund* is suppressed

1848
New constitution combines effective central government with traditional cantonal autonomy

1856
Sep. Unsuccessful uprising of Prussian royalists in Neuchâtel

1857
Jun. Neuchâtel incorporated into Switzerland after Prussia renounces its sovereignty

1873
Dec. Papal nuncio expelled

1874
May Swiss constitution adapted and centralised

1893–1895
Customs war between Switzerland and France

1914–1918
Switzerland remains neutral in the First World War

44. The Turks

1768–1774
Ottoman-Russian War

1774

Jul. *Treaty of Kutchuk-Kainardji*: Russian territorial advance on the Black Sea littoral at the expense of the Ottoman Empire first poses the 'Eastern Question'

1775

Austria annexes Bukovina from Ottoman Empire

1784

Jan. Convention of Constantinople: Ottoman Empire formally recognises Russian acquisition of Crimea and the northern littoral of the Black Sea and the right of Russia to navigate in 'Ottoman waters'

1787–1792

Ottoman-Russian-Austrian War

1789–1807

Reign of Sultan Selim III

1791

Aug. Treaty of Sistova ends Ottoman-Austrian War: Ottomans cede Orsova

1792

Jan. Treaty of Jassy ends Ottoman-Russian War: Dniepr established as the Russian/Ottoman border

1798–1801

Ottoman-French War: Napoleon's Egyptian Campaign

1798

May Napoleon leads French expeditionary force to Egypt
Jul. Napoleon defeats the Mamelukes (rulers of Egypt under Ottoman licence) at Battle of the Pyramids

1799

May Napoleon's invasion of Syria checked at Acre
Jul. Napoleon defeats Ottomans at Aboukir (then returns to France)

1800

Mar. French under Kléber defeat Turks and Mamelukes at Heliopolis

1801

Aug. French surrender after defeat by the British at Alexandria
Sep. French expeditionary force evacuates Egypt
Oct. Peace between Ottoman Empire and France: Egypt restored to the Ottoman Empire

1804–1807

(First) Serb Uprising

1806–1812

Ottoman-Russian War

1807
Jul.   Janissaries dethrone Sultan Selim III

1807–1808
Reign of Sultan Mustafa IV

1808–1839
Reign of Sultan Mahmud II

1811
Feb.   Ottomans lose Belgrade and most of their army to Russia

1812
May   Treaty of Bucharest ends Ottoman-Russian War: Ottomans cede Bessarabia to Russia

Ottoman Retreat before Balkan Nationalism (1815–1914)

1815–1817
Second Serb Uprising

1817
Nov.   Ottomans grant autonomy to Serbia

1821
Mar.   Revolt in Moldavia and Wallachia: rebels appeal to Tsar of Russia for 'Christian aid' against the Ottoman yoke

1821–1829
Greek War of Independence

1826
Janissaries liquidated by Mahmud II

1827
Oct.   Ottoman fleet sunk by British at Navarino

1828–1829
Ottoman-Russian War

1828
Feb.   Peace of Turkmenchai: Ottomans cede parts of northern Armenia to Russia

1829
Sep.   *Treaty of Adrianople* ends Ottoman-Russian War: Ottomans recognise independence of Greece, and Russian acquisition of Georgia and Armenia, occupation of Moldavia and Wallachia, and access through the Straits

1830
Feb.   Treaty of London: independence of Greece from Ottoman Empire guaranteed by Britain, Russia and France

1832–1833
First Mehemet Ali Crisis

1832
Apr. Ottomans declare war on their nominal vassal, Mehemet Ali of Egypt. Mehemet Ali takes Acre
Dec. Mehemet Ali defeats Ottomans at Konieh

1833
May Egypt granted independence (and Syria) by Ottomans
Jun. *Treaty of Unkiar-Skelessi* between Ottoman and Russian Empires: Ottomans permit free Russian passage through the Straits but agree to close them to foreign warships at Russian request
Sep. Agreement of Münchengrätz: Metternich and Tsar Nicholas I agree on joint maintenance of the Ottoman Empire
Oct. Berlin Agreement: Russia, Austria and Prussia agree to maintain the territorial integrity of the Ottoman Empire

1839–1841
Second Mehemet Ali Crisis

1839
Jun. Ottoman forces invade Syria but are defeated by Mehemet Ali at Nezib
Jul. Ottoman fleet surrenders to Mehemet Ali at Alexandria
Nov. New Sultan Abdul Mejid I issues reform decree

1839–1861
Reign of Sultan Abdul Mejid I

1840
Jun. Quadruple Alliance of Britain, France, Austria and Russia formed to support Ottoman Empire against Mehemet Ali
Sep. British Navy bombards Beirut
Nov. British forces capture Acre, forcing Mehemet Ali to withdraw from Syria. Convention of Alexandria: Mehemet Ali agrees to Treaty of London

1841
Jul. Great Powers guarantee Ottoman Empire: Ottomans get Syria back from Egypt; Straits closed to all non-Ottoman warships by the *Straits Convention*

1848
Jul. Russia invades Wallachia to suppress nationalist uprising

1849
May Convention of Balta Liman: joint Russian-Ottoman occupation of Moldavia and Wallachia agreed for seven years. Ottomans agree to allow Christians free exercise of their faith

1852–1853
Ottoman-Montenegrin War

1853
Apr. Russia claims protectorship of the Ottoman Empire's Christian subjects
May Ottomans reject Russian claim
Jul. Russia invades Moldavia and Wallachia
Oct. Ottoman Empire declares war on Russia
Nov. Ottoman fleet destroyed by Russians at Sinope

1854
Mar. Britain and France ally with Ottomans against Russia
Jun. Treaty of Boyadjii-Keuy: Ottoman Empire permits Austria to occupy the Danubian Principalities (to deny them to Russia)

1854–1856
Crimean War: Ottoman Empire, Britain, France and Piedmont- Sardinia fight against the Russian Empire. Ottoman casualties estimated at 35,000 dead

1856
Feb. Hatt-i Humayun: reform edict guaranteeing civil rights to Christian subjects forced upon the Ottoman Empire by Britain, France and Austria
Mar. Treaty of Paris: neutralisation of the Black Sea; Russia returns Bessarabia partly to Ottomans, partly to Danubian Principalities

1858
Feb.–Jul. Ottoman-Montenegrin War
Aug. Paris Agreement: Moldavia and Wallachia formally united as joint Danubian Principalities
Nov. Montenegro granted formal independence by Ottomans

1860
Massacre of Christians in Ottoman Syria
Oct. Ottoman law reforms, based upon *Code Napoléon*

1861–1876
Reign of Sultan Abdul Aziz

1861
Dec. Union of Danubian Principalities of Moldavia and Wallachia into the new Principality of Rumania acknowledged by Sultan Abdul Aziz

1862
Jun. Rising of Serbs in Belgrade. Ottomans bombard the city

1866–1869
Uprising in Crete, unsuccessfully demanding union with Greece

1871

London Conference accepts cancellation of neutralisation of the Black Sea

1875

Jul. Bulgaria and Bosnia-Herzegovina rebel against Ottomans
Oct.–Dec. Reforms promised by Abdul Aziz

1876

Jan. Andrássy Note accepted by Abdul Aziz
Mar. *Bulgarian Massacres* by Ottoman forces
May Berlin Memorandum: Germany, Austria and Russia demand reforms in Ottoman Empire
Jun. Sultan Abdul Aziz is assassinated, and succeeded (briefly) by Murad V. Serbia declares war on Ottomans
Jul. Montenegro joins Serbia against Ottoman Empire
Aug. Sultan Murad V is deposed, and succeeded by Abdul Mejid II
Oct. Ottomans defeat Serbs and Montenegrins at Alexinatz. Russia intervenes with an ultimatum to force an armistice
Dec. New Sultan Abdul Mejid II concedes a constitution, promising parliamentary government and freedom of worship

1876–1909

Reign of Sultan Abdul Hamid II

1877

Jan. Convention of Budapest: Austria-Hungary promises Russia neutrality in the event of war between the Russian and Ottoman Empires
Feb. Peace treaty ends war between Ottomans and Serbs
Mar. Meeting of first Ottoman parliament. London Protocol: Great Powers demand more reforms
Apr. Abdul Hamid defies London Protocol. Russia declares war and invades Ottoman Empire
May Rumania declares war on Ottomans
Dec. Strategically-crucial Ottoman fort of Plevna falls to Russians. Serbia re-declares war on Ottomans

1878

Jan. Adrianople falls to Russians
Feb. Greece declares war on Ottomans
Mar. *Treaty of San Stefano*: Ottoman jurisdiction in Europe greatly reduced by Russian-inspired settlement favouring Bulgaria
Jul. *Congress of Berlin* confirms Ottoman territorial losses (except for the nominal retention of Eastern Rumelia) but redistributes ex-Ottoman territory among Balkan states. Austria-Hungary authorised to occupy Bosnia-Herzegovina and Sanjak of Novi Bazar

1880

Nov. Montenegrin occupation of Duicigno accepted by Sultan

1881

Jul.   Ottomans cede Thessaly and Epirus to Greece

1895

Oct.   Armenian Massacres: an estimated 20,000 Gregorian Christian Armenians killed by Turks. British fleet denied passage of the Straits, prompting British Prime Minister Lord Salisbury to air the question of partitioning the Ottoman Empire

1896–1897

Second Cretan Uprising

1896

Jul.   Ottoman concessions to Cretan autonomy deemed insufficient

1897

Ottoman-Greek War

Feb.   Crete defies Ottoman authority and proclaims its union with Greece

Apr.   Ottomans declare war on Greece

May   Greeks defeated by Ottomans in Thessaly, forcing the Great Powers to intervene to impose an Ottoman-Greek armistice

Dec.   Peace of Constantinople: Ottomans cede Crete to Greece

1899

Dec.   Berlin-Baghdad Railway commissioned, and perceived as consolidation of the German-Austrian-Ottoman political and economic connection

1901

Nov.   Ottomans back down to French ultimatum over treaty violations

1908

Young Turk Revolution

Jul.   Rebellion of army officers in Salonika leads to the creation of the 'Committee of Union and Progress' (or 'Young Turks')

Dec.   Under pressure from the Young Turks, Abdul Hamid II concedes a constitution and convenes a parliament

1908–1909

Bosnian Crisis

Oct.   Bosnia-Herzegovina (occupied since 1878) formally annexed by Austria-Hungary. Ottomans agree in return for Austrian return of the Sanjak of Novi Bazar

1909

Feb.   Serbia forced to yield to Ottoman-Austrian deal

Apr.   Young Turks depose Sultan Abdul Hamid II

1909–1918

Reign of Sultan Mohammed V

1911–1912
Ottoman-Italian War

1912
Oct. Treaty of Ouchy ends Ottoman-Italian War: Ottoman Empire forced to cede Cyrenaica, Tripoli, Rhodes and the Dodecanese to Italy

1912 Oct.–1913 May
First Balkan War: Ottoman Empire attacked by Balkan League of Serbia, Bulgaria, Greece and Montenegro

1913
May Treaty of London ends First Balkan War: Ottoman Empire loses almost all its remaining Balkan territories, and is reduced to a vestigial Turkey-in-Europe around Constantinople
Jun.–Jul. Second Balkan War: Ottoman Empire joins Serbia, Greece and Rumania in attacking Bulgaria
Aug. Treaty of Bucharest ends Second Balkan War: Ottomans receive some territorial recompense for the estimated 70,000 casualties incurred over the two Balkan Wars
Sep. Ottoman-Bulgarian peace treaty
Oct. Ottoman-German military convention
Nov. Ottoman-Greek peace treaty
Dec. Von Sanders arrives in Constantinople to head German Military Mission to the Ottoman Empire

The First World War and the Fall of the Ottoman Empire (1914–1923)

1914
Aug. Ottomans close Dardanelles to foreign warships
Oct. Enver Pasha is appointed commander-in-chief of Ottoman forces
Nov. Britain declares war on Ottoman Empire. Ottomans declare *jihad* (holy war) on Britain, France and Russia

1915
Mar.–Apr. Constantinople Agreements: secret promise from Britain and France that Russia will receive Constantinople and the Straits at the end of the war as reward for joining the Allied side
Apr.–Oct. Gallipoli Campaign: successful Ottoman defence (headed by Mustapha Kemal) against Allied landings. 'Armenian Genocide': Ottoman responsibility for the deaths of up to 1.5 million Armenians
Jun.–Sep. Ottoman defeated by British in Mesopotamia
Nov. Turks defeat British at Ctesiphon

1916
Feb. Russian offensive on Caucasus front: capture of Erzerum
Mar. Allies start to plan the partition of the post-war Ottoman Empire as British force surrenders at Kut
Apr. Russians take Trebizond

May *Sykes-Picot Note:* British and French deal for the territorial partition of the Ottoman Empire after the War. France to receive Syria and Lebanon; Britain to receive Transjordan, Iraq and northern Palestine
Dec. After surrender at Kut, new British offensives in Mesopotamia and Palestine

1917
Mar. British take Baghdad
Apr. Ottoman defeats in Mesopotamia. *Treaty of St Jean de Maurienne:* secret agreement between Britain, France and Russia to permit Italy a share in the partitioned Ottoman Empire (in western Anatolia)
Nov. British capture Gaza and Jaffa in Palestine. *Balfour Declaration:* British support for the establishment of a Jewish homeland in Palestine further complicates the projected partition of the Ottoman Empire
Dec. General Allenby enters Jerusalem

1918
Feb.–Apr. Ottoman offensive on Russian front, retaking Trebizond and Kars and taking Baku
Jul.–Oct. British advance in Palestine, taking Damascua and Aleppo
Oct. *Armistice of Mudros:* Ottomans surrender unconditionally

1918–1922
Reign of Sultan Mohammed VI

1920
May Turkish National Assembly meets in Ankara
Aug. *Treaty of Sèvres* between the Ottoman Empire and Allies: Ottomans renounce all claims to territory occupied by non-Turks, thereby suffering ignominious loss of territory and Allied incursions into the Turkish mainland by Britain, France, Italy and Greece. Irremediably discredits the Ottoman establishment

1921
Mar. Treaty between Turkey and Bolshevik Russia. Mustapha Kemal organises Turkish army

1922
Sep. Turks under Mustapha Kemal take Smyrna and forcibly expel the Greeks. Kemal confronts British expeditionary force authorised by the League of Nations to maintain the de-militarised Straits at Chanak
Oct. Armistice between Turkey and Greece. Convention of Mudania returns the Straits and Constantinople area to Turkish jurisdiction
Nov. Mustapha Kemal proclaims the *Republic of Turkey*

1923
Jul. *Treaty of Lausanne:* renegotiated Treaty of Sèvres to the advantage of Turkey, reclaiming all Asia Minor by expelling all foreign partitionist incursions and establishing the fundamental geopolitical shape and territorial jurisdiction of the Turkish Republic

45. The Ukrainians

1772–1795
Partitions of Poland and retreat of the Ottoman Empire bring most of the 'Greater Ukraine' under Russian jurisdiction

1798
Ivan Kotlyarevsky's *Eneida*, the first book printed in the Ukrainian language

1815
Congress of Vienna effectively partitions 'Ukraine' between Austria (Ruthenia/Galicia/Bukovina) and Russia

1825
Dec. 'Ukrainians' prominent in 'Southern Society' of the Decembrists

1840
Publication of *Kobzar* by Taras Shevchenko, the national poet of Ukraine

1840s
Brotherhood of Saints Cyril and Methodius in Kiev/Kiyiv

1863
Russian limitation on publishing books in Ukrainian

1876
Russian ban on publication or import of all books in Ukrainian

1917
On the fall of tsarism, *Ukrainian nationalists claim autonomy* for Ukraine from the Russian Provisional Government
Jul. Central Council of Ukraine (R.A.D.A.) formed in Kiev/Kyiv, with historian Mykhailo Hrushevsky as president

1918
Jan. Ukrainian National Republic proclaimed in eastern Ukraine
Feb. Central Council of Ukraine (R.A.D.A.) declares independence and signs separate peace treaty with the Central Powers
Mar. Treaty of Brest-Litovsk: Ukraine licensed as a client-state within the eastern empires of Germany and Austria-Hungary
Apr. Puppet Ukrainian Government headed by General Pavlo Skoropadsky established by Central Powers
Nov. On the fall of Austria-Hungary, nationalists in Lvov/Lviv proclaim a Western Ukrainian National Republic
Dec. Following the end of the First World War and withdrawal of the Central Powers, the Skoropadsky government collapses. Red Army attacks Ukraine and the French land in Odessa

1919

Jan. Eastern and Western Ukrainian Republics unite and proclaim a sovereign and independent Ukrainian nation. Ukrainian National Union under Simon Petlyura assumes control

Apr. French withdraw from Odessa

May–Aug. Offensive in Ukraine by Whites under Denikin

Sep. *Treaty of St Germain*: Austria cedes Bukovina (claimed by Ukraine) to Rumania

Oct. Denikin defeated and forced to retreat

Dec. Ukraine forcibly reincorporated into Bolshevik Russia by the Red Army

1920

Apr. Treaty of Warsaw: Poland recognises Ukrainian National Republic and promises aid against the Bolsheviks in return for the acquisition of Galicia/Western Ukraine. *Polish-Russian War*: Poland invades Ukraine/ Bolshevik Russia

May Poles capture Kiev

Jun. *Treaty of Trianon*: Hungary cedes Ruthenia (claimed as Carpatho-Ukraine) to Czecho-Slovakia. Red Army recaptures Kiev

1921

Mar. *Treaty of Riga*: Polish-Russian War ended by the partition of Ukraine: western Ukraine is annexed by Poland, eastern Ukraine remains within Bolshevik Russia

1919–1921

Ukraine is subjected to four-way partition and subordination: Rumania takes Bukovina; Czecho-Slovakia takes Ruthenia; Poland takes Galicia/ western Ukraine; and Bolshevik Russia retains eastern Ukraine

46. The Welsh

1792

Revival of eisteddford by Welsh in London

1811

Two-thirds of Welsh Protestants secede from the Anglican Church

1820s

Eisteddford movement gains support rapidly in Wales

1829

Mass Welsh petition to Parliament protesting at Catholic Emancipation Act

1839–1843

Rebecca (or 'Becky') Riots

1843

Hugh Owen's *Letter to the Welsh* begins campaign for Welsh educational and cultural institutions

1858

Bangor normal teacher training college established

1862

Publication of George Borrow's *Wild Wales*

1867

University College of Wales at Aberystwyth established

1870

Gladstone appoints first Welsh-speaking Bishop in St Asaph since reign of Queen Anne

1881

Welsh Sunday Closing Act: the first parliamentary act to treat Wales separately from England

1895

Bill to disestablish the Anglican Church in Wales (following disestablishment in Ireland in 1869) is defeated

1904–1905

Welsh religious revival, consolidating and extending Non-Conformist ascendancy

1909

Second Bill to disestablish the Anglican Church in Wales is defeated in the House of Lords

1914

Welsh Church Disestablishment Act passed, coming into effect in 1920

Statistical tables

3.7 Comparative populations (in millions) of four ocean states and nations 1850-1920

SECTION 4

Statistical tables

1. Comparative populations (in millions) of European states and nations, 1800–1920

Note the fluctuating populations effected by such factors as mass emigration (notably Ireland), state territorial expansion (notably Greece, Rumania and the Russian Empire) and state territorial contraction (notably Austria, Hungary and the Ottoman Empire).

	1800	1850	1900	1920
Albania	–	–	–	0.8
Austria	14.0	17.5	26.2	6.5
Belgium	3.1	4.4	6.7	7.4
Bulgaria	–	–	3.5	4.8
Czechoslovakia	–	–	–	13.6
Denmark	0.9	1.4	2.5	3.1
Finland	0.8	1.6	2.7	3.2
France	27.4	35.7	38.9	39.2
Germany	23.0	35.2	56.4	61.0
Greece	0.9	1.0	2.5	5.0
Habsburg Empire	19.0	30.7	45.5	–
Hungary	5.0	13.2	19.3	8.0
Iceland	–	0.06	0.08	0.09
Ireland	5.2	6.6	4.5	2.8
Italy	17.2	24.4	33.0	38.0
Montenegro	–	–	0.23	–
Norway	0.9	1.4	2.2	2.6
Ottoman Empire in Europe	–	16.0	5.7	–
Poland	9.0	–	15.1	27.2
Portugal	2.9	3.5	5.4	6.4
Prussia	–	16.4	33.5	–
Rumania	–	3.9	6.0	15.0
Russian Empire	40.0	68.5	130.0	145.0
Scotland	–	2.8	4.4	4.8
Serbia	–	–	2.4	–
Spain	10.5	14.0	18.6	21.0
Sweden	2.4	3.5	5.1	5.8
Switzerland	–	2.4	3.3	3.9
United Kingdom	17.5	27.2	41.0	42.0
Yugoslavia	–	–	–	12.0

2. Most-populated European states (in millions) 1800, 1850, 1900 and 1920

	1800
Russian Empire	40.0
France	27.4
'Germany'	23.0
Habsburg Empire	19.0
United Kingdom	17.5
'Italy'	17.2

	1850
Russian Empire	68.5
France	35.7
'Germany'	35.2
Habsburg Empire	30.7
United Kingdom	27.2
'Italy'	24.4

	1900
Russian Empire	130.0
Germany	56.4
Habsburg Empire	45.5
United Kingdom	41.0
France	38.9
Italy	33.0

	1920
Russia	145.0
Germany	61.0
United Kingdom	42.0
France	39.2
Italy	38.0
Poland	27.2

3. League table of most-populated European states, 1800–1920

Russia	1st in 1800, 1850, 1900 & 1920
France	2nd in 1800, 3rd in 1850, 5th in 1900 & 4th in 1920
Germany	3rd in 1800, 4th in 1850, 2nd in 1900 & 1920
Habsburg Empire	4th in 1800, & 1850, 3rd in 1900
United Kingdom	5th in 1800 & 1850, 4th in 1900 & 3rd in 1920
Italy	6th in 1800, 1850 & 1900, 5th in 1920

4. Ethnic composition of Austria/Cisleithania, 1880 and 1910

Nationality	1880	1910
Germans	36.8%	35.6%
Czechs	23.8%	23.0%
Poles	14.9%	17.8%
Ruthenians	12.8%	12.6%
Slovenes	5.9%	4.5%
Serbs and Croats	2.6%	2.8%
Italians	3.1%	2.7%
Others	0.1%	1.0%

5. Ethnic composition of Hungary/Transleithania, 1890 and 1910

Nationality	1890	1910
Magyars	42.8%	48.1%
Rumanians	14.9%	14.1%
Germans	12.2%	9.8%
Slovaks	11.1%	9.4%
Croats	9.0%	8.8%
Serbs	6.1%	5.3%
Ruthenians	2.2%	2.3%
Others	1.7%	2.2%

6. Ethnic composition of Austria-Hungary (in millions), 1910

Nationality	Population	% of total
Germans	12.0	23.9
Magyars	10.0	20.2
Czechs	6.5	12.6
Poles	5.0	10.0
Ruthenians	4.0	7.9
Rumanians	3.25	6.4
Croats	2.5	5.3
Slovaks	2.0	3.8
Serbs	2.0	3.8
Slovenes	1.25	2.6
Others (incl. Italians)	2.9	3.5
Total	*51.4*	*100.0*

7. Religious affiliation in Austria-Hungary (in millions), 1910

Religion	Population	% of total
Roman Catholic (incl. Uniate)	39.0	77.2
Protestant	4.5	8.9
Orthodox	4.5	8.9
Jewish	2.1	3.9
Muslim	0.5	1.1
Total	**50.6**	**100.0**

8. Ethnic composition of the Russian Empire (in millions), 1897

Nationality	Population	% of total
Russian	55.7	44.3
Ukrainian	22.4	17.8
Polish	7.9	6.3
Belorussian	5.9	4.7
Jewish	5.1	4.0
German	1.8	1.4
Lithuanian	1.7	1.3
Latvian	1.4	1.2
Mordvin	1.0	0.9
Estonian	1.0	0.9
Other Finno-Ugrian	1.5	1.2
Others (mostly Asiatic)	16.4	15.9
Total	**121.8**	**99.9**

9. Comparative populations of leading European cities (in thousands), 1800–1900

	1800	1850	1900
Amsterdam	201	224	515
Athens	12	31	111
Barcelona	115	175	533
Belgrade	20	25	69
Berlin	172	419	1,889
Brussels	66	251	599
Bucharest	–	90	280
Budapest	54	156	732
Christiania	–	37	227
Constantinople	–	600	1,000
Copenhagen	101	127	401
Glasgow	77	357	1,052
Lisbon	180	240	356

Table 9. continued

London	1,117	2,685	7,488
Madrid	160	270	540
Moscow	250	300	1,000
Naples	350	449	564
Paris	547	1,053	2,714
Prague	75	118	202
Rome	153	175	505
Sofia	–	30	80
Stockholm	76	131	301
St Petersburg	220	485	1,400
Turin	78	133	336
Vienna	247	444	1,675
Warsaw	60	114	423

10. Most-populated European cities, 1800, 1850 and 1900

	1800
London	1,117,000
Paris	547,000
Naples	350,000
Moscow	250,000
Vienna	247,000
St Petersburg	220,000

	1850
London	2,685,000
Paris	1,053,000
Constantinople	600,000
St Petersburg	485,000
Naples	449,000
Vienna	444,000

	1900
London	7,488,000
Paris	2,714,000
Berlin	1,889,000
Vienna	1,675,000
St Petersburg	1,400,000
Glasgow	1,052,000

11. League table of most-populated European cities, 1800–1900

Only London, Paris, St Petersburg and Vienna figure among the top six in 1800, 1850 and 1900. The most notable 'risers' are Berlin and Glasgow ; the most notable 'decliners' are Naples and Moscow.

London	1st in 1800, 1850 & 1900
Paris	2nd in 1800, 1850 & 1900
Naples	3rd in 1800 and 5th in 1850
Moscow	4th in 1800
Vienna	5th in 1800, 6th in 1850 and 4th in 1900
St Petersburg	6th in 1800, 4th in 1850 and 5th in 1900
Constantinople	3rd in 1850
Berlin	3rd in 1900
Glasgow	6th in 1900

12. European state production of coal, steel and oil (in thousand tons), 1900

	Coal	Steel	Oil
Belgium	23,463	655	–
Bulgaria	227	–	–
France	33,404	1,565	–
Germany	149,569	6,461	50
Habsburg Empire	39,030	1,170	351
Italy	480	116	2
Luxembourg	–	185	–
Netherlands	320	–	–
Portugal	1	–	–
Rumania	86	–	247
Russian Empire	16,160	2,216	10,684
Serbia	156	–	–
Spain	2,675	122	–
Sweden	252	300	–
United Kingdom	228,794	4,980	–

13. Top coal-producing European states (in tons), 1900

United Kingdom	228,794,000
Germany	149,569,000
Habsburg Empire	39,030,000
France	33,404,000
Belgium	23,463,000
Russian Empire	16,160,000

14. Top steel-producing European states (in tons), 1900

Germany	6,461,000
United Kingdom	4,980,000
Russian Empire	2,216,000
France	1,565,000
Habsburg Empire	1,170,000
Belgium	655,000

15. Top oil-producing European states (in cubic tons), 1900

Russian Empire	10,684,000
Austria	349,000
Rumania	247,000
Germany	50,000
Hungary	2,000
Italy	2,000

16. League table of European coal, steel and oil producing states, 1900

United Kingdom	1st in coal, 2nd in steel
Germany	1st in steel, 2nd in coal, 4th in oil
Russian Empire	1st in oil, 3rd in steel, 6th in coal
Habsburg Empire	2nd in oil, 3rd in coal, 5th in steel
France	4th in both coal and steel
Belgium	5th in coal, 6th in steel

17. Emigration from Europe by state (in thousands), 1860s, 1880s and 1900s

	1860s	1880s	1900s
Belgium	2	21	30
Denmark	8	82	73
Finland	–	26	159
France	36	119	53
Germany	779	1,342	274
Habsburg Empire	40	248	1,111
Italy	27	992	3,615
Netherlands	20	52	28
Norway	98	187	191
Portugal	79	185	324
Russian Empire	–	288	911
Spain	7	572	1,091
Sweden	122	327	324
Switzerland	15	85	37
United Kingdom	1,572	3,259	3,150

18. Top emigrant-despatching European states, 1860s

		% of total for decade
United Kingdom	1,572,000	56
Germany	778,000	28
Sweden	122,000	4
Norway	98,000	3.5
Portugal	79,000	3
Habsburg Empire	40,000	1.5

19. Top emigrant-despatching European states, 1880s

		% of total for decade
United Kingdom	3,259,000	42
Germany	1,342,000	17
Italy	992,000	13
Spain	572,000	7
Sweden	327,000	4
Russian Empire	288,000	3

20. Top emigrant-despatching European states, 1900s

		% of total for decade
Italy	3,615,000	32
United Kingdom	3,150,000	28
Habsburg Empire	1,111,000	10
Spain	1,091,000	10
Russian Empire	911,000	8
Sweden	324,000	3

21. League table of emigrant-despatching European states, 1850–1920

Only two states appear among the top six in the 1860s, 1880s and 1900s: the United Kingdom and Sweden.

United Kingdom	15,879,000 total 1st in 1860s and 1880s, 2nd in 1900s
Italy	8,581,000 total 3rd in 1880s and 1st in 1900s
Germany	4,310,000 total 2nd in 1860s and 1880s
Spain	3,783,000 total 4th in 1880s and 1900s
Habsburg Empire	2,334,000 total 6th in 1860s and 3rd in 1900s
Russian Empire	1,758,000 total 6th in 1880s and 5th in 1900s
Sweden	1,184,000 total 3rd in 1860s, 5th in 1880s and 6th in 1900s

22. Human losses in principal European wars, 1850–1920

The First World War and Russian Civil War together accounted for almost 29 million dead, or 95.5% of the total war losses for the period 1850–1920.

	(Minimum estimated military and civilian deaths)
Crimean War, 1854–1856	253,000
French-Piedmontese-Austrian War, 1859	66,700
Danish-Prussian-Austrian War, 1864	14,500
Austrian-Prussian-Italian War, 1866	145,900
Franco-Prussian War, 1870–1871	710,000
Balkan Wars, 1912–1913	162,500
First World War, 1914–1918	14,959,000
Russian Civil War, 1918-1921	14,000,000
Total	***30,311,600***

23. League table of human losses in war by European states, 1850–1920

	(Minimum estimated military and civilian deaths)
Russia	16,575,000
Germany	2,688,700
Ottoman Empire	2,580,000
France (incl. French Empire)	2,095,600
Habsburg Empire	1,653,500
Britain (incl. British Empire)	960,000
Serbia	808,500
Rumania	612,500
Italy	481,000
Bulgaria	412,000
Greece	144,500
Belgium	44,000
Portugal	7,000

24. European states' relative human losses in war, 1850–1920

	% of total estimated military and civilian deaths
Russia	54.7
Germany	8.9
Ottoman Empire	8.5
French Empire	6.9
Habsburg Empire	5.5
British Empire	3.2
Serbia	2.7
Rumania	2.0
Italy	1.6
Bulgaria	1.4
Greece	0.5
Belgium	0.15
Portugal	0.02

Nationalist biographies

Ali Pasha Tepalene (1741/4–1822): Creator of an early nineteenth-century 'Greater Albanian' principality. Albanian brigand who becomes governor of Epirus from 1788, officially under licence from the Ottomans, in practice independent. Under Ali's capricious patronage, Janina becomes a centre of Greek culture (visited by Byron in 1809). Murdered on orders of Sultan Mahmud II for publicly opposing Ottoman centralisation plans. Ali's reputation as the 'Lion of Janina' inspires all subsequent Albanian nationalists. Biography: William Plomer, *The Diamond of Janina: Ali Pasha, 1741–1822* (1920).

Andrássy, Count Gyula (1823–1890): Hungarian nationalist and Austro-Hungarian statesman. Militant nationalist supporting Kossuth in the campaign for Hungarian independence, 1847–1849. In exile, 1849–1858. On return, campaigns for an *Ausgleich*, achieved in 1867. First Prime Minister of Hungary within the new Dual Monarchy of Austria-Hungary, 1867–1871. Foreign Minister of Austria-Hungary, 1871–1879. Heads Austro-Hungarian delegation to Congress of Berlin in 1878, which licenses Austria-Hungary to occupy Bosnia-Herzegovina. Proponent of pro-German alliance against Russia. Conventionally represented as both a nationalist militant-turned-moderate and a nationalist-turned-imperialist.

Arndt, Ernst Moritz (1769–1860): Early proponent of a 'Big German' state. Journalist and publicist, setting down his anti-French ideas in *Germany and Europe* (1803). Supports a language definition of 'Germany', demanding by 1813 that 'the whole of Germany' be united 'as far and as wide as the German tongue is heard'. Harassed by government of Prussia for his critical views after 1819. Deputy to National Assembly at Frankfurt in 1848. Retires from politics in disillusionment, 1849. Biographies: A.G. Pundt, *Arndt and the National Awakening in Germany* (1935) and H. Scurla, *E.M. Arndt* (1952).

Barrès, Maurice (1862–1923): Extreme French nationalist politician. Strong anti-German animus prompted by the loss to Germany of his native Lorraine in 1871. Supporter of Boulanger and a founder-member of the anti-Semitic *Ligue de la Patrie Française* in 1889. A spokesman for the anti-Dreyfusards after 1895. A major influence on Maurras and *Action Française*. Proponent of the cult of a mystical, heroic French patriotism. A classic example of the 'border-dweller' as typical extreme nationalist.

Bem, Josef (1794–1850): Polish patriot who becomes a hero of the Hungarian Uprising in 1848–1849. Fights for Poland against Russia in 1812 and 1830–1831. Offers his services to Kossuth in 1848, and is given defence of Transylvania. Performs heroically against Austrians, then Russians in 1849. Escapes to Ottoman Empire, adopts Islam and (as Murad Pasha) becomes Governor of Aleppo. The supreme Polish patriot-adventurer.

Beneš, Edvard (1884–1948): Czech politician and Czecho-Slovak statesman. Peasant by birth but educated at the universities of Prague, Dijon and Paris. Collaborates closely with Masaryk in Paris during the First World War, campaigning for Allied recognition of a new state of Czecho-Slovakia. Head of the Czech delegation to the Paris Peace Conference, 1919. Foreign Minister of Czecho-Slovakia, 1918–1935. Also Prime Minister, 1921–1922. Succeeds Masaryk as President of Czecho-Slovakia in 1935, resigning over the Munich Agreement in 1938. President of the Czecho-Slovak government-in-exile in London, 1941–1945. Re-elected President in 1946 but resigns after the Communist coup d'état in 1948. A co-creator of Czecho-Slovakia doomed to see his state twice taken over by neighbouring Great Powers. Memoirs: *My War Memoirs* (1928).

Bernadotte, Jean-Baptiste (1763–1844): Marshal of France turned King of Sweden. Distinguished French soldier, fighting at Austerlitz and Wagram. Promoted to Marshal of France, 1804. Marries into Bonaparte family. Governor of the Hanseatic cities, 1807–1809. Elected heir to the Swedish throne, 1810. Switches camps, encouraging Britain and Russia against France. Leads Swedish army in the defeat of Napoleon at Leipzig, 1813. Formally ascends Swedish throne as Charles/Karl XIV, 1818. Liberal monarch, 1818–1844, accepting ministerial responsibility to parliament and granting concessions to new Norwegian subjects. Extraordinary career as a triumphant survivor of the fall of Napoleon and adoptive Swedish nationalist monarch. Biography: D.P. Barton, *The Amazing Career of Bernadotte* (1929).

Bismarck, Otto von (1815–1898): Prussian-German statesman and architect of German unification. From a *Junker* family in Brandenburg, becomes ultra-royalist member of Prussian Diet, 1847. Hostile to liberal-nationalist revolution, 1848. Prussian member of German Diet at Frankfurt, 1851–1859. Prussian ambassador to St Petersburg, 1859. Prussian Ambassador to Paris, 1862. Chief Minister of Prussia, 1862. Dissolves parliament, forces through reorganisation of army. Seeks unification of 'Germany' under Prussian leadership, excluding the traditional authority of Austria. Provokes wars with Denmark in 1864, Austria in 1866 and France in 1870. Chancellor of North German Confederation, 1867–1871. Created Prince and Imperial Chancellor of German Empire, 1871. Domestic political struggles with Catholic Church (*Kulturkampf*) in 1870s and with socialists in 1880s. Introduces anti-socialist legislation but also provides universal suffrage and social insurance. Foreign policy geared to securing (not expanding) newly-unified Germany. Devises systems of alliances (*Dreikaiserbund* and Triple Alliance) designed to protect Germany and isolate France. Irreconcilable personality clashes with the new Kaiser William/Wilhelm II force resignation in 1890 (prompting the famous *Punch* cartoon 'Dropping the Pilot'). Memoirs: *Bismarck: The Man and the Statesman*

(1898). Leading biographies: Erich Eyck, *Bismarck and the German Empire* (1950); Edward Crankshaw, *Bismarck* (1981); Oscar Pflanze, *Bismarck and the Development of Germany* (1990); Lothar Gall, *Bismarck: The White Revolutionary* (1986) and Bruce Waller, *Bismarck* (1985).

Boulanger, General Georges (1837–1891): French soldier and politician of the Right. Minister of War under the Third Republic, 1886–1887. Elected deputy in 1888, advocating nationalistic and expansionist policies. Demands limitations on republican constitution, attracting the support of militarists and royalists as well as the League of Patriots. Suspected of planning a right-wing coup, flees from France to Belgium, 1889. Condemned for treason in his absence. Wave of 'Boulangism' recedes, 1890. Commits suicide, 1891. Viewed by opponents as representing a rightist threat to the Third Republic, seeking to repeat the career of Louis Napoleon/Napoleon III by overthrowing republican government in favour of a nationalist monarchical empire.

Burns, Robert (1759–1796): National poet of Scotland, writing in the Scottish dialect of English. Restless, Romantic rebel. Enthusiast for Scottish traditional folklore and songs (sometimes credited with 'Auld Lang Syne'). Articulator of the largely anonymous voice of the Scottish people, resulting in his cult status among Scots (especially those in exile). Leading biographies: David Daiches, *Robert Burns and His World* (1971); John M. Lindsay, *Robert Burns: The Man, His Life, The Legend* (1979); and James MacKay, *Burns: A Biography* (1992).

Butt, Isaac (1813–1879): Founder of the Home Rule Association in Ireland in 1870. Lawyer specialising in defence of Young Ireland members and Fenians. First President of Home Rule Confederation of Great Britain, 1873–1877. Overtaken as Home Rule leader by Parnell in 1878. Biography: D. Thornley, *Isaac Butt and Home Rule* (1964).

Byron, Lord George Gordon (1788–1824): Poet and nationalist hero. After a glittering (and scandalous) career as supreme Romantic poet, Byron leads Western Philhellene movement supporting Greek campaign for independence from Ottoman Empire. Patron of the *Carbonari* from 1820. Dies at battle of Missolonghi in 1824 'for Freedom's battle'. In life, the most influential Philhellene; in death, the most celebrated nationalist martyr. Becomes a symbol of altruistic nationalism and the role-model poet-patriot for subsequent nationalist movements, many of which throw up a local equivalent (for example, Petöfi, the 'Hungarian Byron'). Biographies include: Leslie A. Marchand, *Byron* (1957) and Elizabeth Longford, *The Life of Byron* (1976).

Capodistrias, John Antonios (1776–1831): Russian diplomat of Greek origin who becomes the first President of independent Greece. Tsarist Foreign Minister after 1815, promoting a pro-Greek policy. Proves the importance of Great Power backing for nationalist movements. Elected

President of Greece, 1827. Paternalistic, even autocratic style. Assassinated, 1831.

Carson, Edward (1854–1935): Leader of Ulster resistance to Home Rule in Ireland. Born and educated in Dublin. M.P. for Dublin, 1892–1918. Solicitor-General, 1900–1905. Leads Protestant opposition to Home Rule, 1905–1915. Sets up Ulster Unionist Council, 1911. As 'uncrowned king of Ulster', organises Ulster Volunteer Force to resist Home Rule, 1912. Imports arms from Germany, then agrees to Home Rule for Ireland other than Ulster, early 1914. Attorney-General in Asquith Cabinet, 1915–1916. First Lord of the Admiralty, 1916–1917. Member of War Cabinet, 1917–1918. Less militant, seeking compromise over Ulster Question after 1918. M.P. for Belfast, 1918–1921. Lord of Appeal, 1921–1929. Still controversial leader of Ulster Unionism actively opposing the 'surrender' of the British government to Irish Home Rule. Biographies: Edward Marjoribanks and Ian Colvin, *Lord Carson* (1932–1936) and H. Montgomery Hyde, *Carson*(1953).

Casement, Sir Roger (1864–1916): Distinguished British public servant turned Irish nationalist 'martyr'. Dublin-born but serves in British consular service, 1892–1912. Knighted, 1911. Converts to Irish nationalism, 1912. Tries to enlist American, then German aid for Irish nationalist cause, 1914. Attempts to persuade Irish POWs to form 'Irish Brigade' within German Army, 1915. Landed from German U-boat to raise rebellion, arrested, brought to London, tried for treason and hanged, 1916. Prosecution uses private diary (revealing homosexual leanings) to discredit Casement as an Irish patriot-martyr. Biographies: Rene Marie McColl, *Roger Casement: A New Judgement* (1956) and B.L. Reid, *The Lives of Roger Casement* (1976).

Cavour, Count Camillo di (1810–1861): Piedmontese-Italian politician and statesman, credited as the architect of Italian unification. Co-founder of *Il Risorgimento* (Resurrection) newspaper demanding a united liberal Italy, 1847. Piedmont's Minister of Agriculture, 1850. Prime Minister of Piedmont, 1852. Strengthens constitutional government and reduces influence of Catholic Church in Piedmont. Abandons failed *Italia fara da se* (Italy can do it herself) strategy for unification. Commits Piedmontese troops to the Crimean War to curry favour with French and British allies, 1854. Brings 'Italian Question' (unsuccessfully) to Congress of Paris, 1856. Negotiates Pact of Plombières with Napoleon III to expel Austrians from northern Italy, 1858. Resigns when Napoleon III fails to honour Pact in full, ending war with Austria 'prematurely', 1859. Returns as Prime Minister of Piedmont, 1860. Negotiates union of Parma, Modena, Tuscany and the Romagna with Piedmont. First Prime Minister of newly-proclaimed Italy, 1861. Premature death at the juncture when a united Italy is proclaimed but Italian territorial unification is still incomplete.

Conventionally perceived as a diplomat-nationalist, inviting comparisons with Bismarck and contrasts with the adventurer-nationalist Garibaldi. Biographies: Heinrich von Treitschke, *Cavour* (1870); W. Roscoe Thayer, *The Life and Times of Cavour* (1911); and Dennis Mack Smith, *Victor Emmanuel, Cavour and the Risorgimento* (1971) and *Cavour* (1985).

Charles Albert/Carlo Alberto (1798–1849): King of Piedmont-Sardinia and failed unifier of Italy. King of Piedmont-Sardinia, 1831–1849. Grants a reformist government in 1847 and a constitution to Piedmont, 1848. Raises nationalist banner of Italy to expel Austrians from Lombardy, 1848. Defeated by Austrians under Radetzky at Custozza in 1848 and Novara in 1849. Abdicates to Portugal in despair at failure of his *Italia fara da se* (Italy can do it herself) nationalist strategy.

Collins, Michael (1890–1922): Irish nationalist hero murdered for alleged compromise. Born in Cork, works in post office and bank in London. Returns to Ireland to support Easter Rising, 1916. Imprisoned by British for militant nationalism, 1916 and 1918. Elected to first Dail Eireann, 1918. Masterminds nationalist guerrilla warfare operations, 1919–1921. Irish representative in Irish Treaty negotiations, 1921. Supports new Irish Free State, assassinated by anti-Treaty republican nationalists, 1922. Biographies: R. Taylor, *Michael Collins* (1961) and Margaret Forester, *Michael Collins: The Lost Leader* (1971 and 1989).

Crispi, Francesco (1819–1901): Italian nationalist and statesman. Active nationalist in 1848 and 1859–1860. Founder-member of Garibaldi's 'Thousand Redshirts', 1860. Extreme Left deputy in Italian parliament in early 1860s. Converts to monarchism and opposes Garibaldi in late 1860s. Prime Minister of Italy, 1887–1891 and 1893–1896 (when forced to resign by the Italian disaster at Adowa). A mercurial, passionate but controversial nationalist both in opposition before 1870 and in power after 1870. Biographies: W.J. Stillman, *Francesco Crispi* (1899) and M. Gillandi, *Francesco Crispi* (1969).

D'Annunzio, Gabriele (1863–1938): latter-day Italian adventurer-nationalist in the Garibaldi tradition. Scandalous poet and novelist turned militant nationalist. Loses an eye fighting in First World War. Outraged by refusal of Allies in Paris in 1919 to grant Italy the Adriatic territories promised by the Treaty of London in 1915. Seizes Fiume/Rijeka in the name of Italy in defiance of Treaty of St Germain, 1919. Declares war on government of Italy, 1920. Forced into evacuation from Fiume, 1921. Champion of the extreme Italian nationalist demand for *Italia Irredenta*. Subsequently becomes a prominent Fascist.

Davitt, Michael (1846–1906): Irish nationalist leader. Son of a peasant. Member of Fenian movement after 1865. Founder of Irish

Land League, 1879. Imprisoned for seditious speeches, 1881–1882 and 1883. Personal and political quarrels with Parnell. Irish Nationalist M.P., 1892–1893 and 1895–1899. Reputation as uncompromising anti-clericalist and populist nationalist.

Deák, Ferenc (1803–1876): Leading moderate Hungarian nationalist. Aristocrat and lawyer. Reformist member of Hungarian Diet from 1832. Hungarian Minister of Justice and architect of the 'April Laws' of 1848. Non-participant in 1849, opposing militancy of Kossuth. Political educator in 1850s. Acknowledged leader of moderate Hungarian nationalist campaign by 1861. Exploits Habsburg defeat by Prussians to broker *Ausgleich* over 1866–1867, by which Hungary secures a form of 'Home Rule' within Austria-Hungary. Refuses formal political office, deferring to colleague Andrássy after 1867. Reputation as the 'Architect of the *Ausgleich*', representing a pragmatic opportunistic Hungarian nationalism contrasting with the idealistic and heroic nationalism associated with Kossuth. Biography: Béla K. Kiraly, *Ferenc Deák* (1975).

De Valera, Eamon (1882–1975): Irish nationalist politician and statesman. Born in New York of a Spanish father and Irish mother. Leads group of Irish Volunteers in Easter Rising in Dublin, 1916. Imprisoned, then released, 1917. Elected M.P. in 1917. Leader of Sinn Fein, 1917–1926. Elected President of Dail Eireann. Opposes Treaty with Britain, 1921. Leads extreme nationalists during civil war, 1922–1923. Leader of Fianna Fail party from 1926. Reduces links with Britain during prime ministership, 1932–1948. Maintains neutrality of Ireland during Second World War. Re-elected Prime Minister, 1951–1954 and 1957–1959. President of Ireland, 1959–1973. Biographies: Lord Longford and T.P. O'Neill, *Eamonn de Valera* (1970); T. O'Neill and P. O'Fiannachta, *De Valera* (1968 and 1970).

Dmitrievic, Dragutin (1876–1917): Serb nationalist and terrorist. Founds 'Unity or Death' (Black Hand) organisation in Belgrade, 1911. Supports unification of all Serb minorities within Habsburg and Ottoman Empires by the territorial expansion of the state of Serbia. Trains Gavrilo Princip, assassin of Archduke Franz Ferdinand, 1914. Embarrasses Serbian government, 1913–1917. Tried and executed by Serbian government, 1917.

Dmowski, Roman (1864–1939): Polish nationalist politician. Represents Warsaw as M.P. in Russian Duma, 1906. Founds middle-class, right-wing Polish National Democratic Party. Forms Polish National Committee in exile to influence Allies, 1917. Leading Polish delegate to Paris Peace Conference, championing the establishment of a Polish nation-state, 1919. Ill-health forces retirement from politics. Anti-German, pro-Russian orientation (by contrast with Pilsudski).

Fichte, Johann Gottlieb (1762–1814): Early prophet of German nationalism. Philosopher whose 'Addresses to the German Nation' in 1807–1808 are conventionally represented as the clarion call of German cultural and political awakening on the basis of Reason and public education. Co-founder and first rector of University of Berlin, established 1810.

Franz Ferdinand, Archduke (1863–1914): Reformist heir to crown of Austria-Hungary. Nephew to Emperor Franz Josef and heir to Habsburg throne from 1889. Anti-Hungarian and pro-Slav leanings, increasingly associated with schemes to adapt Dual Monarchy into a Tri-Partite Monarchy admitting the Slavs (and especially the Czechs) into political partnership. Disliked by Austrians, hated by Hungarians, favoured by Czechs. Often represented as a reformist last hope for avoiding the disintegration of the Habsburg Empire through expedient granting of autonomy to the Slavs. Assassination in Sarajevo (by a Bosnian Serb) in June 1914 precipitates the First World War.

Gaj, Ljudevit (1809–1872): Croatian leader of Illyrian Movement and precursor of Yugoslavia. Inspired by Napoleonic experience of Illyrian Republic to promote a cultural revival among South Slavs in a spirit of Pan-Slavism. Biography: Elinor M. Despatatović, *Ljudevit Gaj and the Illyrian Movement* (1975).

Garašanin, Ilija (1812–1874): Leading Serbian nationalist politician. Calls for a rising of all Christians against Ottoman rule and the unification of all Serbs, 1844. Disappointed that Serbia could not exploit the 'Habsburg 1848'. Twice Prime Minister of Serbia, 1852 and 1861–1867. Reformer of Serbia's government. Advocate of the strategy of achieving a 'Greater Serbia' through a combination of Serb rebellion and Great Power (especially Russian) patronage. Biography: D. MacKenzie, *Ilija Garašanin: Balkan Bismarck* (1985).

Garibaldi, Guiseppe (1807–1882): Supreme hero of Italian nationalism. Involved in 'Young Italy' movement, 1834. Escapes to South America after sentence of death for role in attempted seizure of Genoa. Fights against Austrians, 1848. Joins revolutionary government in Rome, 1849. Votes for a Roman Republic, repulses French troops but forced to withdraw by Austrians. Summoned by Victor Emmanuel of Piedmont to help liberate Lombardy from Austrians, 1859. Raises expedition of 'One Thousand Redshirts' and takes Sicily and Naples, handing them over to Piedmont, 1860. Marches on Rome but captured at Aspromonte, 1862. Active in Italian campaign against Austrians, 1866. Attempts to seize Rome but thwarted by French, 1867. Helps to secure Rome for Italy during Franco-Prussian War, 1870. Popular hero as 'Maker of Italy'. Impassioned soldier-patriot conventionally contrasted with the intellectual diplomat-patriot Cavour. Supreme example of the romantic (if sometimes politically-embarrassing) nationalist-as-hero, serving (like Byron) as role-model for future generations of nationalists.

Memoirs: *Autobiography of Guiseppe Garibaldi* (1889). Principal biographies: George M. Trevelyan, *Garibaldi and the Making of Italy* (1911); Dennis Mack Smith, *Garibaldi* (1957) and 'Guiseppe Garibaldi' in *History Today*, March 1956 (reprinted August 1991); Christopher Hibbert, *Garibaldi and his Enemies: The Clash of Arms and Personalities in the Making of Italy* (1965); and Jasper Ridley, *Garibaldi* (1974).

Gioberti, Vincenzo (1801–1852): Champion of non-violent Italian unification under the Papacy. Born in Turin, ordained as priest, 1825. From exile in Brussels, publicises idea of Papacy as ideal agency for Italian unification and independence from 1833. Promotes cult of the 'Liberal Pope' Pio Nono (Pius IX), 1846–1848. Prime Minister of Piedmont, 1848–1849. Retires from politics in disillusionment at Pius IX's abandonment of national liberalism after 1849.

Goiri, Sabino de Arana y (1865–1903): Founder of Basque cultural nationalism. Born in Bilbao, educated at Barcelona. Inspired by Catalan nationalism in 1890s. Co-founds P.N.V., 1894. Emphasises unique race, language (*Euzkera*) and culture of Basques. Fear of cultural ethnocide leads to racial and linguistic exclusivity and demands for expulsion of immigrants (*makeros*) from Basque homeland (*Euzkadi*).

Grattan, Henry (1746–1820): Irish orator and politician. Elected to Irish Parliament, 1775. Leads campaign for repeal of Poyning's Law, subjecting the decisions of the Irish Parliament to the approval of the Privy Council in London. Secures the 'Constitution of 1782'. In tribute, the independent Irish Parliament of 1782–1800 is termed 'Grattan's Parliament'. Retires in 1797, then returns to head opposition to the Union of 1800. Campaigns for Catholic emancipation in the House of Commons, 1805–1820. Biography: S. Gwynn, *Henry Grattan and his Times* (1939).

Grimm, Jacob (1785–1863) and Wilhelm (1786–1859): The most celebrated folklorists of Germany, publishing their *Grimms' Fairy Tales* from 1812 to 1822. Perhaps the most well-known example of folklorists in the service of cultural nationalism, pioneering the collection of 'authentic' folk lore and legend to legitimise a sense of unique and exclusive national character. A model much copied outside Germany by cultural nationalists of succeeding generations. Biographies: Muriel E.Hammond, *Jacob and Wilhelm Grimm* (1968) and Murray B. Peppard, *Paths through the Forest: A Biography of the Brothers Grimm* (1971).

Hegel, Georg Wilhelm Friedrich (1770–1831): German philosopher influencing the developing character of nationalism in Germany. Professor at Jena, Nuremburg, Heidelberg and (after 1818) Berlin. Initially welcomes French Revolution and Napoleon, then rejects them absolutely. In his *German Constitution* (1802), Hegel criticises the weakness of the German states and demands a heroic war to discipline and motivate the easy-going German people. Increasingly reverential towards state power. Perceived as a prophet and proponent of the totalitarian German nation-state.

Herder, Johann Gottfried von (1744–1803): Philosopher and pioneering thinker of German nationalism. Publishes collection of German folksongs (anticipating the Grimm brothers), 1778–1779. Emphasises language as the crucial criterion for identifying a solidarity of nationhood: 'If land is the body of the nation, then language is its soul'. Biographies: R.R. Ergang, *Herder and the Foundations of German Nationalism* (1931) and F.M. Barnard, *Herder's Social and Political Thought: From Enlightenment to Nationalism* (1965).

Herzl, Theodor (1860–1904): First Zionist leader. Born of prosperous assimilated Jewish family in Hungary. Follows accommodationist line until attendance as journalist at (first) Dreyfus Trial (1894–1895), which reveals scale of French anti-Semitism and converts Herzl to militant 'Zionist' commitment. Calls for creation of a Jewish state as only protection for Jews in pamphlet 'Judenstaat', 1896. Convenes First Zionist Congress in Basle, 1897. First President of World Zionist Organisation. Attempts to secure Zionist state through personal negotiations with Kaiser William II, Sultan Abdul Mejid II and Russian Prime Minister Sergei Witte, 1899–1904. Early death deprives Zionist movement of his charismatic propagandist leadership. Biographies: Alex Bein, *Theodore Herzl* (1940) and Amos Elon, *Herzl* (1975).

Hrushevsky, Mykhailo S. (1866–1934): Ukrainian nationalist historian and political leader. Forced into exile in Austria from University of Kiev by tsarist persecution, 1894. Produces ten-volume nationalist *History of Ukraine* (1903–1936). Chairman of Ukrainian R.A.D.A. 1917–1918. Emigrates, 1918. Returns to work for Ukrainian autonomy within the Soviet Union 1924. Biography: T. Prymak, 'Hrushevsky and the Ukraine's "Lost" History', *History Today* (January 1989).

Hyde, Douglas (1860–1949): leader of Irish linguistic nationalism. Gaelic scholar and founder of *Gaelic League* to reverse (or at least stem) decline in Irish language, 1893. First Professor of Modern Irish at University College, Dublin, 1909–1932. President of Gaelic League, 1893–1915 (resigning in protest at its separatist politics). Delighted when Irish language given equal status with English in the Irish Free State, 1922. First President of independent Eire, 1937–1944.

Iorga, Nicolae (1871–1940): Leading Rumanian historian and nationalist. Professor of History at University of Bucharest from 1895. Elected to parliament in 1907 and founds National Democratic Party. Prime Minister, 1931–1932. Enormous scholarly, always strongly nationalistic output, notably his monumental ten-volume *History of*

Rumania (1936–1939). Assassinated by the Iron Guard, 1940. Biography: William O. Oldson, *The Historical and Nationalistic Thought of Nicolae Iorga* (1973).

Jahn, Friedrich Ludwig (1778–1852): Early activist of German nationalism and 'Father of the Gymnastic Movement'. Starts *Turnverein*, 1811. Attracts idealistic youth in universities to cause of German nation from 1815. As *Turnvater*, arrested for nationalist (often anti- Semitic) zeal and his movement banned by Prussian government, 1819. Ban on *Turnverein* lifted, 1842. Serves in national parliament, 1848–1849.

Jelačić, Baron Josef/Josip (1801–1859): Croat 'Saviour of the Habsburgs' in 1848–1849. Ban of Croatia, 1848–1849. Instructs Croatian Diet to proclaim independence of Croatia from Hungary. Dismissed by Habsburgs, June 1848. Reinstated and supports Habsburgs by military intervention against Hungarians, 1848–1849. Obedient servant of the Habsburgs from 1849. Embodies an early manifestation of Croat nationalism and its fear of Hungarian imperialism.

Katkov, Mikhail N. (1818–1887): Leading publicist of Russian Pan-Slavism. Russian journalist, editor of *Moskovskie Vedomosti* (Moscow Gazette) from 1851. Pro-reform, then converted to Pan-Slavist enthusiasm by Polish Uprising, 1863. Leading advocate of Russian-sponsored Pan-Slavism in 1870s and 1880s. Close adviser to Alexander III, urging an anti-German, pro-Slav foreign policy.

Kemal, Mustafa (1881–1938): Creator of the nation-state of Turkey. Born in Salonika. Joins Young Turk movement. Army officer, fighting Italians in Tripoli in 1911 and Bulgarians in the Balkan Wars in 1912–1913. Defends Gallipoli against Allied landings, 1915. Leads national resistance to Greek invasion following Ottoman defeat in 1918. Renounces loyalty to Sultan and forms alternative Provisional Government in Ankara, 1920. Leads Turks in war, expelling the Greeks from Anatolia, 1922. Deposes Sultan and establishes Republic of Turkey, 1922. Overthrows punitive Treaty of Sèvres (1920), negotiates Treaty of Lausanne, 1923. First President of Republic of Turkey, 1923–1938. Abolishes Caliphate, 1924. Architect of modern, secularised nation-state, abandoning claims to non-Turkish territories. Avoids neo-Ottoman line, settling for Turkish nationalist horizons. Adopts patronymic Atatürk (Father of the Turks), 1935. Becomes a role-model for nationalist leaders throughout the Middle East. Biographies: H.C. Armstrong, *Grey Wolf: An Intimate Study of a Dictator* (1932); J.P.D. Kinross, *Atatürk: The Rebirth of a Nation* (1964); and A. Kazanagil and E. Ozbudun (eds), *Atatürk: Founder of a Modern State* (1991).

Korais, Adamantios (1748–1833): Founder of modern Greek cultural nationalism. Resident in Paris, effectively creates a new Greek literary language. His advocacy of revived classicism lays the intellectual foundations for the Greek struggle for independence. As a philologist living outside Greece for most of his life, Korais demonstrates that exile may sharpen commitment to the nation despite the disadvantages of physical detachment from the motherland. Biography: Stephen G. Chaconas, *Adamantios Korais: A Study in Greek Nationalism* (1942).

Kościuszko, Tadeusz Andrzej (1746–1817): Polish patriotic leader. Fights in American War of Independence, returning to Poland, 1784. Leads brave but doomed uprising against Russia and Prussia in protest at Second Partition of Poland, 1794. Wounded and imprisoned by Russians, 1794–1796. Settles in France, 1798. Rejects overtures from Napoleon in 1806. Attends Congress of Vienna, 1814. Fails to persuade Tsar Alexander I to grant an independent Poland. A doughty champion for the cause of Poland in its darkest hours, first militarily and then diplomatically. Refuses to compromise with Napoleon and Alexander I, demanding (unsuccessfully) an independent Poland.

Kossuth, Ferenc (1841–1914): Hungarian nationalist politician, son of the celebrated patriot-hero. Leads Hungarian Party of Independence to majority in Hungarian Diet, 1905. Demands for separate Hungarian army breach *Ausgleich* of 1867, prompting military occupation and political crisis of 1905–1906.

Kossuth, Louis/Lajos (1802–1894): Hungarian nationalist revolutionary leader. From an impoverished gentry background, becomes member of Hungarian Diet, 1825–1827. Becomes journalist, campaigning for Hungarian independence. Imprisoned twice, 1837–1840. Returned to Diet, 1832–1836 and 1847–1849. Plays key role in securing 'March Laws' granting autonomy to Hungary, 1848. Insistence on Magyar supremacy within Hungary (despite own Slovak-German blood) antagonises other nationalities, especially Croats. Becomes provisional governor (effectively dictator) of Hungary in 1849. Proclaims independence of Hungary, April 1849. On defeat of Hungarians by Austrian and Russian troops, flees into exile, August 1849. Emigré 'ambassador' for Hungarian cause in Europe and U.S.A. from 1851. Based in Italy, makes unsuccessful attempts to organise uprisings within Hungary in 1859 (abetted by Napoleon III), 1861 and 1866. Retires from politics after *Ausgleich* of 1867. A hero-patriot in the style of Kościuszko and Garibaldi, often accused of needlessly alienating other nationalities by his illiberal espousal of Magyar supremacy in Hungary. Memoirs: *Memories of My Exile* (1880). Biographies: O. Zarek, *Kossuth* (1937) and I. Deak, *The Lawful Revolution: Louis Kossuth and the Hungarians, 1848–1849* (1979).

Lelewel, Joachim (1786–1861): Leading Polish nationalist historian. Harassed by Russian authority for his nationalist views, forced out of Wilno/Vilna in 1824 and Warsaw in 1831. Settles in Brussels, producing works on Polish medieval history and numismatics. Regarded as a martyr to Russian persecution and a founder of modern Polish historical thought. Biography: J.S. Skiernowicz, *Romantic Nationalism and Liberalism: Joachim Lelewel and the Polish National Idea* (1981).

List, Friedrich (1789–1846): German economic nationalist. In *National System of Political Economy* (1841), preaches economic promotion of German national state. Advocates abolition of internal tariffs combined with external tariff protection to stress national welfare over individual undertakings. Claims that 'Germany' is condemned to fall further behind economically unless political and economic unification occurs soon. Driven to suicide by debt, 1846.

Lönnrot, Elias (1802–1884): Finnish folklorist and editor of the national epic *Kalevala* (1835). Collects folk literature on field trips in remote eastern Finland, amalgamating fragments into the *Kalevala*, which assumes immense cultural significance for growing Finnish national self-consciousness. As Professor of Finnish at the University of Helsinki from 1853 to 1861, Lönnrot is a leader of Finnish revivalism against Russian political hegemony and especially Swedish cultural dominance.

Lueger, Karl (1844–1910): Socially progressive but notoriously anti-Semitic Mayor of Vienna, 1897–1910. In some respects liberal, for example supporting universal suffrage and the federalisation of the Habsburg Empire. Also a pioneer politician in exploiting local populist anti- Semitism to own self-interested advantage. Considered a profound influence on the young Adolf Hitler.

MacPherson, James (1736–1796): Scottish poet and perpetrator of the first major cultural nationalist fraud, *Ossian's Poems* (published 1760–1763). Claims to have collected genuine literary fragments written by third-century Gaelic poet Ossian. The degree of deliberate fraud is still debated; but *Ossian* undeniably launched an international trend towards the nationalist 'discovery' of medieval epics (where necessary doctored or fabricated) throughout Europe.

Manin, Daniele (1804–1857): Leader of the Italian *Risorgimento* in Venice. Jewish lawyer. Imprisoned by Habsburgs, 1848. Becomes President of the Venetian Republic and leads the defence of Venice against Habsburg siege, 1849. Spends remainder of his life in exile in Paris. Biographies: George M. Trevelyan, *Manin and the Venetian Republic of 1848* (1923) and C. Ginsborg, *Daniele Manin and the Venetian Revolution of 1848–9* (1979).

Mannerheim, Baron Carl Gustaf Emil (1867–1951): Finnish soldier and statesman. Of aristocratic Swedish origin, serves in Russian Imperial Army, 1889–1917. Commands 'White Guards', retaking Helsinki from Communists in Finnish Civil War, 1918. Regent of independent Finland, 1918–1919. Head of Finnish state, 1919–1920.

President of Finnish Defence Council, 1931–1939. Allies with Germany against Soviet Union, 1941. President of Finland, 1944–1946. Military securer of Finland's independence from Soviet Union. Biography: J.E.O. Screen, *Mannerheim: The Years of Preparation* (1970).

Masaryk, Tomaš Garrigue (1850–1937): Czech statesman and 'Father of Czechoslovakia'. Son of a Slovak coachman, educated at Brno, Vienna and Leipzig. Professor of Philosophy at University of Prague, 1882–1914. Represents 'Young Czech Party' in Austrian Parliament, 1891–1893. Increasingly anti-Austrian, leads 'Czech Realists', 1907–1914. Becomes international celebrity by defending Croats accused of treason in Agram/Zagreb, 1908. Escapes from Austria-Hungary, becomes chairman of emigré Czech National Council in London, 1914. Promotes campaign for Czech independence in journal *The New Europe* from 1916. Travels to Russia to organise Czech Legion from POWs captured by Russia, 1917. Travels to U.S.A. and, with Beneš, wins support of President Woodrow Wilson for independent Czech state, 1918. Organises vote for Czecho-Slovak state among emigré Czechs and Slovaks in U.S.A., 1918. Accepted by U.S.A., then other Allies, as head of an Allied government, 1918. Returns to Czecho-Slovakia as President-elect, 1918. Re-elected President of Czecho-Slovakia twice, 1918–1935. Retires as President, 1935. Reputation as the 'Architect of the Czechoslovak State'. Biographies: V. Cohen, *The Life and Times of Masaryk* (1940) and Emil Ludwig, *Defender of Democracy: Masaryk of Czechoslovakia* (1936).

Maurras, Charles (1868–1952): Founder and leader of *Action Française*. Galvanised by Panama Scandal and Dreyfus Affair into founding royalist, nationalist and anti-Semitic *Action Française*, 1899. Co-editor of newspaper *Action Française* from 1908. Leads the 'integral nationalist' organisation throughout its controversial career (including supporting the Pétain government, 1940–1944).

Mazzini, Guiseppe (1805–1872): Italian patriot and idealist-nationalist. Member of *Carbonari*, 1829. Imprisoned, 1830. Exiled to France, 1831. Founds 'Young Italy' movement to unify 'Italy' under republican government, 1831. Abortive rising in Savoy, 1834. Settles in Marseilles, then London, 1837. In works like *The Duties of Man* develops idea of 'Young Europe', a community of peaceful republican nation-states. Helps liberate Milan, 1848. Member of triumvirate of (brief) Roman Republic, 1849. Loses prestige after fall of Rome, going into exile, again in London. Prompts attempted risings in Mantua (1852), Milan (1853) and Genoa (1857). His idealistic republicanism loses out to unification under monarchist Piedmont. Slips into Italy in disguise to die, 1872. Enjoys a legendary reputation as the 'Prophet-Patriot of Italian Unification', generally accorded a place (with Cavour and Garibaldi) in the triumvirate of honour in the Italian nationalist pantheon. Reputation as the 'Founder of International Nationalism' less secure, especially as evidenced by his controversial map of an 'ideal Europe' in 1857, which included only 11 'true nations' (and excluded such 'nations' as the Slovaks, Irish etc). Biographies: Bolton King, *Mazzini* (1902); Gwilym O.Griffith, *Mazzini: Prophet of Modern Europe* (1932); Gaetano Salvemini, *Mazzini* (1956); E.E.Y. Hales, *Mazzini and the Secret Societies: the making of a myth* (1956).

Mehemet Ali (1769–1849): Ambitious ruler of Egypt and disrupter of Ottoman Empire. Albanian tobacco-merchant by background. Leads Albanian troops against France on behalf of Ottomans, 1799. Governor of Egypt, 1805. Granted supreme authority in Egypt by Sultan Mahmud II, 1811. Promotes military and economic development. Conquers Sudan, 1820–1822. Aids Ottomans during War of Greek Independence, 1823–1828. Rewarded by governorship of Crete. At war with Ottomans, acquiring Syria and Adana, 1832–1833. In second war with Ottomans, forced to surrender earlier conquests by Great Powers concerned to prop up Ottoman Empire, 1839–1841. Mehemet Ali compensated by international recognition as hereditary ruler of Egypt. Insane over last years of his rule.

Michelet, Jules (1798–1874): The leading French nationalist historian. Popularises the term 'Renaissance', articulating the concept of cultural and political national revivalism. Anti-clericalist and anti-monarchist historian promoting an impassioned and broad-spectrum re-creation of the living past. Produces the monumental *Histoire de France*, 1833–1867, earning enormous international respect and influence. Biographies: A.Kippur, *Jules Michelet: a study of mind and sensibility* (1981); R. Barthes, *Michelet* (1987); and A. Mitzman, *Michelet, Historian* (1990).

Michelsen, Christian (1857–1928): Shipping-magnate and lawyer from Bergen. The leading proponent of Norwegian independence from Sweden in the 1890s, he becomes the first prime minister of independent Norway, 1905–1907.

Mickiewicz, Adam (1798–1855): The most celebrated Polish patriot-poet. Deported from Poland to Russia, 1823–1829. His *Pan Tadeusz* (1834) immediately assumes the status of the supreme Polish national epic. Spends most of his life in exile, mostly in Paris. Promotes a humanitarian messianism, particularly the striking (and, to critics, absurdly self-indulgent and Polonocentric) image of Poland as the self-sacrificing 'Christ of Nations'. Biography: D. Welsh, *Adam Mickiewicz* (1966).

Moltke, Helmuth von (1800–1891): Prussian-German general. Enters Prussian army, 1822. Joins Prussian General Staff, 1832. Appointed Chief of Prussian General Staff, 1857. Masterminds major reorganisation of Prussian and then German armies, 1858–1888.

Produces strategic planning facilitating Prussian victories over Denmark (1864), Austria (1866) and France (1870). Chief of Imperial General Staff, 1870–1888. Usually perceived as vital military junior partner to Bismarck in unification then consolidation of Germany under Prussia. Biography: F.E. Whitton, *Moltke* (1921).

Moltke's nephew also called Helmuth von Moltke, (1848–1916), similarly serves as Chief of Imperial General Staff, 1906–1914. Commands German invasion of Belgium and France in late 1914. Made scapegoat for failure of Schlieffen Plan to capture Paris for Germany.

Napoleon Bonaparte (1769–1821): Supreme soldier-statesman, Emperor of the French and disrupter of *ancien régime* Europe. Born in Corsica, enters French army, 1785. Secures military reputation through campaign in northern Italy, 1798. Overthrows Directory, 1799. Consul for life, 1802. Crowns himself Emperor, 1804. Military conquests cover most of Europe, damaging *ancien régime* power of Austrian Empire in particular. Strategy of promoting nations penalised under *ancien régime* (especially Poles, Italians and South Slavs). Patronises new geopolitical constructs as client-states of France (notably Grand Duchy of Warsaw, Italian and Swiss republics, Illyrian Republic and Confederation of the Rhine). Defeated militarily in Russia (1812) and at battles of Leipzig (1813) and Waterloo (1815). Exiled to St Helena, 1815–1821. The Napoleonic experience provides a vital early stimulus to nationalism across most of Europe. In particular, Napoleon has been seen as the 'Godfather' of Italian and German national unification. Modern biographies include: J.M. Thompson, *Napoleon Bonaparte: His Rise and Fall* (1952); Felix Markham, *Napoleon* (1963); Vincent Cronin, *Napoleon* (1971); and Corelli Barnett, *Bonaparte* (1978).

Napoleon III (1808–1873): Emperor of the French, 1852–1870. Born Louis Napoleon, nephew of Napoleon I (Napoleon Bonaparte). Makes two unsuccessful attempts to mount Bonapartist risings against 'July Monarchy' of Louis Philippe, 1836 and 1840. Imprisoned after second attempt, escaping to London, 1845. Exploits 'Napoleonic legend' to secure election as President of Second French Republic, 1848. Launches coup d'état, 1851, to create Second Empire, 1852. Adopts adventurous, opportunist foreign policy. Commits France to Crimean War, 1854–1856. Supports Italian unification and independence first diplomatically (Pact of Plombières, 1858), then militarily (war with Austria, 1859). Angers Italian nationalists by making a premature peace with Austria in 1859 (leaving Venetia outside Italy) and securing the Papal States against Italian unification. Defeated (and captured) in Franco-Prussian War, 1870. Deposed and exiled to England, 1871. Often (perhaps unfairly) dismissed as a 'parvenu monarch' whose headlong pursuit of Napoleonic *'gloire'* led him into unorthodox, even dangerous foreign enterprises (most notably his disastrous Mexican Empire). Played an ambivalent role in the emergence of a united Italy, first promoting and then inhibiting territorial unification. Biographies include: F.A. Simpson, *Louis Napoleon and the Recovery of France, 1848–1856* (1930); J.M. Thompson, *Louis Napoleon and the Second Empire* (1954); J.P.T. Bury, *Napoleon III and the Second Empire* (1964); W.H.C. Smith, *Napoleon III* (1972); and James McMillan, *Napoleon III* (1991).

Nicholas I (1841–1921): Popular, long-ruling monarch of new, then redundant nation-state of Montenegro. Last ruler of native Montenegrin Petrović dynasty. 'Prince Nicola' of Montenegro, 1860–1910. Exhibits considerable military, diplomatic and dynastic expertise. Grants a formal constitution, 1905. King of Montenegro, 1910–1918. Creates Montenegrin capital of Cetinje. Doubles territory of Montenegro through alliance with Serbia against Ottoman Empire, notably in Balkan Wars, 1912–1913. Escapes to France when Montenegro occupied by Austrians, 1916. Dogged by rumours of collusion with Austrians, 1916–1918. Deposed by assembly at Podgorica, voting for union of Montenegro and Serbia under Serb Karageorgević dynasty, 1918. Dies in exile in Italy, 1921.

Nietzsche, Friedrich Wilhelm (1844–1900): Often (inaccurately) represented as exponent of fanatical nationalism. German philosopher developing, in books like *Zarathustra* (1883) and *Beyond Good and Evil* (1886), the idea of need for social élite of 'realists' led by a 'superman' uninhibited by conventional morality. A political maverick too individualistic to endorse nationalism unconditionally. Writings posthumously edited and adapted by fanatically nationalist sister. Insane over last few years.

O'Connell, Daniel (1775–1847): Early Irish nationalist leader, known as 'The Liberator'. A lawyer by profession, opposed to Act of Union from 1801. Founds Catholic Association to campaign for Catholic emancipation, 1823. Elected M.P. for County Clare but, as Roman Catholic, disqualified from taking his seat in House of Commons, 1828. Heads campaign securing the passing of the Roman Catholic Relief Act, 1829. Takes his seat as M.P. for Clare (1830) and Waterford (1832). By supporting the Whigs over 1830s, alienates much of his support in Ireland. Organises meetings in 1842–1843 to secure repeal of Act of Union. Under government pressure, his cancellation of Clontarf meeting discredits him among more militant nationalists (like the 'Young Ireland' Party), 1843. Imprisoned for sedition, 1844. Dies in Genoa, 1847. Reputation as moderate nationalist securing concessions through constitutional means. Biographies: M. Tierney (ed), *Daniel O'Connell: Nine Centenary Essays* (1949); A. Macintyre, *The Liberator: Daniel O'Connell and the Irish Party, 1830–1847* (1965); S. O'Faolain, *King of the Beggars*(1970); R. Moley, *Daniel O'Connell: Nationalism without Violence* (1974); and O. MacDonagh, *The Hereditary Bondsman: Daniel O'Connell, 1775–1829* (1988).

Orlando, Vittorio Emmanuele (1860–1952): Italian nationalist statesman. Professor of constitutional law at Palermo, elected to parliament, 1897. Minister of Justice, 1916. Prime Minister of Italy, 1917–1919. Articulates shift in Italian morale from despair (Italian rout at Caporetto, 1917) to ebullience (belated Italian success at Vittorio Veneto, 1918). Heads Italian delegation to Paris Peace Conference as one of the 'Big Four', 1919. Rows with Woodrow Wilson over claims for *Italia Irredenta*, failing to secure all territories promised to Italy by 1915 Treaty of London. Disgraced by failure to 'deliver' *Italia Irredenta*, resigns as prime minister, 1919. President of Chamber of Deputies, 1919–1925, resigning over Fascist malpractice. Later, President of Constituent Assembly, 1946–1947.

Orsini, Felice (1819–1858): Italian nationalist would-be assassin. Member of Mazzini's 'Young Italy'. After various plots against the Papacy, attempts to assassinate Napoleon III, claiming he is betraying the cause of Italy, 1858. After his execution, press publishes a letter in which Orsini appealed to Napoleon III to help Italy. Napoleon III responds, arranging to meet Cavour at Plombières to discuss French patronage of Italian unification. Biography: Michael St John Packe, *The Bombs of Orsini* (1957).

Palacký, František (1798–1876): Immensely influential Czech nationalist historian regarded as the 'Founder of the Czech Revival'. Promotes sense of historical self-consciousness about Czech lands of Bohemia and Moravia, 1820s. Chairman of Prague Slav Congress, refuses invitation to attend Frankfurt Parliament, 1848. Proponent of 'Austro-Slavism' based not on nationalities but historic provinces, declaring that 'if Austria did not exist, it would be necessary to invent her'. A very Czech combination of cultural nationalist and political realist-autonomist. Biography: O.F. Začek, *Palacký: The Historian as Scholar and Nationalist* (1970).

Parnell, Charles Stewart (1846–1891): Leader of Irish Home Rule movement. Anglo-Irish Protestant gentry background. M.P. for County Meath (1875–1980) and Cork (1880–1891). Succeeds Butt as President of Home Rule Confederation, 1877. Leads agitation for Home Rule, combining political bargaining (including parliamentary obstruction) at Westminster with radical pressure (including boycotting unpopular landlords) in Ireland. Arrested for inciting the Irish, 1881. As part of the 'Kilmainham Treaty', Parnell denounces Irish terrorism of Phoenix Park Murders, 1882. Supports Gladstone's (First) Home Rule Bill, 1886. Career ruined when cited as co-respondent in Kitty O'Shea divorce case, 1890. Irish public opinion scandalised and Irish Home Rule movement split. Writings: Michael Hurst and Alan O'Day (eds), *The Speeches of Charles Stewart Parnell* (1992). Biographies: Conor Cruise O'Brien, *Parnell and his Party, 1880–1890* (1957); J. Abele, *The Parnell*

Tragedy (1966); Roy Foster, *Charles Stewart Parnell: the man and his family* (1976); F.S.L. Lyons, *Charles Stewart Parnell* (1977); and Donal McCartney (ed.), *Parnell: the politics of power* (1991).

Pašić, Nikola (1845–1926): Serb politician and Yugoslav statesman. Co-founder of Serbian Radical Party, 1881. Sentenced to death for plotting against King Milan, but pardoned by King Peter, 1883. In exile, 1883–1889. Chief Minister of Serbia, 1891–1892. Serbian ambassador to Russia, 1893–1894. Exiled again, 1899–1903. Helps establish Karadjordjević dynasty, 1903. Chief Minister of Serbia, 1904–1905, 1906–1908, 1909–1911 and 1912–1918. Suppresses 'Black Hand' terrorist group, 1917. Signs Pact of Corfu with Yugoslav Committee, 1917. Leads joint delegation of Serbs, Croats and Slovenes to Paris Peace Conference, 1919. Chief Minister of Kingdom of Serbs, Croats and Slovenes, 1921–1926. Viewed by Croats and Slovenes as an unreconstructed Serb nationalist, always favouring Serb interests and treating the new Kingdom as 'Greater Serbia'. Biography: Carlo Sforza, *Fifty Years of War and Diplomacy in the Balkans: Pashich and the Union of the Yugoslavs* (1938).

Petlyura, Simon V. (1879–1926): Ukrainian socialist-turned-nationalist leader during the Russian Civil War period. Co-founder of Ukrainian Social-Democratic Workers Party, 1905. Officer in tsarist army, 1914–1917. Minister of War in Ukrainian R.A.D.A., 1917–1918. Ataman of Ukrainian Army and head of five-man directorate of R.A.D.A., 1918–1920. Allies with Pilsudski against Bolshevik Russia, 1920. Flees into exile in Paris, 1921. Assassinated in revenge for pogroms perpetrated under his command, 1926. Sometimes seen as a would-be 'Ukrainian Pilsudski'.

Petöfi, Sandor (1823–1849/1856): Hungarian nationalist poet-martyr. Mixed Magyar/Slovak blood. Passionate anti-aristocratic, anti-monarchist radical. Becomes Romantic nationalist poet with the reputation of the 'Hungarian Byron'. Assumed to have died fighting for Hungary against the Russians at battle of Segesvar in July 1849, instantly converted into a Hungarian national martyr. Recent Soviet research has revealed that Petöfi was actually captured and taken to Siberia as a prisoner-of-war, dying of tuberculosis in 1856. Biography: G. Illyes, *Petöfi* (1973).

Pilsudski, Jozef (1867–1935): Polish nationalist, soldier and statesman. Exiled to Siberia for socialist activities, 1887–1892. Founds Polish Socialist Party, 1892. Increasingly nationalist outlook, 1890s. Seeks Japanese support for Polish uprising during Russo-Japanese War, 1904–1905. Recruited by Austria to lead new Polish Legion against Russia, 1914. Interned by Germans, 1917. On release, becomes commander of all Polish forces, 1918. Elected head of revived state of Poland, 1918. Leads Poles against Red Army in Polish-Russian War,

1919–1920. Effectively dictator, promoting a federal Polish 'common-wealth', until adoption of constitution, 1918–1922. Retires, 1923. Leads military coup, overthrowing constitution and enforcing authoritarian government, 1926. Prime Minister, 1926–1928 and 1930. Retains dictatorial powers, 1926–1935. Socialist-turned-nationalist leader famous for his cynical judgement that 'the nation does not make the state; the state makes the nation'. Memoirs: *Memoirs of a Polish Revolutionary and Soldier* (1931). Biographies: W.F. Reddaway, *Marshal Pilsudski* (1939); M.K. Dziewanowski, *Joseph Pilsudski: A European Federalist, 1918–22* (1969); and Waclaw Jedrzejewicz, *Pilsudski: A Life for Poland* (1982).

Pius IX (1792–1878): Liberal-turned-reactionary pope. Born Giovanni Mastai-Ferretti. Regarded as progressive cardinal. Pontiff, 1846–1878. Seen by Gioberti and others as a 'Liberal Pope' leading cause of Italian unification, 1846–1848. Grants liberal reforms (1846) and constitution (1848) in Papal States. Refuses to take lead as 'Nationalist Pope' of Italy against Austria, 1848. Angry nationalists force Pius to flee from Rome, 1848–1850. Restored by French, 1850. Politically and doctrinally, becomes increasingly reactionary. Attacks liberalism and nationalism in *Syllabus Errararum*, 1864. Convokes first Vatican Council since 1537 in 1869–1870, to declare 'Papal Infallibility' doctrine in *Pastor Aeturnus*, 1870. Considers himself the 'Prisoner in the Vatican' after Rome united with Italy, stripping Papacy of all temporal authority except Vatican City, 1870. 'Pio Nono' is the most controversial of nineteenth-century popes, apparently 'converting' from early patronage to later unqualified condemnation of nationalist unification.

Princip, Gavrilo (1896–1918): Bosnian nationalist assassin. Member of 'Young Bosnia' nationalist terrorist group, trained by Serbian 'Black Hand'. Assassinates Archduke Franz Ferdinand, heir to throne of Austria-Hungary, on state visit to Bosnian capital of Sarajevo, 28 June 1914. Submits to arrest with the claim 'I am a Serbian hero'. Spared execution on grounds of youth (just 18). Dies of tuberculosis in prison, 1918. Perpetrator of the most far-reaching assassination in history, precipitating the First World War.

Redmond, John Edward (1856–1918): Moderate Irish nationalist leader. A follower of Parnell, becomes leader of the reunited Irish Nationalist Party in 1900. Reluctantly agrees to the (temporary) exclusion of Ulster from Home Rule for Ireland, early 1914. His constitutionalist approach is rendered politically redundant by the rise of Sinn Fein and developments in Ireland after 1916. Biography: D. Gwynn, *The Life of John Redmond* (1932).

Renan, Joseph-Ernest (1823–1892): Pioneer thinker about nationalism. Influential French theologian and historian. Initiates academic study of (and debate about) nationalism with his generally sympathetic lecture 'What is a Nation?' (1882). His early liberalism becomes authoritarianism after France's defeat by Prussia in 1870, influencing Barrès and Maurras.

Renner, Karl (1870–1950): Austrian champion of reconciling nationalism and socialism through extra-territorial rights. With Otto Bauer, employs experience of nationalities issue in Austria-Hungary to propose novel accommodation between traditionally antagonistic nationalism and socialism. Subsequently becomes a prominent politician in Austria: Chancellor, 1918–1920; Head of Austrian delegation to Paris Peace Conference, 1919; President 1945–1950.

Rousseau, Jean-Jacques (1712–1778): Early proponent of popular sovereignty doctrine basic to developing nationalism. Swiss-born philosopher attacking social and political order of the *ancien régime.* In *Du Contrat Social* (1762), claims that rulers can only derive their power morally and legitimately from a popular mandate. Immediately after his death, his ideas are influential during the French Revolution in fostering the concept of the nation. Biography: Anne Cohler, *Rousseau and Nationalism* (1970).

Schönerer, Georg von (1842–1921): Leader of German nationalists within Austria-Hungary. Following unification of Germany in 1871, Schönerer articulates view of some Austrians that they should abandon the moribund Dual Monarchy of Austria-Hungary and unite with Germany to create a 'Greater German state'. Founder of pro-Prussian, anti- Semitic Pan-German Party, 1885. Huge personal following among Viennese lower middle class and *burschenschaften.* Supports *Los von Rom* movement after 1898. Influence peaks around 1900, declines to a low ebb after 1907.

Shevchenko, Taras (1814–1861): National poet of Ukraine. Almost single-handedly creates cultural Ukrainian nationalism in the mid-nineteenth century. Exiled 1847. Forbidden to write or paint by tsarist authorities, 1847–1857. Revered by Ukrainians as martyr-poet and towering literary genius of the (re)emergent Ukraine. Biography: G.S.N. Luckyi, *Sherchenko and the Critics, 1861–1980 (1980).*

Sibelius, Jean/Jan (1865–1957): Supreme nationalist composer of Finland. Communicates musically the reality of Finnish identity and nation to the wider world during the experience of Russification: *Finlandia* is a defiant national anthem; the *Karelia Suite* is almost a hymn to Finnish irredentism. A prime example (together with Smetana, Dvořak and Grieg) of a composer promoting the cause of his own small nation. Biographies: Fred Blum, *Jean Sibelius* (1965) and Robert Layton, *Sibelius* (1978).

Sièyes, Abbé Emmanuel Joseph (1748–1836): Pioneer nationalist thinker. Catholic 'secular priest'. Essay 'What is the Third Estate?'

influential in launching political debate, 1789. Becomes a leading 'ideas man' of French Revolution. Proponent of concept of 'nation' as natural social and political community. Participates in all constitutional shifts of 1790s: helps compose constitution, 1791; member of Council of Five Hundred, 1795–1799; member of Directory, 1799; plans Consulate system. Count and Senator under Napoleon. In exile in Belgium, 1814–1830. Returns to France, 1830–1836. Biographies: Glyndon van Deusen, *Sièyes: His Life and His Nationalism* (1932) and Murray Forsyth, *Reason and Revolution: The Political Thought of the Abbé Sièyes* (1987).

Sigurdsson, Jon (1811–1879): Leader of Icelandic autonomist movement against Denmark. Academic, specialising in Old Norse philology and history. Long-serving President of revived Althing (Parliament) of Iceland after 1845. Campaigns tirelessly for constitutional recognition of Iceland, finally conceded by Denmark in 1874.

Stambolisky, Alexander (1879–1923): Bulgarian politician and statesman. Member of Agrarian Union and celebrated orator, 1905–1915. Pro-Russian, imprisoned for opposing Bulgaria's entry into First World War on the side of Germany, 1915. Forces King Ferdinand to abdicate, 1918, Proclaims Republic, 1918. Prime Minister, 1919–1923. Negotiates Treaty of Neuilly, 1919. Uses semi-dictatorial power to impose pro-peasant reform. Provokes Bulgarian nationalists by facilitating moves by the Kingdom of Serbs, Croats and Slovenes to crush Macedonian uprising. Deposed and murdered in putsch, 1923.

Stambulov, Stefan (1854–1895): Bulgarian politician and statesman. Participates in Bulgarian nationalist uprisings, 1875–1878. Becomes national leader of Bulgaria after defying Great Powers (including Russia) and Balkan neighbours to secure union of Bulgaria and Eastern Rumelia, 1885. Appointed Regent, supports newly-elected Ferdinand of Saxe-Coburg as Prince of Bulgaria, 1886–1887. Prime Minister, 1887–1894. Reputation as 'Strong Man of Bulgaria' and even 'The Bulgarian Bismarck' but sensibly attempts to conciliate Ottomans and soft-pedals Bulgarian irredentist claims on Macedonia. His popularity alienates Ferdinand, who dismisses him in 1894. Brutally murdered, 1895.

Štefanik, Milan (1880–1919): Slovak national leader and co-founder of Czecho-Slovakia. Joins Czech liberation movement in First World War, cooperating with Masaryk and Beneš. Minister of War in provisional Czecho-Slovak Government, 1918. Killed in air crash, 1919. Sometimes portrayed as the Slovak dupe of the more worldly-wise Czech leaders in the 'fabrication' of Czecho-Slovakia.

Stein, Baron Heinrich vom (1757–1831): Prussian statesman and German historian. Appointed Prussian minister of trade, 1804. Chief Minister, 1807–1808. Introduces major reform package, including emancipation of serfs and reorganisation of central and local government. Forced out by French, 1808. Enters service of Tsar Alexander I, 1812. Appointed administrator of liberated German territories, 1813–1814. Plan for political unification of German states torpedoed by Metternich at Congress of Vienna, 1815. In 1816, retires to organise documentary *Monumenta Germaniae Historica*, published from 1826. Pioneer of both Prussian power and unification of Germany. Biographies: J.R. Seeley, *The Life and Times of Stein* (1878) and R.C. Raak, *The Fall of Stein* (1965).

Strossmayer, Josip (1815–1905): Croatian priest and 'Prophet of South Slav Unification'. Chaplain to Austrian Emperor, 1838. Bishop of Djakovo, 1849–1905. Establishes South Slav Academy at Agram/Zagreb, 1867. Establishes University of Agram/Zagreb, 1874. Uses influence to curb Magyarisation policies of Hungarian government in Croatia. 'Liberal Catholic' opposed to reactionary Pius IX. Cultivates Western leaders (especially Gladstone), promoting his plans for political unification of the South Slavs.

Šupilo, Franjo (1870–1917): Croatian nationalist and leader of campaign for unification of South Slavs. Draws up Rijeka/Fiume Resolution to create Serb-Croat alliance against Austria-Hungary, 1905. As head of 'Yugoslav Committee' (founded 1914–1915), signs Declaration of Corfu with Serbian Prime Minister Pašić, 1917.

Svinhufvud, Pehr (1861–1944): First head of state of independent Finland. Anti-Russian deputy in *Seim* (Finnish Parliament) from 1894. Exiled by Russians, 1914–1917. Prime Minister of Finland, 1917. Leads Finnish White Government, 1918. Later, Prime Minister in 1930–1931 and President 1931–1937. A committedly anti-Russian, tactically pro-German Finnish nationalist.

Széchenyi, István/Stephen (1791–1860): Hungarian liberal reformer, innovator and scientist. Establishes and finances Hungarian National Academy of Sciences, 1825. Introduces steamship navigation to the Danube, 1830. As 'The Hungarian Benjamin Franklin', campaigns for political, social and technical progress. Opposes Kossuth in 1840s, becoming increasingly pro-Habsburg. Becomes insane in 1848, commits suicide in 1860. Biography: G. Barany, *Stephen Széchenyi and the Awakening of Hungarian Nationalism, 1791–1841* (1968).

Tisza, István (1861–1918): Hungarian politician. Son of Kálmán Tisza. Prime Minister of Hungary/Transleithania, 1903–1905 and 1913–1917. Uncompromisingly continues father's legacy of Magyar ascendancy and Magyarisation. Reluctant to commit Hungary to war during 1914 crisis. Facilitates succession of Charles/Karl as Emperor of Austria-Hungary and King of Hungary to guarantee Hungarian jurisdiction, 1916. Resigns over Charles's extension of the suffrage in Hungary, 1917.

Murdered in turmoil of collapse of Austria-Hungary, 1918. Biography: G. Vermes, *István Tisza: The Liberal Vision and Conservative Statecraft of a Magyar Nationalist* (1985).

Tisza, Kálmán (1830–1902): Hungarian politician and leading proponent of Magyarisation. Exiled after fighting for Hungary in 1848–1849. Founds Hungarian Liberal Party, 1875. Prime Minister of Hungary/Transleithania, 1875–1890. Creates and personifies the 'Magyar Ascendancy' in post-*Ausgleich* Hungary. Energetic prosecutor of the Magyarisation of the non-Magyar nationalities within Hungary.

Tone, Theobald Wolfe (1763–1798): Irish revolutionary patriot and nationalist martyr. Founds 'United Irishmen' in Belfast, 1791. Seeks aid for rebellion against Britain in U.S.A. and France, 1794–1796. Leads rebellion of United Irishmen, 1796–1798. Captured, imprisoned, commits suicide awaiting execution, 1798. Biographies: F. MacDermot, *Theobald Wolfe Tone* (1939) and Marianne Elliott, *Wolfe Tone: Prophet of Irish Independence* (1989).

Treitschke, Heinrich von (1834–1896): German nationalist historian. Professor of History at Heidelberg and (succeeding Ranke) Berlin. Conservative deputy to Reichstag, 1871–1884. Strong supporter of Bismarck. Embarks upon monumental *History of Germany in the Nineteenth Century*, 1879. By his death (in 1896), completes seven volumes but only reaches 1848. Emphasises historical necessity and inevitability of Prussian domination of Germany. Pro-Prussia, pro-Bismarck, pro-state power. Reputation as triumphalist 'historian-laureate' of Bismarckian Germany. Biography: A. Dorpalen, *Heinrich von Treitschke* (1957).

Trumbić, Ante (1864–1938): Croatian nationalist and leading proponent of South Slav state. Helps to draft Rijeka/Fiume Resolution, 1905. President of Yugoslav Committee, formed in Florence, then relocated in London by emigrés from Austria-Hungary, 1914–1915. Signs Pact of Corfu with Serbian Prime Minister Pašić, 1917. First Foreign Minister of the Kingdom of the Serbs, Croats and Slovenes, leading its delegation to the Paris Peace Conference.

Venizelos, Eleutherios (1864–1936): Greek nationalist politician and statesman. Cretan by birth, participates in rising against Ottomans, 1896. President of Cretan Assembly, declares union of Crete with Greece, 1905. Prime Minister of Greece, 1910. Imposes package of constitutional, administrative and military reforms. Takes Greece into Balkan Wars, gaining Macedonia in peace settlement, 1912–1913. Attempts to join Allies in First World War but dismissed by King Constantine, 1915. Forms alternative government, first in Crete, then in Salonika, 1916. Declares war on Bulgaria and Germany. Secures abdication of Constantine, becomes legitimate prime minister again,

1917. Heads Greek delegation at Paris Peace Conference, 1919. As champion of 'Greater Greece', insists on Greek acquisition of western Anatolia, provoking Greek-Turkish War in which Greeks are defeated and expelled. Defeated in elections, 1920. Prime Minister again, 1924, 1928–1932 and 1933. Attempted coup leads to short civil war, 1935. Flees into exile in France, 1935–1936. Biographies: C. Kerofilas, *Eleutherios Venizelos: his life and work* (1915); E.B. Chester, *Life of Venizelos* (1921); and D. Alastos, *Venizelos: Patriot, Statesman, Revolutionary* (1942).

Victor Emmanuel II (1820–1878): King of Piedmont, then Italy. Son of Charles Albert of Savoy, succeeding to throne on his father's abdication, 1849. King of Piedmont-Sardinia, 1849–1861. Proclaimed King of United Italy, 1861. Remains a constitutional monarch, upholding liberal Piedmontese constitution of 1849. King of Italy, 1861–1878. Conventionally assigned a ceremonial role in Italian unification similar to that of William I in German unification. In reality, Victor Emmanuel was no mere figurehead of Italian unification but actively promoted (and acted as peacemaker between) Cavour and Garibaldi.

Weizmann, Chaim (1874–1952): Zionist leader. Born near Pinsk in Russian Poland. Studies in Germany before emigrating to England. Reader in Biochemistry at University of Manchester, 1906. Naturalised British subject, 1910. Heads British Zionist movement before First World War. Director of British Admiralty Laboratories, 1916–1919. Advises British government over Balfour Declaration, 1917. President of World Zionist Organisation after 1920. President of Jewish Agency in Palestine, 1921–1931 and 1935–1946. Elected first President of Israel, 1948–1952. Memoirs: *Trial and Error: The Autobiography of Chaim Weizmann* (1949). Biographies: Meyer Weisgal and Joel Carmichael, *Chaim Weizmann* (1962) and Harold M. Blumberg, *Weizmann: His Life and Times* (1975).

William I (1797–1888): King of Prussia, then German Emperor. Son of Frederick William IV of Prussia. King of Prussia alone, 1861–1871. Appoints and supports plans of Bismarck, 1862. King of Prussia and German Emperor, 1871–1888. Conventionally assigned a low-profile, ceremonial role in German unification comparable to that of Victor Emmanuel II in Italian unification.

William II (1859–1941): King of Prussia and German Emperor, 1888–1918. Son of Emperor Frederick II (and grandson of Queen Victoria). Dismisses Bismarck as Chancellor ('Dropping the Pilot') to pursue own ebullient 'New Course', 1890. Asserts German claims to Great Power status, even dominance. Provokes a succession of tension-raising incidents in 1900s, acquiring reputation as warmonger. Increasingly dominated by German High Command. Forced by High Command to abdicate after German defeat in First World War, 1918. Lives in exile in Doorn in Holland, 1918–1941. Judged harshly by contemporaries ('Hang the Kaiser') and frequently condemned by historians as a criminally-irresponsible poseur. Memoirs: *My Memoirs, 1878–1918* (1922). Biographies: Virginia Cowles, *The Kaiser* (1963); M.L.G. Balfour, *The Kaiser and His Times* (1964); and Alan W. Palmer, *The Kaiser: Warlord of the Second Reich* (1978).

Yeats, William Butler (1865–1939): Irish nationalist poet and most celebrated exponent of the Irish revival of cultural nationalism. Publishes *The Celtic Twilight*, 1893. Founds Abbey Theatre in Dublin, 1904. Responds to the 1916 Easter Rising with a poem proclaiming that 'a Terrible Beauty is born'. Awarded Nobel Prize for Literature, 1923. A towering but contradictory and controversial figure in Irish cultural nationalism. Biographies: Richard Ellmann, *Yeats: The Man and the Masks* (1948) and A. Norman Jeffares, *W.B. Yeats: a new biography* (1988).

Ypsilanti Family: Activists from a privileged Phanariot background in the Greek and Serb struggles for independence against the Ottoman Empire. Alexander (I), 1725–1805: Hospodar of Wallachia executed for promoting a Greek uprising. Constantine: Hospodar of Moldavia and Wallachia who sponsors rebellion in Serbia. Alexander (II), 1792–1828: elected head of the Greek National Society in 1820. Demetrius, 1793–1832: commander of the Greek armies in eastern Greece in 1825. A dynasty of Ottoman servants turning rebels against Ottoman authority in the Balkans.

Political glossary

Absolutism Term derived from Latin *legibus absolutus* (absolved from laws). A system of constitutionally unlimited government in which the governed possess no representation or participation in the administration, exercising no legal or constitutional restraints on the ruler.

Acculturation The process by which a minority voluntarily adopts the language, culture and social conventions of the majority or host community while retaining its own self-conscious identity. Note the acculturation/assimilation distinction.

Action Française French right-wing political movement founded by Charles Maurras in 1899, promoting a nationalist, monarchist and anti-Semitic programme. Newspaper *Action Française*, with Maurras and Leon Daudet as joint editors, launched 1908. Attacked alleged decadence and non-patriotism of Third French Republic, preaching a robust but often mystical French nationalism. Although claiming to support the Roman Catholic Church, the movement was banned by the Papacy in 1926. The movement persisted until after the Second World War, when it was banned in France for active collaboration with the Vichy régime.

Activist Member of a political movement prepared to take direct and public action, as opposed to one whose participation is passive and private (perhaps only involving the payment of membership dues). Not a nineteenth-century term but one passing into common currency from the 1960s.

Ancien régime French for 'old order'. A pejorative term describing the overall structure of government and society prevailing in Europe prior to the French Revolution. Among its cardinal characteristics were absolutist monarchy and the rigid division of society into three 'orders' or 'estates': aristocracy, clergy and – in the 'Third Estate' – everybody else.

Annexation The process by which a state unilaterally assumes possession of a territory without the consent of its (former) owner, by diplomatic, political or military means.

Anticlericalism Term applied to opposition to ecclesiastical political and temporal power and privilege, especially as exercised by the Roman Catholic Church. Featured in virtually all Catholic societies in the course of the nineteenth century but especially France, Spain, Italy and Germany.

Anti-Semitism Term used to describe antagonism towards the Jews, whether motivated by religious, racial, social or economic considerations. The term emerged around 1860 and is associated (not always fairly) with early racial theorists like Joseph de Gobineau and Houston Stewart Chamberlain. From the 1870s, the phenomenon of anti-Semitism became widespread, being especially overt in Russia, Austria-Hungary, France and Rumania (and in turn prompting the rise of Zionism). Became a central tenet of Nazi ideology.

Apostles of Liberty Self-chosen title of a group of Balkan nationalists including Delchev in the 1870s, inspired by the emancipatory *Risorgimento* of Mazzini and Garibaldi to bring the 'Gospel of the Nation' as latter-day missionaries to benighted and backward societies. Often cited as evidence that nationalism plays the role of a surrogate religion in an increasingly secular age.

Armistice A temporary suspension of military hostilities pending the negotiation and signing of a definitive peace settlement.

Assimilation Term employed for the process by which an ethnie or nation is culturally, socially and politically absorbed by a more dominant ethnie or nation. The term is usually, but not necessarily, employed pejoratively. The most notorious examples of nineteenth-century attempts at forced assimilation were Russification within the Russian Empire after 1890 and Magyarisation within Hungary after 1867. Note the assimilation/acculturation distinction.

Ausgleich German for 'compromise'. An agreement reached between the Habsburg establishment (headed by Count Beust) and moderate Hungarian politicians (led by Deák and Andrássy) over 1866–1867 to transform the Austrian Empire into the Dual Monarchy of Austria-Hungary. This system, lending Austria/Cisleithania senior partnership status and Hungary/Transleithania junior partnership status, remained in operation until the collapse of Austria-Hungary in 1918.

Autarchy Greek for 'self-sufficiency'. A condition of national economic self-sufficiency, rendering import from abroad unnecessary. The economic equivalent of total political sovereignty, both of which are prized as ideals by and for the nation-state.

Autochthonous Greek for 'from the land itself'. Term for the aboriginal settlers of a territory, who have maintained continuous and unbroken residence throughout recorded history. The historical pedigree of autochthonous residence was (and still is) regarded by nationalists as a morally-unchallengeable claim to the 'ownership' of territory.

Autonomy Greek for 'self-law'. Self-government of a nation or national grouping within a larger political entity, stopping short of independence. Various degrees (as well as varieties) of autonomy are possible. Autonomy is generally perceived as a transitory or unstable condition, either encouraging nationalists into pressing for complete independence or provoking the existing establishment into cancelling past concessions.

Awakeners The better-educated, enthusiastic and idealistic first generation of nationalists who communicated the sense of nationhood from an academic to a popular mass audience. Historians, philologists, writers, poets, academics and the lower clergy typically loomed large among the nationalist 'awakeners' committed to recalling the slumbering nation to renewed endeavour.

Babel concept Pre-modern and pre-nationalist perception of the multiplicity of languages as representing not a natural organic phenomenon but an enduring demonstration of divine punishment (Genesis XI: 1–9).

Balance of power A system of international relations based on the strategy that peace can only (or perhaps best) be secured by ensuring that the threat of excessive dominance by any one state (or alliance) is countered by the deliberate creation of another alliance or counter-force of cumulatively equal strength. A cardinal principle of British foreign policy in the nineteenth century, notably against Napoleonic France.

Balfour Declaration A communication by British Foreign Secretary Arthur J. Balfour to Lord Rothschild on 2 November 1917, declaring British support for the establishment of a Jewish homeland in Palestine, provided that the rights of resident non-Jewish communities were safeguarded. Brokered by Chaim Weizmann, the Declaration identified Britain as the principal state-backer of Zionism, and was universally regarded as a breakthrough for the Zionist cause, particularly as it was soon formally adhered to by all Allied governments.

Balkanization A term popular at the Paris Peace Conference of 1919–1920 expressing the fear that if national self-determination were allowed free rein, the result would be a chaotic hotchpotch of mini-states, micro-states and statelets across eastern Europe. This apprehension was influential in persuading the victorious Allied Great Powers to fudge the issue of nation-statehood in the new geopolitical settlement.

Black Hand Popular name for the Serbian nationalist secret society *Ujedinjenje ili Smert* (Unity or Death), founded in Belgrade in May 1911. Led by Dragutin Dmitriević ('Apis'), the society consisted mainly of Serbian army officers and aimed to unite all 'outposted' Serb minorities within Austria-Hungary and the Ottoman Empire into an enlarged independent state of Serbia. Trained Gavrilo Princip, who assassinated Archduke Franz Ferdinand on 28 June 1914 and so precipitated the First World War. Embarrassed by the society, the Serbian government first disowned and then banned the 'Black Hand'. Its three leaders (including Dmitriević) were arrested, tried and executed by the Serbian government in June 1917.

Blut und Eisen German for 'blood and iron'. A slogan taken from an early speech by Bismarck in September 1862, in which he declared that 'the great questions of the day will be decided, not by speeches and majority votes ... but by blood and iron'. Perceived as a contemptuous condemnation of earlier attempts (notably in 1848–1849) to effect German unification by liberal, democratic means. Bismarck's phrase, asserting the combination of human self-sacrifice and material might as the supreme nationalist winning formula, instantly became the prime slogan of the Prussian vision of a unified Germany.

Bourgeoisie An analytical (and subsequently derogatory) Marxist term for the middle and upper classes who own property and capital and therefore have a vested, profit-motivated interest in maintaining capitalism. Having displaced the feudal estates, the bourgeoisie is, according to the prescriptive Marxist dialectic, itself doomed to be displaced by the proletariat.

Boycott The organised refusal by a body of people to have any dealings with a targeted individual. Term derived from the 1880 case of Captain C.C. Boycott, who was 'sent to Coventry' by the Irish Land League for evicting his tenants. The practice of 'boycotting' was employed by Charles Stewart Parnell in the 1880s as part of his campaign for Irish Home Rule.

Brest-Litovsk Empire The expanded territorial jurisdiction of the Central Powers of Germany and Austria-Hungary at the expense of Russia, effected by the Treaty of Brest-Litovsk in March 1918. Representing the geopolitical reconstruction of eastern Europe by the self-interested Central Powers, this 'empire' lasted only eight months, being automatically forfeit with the defeat (and military with- drawal) of the Central Powers in November 1918.

Buffer state A small state created or maintained between larger states for the purpose of reducing the likelihood of armed conflict by removing their common border. An intriguing nineteenth-century example is Belgium. A collection of buffer states may constitute a *cordon sanitaire*. By the very nature of their predicament, buffer states may be unstable and short-lived entities, often taken over by one or other of their powerful neighbours or partitioned between them.

Bundestag German for 'Federal Assembly'. Federal Diet of the German Confederation, established by the Congress of Vienna in 1815 and superseded by the North German Confederation in 1866.

Burschenschaft German for 'student society'. Student youth organisation founded at University of Jena in 1813. Became a vehicle for the nationalism of German youth, disappointed that the Congress of Vienna advanced the cause of 'Germany' so little in post-Napoleonic Europe. Staged famous demonstration at Wartburg Festival in 1817. A member assassinated Kotzebue in 1819. The Carlsbad Decrees were promulgated as an attempt to suppress the movement which, however, operated secretly until 1848, openly over 1848–1849, and became increasingly militaristic, Pan-German and anti-Semitic thereafter. The prototype nationalist youth movement, much copied elsewhere in Europe.

Carbonari Italian for 'charcoal-burners'. Italian secret society with republican and masonic influences, founded in Calabria in 1807. Set out after 1815 to overthrow the régimes restored by the Vienna Settlement and, more modestly, to establish Italian unity. Instigated unsuccessful revolts in Naples (1820), Piedmont (1821) and elsewhere in 'Italy' (1831). Later absorbed into Mazzini's 'Young Italy' movement. Regarded as a model for a nationalist secret society, despite its poor leadership and lack of success.

Castle-and-Border A geopolitical distinction, popularised by Robert Ardrey in *The Territorial Imperative* (1962), between the 'core-dwellers' of a nation, who tend to be complacent non-nationalists, and 'border-dwellers', who are likely to become nationalists out of either insecurity or ambition.

Central Powers Initially members of the Triple Alliance created by Bismarck in 1882; namely Germany, Austria-Hungary and Italy. As Italy first remained neutral and then joined the Allied camp in the First World War, the term was applied to Germany and Austria-Hungary and their Ottoman and Bulgarian allies over the period 1914–1918.

Chauvinism Pejorative term for aggressive and excessive populist nationalism. Derived from Nicholas Chauvin, whose exaggerated public devotion to Napoleon exposed them both to general ridicule. The French (but more self-serving) equivalent of the British 'jingoism'.

Comity The sense of an international community of states, representing a broad consensus regarding generally acceptable norms of behaviour. In many ways, a secular updating of 'Christendom'.

Concert of Europe Term used to describe the workings of the Congress System after 1815, whereby treaties were made and guaranteed by the European Great Powers meeting together. The idea of the 'summit meeting' extended from the immediate post-Vienna Settlement period to the era of the Eastern Question and colonial disputes in the later nineteenth century.

Concordat A specialised term for an agreement between the Pope, as head of the Roman Catholic Church, and the secular authority of a state on the rights, privileges and obligations of the Church within the jurisdiction of that state. A famous nineteenth-century example was the Concordat between Pope Pius VII and Napoleon in 1801.

Confederation A multi-national or multi-regional association of states, retaining sovereignty for the individual contracting partners but voluntarily delegating certain powers to a central confederal executive. Note the federation/confederation distinction: in a federation, constitutional sovereignty lies with the central executive; in a confederation, sovereignty lies with the 'component' states. For example, the German Confederation (1815–1866) was a true confederation but the North German Confederation (1866–1871) was not.

Congress System A system for settling international disputes and maintaining peace in Europe through regular diplomatic conferences between the Great Powers. Initiated after the Congress of Vienna through Article VI of the Quadruple Alliance (between Austria, Britain, Prussia and Russia) signed in Paris in November 1815. Further congresses were convened in Aix-la-Chapelle (1818), Troppau (1820), Laibach (1821), Verona (1822) and St Petersburg (1825). The system was increasingly perceived as a reactionary compact of autocratic monarchs dedicated to maintaining the status quo through the suppression of all nationalist and liberal movements, where necessary by military intervention. Britain withdrew from the Verona Congress in protest and refused to attend the St Petersburg Congress. At the St Petersburg Congress, Austria and Russia quarrelled, leading to the abandonment of the formal system.

Cordon sanitaire French for 'sanitary line'. A ring or band of buffer states designed to separate antagonistic Great Powers or contain a threatening Great Power. The best historical example is probably the Successor States of eastern Europe established by the Paris Peace Settlement in 1919–1920 against the expansionist threat of Bolshevik Russia.

Coup d'état French for 'strike of state'. A sudden change in government brought about by unconstitutional means at the hands of individuals already in positions of considerable political or military power. A coup does not typically involve mass or even popular participation. A famous example is Louis Napoleon's coup of December 1851, which prepared the ground for the establishment of the Second French Empire.

Cradle of nationality A phrase of Lord Acton encapsulating the proposition that involuntary exile is a prime motivator for nationalists. By this interpretation, a spell in exile sharpens the emigré's appreciation of his homeland and increases his commitment to the realisation of a nation-state. Represents an optimistic viewpoint, implicitly arguing that (despite much anecdotal testimony to the contrary) exile is never a wasted experience for the nationalist activist.

Darwinism The corpus of ideas associated with Charles Darwin (1809–1882). In his *Origin of Species* (1859), Darwin introduced such concepts as the 'law of the jungle', 'natural selection', 'adapt or die' and 'the survival of the fittest'. These ideas about the animal world were almost instantly applied (though not by Darwin himself) to the world of human society and politics. Such 'social Darwinism' profoundly influenced the development of nationalism in the later nineteenth century, lending a 'biological justification' to hardening nationalist policy.

Demagogue Greek for 'people-leader'. A derogatory term for a popular personality who unscrupulously and self- interestedly appeals to the baser instincts of the unsophisticated masses, pandering to their prejudice and passion. An accusation commonly levelled at nationalist leaders, often by alarmed élitist establishments.

Despotism In Montesquieu's definition, 'power without restraint'. To the nineteenth-century democrat, despotism – the wielding of state power without constitutional limitation – could never be approved, though degrees of disapproval were admissible. 'Tyranny' or (later) 'dictatorship' was the personal power-system of an individual enforced by state violence. 'Enlightened despotism' raised at least the possibility that state power could be harnessed to an admirable cause.

Devolution A process of 'devolving' power down from higher and central authority to lower and regional levels, whether voluntarily or under duress. The granting of autonomy or home rule to a region by imperial government is an act of 'devolution'. A famous example was the Habsburg granting of autonomous status to Hungary by the *Ausgleich* of 1867.

Diaspora Greek for 'dispersal'. A term traditionally restricted to the scattering of the Jews from their original historic heartland of Palestine. Zionism proclaimed a reversal of the Diaspora, a regathering and concentration of Jewish settlement in a Jewish nation-state of Israel. More recently, the exclusive connotation of diaspora with the Jewish experience has been lost: to refer to the 'diaspora' of such demographically-scattered nations as the Armenians and Gypsies is now acceptable.

Diet A general term for a political assembly with at least some claims to parliamentary and representative functions (for example, the Diet of the German Confederation, 1815–1866).

Diktat German for 'command'. A diplomatic, political or military settlement forcibly imposed on a state, typically as a punitive measure at the end of a war. The treatment of Germany by the Versailles Treaty of 1919 is probably the most well-known example, though the treatment of Hungary by the Treaty of Trianon of 1920 fits the definition even better.

Divide et impera Latin for 'divide and rule'. The classic imperial tactic, as exercised by all empires from the Roman to the Soviet, of retaining overall authority by deliberately setting subject peoples against each other, thereby deflecting rebellion and rendering an alliance of rebellious peoples against the empire unlikely.

Drang nach Osten German for 'drive to the East'. An historically long-established German ambition, only partly-realised, to seek territorial gains through colonisation in eastern Europe. The high incidence of German enclaves throughout eastern Europe provided both evidence of past prosecution of the 'drive to the East' and encouragement to the new Germany to revive the strategy. The Brest-Litovsk Empire of 1918 may be seen as a manifestation of the revived 'drive to the East'.

Dreyfus Affair A protracted scandal in France between 1894 and 1899 (and extending to 1906) involving Alfred Dreyfus, a Jewish army officer sentenced to life imprisonment on Devil's Island on trumped-up espionage charges. Exercised a profound effect on French society, dividing opinion into liberal and anti-clerical 'Dreyfusards' (including Zola and Clemenceau) and clerical, right-wing 'Anti-Dreyfusards' (like Maurras and Barrès). The scale and depth of anti-Semitism exposed by the affair deeply shocked many European Jews and indirectly promoted the cause of Zionism.

Duma Russian for 'thought'. An assembly of the Russian Empire conceded under revolutionary duress by Tsar Nicholas II by the October Manifesto of 1905. The First and Second Dumas (1906 and 1907) were freely elected, resulting in radical demands and early dissolution. Government fixing of the electoral laws under Peter Stolypin produced the more right-wing and submissive Third Duma (1907–1912) and Fourth Duma (1912–1917), both of which were permitted to run their full constitutional terms. The first two Dumas had a high representation of non-Russians. The Third and Fourth Dumas featured an artificially-boosted Russian representation and endorsed the Russification strategy of the tsarist government. Whether to term the Duma a genuine 'parliament' remains a matter of controversy.

Eastern Question The name given to the clutch of problems created in south-eastern Europe by the decline of the Ottoman Empire over the nineteenth century. There were three basic problems: (1) The territorial shrinkage of the Ottoman Empire, raising the question of the political viability or desirability of the 'Sick Man of Europe'; (2) The intervention of the Great Powers, with all Powers having either direct ambitions (like Russia and Austria-Hungary) or indirect concerns (like Britain and France) in the ex-Ottoman Balkan area; (3) The emergence of independent, self- proclaimed nation-states (Greece, Serbia, Rumania, Bulgaria and Albania) to replace Ottoman authority.

The Eastern Question is conventionally viewed as starting in 1774 (with Russian territorial gains at Ottoman expense by the Treaty of Kutchuk-Kainardji) and ending in 1923 (with the Treaty of Lausanne securing a nation-state of Turkey). By the late nineteenth century, the Eastern Question had assumed proportions of mind-boggling complexity, making a major contribution to precipitating the First World War.

Easter Rising An armed insurrection in Dublin in April 1916 with the aim of achieving immediate independence for Ireland, led by Patrick Pearse of the Irish Republican Brotherhood and James Connolly of the Sinn Fein Citizen Army. Surrendering after five days of heavy street fighting, 12 ringleaders were executed by the British. Although many Irish people regarded the Rising as a treacherous stab in the back at a time when Britain was heavily engaged in the First World War (and many Irish troops were serving with the British Army), the courage of the rebels and their summary execution increased public sympathy for their cause. The Rising instantly became nationalist legend and its leaders were canonised as nationalist martyrs.

Emancipation The freeing of religious groups, especially Roman Catholics and Jews, from institutionalised legislative and judicial disadvantage. The acquisition of full political and civil rights for religious minorities was an important motif throughout nineteenth-century Europe.

Emigrant An individual quitting his/her native land to settle in another state, usually with a sense of permanent commitment. Note the emigrant/emigré distinction.

Emigration The process or experience of quitting domicile in one's native land to resettle permanently in another state. Over the late nineteenth century, a rising tide of emigration (for religious, political but especially economic reasons) flowed from Europe to the wider world, with the U.S.A. as the favourite destination. The historical controversy over whether mass emigration debilitated nationalism in Europe remains unresolved. Note the emigration/immigration distinction.

Emigré French for 'emigrant'. Originally a term to describe an aristocratic opponent of the French Revolution forced to flee France in fear of the guillotine, settling abroad temporarily in anticipation of an early return home when the political climate moderated. Over the nineteenth century, the term was broadened to cover any temporary refugee from (especially) political persecution with a commitment to return home.

Empire A term with at least three distinct historical meanings: (1) A multi-national political entity, a state incorporating more than one national group; (2) A synonym for 'Great Power' (for example, the German Empire, 1871–1918); (3) A power system by which a founding 'imperial' power subordinates and exploits the colonies within its jurisdiction to its own (sometimes exclusive) advantage.

Ems telegram Telegram sent by William I, King of Prussia, to Bismarck from the German spa town of Ems in July 1870, reporting on his conversations with the French ambassador over the Hohenzollern candidature for the Spanish throne. The text was doctored by Bismarck to suggest that the French ambassador had been insulted, in the calculation that French public opinion would be outraged on the release of the text to the press. French national pride was indeed inflamed, leading to a French declaration of war against Prussia only four days later. Always cited as proof of the Machiavellian plotting of Bismarck, the 'Wizard of the Wilhelmstrasse'.

Enclave A national settlement physically distanced from the 'heartland' of that nation, set within the community or state of a different nation. Examples include the Turkish communities within Bulgaria after 1878 and the Hungarian and German communities within Rumania after 1920. Enclaves made the task of fitting state boundaries to national settlement, as attempted by the Paris Peace Conference of 1919–1920, completely impossible.

Enlightened despotism Term employed to describe a style of government prevalent in the later eighteenth century in which absolute rulers claimed to act for the general welfare of their subjects rather than either their own exclusive benefit or the privileges of the established estates. Supposedly influenced by the Enlightenment, this government was characterised by administrative reform (often of a centralising intent), weakening of feudalism (involving both the reduction of aristocratic privilege and undermining of serfdom) and religious toleration. Monarchs dubbed 'enlightened despots' include Catherine the Great of Russia (least convincingly), Frederick the Great of Prussia (more convincingly) and Josef II of Austria (most convincingly). Some historians regard the term (which was only invented in the mid-nineteenth century) as at least misleading and possibly self-contradictory.

Enlightenment A widespread but French-centred intellectual movement of the eighteenth century based on the belief that through reason Man could achieve true knowledge and therefore human progress. Through such *'Philosophes'* as Voltaire, Diderot, Montesquieu and especially Rousseau, the applications of the Enlightenment to the world of politics were increasingly stressed.

Entente Cordiale French for 'cordial understanding'. Term first used in the 1840s to express a 'special relationship' between Britain and France but only institutionalised with the Anglo-French agreement of April 1904. Britain and France (and Russia after 1907) were subsequently known generally as the 'Entente Powers' (as against the 'Central Powers').

Epic A substantial literary work of ancient provenance illuminating the history and identity of a nation. By the mid-nineteenth century, all self-respecting nations were attempting to establish their politico-cultural credentials by discovering or (on occasion) inventing or even forging a national epic. Examples include the Scottish *Ossian* epic 'located' by MacPherson and the Finnish *Kalevala* epic 'edited' by Lönnrot.

Étatisme French for 'state-ism'. The extension of the moral authority and practical power of the state over society and the individual, amongst the most striking and significant developments in nineteenth-century Europe.

Ethnicity The character or quality of ethnic identity, self-ascription and allegiance. The phenomenon of ethnicity, though not absent before the nineteenth century, is seen as growing dramatically over the nineteenth century, being both a stimulus to and a product of the rise of nationalism.

Ethnie A recent term meaning the 'natural' ethnic base-unit or fundamental community of society.

Ethnocentrism A recent term meaning the essentially nationalist perception of ethnicity as the most fundamental and all-important determinant of identity and purpose for an individual or group.

Ethnocide The deliberate destruction of the identity of an ethnic community, usually by the suppression of indigenous culture by a foreign or alien power. Note the ethnocide/genocide distinction.

False consciousness A term applied to national sentiment by its critics, especially socialists in competition with nationalists for recruitment of the lower classes. According to the socialist viewpoint, the awakening masses were all too often diverted from the 'true consciousness' of international working-class solidarity by the divisive 'false dawn' of nationalism, from which the masses could never benefit.

Federation A multi-national or multi-regional political entity in which an equitable balance between the central and local distribution of power is voluntarily and constitutionally agreed by the contracting partners. In an age of nationalism, there is a dearth of successful examples of federation in Europe. Note the federation/confederation distinction.

Fenians Irish for 'warriors'. An Irish nationalist terrorist society founded in the U.S.A. by James Stephens in 1858. Largely manned by Irish emigrants in the U.S.A., the 'Irish Republican Brotherhood' was active in Britain in the late 1860s. The objective of the Fenians was to foment disturbances in order to render Ireland ungovernable by Britain. Outrages in England included an attempt to seize Chester and blow up Clerkenwell Jail in 1867. Attempts to raise a general uprising in Ireland in 1867 failed. Unsuccessful raids into Canada were launched in 1866, 1869 and 1870–1871. Fenian activity declined over the 1870s, restricted to isolated outrages. The only success for the Fenians was in drawing the attention of Gladstone to the urgency of the Irish Question.

Fourteen Points A statement of war aims advanced by President Woodrow Wilson to the U.S. Congress on 8 January 1918, accepted as the basis for an armistice by Germany and Austria-Hungary in November 1918, and subsequently recognised as an Allied blueprint on which to build the Paris Peace Settlement. The 'Fourteen Points' were: (1) renunciation of all secret diplomacy; (2) freedom of the seas; (3) removal of economic barriers between states; (4) reduction of armaments; (5) impartial settlement of colonial disputes; (6) evacuation of Russian territory by the Central Powers; (7) restoration of Belgium; (8) German withdrawal from France (including Alsace-Lorraine); (9) readjustment of the Italian frontier following the principle of nationality; (10) autonomous development for the peoples of Austria-Hungary; (11) evacuation of Rumania, Serbia and Montenegro by the Central Powers and guarantee of Serbian access to sea; (12) self-development of the non-Turkish peoples of the Ottoman Empire and free passage of the Dardanelles; (13) creation of an independent Poland with access to sea; (14) creation of an association of states to guarantee peace. The degree to which the Paris Peace Settlement embodied or reneged on the Fourteen Points has always been controversial (especially for Germans, Hungarians and Italians).

Gallicanism A term coined in nineteenth-century France for opposition to ultramontanism or, in other words, an alliance of secular and clerical forces to resist interference from the Papacy in France.

Genocide Deliberate physical liquidation of a targeted national group through the exercise of state power. The most well-known examples are the (alleged) destruction of the Armenians by the Ottomans in 1915–1916 and the Jewish Holocaust at the hands of the Nazis in the Second World War. Note the genocide/ethnocide distinction.

Geopolitics The area where geography and politics not only meet but overlap. The term was introduced in the late nineteenth century and popularised in the early twentieth century by proponents like H.L. Mackinder. The concept was especially influential in Germany, with its concern for 'national space' and later *lebensraum*. Recognition of the intimate and frequently decisive relationship between geography and politics has become a commonplace for historians.

Ghetto Italian for 'foundry' (the site of the first European ghetto, in Venice in 1516). Originally, the area of a city designated by authority for predominant or exclusive Jewish settlement. A Jewish ghetto typically combined the functions of prison and refuge, prompting an ambivalent attitude on the part of both Jews and non-Jews. More recently, the term has been more widely applied to the concentrated urban settlement of almost any national or racial minority.

Grattan's Parliament Irish Parliament operating independently of Britain, 1782–1800. Henry Grattan led the movement to repeal Poyning's Law, which subjected the decisions of the Irish Parliament to the approval of the Privy Council in London. Secured by the 'constitution of 1782', the independent Parliament was brought to an end by the Act of Union in 1800. The 'restoration' of Grattan's Parliament was a key objective of the nineteenth-century Home Rulers.

Grievance A general term meaning unfocussed complaint. Its more specific sociological meaning is an agitated sense of protest at a perceived infringement of natural justice. The French Revolution is generally seen as 'consciousness-raising experience' fostering a widespread sense of legitimate grievance, which in turn promoted the cause of nationalism.

Grossdeutsch German for 'big German'. A central issue for German nationalists before unification was whether the future Germany should include all Germans, particularly those within the Austrian Empire (the *grossdeutsch* option) or settle for a German 'heartland' which excluded both German enclaves and Austria (the *kleindeutsch* option). In the event, a *Kleindeutsch* German Empire was established in 1871 but the ambition to expand territorially towards a *Grossdeutsch* Germany never disappeared from the nationalist agenda. The reduced state of Austria voted for *Anschluss* (merger) with Germany in 1920, a move towards a *Grossdeutsch* Germany realised in 1938.

Gymnastic movement Nationalist youth associations employing sports societies as front organisations to minimise official harassment. The most celebrated examples were the German *Turnerbund* and Czech *Sokol* clubs. In Germany, gymnastic prowess became less a cover for nationalist ambition than a desirable adjunct. A related phenomenon was the *Sängerbewegung* or 'singing movement', by which local choirs became a vehicle for promoting German national self-consciousness.

Habsburgs The family of Habsburg-Lorraine, the royal dynasty of Austria ruling from 1282 to 1918. Held the title of Holy Roman Emperor, 1438–1740 and 1745–1806. Anticipating the dissolution of the Holy Roman Empire in 1806, the Habsburgs assumed the title of Emperor of Austria, 1804–1867. After the *Ausgleich* of 1867, the Habsburgs became Emperors of Austria-Hungary. The assassination of the heir to the Habsburg throne, Archduke Franz Ferdinand, on 28 June 1914 precipitated the First World War. The last ruling Habsburg Emperor, Charles/Karl I was forced to quit the throne in November 1918. The nineteenth-century Habsburg Emperors were: Josef II (1780–1790), Leopold II (1790–1792), Francis I (1792–1835), Ferdinand I (1835–1848), Franz Josef (1848–1916) and Karl I (1916–1918).

Haskala Hebrew for 'enlightenment'. A movement of acculturation originating in late eighteenth-century Germany proposing that Jews should play down the more overt manifestations of their traditional distinctive culture, instead making more concessions to adaptation to the cultures of their host Gentile communities. Condemned as collaborationist assimilationism by Orthodox Jewry in the nineteenth century and by Zionists in the early twentieth century.

Heartland The territorial bastion of a nation, occupied by the majority of the nation in broadly homogeneous settlement. The heartland is the minimum jurisdiction acceptable to any self-respecting nation-state. For German nationalists, for example, the German heartland became the *Kleindeutsch* German Empire of 1871–1918.

Hegemony The dominance of one individual in the company of others or, most commonly, the dominance of one nation or interest-group over others within a political entity. Leading examples of hegemony are Prussia within Germany after 1871, Piedmont within Italy after 1862 and Serbia within 'Yugoslavia' after 1918.

Hohenzollern candidature The candidature of Prince Leopold of Hohenzollern to the vacant throne of Spain precipitated war between France and Prussia in 1870. With a cadet branch of the Hohenzollern dynasty, the Hohenzollern-Sigmaringens, only recently (1866) installed as the royal family of Rumania, the prospect of another branch taking over the Spanish monarchy was condemned as 'dynastic imperialism' by France.

Hohenzollerns The family of Hohenzollern, the ruling dynasty of Prussia (1701–1918) and Germany (1871–1918). The nineteenth-century Hohenzollern Kings of Prussia alone were: Frederick William II (1786–1797), Frederick William III (1797–1840), Frederick William IV (1840–1858) and William I (1861–1871). After 1871, the Hohenzollerns were both Kings of Prussia and German Emperors: William I (1871–1888), Frederick III (1888) and William II (1888–1918). The ruling Hohenzollern dynasty came to an end with the abdication of William II in November 1918.

Holy Alliance Accord agreed by the monarchs of Russia, Prussia and Austria in September 1815, instigated by Tsar Alexander I, to conduct future policy on Christian principles. Famously dismissed by British

Foreign Secretary Castlereagh as 'a piece of sublime mysticism and nonsense', the Holy Alliance was eventually signed by most European monarchs (though not the Muslim Sultan of the Ottoman Empire or the British Prince Regent). In practice, the 'Alliance' merely provided a form of justification for the repression of national and liberal movements.

Homeland   The nationalist tenet that all self-respecting nations must have an historically and culturally-legitimised claim to a national territory central to their sense of identity and purpose. The sense of *Heimat* has been especially sacred to German nationalists. Note the homeland/heartland distinction.

Home Rule   The repeal of the Act of Union of 1800 and the (re)establishment of a parliament in Dublin responsible for Irish domestic affairs. The Irish Home Rule Association was founded by Butt in 1870. Under Parnell, Irish Nationalist MPs employed obstruction tactics to force the Irish Question upon the House of Commons. Gladstone introduced two Home Rule bills, the first in 1886 defeated in the Commons, the second in 1893 defeated in the Lords. Asquith introduced a Third Home Rule Bill in 1912. Despite determined Protestant Ulster opposition, the Bill was passed in 1914 (but its implementation held over until after the First World War). In 1921, southern Ireland received dominion status as the 'Irish Free State' and 'Northern Ireland' received local home rule in the form of the Stormont Parliament. Home Rule was therefore never (re)instituted throughout Ireland.

Honvéd   Originally, the early Magyar warriors. By the later nineteenth century, the Hungarian military reserve within the Austrian, later Austro-Hungarian Imperial Army. As the Austro-Hungarian crises of 1848–1849 and 1905–1906 demonstrated, the *Honvéd* was regarded by Hungarian nationalists as the military means by which full independence from Austria might be achieved.

Illyrianism   A nineteenth-century Croatian-based cultural movement asserting the fraternity of the South Slav peoples. Initially an attempt to keep both Germanisation and Magyarisation at bay, Illyrianism (or Illyrism) is often portrayed as the cultural precursor to political 'Yugoslavism', the inspiration for the creation of 'Yugoslavia' after the First World War.

Imagined Communities   A term coined by Benedict Anderson (in his 1983 work of the same title) to describe the earliest shared perception of the 'nation', a communal 'state of mind' fundamental to the subsequent pursuit of the nation-state.

Imperialism   The acquisition and administration of an empire, a multi-national and often geographically far-flung political entity, for the (sometimes exclusive) benefit of the imperial power. The 'New Imperialism' is usually dated from the 1870s and especially the European Great Powers' 'Scramble for Africa' in the 1880s. Late nineteenth-century imperialism outside Europe is often seen as a logical development from successful nationalism within Europe (especially in the cases of Germany and Italy).

I.M.R.O. 'Internal Macedonian Revolutionary Organisation'. Established in 1895 to campaign for the autonomy of Macedonia within either the Ottoman Empire or a Balkan federation. The original Macedonian nationalists came under increasing pressure from the 'Supreme Macedonian Committee', a Bulgarian terrorist group bent on incorporating Macedonia into 'Greater Bulgaria'. By 1921, I.M.R.O. had been effectively converted into a front organisation for extreme Bulgarian nationalists. Earned the reputation of being the earliest nationalist terrorist organisation.

Indemnities Payments demanded by the victors from the defeated at the conclusion of a war to defray the expenses of victory. Examples include the 'war bills' presented for payment to France in 1815 and 1871. After the First World War, the term 'indemnities' was replaced by 'reparations'.

Independence Self-government within and by a sovereign state, rejecting the jurisdiction of all external authority. In an era of increasing internationalism, 'independence' has in practice become a less absolute and more relative term but its essential reality for the nation-state is sacrosanct for nationalists.

Instrumentalist A term applied to specialists who contend that modern nationalism is essentially an artificial construct dictated by, and attuned to, the pressing needs of rapidly-modernising society. 'Instrumentalists' play down the role of pre-modern 'natural' factors in 'nation-building', thereby conflicting with the 'primordialist' school of interpretation.

Integral nationalism A term used to describe the later form of nationalism, when state authority is employed to consolidate the position of the dominant nationality, invariably at the expense of any national minorities within the self-proclaimed nation-state. Later nineteenth-century examples of 'integral' or 'integrationist' nationalism are Russification in the Russian Empire and Magyarisation in Hungary.

Intelligentsia Originally a Russian term of the 1860s describing a community of university students of diverse (often lower-class) social origins committed to a radical cause. Such 'intelligentsias' played important, sometimes dominant, roles in the middle phase of liberal, socialist and nationalist movements of the nineteenth century.

Invention of tradition A provocatively paradoxical concept, popularised by Hobsbawn and Ranger's 1983 essay collection of the same name, which promotes the 'instrumentalist' line that the national traditions revered by 'primordialists' are typically novel constructs invented and propagated in the interests of state 'nation-building'.

Irredentism Named after an Italian nationalist party founded in 1877 to reclaim 'unredeemed' Italy and unite all neighbouring foreign-ruled Italian territories in a complete nation-state of 'Greater Italy'. More generally, 'irredentism' signifies an extreme nationalist movement that declares the nation-state is incomplete until all previously-held national territories are reunited with the motherland. Perhaps the most famous example of irredentism (other than the Italian) is the French campaign for the return of Alsace-Lorraine, 1871–1919.

Italia fara da se Italian for 'Italy will do it herself'. The principal Italian nationalist slogan up to 1849, proclaiming the proud boast that the Italian people would accomplish unification unaided. The concept was perhaps the principal casualty of 1848–1849, dying with Charles Albert of Piedmont's defeats at Custozza and Novara. Thereafter Cavour was persuaded that Piedmont needed outside aid (notably from France) if Italian unification was to be achieved.

Italia Irredenta Italian for 'Unredeemed Italy'. Term applied by Italian nationalists to the territories of Trentino, Istria and South Tyrol sought for 'Greater Italy' from 1870 but only secured from Austria by the Treaty of St Germain in 1919. According to the Irredentist Party founded by Matteo Imbriani in 1877, until these Italian lands were united to Italy, the Italian nation-state was incomplete. To the most extreme Italian irredentists, even these additions were not enough: areas on the eastern Adriatic littoral promised to Italy by the 1915 Treaty of London were not transferred to Italy by the Treaty of St Germain. This led to Gabriele d'Annunzio seizing Fiume/Rijeka 'for Italy', 1919–1921.

Jingoism A pejorative term to describe populist British nationalism in the late nineteenth century. Derived from a hit music-hall song by 'The Great McDermott' inspired by the Russo-Ottoman War of 1877–1878: 'We don't want to fight, but by jingo if we do, we've got the ships, we've got the men, we've got the money too'. Note the distinction between the more witless 'jingoism' and the more sinister 'chauvinism'.

Junkers Name applied to Prussian aristocrats whose power rested on their large estates and who provided Prussia with most of her administrators and army officers. With actions proverbially limited to the defence of narrow self-interest, the conservative Junkers constituted a bastion against liberalism. The term originated as *Jungherr*, a son of the nobility serving as an officer-cadet. Under the German Empire, the power of the Junkers declined under the twin assaults of industrialisation and state power.

Kaiser German for 'Caesar'. Title of 'Emperor' employed by the Habsburgs throughout the nineteenth century and adopted by the Hohenzollerns on the creation of the German Empire in 1871.

Kaisertreu German for 'loyal to the Emperor'. The concept of personal loyalty to the ruling dynasty overriding all other (especially national) allegiances. Most relevant to the Habsburg Empire and especially to the personal respect accorded the long-reigning Emperor Franz Josef.

Kulturkampf German for 'culture-struggle'. A term used to describe the period in Germany between 1873 and 1887 when Bismarck came into conflict with the Roman Catholic Church. Ostensibly a reaction against the Declaration of Papal Infallibility in 1870, which implied that the Church had prior claim over the state to the citizen's obedience. The Falk Laws in Prussia in 1873 were designed to subordinate the Church to state control. The aim was to discipline the Roman Catholic population in general and the Polish minority in particular within the new German Empire. After the death of Pius IX in 1878, negotiations with the new Pope Leo XIII led to compromise and the restoration of most Catholic rights by 1887.

Latinism A pan-movement promoting the well-being and especially the political independence of all members of the Latin community of nations. Out of manifest self-interest, such disadvantaged Latin nations as the Italians and Rumanians were most attracted to the movement. Napoleon III of France readily assumed the role of champion of Latinism, promoting the cause of Rumanian independence and Italian unification over the 1850s.

Lebensraum German for 'living-space'. A term coined by General K. Haushofer of the German Institute of Geopolitics in 1923. Taken up by the Nazis in the 1920s and 1930s to justify German territorial expansion to the East on grounds of population-growth. Now employed more generally to describe the 'demographic-imperative' claim to extra territory advanced by many ebullient nation-states.

Levant A vague geographical term employed in the nineteenth century to describe collectively the regions of the Asian littoral of the eastern Mediterranean, notably Anatolia, Syria, Lebanon and Palestine. More generally, the part of Asia closest to Europe.

Littoral Coastal territory and hinterland adjoining the sea. States have traditionally coveted access to the sea, many viewing possession of a littoral as so important for communication and trade with the wider world as to constitute an essential prerequisite for a nation-state. Examples of national 'drives to the sea' in the nineteenth century include Russia (to the Black Sea), Serbia (to the Adriatic) and Poland (to the Baltic).

Los von Rom German for 'away from Rome'. A movement launched by Pan-German activists from 1899 to detach Roman Catholic German-speaking areas of Austria-Hungary from allegiance to the Papacy. The objective was to make a merger of the German areas of Austria into a 'Greater Germany' (in the event of the disintegration of Austria-Hungary) more acceptable to Germany.

Machtpolitik German for 'power-policy'. A term associated with Germany in the late nineteenth century to describe politics of the most brutal 'might is right' variety, militarily-based and without diplomatic niceties.

Magyar A Hungarian term with two distinct (but cognate) meanings: (1) The Hungarian word for 'Hungarian'; (2) A landowner exempted from land tax, with the right to attend county assemblies and participate in elections to the Hungarian Diet. 'Magyar' is therefore both a neutral linguistic term and a definition of the politically-enfranchised gentry.

Magyarisation A policy adopted by the Magyar establishment in Hungary/Transleithania after the *Ausgleich* of 1867 to ensure Magyar social, economic and political hegemony by repression of the non-Magyar minorities. The policy assumed linguistic, educational, occupational and political forms. As a consequence, the non-Magyars (who together comprised almost half the population of Hungary) were increasingly penalised from the 1870s onwards, contributing to the rising tide of emigration from Hungary.

Mandate A term with two distinct meanings: (1) The democratic right to rule, the moral commission conferred by the electorate at a general election; (2) The licence granted to Great Powers (notably the victors in the First World War) to administer territories (usually confiscated from the losers in the First World War) by the authority of the League of Nations in 1919–1920.

Metternichian Europe The conventional label attached to Europe over the generally reactionary period between the fall of Napoleon and the 1848 Revolutions, 1815–1848. Klemens Metternich (Austrian Foreign Minister, 1809–1848 and Chancellor, 1821–1848) is often represented as the presiding 'genius of reaction' at the Congress of Vienna and the architect of the repressive 'Metternich System' against nationalism and liberalism. Whether Metternich dominated the international politics of the period to the degree suggested by the label remains a matter of historical controversy.

Millet A non-Muslim, usually Christian, community of faith accorded a measure of recognition and autonomy by the Ottoman Empire (usually paid for by a higher rate of taxation). The 'millet' (or 'millyet') was typically the religious fundament from which secular nationalism developed in Ottoman south-eastern Europe.

Mitteleuropa German for 'Middle-Europe'. The idea of a German-speaking supra-national state in Europe was pioneered by Austrian Minister Schwarzenberg in 1848. The concept was later rejected by Bismarck as too *Grossdeutsch* and a pretext for German domination of the Balkans. The idea was revived during the First World War, especially with the publication in October 1915 of Friedrich Naumann's bestseller *Mitteleuropa.*

Mythomoteur A modern specialist term meaning the central concept or role serving as the self-perceived *raison d'être* of a nation or state. The basic mythic role legitimising a nation-state to itself.

Nagodba An agreement undertaken between the Magyars and Croats in 1868 to effect devolution of power within post-*Ausgleich* Hungary/Transleithania. The arrangement was intended to be the local counterpart of the *Ausgleich* between Austria and Hungary agreed in 1867. This promise of a liberal Hungary was soon cancelled, with the *Nagodba* between Magyars and Croats revoked in 1883 and a policy of Magyarisation introduced.

Nation A term with a long history and various meanings. To the Romans, a 'nation' was a barbarian tribe outside the civilised world. In the medieval period, a 'nation' was a traditional, region-based, student fraternity at a university. The French Revolutionary debate clarified the concept of the 'nation' as the moral alternative to the artificial power divisions of the *ancien régime*. By the early nineteenth century, the 'nation' was perceived by its advocates as the 'natural' and therefore sole legitimate community. The criteria by which the 'nation' was defined were controversial to the point of being unresolvable throughout the nineteenth century.

Nationalism The increasingly-authoritative movement over the nineteenth century to convert a society 'naturally' divided into the culture-communities of 'nations' into geopolitical 'nation-states'.

Nation-State The supreme nationalist objective, whereby the ethnic 'nation' naturally acquires political expression and fulfilment in an independent state. According to nationalist orthodoxy, every nation must become a state, and there should be no states except nation-states. Ideally (but rarely in practice), the borders of the 'nation' and 'nation-state' exactly coincide, simultaneously including all co-nationals while excluding all non-nationals. Note the nation-state/state-nation distinction.

Oligarchy Greek for 'rule by the few'. A pejorative term for the rule of a privileged minority, generally a proportionately-small, self-interested, self-perpetuating and unrepresentative power-élite.

Omladina A Pan-Slavist nationalist secret society based in Serbia, influential over the late nineteenth century. With its republican and irredentist appeal, the society helped to push Serbia and Montenegro into war with the Ottoman Empire in 1876. Later responsible for sporadic outbursts of Slav anti-Habsburg unrest, notably in Bohemia in 1891.

Orange Order Organisation founded in 1795, committed to the maintenance of the Protestant Ascendancy in Ireland. Name taken from the Protestant William III, Prince of Orange, who defeated the Catholic James II at the Battle of the Boyne in 1690. Constituted an influential and often bitterly anti-Catholic establishment in Ulster, with branches elsewhere in the United Kingdom (especially Glasgow and Liverpool).

Ottomans Muslim dynasty founded by Osman, ruling the Ottoman Empire from the late thirteenth century until the abolition of the Empire and its Sultanate in 1922. The Ottoman Sultans in the nineteenth century were: Selim III (1789–1807), Mustafa IV (1807–1808), Mahmud II (1808–1839), Abdul Mejid I (1839–1861), Abdul Aziz ((1861–1876), Murad V (1876), Abdul Mejid II (1876–1909), Mohammed V (1909–1918) and Mohammed VI (1918–1922).

Pale of Settlement The western borderlands of the Russian Empire (including Poland, Ukraine and Belorussia) to which the Jews were confined by tsarist law, 1815–1917.

Pan-movements A generic term given to the increasingly influential movements for closer union between peoples of a distinctive race in the interests of self-protection and self-promotion. By the end of the nineteenth century, examples included Pan-Germanism, Pan-Slavism, Pan-Turanianism and Latinism.

Pan-Germanism An imperialist movement aimed at uniting all Germans in a common empire. The *All-Deutschtum* movement only developed at the very end of the nineteenth century, fostered by the *Alldeutscher Verband* headed by Heinrich Class. Its programme, demanding territorial expansionism to the East, was well supported in the German areas of Austria-Hungary. Related to the *Grossdeutsch* philosophy (with its sympathy for the *Drang nach Osten* and concept of *lebensraum*).

Pan-Slavism A movement in the mid-nineteenth century to develop the sense of racial community between the Slav peoples for the purpose of mutual protection against Germanisation and later Magyarisation. By the late nineteenth century, pan-Slavism was increasingly regarded as a cynical ploy by the Russian Empire to expand territorially at the expense of the Ottoman and Habsburg Empires: under the cover of their self-proclaimed mission to liberate all captive Slavs from the German, Magyar and Turkish yokes, the tsars were intent on establishing a Greater Russian Empire throughout eastern Europe. Pan-Slavist sentiment in both Russia and Serbia contributed to the Balkan events precipitating the First World War.

Papacy The Holy See, supreme authority of the Roman Catholic Church, located in Rome. The nineteenth and early twentieth-century Popes were: Pius VI (1775–1799), Pius VII (1800–1823), Leo XII (1823–1829), Pius VIII (1829–1830), Gregory XVI (1831–1846), Pius IX (1846–1878), Leo XIII (1878–1903), Pius X (1903–1914) and Benedict XV (1914–1922).

Papal Infallibility A new doctrine of the Roman Catholic Church proclaimed at the Vatican Council in July 1870. Inspired by Pius IX, *Pastor Aeternus* insisted that papal pronouncements *ex cathedra* on matters of faith and morals were not open to question by Catholics. This claim to enhanced spiritual authority was seen by some as an attempt to compensate for the Papacy's recent deprival of temporal authority (by the loss of all the Papal States except the Vatican City to Italy). The doctrine was interpreted by many states with substantial Catholic populations as a direct challenge to state authority, leading to church-state confrontations (notably the *Kulturkampf* in Germany).

Patriotism A willingness to defend the motherland against attack or a devotion to one's own country of an unaggressive and therefore generally admirable kind. By this definition, one can be a patriot without ever becoming a nationalist. For example, in eighteenth-century Ireland, a 'patriot' was a member of the Protestant upper and middle classes campaigning for greater commercial and political privilege and autonomy.

Philhellenism Greek for 'love of Greece'. Enthusiasm in western Europe for classical Greek culture which became, after 1815, support for the cause of Greek independence from the Ottoman Empire. The most prominent and influential Philhellene, in life and death, was Lord Byron (who died 'for Freedom's battle' at Missolonghi in 1824).

Philosophes Generic term for the leading French thinkers of the Enlightenment (including Voltaire, Montesquieu, Diderot and Rousseau). Basing their philosophies on the rigorous application of Reason, the *Philosophes* became increasingly critical of existing privilege and power abuse under the *ancien régime*. Hailed by many historians (and condemned by all conservatives) as providing the critical intellectual climate which promoted the French Revolution.

Plantation   A term with two distinct meanings. (1) A form of social and economic organisation geared to agricultural production. (2) Human settlement facilitated by state intervention to serve geopolitical interests, especially the dilution of rebellious peripheral territories with settlers dependent upon the imperial establishment. Examples of this characteristic imperial *divide et impera* strategy are the seventeenth-century British plantations of Scots and English in Ulster and the eighteenth-century Habsburg plantations of Germans and Serbs in Hungary. Such early imperial exercises in 'demographic engineering' only further complicated the later attempted conversion of the empires into nation-states.

Plebiscite   The direct vote of the electorate on a fundamental constitutional issue, usually with binding political force.

Pogrom   Russian for 'destruction'. A violent anti-Semitic riot in Russia, sometimes incited and often condoned by the tsarist authorities but usually possessing a genuinely populist dynamic. The most notorious pogroms occurred in 1881 and 1903–1906. The term has become generalised to cover any violent outrage directed against Jews.

Polish Corridor   The Versailles Treaty of 1919 insisted that the revived Polish state have direct territorial access to the Baltic, a prime example of the nationalist 'littoral fixation'. In order to provide this, a large area of west Prussia and Posen was assigned to Poland. This 'Corridor' was bitterly resented by German nationalists, who claimed that the majority of its inhabitants were German and therefore the Corridor directly contravened the principle of national self-determination.

Pragmatism   Advocacy of dealing with issues in a practical and realistic manner, uncluttered and uncomplicated by allegiance to ideology.

Primordialist   A (derogatory) term applied to specialists who maintain that nationalism is a natural modern development of a fundamental and abiding sense of national identity. Interpreters of the historical phenomenon of nationalism are commonly consigned (usually involuntarily and under protest) to either the 'primordialist' or 'instrumentalist' schools of explanation.

Principality   The geopolitical jurisdiction of a prince. A principality is generally either a monarchical jurisdiction too small to warrant a kingdom (for example, Monaco) or a transitional stage in political progress between colonial and independent status (for example, the formally autonomous principality of Rumania was promoted to an independent monarchy in 1878).

Progressive   Advocate of reform based upon the optimistic principle of 'change for the better'. The concept of 'Progress' is essentially modern, dating from the *Philosophes* of the eighteenth-century Enlightenment.

Proto-nationalism The stage before nationalism proper, when features identifiable as indicative of later nationalism are discernible. The phase of 'nations before nationalism' often features religion and sometimes language as factors conducive to development towards 'real' nationalism.

Provisional Government The politically enfeebled government of the Russian Empire between the abdication of Tsar Nicholas II in March 1917 and the Bolshevik takeover in November 1917. Comprised of leaders of the Progressive Bloc in the Fourth Duma headed by George Lvov, Paul Milyukov and later Alexander Kerensky. The Government was 'provisional' because it was constitutionally only a caretaker administration until the convocation of a Constituent Assembly (which was in any case forcibly suppressed by the Bolsheviks after its opening session in January 1918).

Putsch A right-wing seizure of power characterised by military action against the civil government.

Quadrilateral The military stronghold of Austrian power in Lombardy-Venetia, comprising the fortress-towns of Peschiera, Verona, Mantua and Legnano. In 1848, Peschiera was (briefly) captured by the Piedmontese but soon reclaimed by the Austrians under Marshal Radetzky. The Quadrilateral featured prominently in the French-Piedmontese-Austrian War of 1859 and was lost (with Venetia) to Italy in 1866.

Quai d'Orsay The embankment of the River Seine in central Paris where the French Foreign Office is located. A term employed in diplomatic jargon to signify official French foreign policy.

Radical Latin for 'root'. A proponent of fundamental reform of the existing political and/or social system.

Reactionary Literally, a proponent of setting the political clock back to an earlier period and system (for example, Charles X of France, who hoped to restore the *ancien régime* as though the French Revolution and Napoleon had never happened). More generally, a pejorative term for a conservative of the deepest dye.

Realpolitik German for 'policy of realism'. A term coined by the liberal historian Rochau in 1859 and later applied to Bismarck's attitude to politics as a naked struggle for power. Now employed ironically and mock-euphemistically to signify that the ruthless pursuit of self-interest is the only pragmatic policy for a Great Power.

Redshirts The followers of Garibaldi during the Italian *Risorgimento*, and specifically the 'One Thousand' activists who participated in the expedition which secured Sicily and Naples for Italy, May to September 1860. More generally, zealots for the nationalist cause.

Referendum   The referral of a national issue directly to the electorate, rather than permitting its resolution indirectly through parliamentary representation.

Reich   German for 'rule'. A term employed to describe the German empire. The Holy Roman Empire (dissolved in 1806) was considered the First Reich. The newly-unified German Empire of 1871–1918 was dubbed the Second Reich or *Kaiserreich.* In its early years, Nazi Germany was called the Third Reich.

Reichstag   German for 'rule assembly'. The parliament of the German Empire established in Berlin by the Constitution of 1871. Representatives were elected by universal suffrage, representing a concession to democracy, but the Reichstag could not initiate legislation and could only veto certain executive measures. Government ministers were neither appointed by nor responsible to the Reichstag. Played an important, sometimes petulant but always essentially subordinate role in Germany, 1871–1918.

Reparations   Payments imposed on powers defeated in war to recompense the victors, nearly always causing more political resentment than the financial returns warranted. Replacing the term 'indemnities' in common usage after the First World War, long-term 'reparations' were imposed upon Germany, Austria, Hungary and Bulgaria by the Paris Peace Settlement of 1919–1920.

Republic   A state based upon popular sovereignty, usually with a democratic constitution, with an elected president rather than a dynastic monarch as head of state.

Revanche   French for 'revenge'. A determination to regain territory recently lost. Perhaps the most well-known nineteenth-century example was France's obsession with the recovery of Alsace-Lorraine, annexed and absorbed into the German Empire after the Franco-Prussian War of 1870–1871.

Revivalism   A universal nationalist predisposition to view the nation as essentially primordial, often with a glorious 'Golden Age' in the remote past. An (ostensibly) unassailable historical pedigree for the nation enabled nationalist 'awakeners' to portray the nineteenth century as an era of national 'revival', 'regeneration' or 'resurrection'.

Risorgimento   Italian for 'resurrection'. An Italian literary term of the eighteenth century, taken up as the title of a nationalist newspaper co-founded by Cavour in 1847. The most celebrated of all revivalist nationalist slogans, '*Risorgimento*' expressed the spirit of Italian unification over the 1850s and 1860s. More recently, '*Risorgimento*' has been employed as a generic term to describe all varieties of classic emancipatory nationalism.

Romanovs The ruling tsarist dynasty of the Russian Empire from 1613 to 1917, finally ended with the abdication of Nicholas II in March 1917. The nineteenth-century Romanov tsars were: Catherine (II) the Great (1762–1796), Paul I (1796–1801), Alexander I (1801–1825), Nicholas I (1825–1855), Alexander II (1855–1881), Alexander III (1881–1894) and Nicholas II (1894–1917).

Romanticism A movement exalting the voluntaristic role and importance of the individual in late eighteenth to mid-nineteenth-century European society. Proclaiming an aristocracy of talent, Romanticism promoted a cult of artistic and political genius. Both Napoleon and Byron can be seen as quintessential Romantic heroes.

Russification A policy of imposing Russian power and culture upon the non-Russians, increasingly favoured by the tsarist state over the later nineteenth century. The policy had some beneficial aspects (notably in the modernisation of the Empire's recently-acquired Asian territories). However, by an overwhelming consensus, Western historical opinion has always condemned the policy as both iniquitous and mistaken, simultaneously morally reprehensible and politically counter-productive. According to the latter argument, Russification may have sharpened (or even created) non-Russian national consciousness rather than suppressed it.

Sanjak Turkish for 'banner'. An administrative division of the Ottoman Empire. According to the post-1864 reformed Ottoman system, the largest territorial jurisdiction was the 'vilayets' (province), within which were a variable number of 'sanjaks' (districts).

Scandinavianism A pan-movement of northern Europe growing in authority over the nineteenth century. In the early nineteenth century, the movement was limited to a literary and academic fashion influenced by Romanticism. The defeat of Denmark by Prussia and Austria in 1864 generated a defensive campaign of political and economic unity between Denmark, Norway and Sweden. Although the independence of Norway from Sweden in 1905 represented a setback, Scandinavianism developed further with the establishment of the Nordic Interparliamentary Union in 1907.

Schlieffen Plan German military strategy named after Count Alfred von Schlieffen (Chief of German Imperial General Staff, 1891–1905) for employment in the event of a two-front war against the Entente Powers of France and Russia. First produced in 1905, the plan was premissed on rapid German defeat of France through invasion to the West in order to forestall invasion from the East by slower-mobilising Russia. As revised in 1908, the Plan depended on a 'knock- out' blow to France effected by full-scale invasion through neutral and lightly-armed Belgium and Luxembourg. An expression of *Machtpolitik*, the plan was implemented in 1914 but, despite provoking Britain into entering the First World War by the invasion of Belgium, failed to achieve its objectives.

Secessionism The movement for political independence demanding geopolitical secession of a territorial nation from a larger, multi-national entity to form a sovereign nation-state. Also termed 'separatism', secessionism was never as universal a nationalist preoccupation in nineteenth-century Europe as has subsequently been suggested.

Self-determination The classic nationalist insistence that any self-respecting nation must determine its own fate, ultimately by securing a sovereign and independent nation-state.

Shibboleth concept A Biblical metaphor (derived from Judges XII: 4–6) promoting the belief that language is so crucial a determinant of identity as to dictate the individual's destiny. The opposite of the Babel concept, the Shibboleth concept exalted the language factor in national identity to supremacy above all other indicators. First influential in Germany and then throughout eastern Europe.

Short-war mentality The consensus before the outbreak of the First World War that the probably inevitable Great Power conflict would be massive in scale but brief in duration. The Great Powers planned and budgeted for a six-month war in 1914: Britain was not alone in expecting a 'Mince-Pie War' which would be over by Christmas. The degree to which this (mistaken) general assumption predisposed the Great Powers to undertake commitment to war is still debated by historians. The extent to which the Powers were capable of adapting to a war which was to last four years proved crucial to the political survival of many of the combatants (especially the Russian, Habsburg and Ottoman Empires).

Sinn Fein Gaelic for 'we ourselves'. Irish nationalist party founded in 1902–1905 by Arthur Griffith, originally to secure the same auto-nomous status for Ireland within the United Kingdom that Hungary enjoyed within post-1867 Austria-Hungary. Formed into the Sinn Fein League in 1907–1908 by absorbing other nationalist groups. Rose to prominence during Home Rule crisis of 1913–1914, when many Dublin workers became members of Sinn Fein and joined the Irish Volunteers. The moderate tactics of Griffith were largely superseded by the more militant Connolly, Pearce, Plunkett and de Valera. Sinn Fein was involved in the Easter Rising of 1916 and, under de Valera's leadership, the establishment of a *Dail Eireann*, 1917–1919.

Slavophiles A select group of Russian intellectuals in the 1830s to 1850s who resisted what they believed to be the undesirable and servile Westernisation of Russian society. Deeply nationalistic, they believed in patriarchal and paternalistic tsarism and demanded a return to the traditional values of Russia observed prior to Peter the Great. More generally, a reactionary current of opinion insisting that Western values were inappropriate and alien to Russia.

Sonderbund German for 'southern league'. An alliance formed by seven Roman Catholic cantons of Switzerland over 1843–1845 to protect their interests against liberal moves to strengthen the mainly Protestant federal government. The Swiss Federal Diet condemned the Sonderbund as secessionist. Austria and France both considered intervention to support their Catholic co-religionists (and acquire territory). A brief civil war in late 1847 led to the suppression of the Sonderbund. The Jesuits, alleged to have organised the Sonderbund in the interests of French or Austrian expansionism, were subsequently expelled from Switzerland.

Sovereignty According to nationalists, the absolute and inalienable moral right of a nation to independence. Note the distinction between 'sovereignty' and 'independence': any self-respecting nation has the inalienable 'right' of sovereignty but may voluntarily decline or defer the realisation of its independence as a nation-state.

Springtime of Nations The favourite nationalist term for the events of 1848. Predictably, the metaphor is revivalist, suggesting a natural progression of nations from the hard winter of post-Napoleonic reaction towards a balmy summer of national fulfilment.

State-nation A state which sets out to create a nation within its frontiers by the exercise of state power for the purpose of self-legitimation. Note the distinction between the 'nation-state', which develops organically from a cultural nation into a political state, and the 'state-nation', in which nationhood is artificially promoted by the existing state. Nationalists claim that nationalism is the international movement to promote 'nation-states' but the degree to which newly-unified Germany and Italy (let alone Britain and France) were really 'state-nations' masquerading as 'nation-states' is still an unresolved controversy among historians. Many nationalists declared themselves outraged at the cynical remark of the Polish nationalist leader Pilsudski that 'the nation does not make the state; the state makes the nation'.

Straits Question 'The Straits' is the collective geopolitical term for the Bosphorus and Dardanelles, connecting the Black Sea and Aegean Sea. The Bosphorus is the eastern waterway link between the Black Sea and the Sea of Marmora, with the Ottoman capital Constantinople (Istanbul) situated on the northern (European) littoral. The Dardanelles is the western waterway link between the Aegean and the Sea of Marmora, the Hellespont of classical times. The strategic importance of the Straits provided a vital component in the Eastern Question as Russia attempted to gain free access to the Mediterranean while the other Great Powers combined to bottle up Russia by supporting Ottoman control of the Straits. By the Constantinople Agreements of 1915, Russia was promised the Straits at the end of the First World War, a claim nullified by the Bolshevik separate peace with Germany in 1918. The Straits were demilitarised under the Treaty of Lausanne in 1923.

Sturm und Drang German for 'storm and stress'. Romantic term employed to describe the intellectual ferment of the late eighteenth century, both before and after Europe was thrown into turmoil by the French Revolution.

Sublime porte French for 'high gate'. An architectural feature of the Ottoman Foreign Ministry in Constantinople employed as diplomatic jargon for the government of the Ottoman Empire.

Successor states The new (or nearly new) states formed or expanded after the First World War under licence from the Paris Peace Settlement out of at least part of the territory of the defunct Austro-Hungarian Empire i.e. Austria, Hungary, Czechoslovakia, Poland, Romania, and the Kingdom of the Serbs, Croats and Slovenes (later Yugoslavia). Technically speaking, Italy (which received the South Tyrol and the Julian March from Austria by the 1919 Treaty of St Germain) was a 'Successor (or Succession) State' but is not conventionally placed into this politically-patronised category.

Suffrage Eligibility to vote (normally applicable to national elections). Campaigns to extend the suffrage socially, religiously and nationally were a common motif of the nineteenth century, often resulting in the enfranchisement of such hitherto excluded groups as the working classes, religious minorities and—eventually—women.

Territorial imperative A recent term expressing the concept of the possession of territory as the prime motivation and principal dynamic for living organisms. As popularised by Robert Ardrey in his 1962 book of the same name, the territorial imperative applies to animal species, humans individually or in groups, and to nations and states. By this bold interpretation, appetite for territory or land is the supreme classic element in nationalism.

Territorialism The belief that for a nation to prosper or perhaps even survive, the possession of territory is essential. The concept was particularly relevant to the predicaments of the 'landless' Jews and Gypsies. By the turn of the nineteenth century, many Jews believed that, faced with growing anti-Semitism, any territory was better than none and the only guarantee against imminent ethnocide. They were therefore prepared to consider the possibility of establishing a Jewish homeland in such (unlikely) locations as Uganda and Mozambique. This 'territorialist heresy' was roundly condemned by Zionists, who uncompromisingly insisted upon the (re)acquisition of the historical Jewish homeland in Palestine.

Triple Alliance The military alliance between Germany, Austria-Hungary and Italy formed on Bismarck's initiative in 1882.

Triple Entente The developing accord between France, Russia and Britain in response to the Triple Alliance. France and Russia signed commercial and military accords over 1891–1893, France and Britain came to an *Entente Cordiale* in 1904 and Britain and Russia signed an agreement over colonial spheres of influence in 1907. Although not a full-scale military alliance until 1914, the 'Entente Powers' were identified from 1907.

Tsar or Czar Russian for 'Caesar'. Monarch of Russia, and subsequently the Russian Empire, from 1547 to 1917. The Romanov tsars (1613–1917) accumulated a concentration of political, military and even sacerdotal authority unmatched elsewhere in Europe by the nineteenth century. The autocratic or absolutist authority of tsarism remained unchallenged through the nineteenth century, only coming into question in the period of the '*Duma* Monarchy', 1906–1917.

Überfremdung German for 'over-foreignness'. The demographic swamping of the native population of a territory by outsiders. The threat or fear of deliberate or accidental ethnocide through the influx of a flood of alien immigrants has always been a classic prompter of defensive nationalism.

Ultramontanism Latin for 'beyond the mountains'. A belief in the ultimate authority of the Roman Catholic Church, as wielded by the Papacy 'across the Alps' in Rome. Reinforced by the Vatican decree of Papal Infallibility in 1870, the ultramontanist doctrine asserted that the Church had prior claim over the state to the loyalty of the citizen. Confrontations ensued between the Papacy and states with proportionately-high Catholic populations, notably France, Italy and Germany ('*Kulturkampf*'). A doctrine rejected absolutely by nationalists, who claimed at very least the primacy (and sometimes the monopoly) of authority for the nation-state.

Unionist A supporter of any multi-regional or multi- national political union. The term has increasingly assumed an Irish connotation, meaning a supporter of the United Kingdom established by the Act of Union in 1800–1801. The label became current following the introduction of the (first) Irish Home Rule Bill in 1886. The Ulster Unionist Council was established in 1905 and in 1912 the Conservative Party officially adopted the title of 'Conservative and Unionist Party'.

United Irishmen A society of predominantly Protestant, middle-class radicals formed by Wolfe Tone in 1791 to urge reform on Grattan's

Parliament. Turned to the Catholic population and increasingly revolutionary tactics after 1793, engaging French assistance for the cause of independence in 1796–1798. Uprising defeated at Battle of Vinegar Hill, 1798. The movement was suppressed but alarmed the British government into passing the Act of Union in 1800.

Voluntarism A belief in both the moral justification and historical authority of voluntary action by the individual in society. Perceived as a novel, Romantic nineteenth-century attitude vital to the rise of nationalist movements.

Weltpolitik German for 'world policy'. A trend in German foreign policy promoted by Kaiser William II following his dismissal of Bismarck in 1890. Nationalist pressures, socio-economic factors and the personal ambition of William II combined to press for colonial expansion (especially in Africa and China), a powerful navy and the transformation of Germany from a European Great Power into a globally-acknowledged World Power.

Westminster Political jargon for the Parliament of the United Kingdom. Both the lower House of Commons and the upper House of Lords are accommodated in the Palace of Westminster, located in central London.

Whitehall Political jargon for the government of the United Kingdom, many of whose principal institutions (including the Foreign Office) are located off Whitehall in central London.

White Russians A label with two entirely separate meanings, one ethnic, the other political. (1) The Eastern Slavonic sub-group settled in Belorussia/Belarus on the borderland of Russia in the vicinity of Minsk. (2) All Russians fighting against the Bolshevik 'Reds' over the Russian Civil War, 1918–1921.

Young Europe An embryonic international nationalist organisation on idealist, republican principles founded in Berne in 1834, sponsored by Mazzini and the 'Young Italy' movement. Enjoyed very limited success, never developing into a 'Nationalist International' (or *Natintern*).

Young Ireland An Irish nationalist organisation of the 1840s. Led by Smith O'Brien and John Mitchel, 'Young Ireland' overshadowed the more cautious line represented by the aging O'Connell. The leaders quarrelled, then attempted an uprising in Tipperary to demonstrate Ireland's participation in the 'Springtime of Nations' in 1848. The uprising was easily suppressed and O'Brien and Mitchel were transported to Australia.

Young Italy *Giovine Italia* in Italian. Pioneering nationalist organisation founded in Marseilles in 1831 by Mazzini, with the principal aim of establishing a free, independent and unified Italian republic. Developing out of the *Carbonari* secret society, 'Young Italy' headed its statutes with the motto 'Freedom, Equality, Humanity, Independence, Unity'. Acted as a pressure group supporting Cavour in the 1850s, facilitating the territorial unification of Italy. A much-imitated prototype campaigning nationalist organisation.

Young Turks A reform movement among young army officers of the Ottoman Empire between 1903 and 1909. Started as an emigré Turkish organisation hoping to compel Abdul Hamid II to restore the liberal constitution of 1876. A rebellion in Salonika in 1908 led to the creation of a 'Committee of Union and Progress' headed by Enver Bey, Ahmed Djemal and Mehmed Talaat. The 'Committee' forced Abdul Hamid II to convene a parliament in 1908 (before ousting him as Sultan in 1909). The movement then split between its broadly liberal emigré and nationalist officer constituencies into factions headed by its three leaders. Retained a strong influence throughout the Balkan Wars, demanding close alliance with Germany. Contributed to the demise of the Ottoman Empire and emergence of the new Turkey.

Zealot Originally a member of a Jewish theocratic sect defying Roman authority in the first century AD. Now employed as a general term for a militant partisan for a cause, uncompromising to the point of fanaticism.

Zionism Jewish nationalism directed towards the (re)creation of a Jewish state in Palestine. Though far from new, the concept was popularised in the 1890s by Theodor Herzl, convinced by the Dreyfus Affair that only a territorial homeland could afford the Jews security in an increasingly anti-Semitic Europe. Opposed by many assimilated Jews, who dismissed Zionism as merely sentimental 'Palestinophilism'. A Zionist headquarters was established in Vienna (until 1904), then Cologne and finally Berlin (after 1911). A relatively minor movement in the nineteenth century (and arguably even up to the Second World War). The Jewish state of Israel was proclaimed in May 1948.

Zollverein German for 'customs union'. Established within Prussia after 1815, this customs union gradually incorporated most of the smaller German states by 1833. The abolition of internal customs established a large free trade bloc which encouraged Prussian-centred industrialisation. Conventionally represented as an economic precursor to the political unification of Germany, identifying Prussia rather than Austria as the focus of German nationalism.

SECTION VIII
Select bibliography

1. Analytical

The traditional canon of first-generation studies of the phenomenon of nationalism is dominated by the names of four American writers: Hayes, Kohn, Shafer and Snyder. Among their many publications on nationalism are the following major works. C. Hayes, *Essays on Nationalism* (1926), *The Historical Evolution of Modern Nationalism* (1931) and *Nationalism: A Religion* (1960). H. Kohn, *The Idea of Nationalism: A Study in its Origin and Background* (1944), *Nationalism: Its Meaning and History* (1955) and *The Age of Nationalism* (1962). B.C. Shafer, *Nationalism: Interpreters and Interpretations* (1963), *Faces of Nationalism: New Realities and Old Myths* (1972), *Nationalism: Its Nature and Interpreters* (1976) and *Nationalism and Internationalism: Belonging in Human Experience* (1982). L.L. Snyder, *The Meaning of Nationalism* (1954), *The Dynamics of Nationalism* (1964) and *Varieties of Nationalism: A Comparative Study* (1976).

The post-Second World War debate on the phenomenon of nationalism was prompted partly by E.H. Carr's valedictory *Nationalism and After* (1948) but especially K.W. Deutsch's seminal *Nationalism and Social Communication: An Enquiry into the Foundations of Nationality* (1953). A spate of studies of individual aspects of nationalism appeared in the course of the early 1960s: S.W. Baron, *Modern Nationalism and Religion* (1960), K.W. Deutsch and W.J. Foltz (eds), *Nation-Building* (1963), E. Gellner, *Thought and Change* (1964), L. Doob, *Patriotism and Nationalism: Their Psychological Foundations* (1964), A. Kemilainen, *Nationalism: Problems Concerning the Word, Concept and Classification* (1964) and B. Akzin, *State and Nation* (1964). Two more general and synoptic attempts to sum up current thinking on nationalism were E. Kedourie, *Nationalism* (1960) and K.R. Minogue, *Nationalism* (1967).

The later 1960s and 1970s witnessed the publication of a rich variety of studies of nationalism, with a particular contribution from the anthropological viewpoint which included F. Barth (ed.), *Ethnic Groups and Boundaries* (1969), R. Ardrey, *The Territorial Imperative* (1962 and 1970), J.A. Fishman, *Language and Nationalism* (1973) and H.R. Isaacs, *Idols of the Tribe: Group Identity and Political Change* (1975). The relationship of nationalism and Marxism was also considered in C.C. Herod, *The Nation in the History of Marxian Thought* (1976) and H.B. Davis, *Toward a Marxist Theory of Nationalism* (1978). E. Kamenka (ed.), *Nationalism: The Nature and Evolution of an Idea* (1976) again attempted a more general interpretation of the phenomenon.

The 1980s were opened by three useful studies: L.C. Bucheit, *Secession: The Legitimacy of Self-Determination* (1981), P. Grillo, *Nation and State in Europe: Anthropological Perspectives* (1981) and M. Olson, *The Rise and Decline of Nations* (1982). They were followed almost immediately by three modern classics which became seminal to the ongoing debate by pressing an 'instrumentalist' view of nationalism: John Breuilly, *Nationalism and the State* (1982), Benedict Anderson, *Imagined Communities: Reflections on the Origin and Spread of Nationalism* (1983) and Ernest Gellner, *Nations and Nationalism* (1983). The essay collection *The Invention of Tradition* (1983), edited by Eric Hobsbawm and Terence Ranger, popularised the 'instrumentalist' line.

By contrast to the 'instrumentalist' critics of nationalism, the least reconstructed 'primordialist' view has been projected over the last 20 years by the most prolific specialist on the worldwide phenomenon of nationalism, Anthony D. Smith: from *Theories of Nationalism* (1971) through *The Ethnic Origins of Nations* (1986) to *National Identity* (1991). Smith has also produced three valuable historiographical articles, 'Nationalism: A Trend Report and Annotated Bibliography' in *Current Sociology* (1973), 'Nationalism' in *History Today* (1984) and 'Nationalism and the Historians' in *International Journal of Comparative Sociology* (1992) to provide much-needed supplements to the rather outdated volumes by K.S. Pinson, *A Bibliographical Introduction to Nationalism* (1935) and K.W. Deutsch, *An Interdisciplinary Bibliography on Nationalism, 1935–1953* (1956).

The explosion of nationalist ambition and activity throughout the ex-Soviet Bloc in the early 1990s has ensured that the debate between the 'instrumentalist' and 'primordialist' camps of specialists attempting to explain the arcane dynamics and supernatural resilience of both nineteenth and twentieth-century nationalism shows no signs of flagging.

2. General

Leading single-volume general surveys of the broad sweep of historical developments in nineteenth-century Europe include D. Thompson, *Europe since Napoleon* (1966), T.S. Hamerow, *The Birth of a New Europe: State and Society in the Nineteenth Century* (1983), M.S. Anderson, *The Ascendancy of Europe, 1815–1914* (1986) and R. Gildea, *Barricades and Borders: Europe, 1800–1914* (1987). A long-respected two-volume work is A.J. Grant and H. Temperley, *Europe in the Nineteenth and Twentieth Centuries* (1984).

Perhaps the best single-author multi-volume work on nineteenth-century Europe is E. Hobsbawm, *The Age of Revolution, 1789–1848* (1962), *The Age of Capital, 1848–1875* (1975) and *The Age of Empire, 1875–1914* (1987), all of which contain chapters on nationalism.

Multi-volume multi-authored histories covering nineteenth-century Europe are available. The 'Rise of Modern Europe' series, edited by

R.L. Langer, is a touch dated but still valuable: C. Brinton, *A Decade of Revolution, 1789–1799* (1934), G. Brunn, *Europe and the French Imperium, 1799–1814* (1938), F.B. Artz, *Reaction and Revolution, 1814–1832* (1953), R.C. Brinkley, *Realism and Nationalism, 1852–1871* (1951) and C.J.H. Hayes, *A Generation of Materialism, 1871–1900* (1951). Volumes VIII-XII (1950–1965) of *The New Cambridge Modern History* provide a more modern multi-authored survey. The still more recent 'Fontana History of Europe' includes O. Hufton, *Europe: Privilege and Protest, 1730–1789* (1980), G. Rudé, *Revolutionary Europe, 1789–1815* (1964), J. Droz, *Europe between Revolutions, 1815–1848* (1967), J.A.S. Grenville, *Europe Reshaped, 1848–1878* (1976) and N. Stone, *Europe Transformed, 1878–1919* (1983).

Useful general works on shorter periods within the nineteenth century include J.M. Roberts, *Revolution and Improvement: The Western World, 1775–1847* (1976), F.L. Ford, *Europe, 1780–1830* (1970), I. Collins, *The Age of Revolution, 1789–1848* (1962), L.W. Cowie and R. Wolfson, *Years of Nationalism: European History, 1815–1890* (1985), H. Hearder, *Europe in the Nineteenth Century, 1830–1880* (1988), W.E. Mosse, *Liberal Europe: The Age of Bourgeois Realism, 1848–75* (1974), J. Joll, *Europe since 1870* (1973) and J.M. Roberts, *Europe, 1880–1945* (1967).

The most accessible general introductions to nationalism in nineteenth-century Europe include C.B. Hayes, *The Historical Evolution of Modern Nationalism* (1931), F.G. Stambrook, *European Nationalism in the Nineteenth Century* (1969), H. Seton-Watson, *Nations and States: An Enquiry into the Origins of Nations and the Politics of Nationalism* (1977) and especially P. Alter, *Nationalism* (1989) and E. Hobsbawm, *Nations and Nationalism since 1780* (1990, revised edition 1993).

Other works covering aspects of nationalism throughout nineteenth-century Europe include A. Cobban, *The Nation-State and National Self-Determination* (1969), M. Hroch, *Social Preconditions of National Revival in Europe* (1985), H. Kohn, *Prophets and Peoples: Studies in Nineteenth-Century Nationalism* (1946), A.D. Smith (ed.) *Nationalist Movements* (1976) and E. Hobsbawm and T. Ranger (eds), *The Invention of Tradition* (1983).

Considering nationalism within an international European context come M.S. Anderson, *The Eastern Question, 1774–1923* (1966), R. Bridge and R. Bullen, *The Great Powers and the European States System, 1815–1914* (1980), F.H. Hinsley, *Nationalism and the International System* (1973) and J. Lowe, *Rivalry and Accord: International Relations, 1870–1914* (1992).

Publications on nationalism throughout western Europe are not plentiful but include R. Mitchison (ed.), *The Roots of Nationalism: Studies in Northern Europe* (1980), H. Schulze (ed.), *Nation-Building in Central Europe* (1987) and C. Tilly (ed.), *The Formation of National States in Western Europe* (1979).

By contrast, nationalism throughout eastern Europe is covered in E. Niederhauser, *The Rise of Nationality in Eastern Europe* (1982), R. Pearson, *National Minorities in Eastern Europe, 1848–1945* (1983) and R. Sussex and J.C. Eade (eds), *Culture and Nationalism in Nineteenth-Century Eastern Europe* (1984).

Nationalism in regions within eastern Europe is treated in I. Lederer and P.F. Sugar, *Nationalism in East-Central Europe* (1969), A.W. Palmer, *The Lands Between: A History of East-Central Europe since the Congress of Vienna* (1970), M. Hroch, *Social Preconditions of National Revival in Europe* (1985), W.M. Geweher, *The Rise of Nationalism in the Balkans, 1800–1930* (1931), L.S. Stavrianos, *The Balkans, 1815–1914* (1963), and B. and C. Jelavich, *The Establishment of the Balkan National States, 1804–1920* (1977).

Different periods within the nineteenth century have received varying (and variable) coverage from historians. The question of whether nations or nationalism existed before the nineteenth century has attracted some attention, for example, L. Tipton (ed.), *Nationalism in the Middle Ages* (1972), E.D. Marcu, *Sixteenth-Century Nationalism* (1976) and, most recently, J.A. Armstrong, *Nations Before Nationalism* (1982).

Nationalism in the 1789–1815 period is considered in O. Dann and J. Dinwiddy (eds), *Nationalism in the Age of the French Revolution* (1988), H. Kohn, *Prelude to Nation-States: The French and German Experience, 1789–1815* (1967), B.C. Shafer, *Nationalism: Myth and Reality* (1955) and S. Woolf's recent *Napoleon's Integration of Europe* (1991).

The period of 'Metternichian Reaction' between 1815 and 1848 is poorly served, partly because of the poor showing of nationalism itself. Exceptions include H.A. Straus, *The Attitude of the Congress of Vienna towards Nationalism in Germany, Italy and Poland* (1949), H. Kohn, 'Romanticism and the Rise of Nationalism' in *Review of Politics* (1956), A.J. May, *The Age of Metternich, 1814–1848* (1963) and R. Clogg (ed.), *Balkan Society in the Age of Greek Independence* (1985).

'The Springtime of Nations' in 1848–1849 is well-covered. Early examples greeting the centenary include the classic by L.B. Namier, *1848: The Revolution of the Intellectuals* (1944), F. Fejto, *The Opening of an Era: 1848* (1948), A. Whitridge, *Men in Crisis: The Revolutions of 1848* (1949), P. Robertson, *Revolution of 1848: A Social History* (1952) and M. Kranzberg, *1848: A Turning-Point?* (1959). More recent publications include P. Stearns, *The Revolutions of 1848* (1974), J. Sigmann, *1848: The Romantic and Democratic Revolutions in Europe* (1973), P. Jones, *The 1848 Revolutions* (1982) and R. Price, *The Revolutions of 1848* (1988).

The period 1850–1870 is dominated by studies of individual nationalist campaigns, especially those of Italy and Germany. A rare exception is O. Pflanze, 'Characteristics of Nationalism in Europe, 1848–1871' in *Review of Politics* (1966).

General studies of nationalism in the later nineteenth century (1870–1914) cover a variety of topics, for example, I. Cummins, *Marx, Engels and National Movements* (1980), E.L. Benner, 'Marx and Engels on Nationalism and National Identity: A Reappraisal' in *Millenium: Journal of International Studies* (1988) and P. Kennedy and A.J. Nicholls, *Nationalist and Racialist Movements in Britain and Germany before 1914* (1981).

Coverage of the First World War period concentrates on the degree to which nationalism but more especially individual nations may be held responsible for the outbreak of war. From an enormous literature, sample the more general works by J. Joll, *The Origins of the First World War* (1984 and 1992) and R. Henig, *The Origins of the First World War* (1989).

The period of the Paris Peace Settlement (1919–1920) is again dominated by studies of individual nations rather than comparative works on the phenomenon of nationalism. A rare broader study is W. Sukiennicki, *East Central Europe during World War I: From Foreign Domination to National Independence* (1982).

3. National

Albania The best available general account is S. Pollo and A. Puto, *History of Albania* (1981). J. Swire, *Albania: The Rise of a Kingdom* (1929) covers the period 1878 to 1928 but the pioneering scholarly monograph remains S. Skendi, *The Albanian National Awakening, 1878–1912* (1967).

Armenia D. Marshall Lang, *Armenia, Cradle of Civilisation* (1982) provides a useful general introduction. Three outstanding specialist studies are F. Kazemzadeh, *The Struggle for Transcaucasia, 1917–1921* (1951), L. Nalbandian, *The Armenian Revolutionary Movement: The Development of Armenian Political Parties through the Nineteenth Century* (1963) and R.G. Hovannisian, *Armenia: The Road to Independence* (1967). See also R.G. Hovannisian (ed.), *The Armenian Genocide: History, Politics, Ethics* (1992).

Austria Authoritative surveys of Austria over the nineteenth century include A.J.P. Taylor, *The Habsburg Monarchy, 1809–1918: A History of the Austrian Empire and Austria-Hungary* (1948), C.A. Macartney, *The Habsburg Empire, 1790–1918* (1968), R.A. Kann, *A History of the Habsburg Empire, 1526–1918* (1974), A.J. May, *The Habsburg Monarchy, 1867–1914* (1978), B. Jelavich, *Modern Austria: Empire and Republic, 1800–1986* (1987) and, most recent, A. Sked, *The Decline and Fall of the Habsburg Empire, 1815–1918* (1989).

Austria's relations with the other Great Powers are covered in F.R.

Bridge, *The Habsburg Monarchy among the Great Powers, 1815–1918* (1990), P.J. Katzenstein, *Disjointed Partners: Austria and Germany since 1815* (1976), K.J. Calder, *Britain and the Origins of the New Europe, 1914–1918* (1976) and S.R. Williamson, *Austria-Hungary and the Origins of the First World War* (1991).

Studies of the Habsburg 'nationalities question' range from scholarly monographs like R. Donia, *Islam under the Double Eagle: The Muslims of Bosnia and Hercegovina, 1878–1914* (1981) through historical travelogues like E. Roth, *A Tale of Three Cities* (1970) to the monumental two-volume R.A. Kann, *The Multinational Empire: Nationalism and National Reform in the Habsburg Monarchy, 1848–1918* (1950).

Interpretations of the fall of Austria-Hungary include the classic by O. Jaszi, *The Dissolution of the Habsburg Monarchy* (1929) and the valuable studies by Z.A.B. Zeman, *The Break-Up of the Habsburg Empire, 1914–1918* (1961), E. Crankshaw, *The Fall of the House of Habsburg* (1963) and A.J. May, *The Passing of the Habsburg Monarchy, 1914–1918* (1966).

Azerbaidzhan Only F. Kazemzadeh, *The Struggle for Transcaucasia, 1917–1921* (1951) and T. Swietochowski, *Russian Azerbaijan, 1905–1920* (1985) can be recommended.

Basques S.G. Payne, *History of Basque Nationalism* (1982) makes an excellent standard account. Perhaps the most comprehensive account is J.L. Sullivan, *ETA and Basque Nationalism: The Fight for Euskadi, 1890–1986* (1988). For useful comparative studies, read S. Payne, 'Catalan and Basque Nationalism' in *Journal of Contemporary History* (1971) and K. Medhurst, *The Basques and Catalans* (rev. ed. 1982). See also R. Barahona, 'Basque Regionalism and Centre-Periphery Relations, 1759–1833' in *European Studies Review* (1983) and J. Harrison, 'Big Business and the Rise of Basque Nationalism' in *European Studies Review* (1979).

Belgium A standard history is F.E. Huggett, *Modern Belgium* (1969). J.L. Polasky, *Revolution in Brussels, 1787–1793* (1987) is a solid recent monograph. By contrast, a useful brief introduction is A.R. Zolberg, 'The Making of Flemings and Walloons: Belgium, 1830–1914' in *Journal of Interdisciplinary History* (1974). Partisan accounts include S.B. Clough, *A History of the Flemish Movement in Belgium: A Study in Nationalism* (1930) and T. Hermans (ed.), *The Flemish Movement: A Documentary History, 1790–1990* (1991).

Belorussia/Belarus Virtually the only survey account available is N.P. Vakar, *Belorussia: The Making of a Nation* (1956).

Bulgaria A generally neglected area in western historiography but S. Evans, *A Short History of Bulgaria* (1960) and R.J. Crampton, *Bulgaria, 1878–1918* (1983) are very serviceable accounts. J.D. Bell, *Peasants in Power: Stamboliski and the Bulgarian Agrarian National Union, 1899–1923* (1977) and V. Tamir, *Bulgaria and Her Jews: The History of a Dubious*

Symbiosis (1979) offer vivid impressionistic views of late nineteenth-century Bulgaria.

Catalans J. Read, *The Catalans* (1978) and V. Alba, *Catalonia: A Profile* (1975) make useful introductions. Effective comparative works are S. Payne, 'Catalan and Basque Nationalism' in *Journal of Contemporary History* (1971) and K. Medhurst, *The Basques and Catalans* (1982). See also J. Harrison, 'Catalan Business and the Loss of Cuba, 1898–1914' in *Economic History Review* (1974) and 'Big Business and the Failure of Right-Wing Catalan Nationalism, 1901–1923' in *Historical Journal* (1976).

Croatia Single-volume accounts include the standard S. Gazi, *A History of Croatia* (1973) and A. Kadic, *From Croatian Renaissance to Yugoslav Socialism* (1969). A recommended two-volume general history is F. Eterovich, *Croatia* (1964). Survey articles include B. Krizman, 'The Croats in the Habsburg Monarchy in the Nineteenth Century' and C. Jelavich, 'The Croatian Problem in the Habsburg Empire in the Nineteenth Century', both in *Austrian History Yearbook* (1967). More specialist articles include G. Rothenberg, 'The Croatian Military Border and the Rise of Yugoslav Nationalism' in *Slavonic and East European Review* (1964–1965) and M. Gross, 'On the Integration of the Croatian Nation: a case-study in nation-building' in *East European Quarterly* (1981).

Czechs The best introduction is probably J.F. Bradley, *Czech Nationalism in the Nineteenth Century* (1984). Longer-range standard histories include R.W. Seton-Watson, *A History of the Czechs and Slovaks* (1943) and S.K. Thomson, *Czechoslovakia in European History* (1965). W.V. Wallace, *Czechoslovakia* (1981) covers the period after 1848.

Studies of individual aspects of Czech cultural nationalism include J. Kalvoda, *The Genesis of Czechoslovakia* (1986) and P. Brock and H.G. Skilling (eds), *The Czech Renascence of the Nineteenth Century* (1970). Two valuable monographs on the 'Czech 1848' are S.J. Pech, *The Czech Revolution of 1848* (1969) and L.D. Orton, *The Prague Slav Congress of 1848* (1978). Two studies of emerging Czech political nationalism are P. Vysny, *Neo-Slavism and the Czechs, 1898–1914* (1977) and D. Perman, *The Shaping of the Czechoslovak State* (1962).

Denmark Aside from standard histories like W.G. Jones, *Denmark* (1970), perhaps the only relevant accessible study is W. Carr, *Schleswig-Holstein, 1815–1848: A Study in National Conflict* (1963).

England Whether English (as distinct from British) nationalism exists at all was posed by H. Kohn, 'The Origins of English Nationalism' in *Journal of the History of Ideas* (1940). The topic developed into a lively debate in the 1980s. A selection of publications include P. Corrigan and D. Sayer, *The Great Arch: English State Formation as Cultural Revolution*

(1985), J.H. Grainger, *Patriotisms: Britain 1900–1939* (1986), R. Colls and P. Dodd (eds), *Englishness: Politics and Culture, 1880–1920* (1986), G. Newman, *The Rise of English Nationalism: A Cultural History, 1740–1830* (1987) and R. Samuel (ed.), *Patriotism: The Making and Unmaking of British National Identity* (1989). The most recent contributions are K. Robbins, *Nineteenth-Century Britain: England, Scotland, Wales: the making of a nation* (1989) and L. Colley, *Britons: Forging the Nation, 1707–1837* (1992).

Estonia Aside from standard accounts like E. Uustalu, *The History of the Estonian People* (1952), a useful brief introduction is O. Loorits, 'The Renascence of the Estonian Nation' in *Slavonic and East European Review* (1954).

Finland General histories with relevant sections include E. Jutikkala and K. Pirinen, *A History of Finland* (1962), J.H. Wuorinen, *A History of Finland* (1965) and L.A. Puntila, *The Political History of Finland, 1809–1966* (1974). More specific studies are J.H. Wuorinen, *Nationalism in Modern Finland* (1931), D. Kirby, *Finland and Russia, 1808–1920: from autonomy to independence* (1975), W.A. Wilson, *Folklore and Nationalism in Modern Finland* (1976) and M. Branch (ed.), *Kalevala: The Land of Heroes* (1985).

France Standard histories include A. Cobban, *A History of Modern France, 1715–1945* (3 vols, 1961–1965), the older, single-volume J.P.T. Bury, *France, 1815–1940* (1949) and B. Jenkins, *Nationalism in France: Class and Nation since 1789* (1990).

Works on periods within the nineteenth century include P. McPhee, *A Social History of France, 1789–1880* (1992), K. Randall, *France: Monarchy, Republic and Empire, 1814–1870* (1992), D.W. Brogan, *The Development of Modern France, 1870–1939* (rev. ed. 1967) and R.D. Anderson, *France, 1870–1914* (1977). The 'Fontana History of Modern France' comprises two nineteenth-century volumes: D.M.G. Sutherland, *France, 1789–1815: Revolution and Counter-revolution* (1985) and R. Magraw, *France, 1815–1914: The Bourgeois Century* (1984).

Studies of the Revolutionary and Napoleonic period include B.F. Hylop, *French Nationalism in 1789* (1934), R. Palmer, 'The National Idea in France before the Revolution' in *Journal of the History of Ideas* (1940), N. Hampson, *A Social History of the French Revolution* (1963) and F. Markham, *Napoleon and the Awakening of Europe* (1954).

For the 1815–1871 period, see H.A.C. Collingham, *The July Monarchy: A Political History of France, 1830–1848* (1988), W.H.C. Smith, *Second Empire and Commune: France, 1848–1871* (1985), T. Zeldin, *The Political System of Napoleon III* (1958), M. Howard, *The Franco-Prussian War* (1961), F. Jellinek, *The Paris Commune of 1871* (1937) and S. Edwards, *The Paris Commune, 1871* (1971).

Survey works concerned with the period after 1871 include R.

Gildea, *The Third Republic from 1870 to 1914* (1988) and K. Randall, *France: The Third Republic, 1870–1914* (1992). A useful collection is R. Tombs (ed.), *Nationhood and Nationalism in France: from Boulangism to the Great War, 1889–1918* (1991). Recommended specialist studies are P.M. Rutkoff, *Revanche and Revision: The Ligue des Patriotes and the Origins of the Radical Right in France, 1882–1900* (1981), G. Chapman, *The Dreyfus Case* (1955), D. Johnson, *France and the Dreyfus Case* (1967), E.R. Tannenbaum, *The Action Française* (1962) and the seminal work by E. Weber, *Peasants into Frenchmen: The Modernization of Rural France, 1870–1914* (1976).

Georgia Superior surveys include W.E.D. Allen, *History of the Georgian People* (1932), D.M. Lang, *A Modern History of Georgia* (1962) and K.Salia, *History of the Georgian Nation* (1983). Narrower studies feature J.F. Baddeley, *The Russian Conquest of the Caucasus* (1908), F. Kazemzadeh, *The Struggle for Transcaucasia, 1917–1921* (1951) and Z. Avalishvili, *The Independence of Georgia in International Politics, 1918–1921* (1940).

Germany Recommended single-volume standard works include G. Mann, *The History of Germany since 1789* (1968), A. Ramm, *Germany, 1789–1919* (1967), W. Carr, *A History of Germany, 1815–1985* (1987), D.S. Detwiler, *Germany: A Short History* (1976) and M. Hughes' excellent *Nationalism and Society: Germany, 1800–1945* (1988).

Studies of particular periods in nineteenth-century Germany include H. Schulze, *The Course of German Nationalism: from Frederick the Great to Bismarck, 1763–1867* (1991), T.S. Hamerow, *Restoration, Revolution, Reaction: Economics and Politics in Germany, 1815–71* (1958), W. Henderson, *The Rise of German Industrial Power, 1834–1914* (1964), G.A. Craig, *Germany, 1866–1945* (1978), H.U. Wehler, *The German Empire, 1871–1918* (1985), R.J. Evans (ed.), *Society and Politics in Wilhelmine Germany* (1978), M. John, *The German Empire, 1871–1918* (1991) and T.F. Cole, *Germany in the Age of Wilhelm II, 1888–1918* (1992).

Introductory works on nationalism in Germany include A. Ashkenasi, *Modern German Nationalism* (1976), R.M. Berdahl, 'New Thoughts on German Nationalism' in *American Historical Review* (1972), J.J. Sheehan, 'What is German History? Reflections on the Role of the Nation in German History and Historiography' in *Journal of Modern History* (1981) and J. Breuilly, 'Nation and Nationalism in Modern German History' in *The Historical Journal* (1990). Highly recommended are A. Stiles, *The Unification of Germany, 1815–90* (1992) and especially M. Hughes, *Nationalism and Society: Germany, 1800–1945* (1988).

Specialist monographs on aspects of German nationalism have become legion. For the 1789–1815 period, consult L.L. Snyder, *Roots of German Nationalism* (1978), H. Kohn, *Prelude to Nation States* (1967), T.C.W. Blanning, *The French Revolution in Germany: Occupation and Resistance in the Rhineland, 1792–1802* (1983), H.S. Reiss (ed.), *The Political Thought of the German Romantics, 1793–1815* (1955), E.N. Anderson, *Nationalism and the Cultural Crisis in Prussia, 1806–1815*

(1939) and P. Paret, *Yorck and the Era of Prussian Reform, 1807–1815* (1966).

For the 1815–1848 period, see R.H. Thomas, *Liberalism, Nationalism and the German Intellectuals, 1822–1847* (1951), A.H. Price, *The Evolution of the Zollverein* (1949), W.O. Henderson, *The Zollverein* (1939) and F. Eyck, *The Frankfurt Parliament, 1848–1849* (1968).

For the 1850–1870 period, read R.A. Austensen, 'Austria and the Struggle for Supremacy in Germany, 1848–1864' in *Journal of Modern History* (1980), T. Hamerow, *The Social Foundations of German Unification, 1858–1871* (1960 and 1972), W. Carr, *The Origins of the Wars of German Unification* (1991) and O. Pflanze, *The Unification of Germany, 1848–1871* (1969).

For the increasingly well-served 1870–1914 period, see D.P. Silverman, *Reluctant Union: Alsace-Lorraine and Imperial Germany, 1871–1918* (1972), J.E. Craig, *Scholarship and Nation-Building: The Universities of Strasbourg and Alsatian Society, 1870–1939* (1984), K.H. Jarausch, *Students, Society and Politics in Imperial Germany: The Rise of Academic Illiberalism* (1982), F. Stern, *Gold and Iron: Bismarck, Bleichroder and the Building of the German Empire* (1977), R. Chickering, *We Men Who Feel Most German: A Cultural Study of the Pan-German League, 1886–1914* (1984) and G. Eley, *Reshaping the German Right: Radical Nationalism and Political Change after Bismarck* (1980).

A final category of recommended extended-period studies might feature W.W. Hagen, *Germans, Poles and Jews: The Nationality Conflict in the Prussian East, 1772–1914* (1980), A.L. Hoover, *The Gospel of Nationalism: German Patriotic Preaching from Napoleon to Versailles* (1986), F. Hertz, *The German Public Mind in the Nineteenth Century* (1975), H. Kohn, *The Mind of Germany: The Education of a Nation* (1962) and G.L. Mosse, *The Nationalization of the Masses: Political Symbolism and Mass Movements in Germany from the Napoleonic Wars through the Third Reich* (1975).

Greece General histories include C.M. Woodhouse, *Modern Greece: A Short History* (1968), D. Dakin, *The Unification of Greece, 1770–1923* (1972), D.A. Zakynthinos, *The Making of Modern Greece: From Byzantium to Independence* (1976) and R. Clogg, *A Concise History of Greece* (1992).

Studies of pre-independent Greece include such 150–year anniversary publications as D. Dakin, *The Greek Struggle for Independence, 1821–1833* (1973) and R. Clogg (ed.), *The Struggle for Greek Independence* (1973). Works on the Greek national identity include J. Braddock, *The Greek Phoenix* (1972), M. Herzfeld, *Ours Once More: Folklore, Ideology and the Making of Modern Greece* (1982) and C. Carras, *3,000 Years of Greek Identity: Myth or Reality?* (1983). Studies on the campaign for 'Greater Greece' range from the A. Bryer's introductory 'The Great Idea' in *History Today* (1965) to D. Dakin's specialist *The Greek Struggle in Macedonia, 1897–1913* (1966) and M. Llewellyn Smith, *Ionian Vision: Greece in Asia Minor, 1918–1922* (1973). See also the special issue on

'Modern Greece: nationalism and nationality' in *European History Quarterly* (April 1989).

Greece in its international context is covered in partisan works by A.I. Psomas, *The Nation, The State and the International System: The Case of Modern Greece* (1978), G. Leon, *Greece and the Great Powers, 1914–1917* (1973) and N. Petsalis-Diomidis, *Greece at the Paris Peace Conference, 1919* (1978).

Gypsies With Gypsy/Roma nationalism virtually non-existent over the nineteenth century, relevant literature is meagre. General surveys like J.P. Clebert, *The Gypsies* (1963), I. Hancock, *The Pariah Syndrome: An Account of Gypsy Slavery and Persecution* (1987) and A. Fraser, *The Gypsies* (1992) must suffice.

Hungary For standard histories, see D. Sinor, *History of Hungary* (1959), C.A. Macartney, *Hungary: A Short History* (1962) and J.K. Hoensch, *A History of Modern Hungary, 1867–1986* (1988).

Works on individual aspects of Hungarian nationalism include I. Deak, *The Lawful Revolution: Louis Kossuth and the Hungarians, 1848–1849* (1979), L. Deme, *The Radical Left in the Hungarian Revolution of 1848* (1976) and A. Siklos, *Revolution in Hungary and the Dissolution of the Multinational State, 1918* (1988). J. Lukacs, *Budapest 1900* (1988) is also recommended.

Iceland K. Gjerset, *History of Iceland* (1923) is virtually the only relevant work readily available in English apart from S. Magnusson, *Northern Sphinx: Iceland and the Icelanders from the Settlement to the Present* (1972 and 1984).

Ireland Recommended single-volume histories of modern Ireland include J.C. Beckett, *The Making of Modern Ireland, 1603–1923* (1966) and especially R.F. Foster, *Modern Ireland, 1600–1972* (1988).

Treatments of the nineteenth century include P.S. O'Hegarty's partisan *Ireland under the Union, 1801–1922* (1952), L.J. McCaffrey, *The Irish Question, 1800–1922* (1968), N. Mansergh's magisterial *The Irish Question, 1840–1921* (1965) and K.T. Hoppen, *Ireland since 1800: Conflict and Conformity* (1988). Volumes 9, 10 and 11 of the Gill 'History of Ireland' are very accessible surveys: G. O'Tuathaigh, *Ireland before the Famine, 1798–1848* (1972), J. Lee, *The Modernization of Irish Society, 1848–1918* (1973) and J.A. Murphy, *Ireland in the Twentieth Century* (1975). For the later nineteenth century, see P. Travers, *Settlements and Divisions: Ireland 1870–1922* (1988), while F.S.L. Lyons, *Ireland since the Famine* (1971) remains the classic account.

Recent works on the general phenomenon of Irish nationalism include R. Kee, *The Green Flag: A History of Irish Nationalism* (3 vols, 1972), S. Cronin, *Irish Nationalism: A History of its Roots and Ideology* (1980), D.G. Boyce, *Nationalism in Ireland* (1982 and 1991) and J.E. Hackry and L.J. McCaffrey (eds), *Perspectives on Irish Nationalism* (1989).

A selection of studies of aspects of early Irish nationalism might include R. Jacob, *The Rise of the United Irishmen, 1791–4* (1937), F. Pakenham, *The Year of Liberty: The Great Irish Rebellion of 1798* (1969), G.C. Bolton, *The Passing of the Irish Act of Union* (1966), O. MacDonagh, *Ireland: The Union and its Aftermath* (1968), R. Davis, *The Young Ireland Movement* (1954), T.W. Moody (ed.), *The Fenian Movement* (1968) and R.V. Comerford, *The Fenians in Context* (1978).

A similar selection on later Irish nationalism should include T. Garvin, *The Evolution of Irish Nationalist Politics* (1981) and *Nationalist Revolutionaries in Ireland, 1858–1928* (1986), C.H.E. Philbin (ed.), *Nationalism and Popular Protest in Ireland* (1987), A. O'Day (ed.), *Reactions to Irish Nationalism* (1987), D.G. Boyce (ed.), *The Revolution in Ireland, 1879–1923* (1967), W.F. Mandle, *The Gaelic Athletic Association and Irish Nationalist Politics, 1884–1924* (1987), J. Hutchinson, *The Dynamics of Cultural Nationalism: The Gaelic Revival and the Creation of the Irish Nation State* (1987), F.S.L. Lyons, *Culture and Anarchy in Ireland, 1890–1930* (1979), F.X. Martin (ed.), *Leaders and Men of the 1916 Rising* (1967), K.B. Nowlan (ed.), *The Making of 1916* (1969), B. Farrell, *The Founding of Dail Eireann* (1971) and F. Pakenham, *Peace by Ordeal* (1935).

For the Ulster Question, see A.T.Q. Stewart, *The Ulster Crisis* (1967) and D. Miller, *Queen's Rebels: Ulster Loyalism in Historical Perspective* (1974). For a Unionist perspective, read W.A. Phillips, *The Revolution in Ireland, 1906–1923* (1926).

Italy Useful standard single-volume histories include R. Albrecht-Carrié, *Italy from Napoleon to Mussolini* (1950) and H. Hearder, *Italy: A Short History* (1991).

Histories of the pre-1870 period include D. Mack Smith (ed.), *The Making of Italy, 1796–1870* (2nd ed. 1978), H. Hearder, *Italy in the Age of Risorgimento, 1790–1870* (1983), A. Stiles, *The Unification of Italy, 1815–1870* (1991) and S. Woolf, *A History of Italy, 1700–1860* (1979).

Histories of the post-1870 period include the classic account by B. Croce, *A History of Italy, 1871–1915* (1929), D. Mack Smith, *Italy: A Modern History* (1959), J.A. Thayer, *Italy and the Great War: Politics and Culture, 1870–1915* (1964), C. Seton-Watson, *Italy from Liberalism to Fascism, 1870–1925* (1967), M. Clark, *Modern Italy, 1871–1982* (1984) and the concise J. Gooch, *The Unification of Italy* (1986).

Studies of the *Risorgimento* include R. Grew, *A Sterner Plan for Italian Unity: The Italian National Society in the Risorgimento* (1963), G. Martin's lively *The Red Shirt and the Cross of Savoy: The Story of Italy's Risorgimento* (1969), S.J. Woolf's sober *The Italian Risorgimento* (1969), E. Holt, *Risorgimento: the Making of Italy, 1815–1870* (1970), I. Scott, *The Rise of the Italian State: A Study of Italian Politics during the Period of Unification* (1980), D. Beales, *The Risorgimento and the Unification of Italy* (2nd ed. 1982) and F.J. Coppa, *The Origins of the Italian Wars of Independence* (1992).

Other useful studies are J.A.Thayer, *Italy and the Great War: Politics and Culture, 1870–1915* (1964), R. Bosworth, *Italy and the Approach of the First World War* (1983), A. Salandra, *Italy and the Great War: from neutrality to intervention* (1932), R. Albrecht-Carrié, *Italy at the Paris Peace Conference* (1938) and D. Mack Smith, *Italy and Its Monarchy* (1991).

Jews Noted works on late nineteenth-century Zionism include A. Hertzberg (ed.), *The Zionist Idea: A Reader* (1960), D. Vital, *The Origins of Zionism* (1975) and S. Avineri, *The Making of Modern Zionism: The Intellectual Origins of the Jewish State* (1981).

Jews in the Habsburg Empire are covered in J.Frankel, *The Jews of Austria* (1968) and W. McCagg, *A History of Habsburg Jews, 1670–1918* (1988). Jews in the Russian Empire are treated in S.W. Baron, *The Russian Jew under Tsars and Soviets* (1976) and L.S. Greenberg, *The Jews in Russia: the struggle for emancipation* (1976). Jews in Germany are considered in R. Gay, *The Jews of Germany: an historical portrait* (1992).

Other related studies include H. Trevor-Roper, *Jewish and Other Nationalisms* (1962) and A.S. Lindemann, *The Jew Accused: Three Anti-Semitic Affairs (Dreyfus, Beilis, Frank), 1894–1915* (1991). See also F. Malino and D. Sorkin (eds), *From East and West: Jews in a Changing Europe, 1750–1870* (1991) and J. Frankel and S.J. Zipperstein (eds), *Assimilation and Community: the Jews in Nineteenth-Century Europe* (1992).

Latvia The standard accounts are A. Bilmanis, *A History of Latvia* (1951) and A. Spekke, *History of Latvia: an outline* (1951). For Latvian nationalism, see A. Plakans, 'Peasants, Intellectuals and Nationalism in the Russian Baltic Provinces, 1820–1890' in *Journal of Modern History* (1974).

Lithuania Standard accounts are the partisan T.G. Chase, *The Story of Lithuania* (1946) and C.R. Jurgela, *History of the Lithuanian Nation* (1948). See also A. Plakans, 'Peasants, Intellectuals and Nationalism in the Russian Baltic Provinces, 1820–1890' in *Journal of Modern History* (1974) and J.J. Stukas, *Awakening Lithuania* (1966).

Macedonia A fascinating early western account is H.N. Brailsford, *Macedonia: Its Races and Their Future* (1906). More recent scholarly studies include D.M. Perry, *The Politics of Terror: The Macedonian Revolutionary Movements, 1893–1903* (1988), I. Mihailov, *Macedonia: A Switzerland of the Balkans* (1950) and E. Barker, *Macedonia: Its Place in Balkan Power Politics* (1950).

Montenegro Compare F.S. Stevenson, *A History of Montenegro* (1913) with J.D. Treadway, *The Falcon and the Eagle: Montenegro and Austria-Hungary, 1908–1914* (1983).

Netherlands For standard histories, see G. Edmunson, *A History of Holland* (1922), B.H.M. Vlekke, *Evolution of the Dutch Nation* (1951), G.J. Renier, *The Dutch Nation* (1944) and E.H. Kossman, *The Low Countries,*

1780–1940 (1978). S. Schama, *Patriots and Liberators: Revolution in the Netherlands, 1780–1830* (1977) is a valuable study of an historiographically neglected historical topic.

Norway A useful introduction is C. Falls, 'The Independence of Norway' in *History Today* (1955). The best standard account is T.K. Derry, *A History of Modern Norway, 1814–1972* (1973), largely replacing the older two-volume K. Gjerset, *History of the Norwegian People* (1915) and K. Larsen, *A History of Norway* (1948). Useful contributions on cultural nationalism are A. Elviken, 'The Genesis of Norwegian Nationalism' in *Journal of Modern History* (1931) and O.J. Falnes, *National Romanticism in Norway* (1933). For Norway's relations with its neighbours, see F. Nansen, *Norway and the Union with Sweden* (1905), T. Jorgenson, *Norway's Relations to Scandinavian Unionism, 1815–1871* (1935) and R.E. Lindgren, *Norway-Sweden: Union, Disunion and Scandinavian Integration* (1959).

Poland The most recent standard histories are by N. Davies: volume 2 (1795 to present) of *God's Playground: A History of Poland* (1981) and *Heart of Europe: A Short History of Poland* (1984). Other useful long-period accounts are H. Frankel, *Poland: The Struggle for Power, 1772–1939* (1946), P.S. Wandycz, *The Lands of Partitioned Poland, 1795–1918* (1975) and R.F. Leslie et al., *The History of Poland since 1863* (1980).

On the phenomenon of Polish nationalism, see P. Brock, *Polish Nationalism* (1968) and *Nationalism and Populism in Partitioned Poland* (1973). Studies of aspects of Polish nationalism include R.F. Leslie, *Polish Politics and the Revolution of 1830* (1956) and *Reform and Insurrection in Russian Poland, 1856–1865* (1963), T. Komarnicki, *Rebirth of the Polish Republic: A Study in the Diplomatic History of Europe, 1914–1920* (1957), N. Davies, *White Eagle, Red Star: The Polish-Soviet War, 1919–1920* (1972) and K. Lundgren-Nielsen, *The Polish Problem at the Paris Peace Conference* (1979).

Portugal Very little is available in English on nineteenth-century Portuguese domestic (as against imperial) politics, so A.H. de Oliveira Marques, *History of Portugal* (1972–1976), C. Nowell, *History of Portugal* (1952) and H.V. Livermore, *A History of Portugal* (1947) must serve.

Rumania Two deterministic Rumanian histories are C.C. Giurescu, *The Making of the Romanian National Unitary State* (rev. ed. 1975) and S. Pascu, *The Independence of Romania* (1977).

More scholarly studies include V. Georgescu, *Political Ideas and the Enlightenment in the Romanian Principalities, 1750–1831* (1971), B. Jelavich, *Russia and the Formation of the Romanian National State, 1821–1878* (1984), J.C. Campbell, *French Influence and the Rise of Roumanian Nationalism* (1940, repr. 1971) and G.J. Bobango, *The Emergence of the Romanian National State* (1979).

Nationalism in Transylvania is covered in the partisan C.C. Giurescu,

Transylvania in the History of Romania (1967) and the more scholarly K. Hitchens, *The Rumanian National Movement in Transylvania, 1780–1849* (1969) and S. Pascu, *A History of Transylvania* (1982).

Russia Recommended single-volume histories of the Russian Empire include H. Seton-Watson, *The Russian Empire, 1801–1917* (1967), G. Stephenson, *A History of Russia, 1812–1945* (1969), J.N. Westwood, *Endurance and Endeavour: Russian History, 1812–1971* (1973) and L. Kochan and R. Abraham, *The Making of Modern Russia* (1983).

Accounts of shorter periods within the nineteenth century include D. Saunders, *Russia in the Age of Reaction and Reform, 1801–1881* (1992), R. Sherman, *Russia, 1815–1881* (1992), E. Crankshaw, *The Shadow of the Winter Palace* (1978), H. Rogger, *Russia in the Age of Modernization and Revolution, 1880–1917* (1983), L. Kochan, *Russia in Revolution, 1890–1918* (1966) and M. Lynch, *Reaction and Revolution: Russia, 1881–1924* (1992).

Russian nationalism is not well covered historiographically. Exceptions are the studies by E.C. Thaden, *Conservative Nationalism in Nineteenth-Century Russia* (1964), *Russification in the Baltic Provinces and Finland, 1855–1914* (1981) and *Russia's Western Borderlands, 1710–1870* (1985). Tsarist promotion of Pan-Slavism is considered in H. Kohn, *Pan-Slavism: Its History and Ideology* (rev. ed. 1960), M.B. Petrovich, *The Emergence of Russian Pan-Slavism, 1856–70* (1956), J. Erickson, *Pan-Slavism* (1964) and B. Jelavich, *Russia's Balkan Entanglements, 1806–1914* (1991).

Russian responsibility for the outbreak of war is considered in I. Nish, *The Origins of the Russo-Japanese War* (1985) and D.C.B. Lieven, *Russia and the Origins of the First World War* (1983). A concise and accessible study of the 'Duma Monarchy' period is R.B. McKean, *The Russian Constitutional Monarchy, 1907–1917* (1977). The Russian experience of the First World War and Revolution may be sampled from N. Stone, *The Eastern Front, 1914–1917* (1978). Russian, as against anti-Russian, nationalism is not a common motif in the plethora of literature published on the era of the Russian Revolution and Civil War.

Scotland Standard histories covering all or part of the nineteenth century include W. Ferguson, *Scotland, 1689 to the Present* (1968) and T.C. Smout, *A History of the Scottish People, 1560–1830* (1969).

A lively, present-minded debate on the Scottish past has developed over the last 20 years, and may be sampled from the following selection: H.J. Hanham, *Scottish Nationalism* (1969), N. MacCormick (ed.), *The Scottish Debate: Essays in Scottish Nationalism* (1970), M. Hechter, *Internal Colonialism: The Celtic Fringe in British National Development, 1533–1966* (1975), C. Harvie, *Scotland and Nationalism* (1977), K. Webb, *The Growth of Nationalism in Scotland* (1977), J. Brand, *The National Movement in Scotland* (1978), J.G. Kellas, *Modern Scotland: The Nation since 1870* (1980) and L. Colley, *Britons: Forging the Nation, 1707–1837* (1992).

For studies of individual aspects, see H.W. Meikle, *Scotland and the French Revolution* (1912), L.J. Saunders, *Scottish Democracy, 1815–1840* (1950), A.O.J. Cockshut, *The Achievement of Walter Scott* (1969) and M. Chapman, *The Gaelic Vision in Scottish Culture* (1973).

Serbia The nearest to introductory general accounts of nineteenth-century Serbia are I. Banac, *The National Question in Yugoslavia: Origins, History, Politics* (1984) and R.G.D. Laffan, *The Serbs: The Guardians of the Gate* (reissued 1990).

Scholarly monographs on aspects of Serbian nationalism include G. Stokes, *Legitimacy through Liberation: Vladimir Jovanovic and the Transformation of Serbian Politics* (1975) and *Politics as Development: The Emergence of Political Parties in Nineteenth-Century Serbia* (1990), and W.S. Vucinich, *Serbia Between East and West, 1903–1908* (1954).

Useful articles (in chronological order of subject) are R.V. Paxton, 'Nationalism and Revolution: A Re-examination of the Origins of the First Serbian Insurrection, 1804–7' in *East European Quarterly* (1972), C. Jelavich, 'Serbian Nationalism and the Question of Union with Croatia in the Nineteenth Century' in *Balkan Studies* (1962) and G. Stokes, 'The Absence of Nationalism in Serbian Politics before 1844' in *Canadian Review of Studies in Nationalism* (1976) and 'Yugoslavism in the 1860s?' in *Southeastern Europe* (1974).

For Serbs outside Serbia, see W.S. Vucinich, 'The Serbs in Austria-Hungary' in *Austrian History Yearbook* (1967) and P. Adler, 'Nations and Nationalism among the Serbs of Hungary, 1790–1870' in *East European Quarterly* (1979).

Slovakia Four recommended works are R.W. Seton-Watson, *A History of the Czechs and Slovaks* (1943) and *Slovakia Then and Now* (1931), J. Lettrich, *A History of Modern Slovakia* (1955) and P. Brock, *The Slovak National Awakening: An Essay in the Intellectual History of East Central Europe* (1976).

Slovenia In a sparse field, three recommended works are D. Loncar, *The Slovenes* (1931), F. Zwitter, 'The Slovenes in the Habsburg Monarchy' in *Austrian History Yearbook* (1967) and C. Rogel, *The Slovenes and Yugoslavism, 1890–1914* (1977).

Spain Early single-volume accounts of nineteenth-century Spain include M.A.S. Hume, *Modern Spain, 1788–1898* (1900), H.B. Clarke, *Modern Spain, 1815–1898* (1906) and G.F. White, *A Century of Spain and Portugal, 1788–1898* (1909). More modern accounts include S. de Madariaga, *Spain: A Modern History* (1957), R. Carr's exhaustive *Spain, 1808–1975* (1982) and more accessible *Modern Spain, 1875–1980* (1980), P. Vilar, *Spain: A Brief History* (1977), J.M. Roldan, *A Short History of Spain* (1987) and Volume 2 of S.G. Payne, *A History of Spain and Portugal* (1973).

Studies of particular aspects include (in chronological order of topic) G. Lovett, *Napoleon and the Birth of Modern Spain* (1965), E. Holt, *The Carlist Wars in Spain* (1967), V.G. Kiernan, *The Revolution of 1854 in Spanish History* (1966), E.H. Strobel, *Spanish Revolution, 1868–75* (1898), J.C. Ullman, *The Tragic Week: A Study of Anti-Clericalism in Spain, 1875–1912* (1968) and J. Romera Maura, 'Terrorism in Barcelona and its Impact on Spanish Politics, 1904–1909' in *Past and Present* (1968).

Sweden Introductory accounts include I. Andersson, *A History of Sweden* (1956) and S. Oakley, *The Story of Sweden* (1966).

Studies include D. Verney, *Parliamentary Reform in Sweden, 1866–1921* (1957), F. Lindberg, *Scandinavia in Great Power Politics, 1905–1908* (1958) and R.E. Lindgren, *Norway-Sweden Union, Disunion and Scandinavian Integration* (1959).

Switzerland Apart from the standard *Short History of Switzerland* (1952) by H.S. Offler, G.R. Potter and E. Bonjour, three recommended recent works are H. Kohn, *Nationalism and Liberty: The Swiss Example* (1957), C.L. Schmidt, *Conflict and Consensus in Switzerland* (1981) and especially J. Steinberg, *Why Switzerland?* (1976).

Turkey Perhaps the best general accounts are B. Lewis, *The Emergence of Modern Turkey* (1968) and S.J. Shaw, *History of the Ottoman Empire and Modern Turkey* (2 vols, 1977–1978).

The predicament of the Ottoman Empire within the 'Eastern Question' is covered in the classic J.A.R. Marriott, *The Eastern Question* (1917) and M. Miller, *The Ottoman Empire and Its Successors, 1801–1927* (1936) as well as the more modern M.S. Anderson, *The Eastern Question, 1774–1923* (1966), A.L. MacFie, *The Eastern Question, 1774–1923* (1976), M. Kent, *The Great Powers and the End of the Ottoman Empire* (1984) and, most recently, A. Palmer, *The Decline and Fall of the Ottoman Empire* (1992).

Studies of Turkish nationalism include D. Kushner, *The Rise of Turkish Nationalism, 1876–1908* (1976), U. Heyd, *Foundations of Turkish Nationalism* (1979) and J. Landau, *Pan-Turkism in Turkey* (1981). A valuable related work is K.H. Karpat, *An Inquiry into the Social Foundations of Nationalism in the Ottoman State: From Social Estates to Classes, from Millets to Nations* (1973).

Ukraine Partisan nationalist volumes include the classic M. Hrushevsky, *A History of Ukraine* (1941) and D. Doroshenko, *History of the Ukraine* (1939). W.E.D. Allen, *The Ukraine: A History* has been denounced as 'Great Russian propaganda' by Ukrainian nationalists. A more objective and scholarly work is I.L. Rudnytsky, *Rethinking Ukrainian History* (1981).

Wales Standard surveys include *A Short History of Modern Wales* (1961) and *A History of Modern Wales* (rev. ed. 1977), both by D. Williams; and P. Jenkins, *A History of Modern Wales, 1536–1990* (1991).

Introductory articles include R.T. Jenkins, 'The Development of Nationalism in Wales' in *Sociological Review* (1935) and K.O. Morgan, 'Welsh Nationalism: The Historical Background' in *Journal of Contemporary History* (1971).

Four recent useful publications are D. Smith (ed.), *A People and a Proletariat: Essays in the History of Wales, 1780–1980* (1980), K.O. Morgan, *Rebirth of a Nation: Wales, 1880–1980* (1981), G.A. Williams, *The Welsh in their History* (1982) and D. Gareth Evans, *A History of Wales, 1815–1906* (1989). Studies considering Wales in a broader context include R. Coupland, *Welsh and Scottish Nationalism* (1954), M. Hechter, *Internal Colonialism: The Celtic Fringe in British National Development, 1533–1966* (1975) and, most recently, K. Robbins, *Nineteenth-Century Britain: England, Scotland, Wales: the making of a nation* (1989).

Index

References in **bold** type indicate main entries.